Reappraisals in Irish History

Editors
Enda Delaney (University of Edinburgh)
Maria Luddy (University of Warwick)
Ciaran O'Neill (Trinity College Dublin)

sals in Irish History offers new insights into Irish history, society
ure from 1750. Recognising the many methodologies that make
ical research, the series presents innovative and interdisciplinary
is conceptual and interpretative, and expands and challenges the
understandings of the Irish past. It showcases new and exciting
ip on subjects such as the history of gender, power, class, the
dscape, memory and social and cultural change. It also reflects the
of Irish historical writing, since it includes titles that are empirically
ted together with conceptually driven synoptic studies.

Begging, Charity a

in Pre-Famine

Reappra
and cult
up histo
work tha
common
scholarsh
body, lan
diversity
sophistic

Begging, Charity and Religion in Pre-Famine Ireland

CIARÁN McCABE

LIVERPOOL UNIVERSITY PRESS

First published 2018 by
Liverpool University Press
4 Cambridge Street
Liverpool
L69 7ZU

British Library Cataloguing-in-Publication data
A British Library CIP record is available

ISBN 978-1-78694-157-2

Typeset by Carnegie Book Production, Lancaster
Printed and bound by TJ International Ltd, Padstow, Cornwall, PL28 8RW

For Anne Maree

There is scarcely a greater plague that can infest a society than swarms of beggars; and the inconveniences to individuals arising from them are so generally, and so severely, felt that relief from so great an evil cannot fail to produce a powerful and lasting effect upon the minds of the public.

Anon., *Arguments in proof of the necessity and practicality of suppressing street begging in the city of Dublin* ... (Dublin, 1817), p. 10

[T]he beggar is not in Ireland – as he is in England – an outcast, whose apparent misery is ascribed to imposture or vice – whose contact is degradation to the humblest labourer – and who is relieved, not so much to satisfy his wants as to get rid of his presence. The Irish cottier considers the beggar as his equal – indeed, as acting a part in the great drama of life which he may have to perform erelong himself. The beggar is not an occasional and unwelcome intruder; he makes a part, and probably not the least agreeable part, of the society of the family. He has his regular seat before the potatoe-bowl, his nook near the chimney where a chimney exists, and the corner in which he sleeps, on the straw which he has begged during the day. He brings with him news, flattery, conversation, prayers, the blessing of God, and the good-will of men.

[Nassau William Senior], 'Mendicancy in Ireland' in *Edinburgh Review*, lxxvii, no. 156 (Apr. 1843), pp. 400–1

I trouble the gentlemen little; they do not know our miserable condition, when God has made us poor, as well as the very small farmers and labourers, who give us all they have for God's sake; they know they may soon be in our state, and feel more for us.

Mary O'Brien, 'An old beggar-woman', Buncrana, County Donegal, *PI, Appendix A*, p. 744

Contents

Figures

Tables

Acknowledgements

This book is the result of a number of years of research, writing and reflection, and many people have helped me in countless ways during this period. While it is not feasible in this short space to thank every single person, I am delighted to take this opportunity to acknowledge the assistance and support received from the following individuals.

I want to first thank my doctoral supervisor at Maynooth University, Dr Jacinta Prunty, whose kindness, generosity and encouragement have been inspirational. It was a pleasure to work closely with Jacinta and I could not have wished for a better teacher than she. During my time at Maynooth, I benefited from the knowledge and support of many colleagues: Professor Marian Lyons, Professor Jacqueline Hill, Professor Terence Dooley, Professor Raymond Gillespie and Professor Emeritus R.V. Comerford, as well as Dr Georgina Laragy, Dr Miriam Moffitt, Dr Ciarán Reilly, Dr Adrian Kirwan and Dr Fiona Gallagher, among many others, while I will be eternally grateful to the late Dr Caroline Gallagher for sparking my interest in vestry minute books as source material. The efficiency and kindness of Ann Donoghue and Catherine Heslin were constant sources of support and assurance.

This book arises from a PhD thesis completed at Maynooth University and the revision of the original thesis into this monograph was carried out under the guidance of Dr Niall Ó Ciosáin at NUI Galway. Niall inspired me to consider and develop new approaches to my topic, and I am in no doubt that my historical understanding has been developed by his Socratic method of questioning. Professor Catherine Cox and Professor Lindsey-Earner Byrne have encouraged my research since my MA days in UCD, while Professor Peter Gray and Dr Jonathan Wright provided important and valued feedback on earlier stages of this work.

As a historian, I am ever-cognisant of the saying 'Researchers come and go; archives are forever', which speaks of the eternal debt which researchers pay to custodians of archives. I am indebted to many archivists and librarians, and I am happy to acknowledge their assistance. I would like to thank Dr

Raymond Refaussé, Dr Susan Hood, Jennifer Murphy and Mary Furlong at the Representative Church Body Library for their assistance. Dr Brian Donnelly and his colleagues at the National Archives of Ireland have been helpful, as have the staff members at the National Library of Ireland. I wish to thank Dr Bernadette Cunningham, Siobhán Fitzpatrick and their colleagues in the Royal Irish Academy Library, as well as Penny Woods, Audrey Kinch and Barbara McCormack in the Russell Library, Maynooth; Rev. Robin Roddie and Jennifer Stutt in the Methodist Library and Archives in Belfast; Valerie Adams in the library of the Presbyterian Historical Society of Ireland; Noelle Dowling in the Dublin Diocesan Archives; Sister Marie Therese in the Presentation Convent, George's Hill Archive in Dublin; Sister Marie Bernadette in the Religious Sisters of Charity Archive in Caritas, Sandymount; Christopher Moriarty and colleagues in the Friends Historical Library, Dublin; the Abbey Presbyterian Church, Dublin; Mary Guinan Darmody in Thurles Library; the staff at the Public Record Office of Northern Ireland, the Linen Hall Library, Belfast, the British Library, the National Archives (Kew) and the National Records of Scotland. Much of this book has been researched and written in university libraries across Ireland, and I wish to thank the staff at the James Joyce Library in UCD, the John Paul II Library in Maynooth, the McClay Library in QUB, the James Hardiman Library at NUIG and the library at Trinity College Dublin. Much of the final draft of this book was compiled in the Local Studies room in Mullingar Library and I am grateful to Greta Connell and her colleagues for their assistance. Facilities were also provided to me by An Foras Feasa in Maynooth University and the Moore Institute at NUI Galway. The doctoral research was carried out with the support of an Irish Research Council (IRC) Government of Ireland Postgraduate Scholarship, while much of the book was written at NUIG on foot of an IRC postdoctoral fellowship, and I am most grateful to the IRC for this financial support.

Raymond Gillespie and Niall Ó Ciosáin read draft chapters from this book, and their comments, which have been most valuable, greatly broadened my understanding of this period and of some of the historical dynamics at play. This book has benefited greatly from the comments of Liverpool University Press's anonymous readers, to whom I am grateful, while Alison Welsby has been a most efficient and amiable editor at LUP, with whom it has been a pleasure to work.

The research and writing of this book has not been a solo project and throughout this process I have been lucky to be surrounded by loving family and friends. My parents-in-law, Tommy and Chris Jones, have proved most supportive, most practically in allowing me to stay for prolonged periods in their 'bolt-hole' to 'get some writing done'. To my parents, Noel and Marian, I owe my gratitude, not only for a lifetime of love and support, but for instilling in me the confidence and self-belief to undertake postgraduate research and the commitment to write this book. I have no doubt they will be delighted that the book will see the light of day.

In the course of bringing this book to completion, my wife Anne Maree and I were blessed by the birth of our daughter Alannah. She has enriched our lives beyond comprehension. Finally, and most appropriately, I wish to thank my wife, Anne Maree, who has shared the past few years, including the early years of our marriage, with 'idle vagrants and sturdy beggars' from two centuries ago, and has displayed heroic levels of patience with 'The Book'. Throughout this process, her constant support, encouragement and love have been unshakeable, for which I will always be thankful. To Anne Maree, for her support, encouragement, patience, sacrifice and love, this book is dedicated.

Abbreviations

BL	British Library
BNL	*Belfast News-Letter*
CSOOP	Chief Secretary's Office Official Papers, National Archives of Ireland
CSORP	Chief Secretary's Office Registered Papers, National Archives of Ireland
DIB	James McGuire and James Quinn (eds), *Dictionary of Irish biography: from the earliest times to the year 2002* (9 vols, Cambridge, 2009)
DDA	Dublin Diocesan Archives
DMP	Daniel Murray papers, Dublin Diocesan Archives
DMSP	Dublin Mendicity Society papers, National Library of Ireland
FHLD	Friends Historical Library, Dublin
FJ	*Freeman's Journal*
IHS	*Irish Historical Studies*
IMC	Irish Manuscripts Commission
JHP	John Hamilton papers, Dublin Diocesan Archives
NAI	National Archives of Ireland
NLI	National Library of Ireland
ODNB	H.C.G. Matthew and Brian Harrison (eds), *Oxford dictionary of national biography, from the earliest times to the year 2000* (60 vols, Oxford, 2004)
OSM	Angélique Day and Patrick McWilliams (eds), *Ordnance Survey memoirs of Ireland* (40 vols, Belfast, 1990–8)
PI, Appendix A	[*Poor Inquiry (Ireland)*], *First report from His Majesty's Commissioners for inquiring into the condition of the poorer classes in Ireland, with Appendix (A) and supplement,* H.C. 1835 (369), xxxii, 1

PI, Appendix C   [*Poor Inquiry (Ireland)*], *Royal Commission for inquiring into the condition of the poorer classes in Ireland: Appendix (C) – Part I. Reports on the state of the poor, and on the charitable institutions in some of the principal towns; with supplement containing answers to queries; Part II. Report on the city of Dublin, and supplement containing answers to queries; with addenda to Appendix (A), and communications*; *The report upon vagrancy and mendicity in the City of Dublin*, H.C. 1836 [C 35], xxx, 35

PRONI   Public Record Office of Northern Ireland

RCBL   Representative Church Body Library

RSCA   Religious Sisters of Charity Archives, Caritas, Sandymount

TNA   The National Archives, Kew

Note on Editorial Conventions

The italicisation of words in primary sources has been retained in quotations. Where emphasis results from editorial intervention, this is acknowledged. Interventions in editorial matter are illustrated by the use of square brackets. The spelling in primary sources has not been modernised. The use of [*sic*] has been kept to a minimum. Certain contractions, such as w^{ch}, have been silently expanded.

Place names have been presented in their nineteenth-century form, with modern versions presented in round brackets in the first instance of use: for example, King's County (County Offaly). This book refers to the city of Derry and the county of Londonderry but retains the name for the city's mendicity charity as the Londonderry Mendicity Society.

Sums of money are retained in the pre-decimal format (pounds (£), shillings (*s.*) and pence (*d.*)), whereby:

240*d.* = £1
12*d.* = 1*s.*
20*s.* = £1

Introduction

Begging was a ubiquitous feature of life in pre-Famine Ireland. Accounts of social conditions in the country invariably refer to the prevalence of mendicants, while travellers' narratives inevitably present descriptions of the colourful and menacing beggars they encountered. Urban streets and country roads were frequently described as being 'infested' with 'swarms' of mendicants and the use of such language affirmed the widespread association of mendicancy with disease. Indeed, beggary was seen as a threat to society on a number of fronts. Yet, the practices of mendicancy and alms-giving were also framed by a universal sense of Christian obligation amongst all classes of society to assist those poorer than themselves. The example and teaching of Christ, as expounded in the New Testament, was intrinsic to the language of private and public charity in this period and deeply influenced how individuals and corporate bodies perceived and responded to begging. Indiscriminate charity was widely believed, especially by members of the 'respectable' middle classes who drove the philanthropic impulse of this period, to constitute a considerable evil, undermining industry, thrift and self-help, and encouraging idleness and pauperism. The long-held distinction between the 'deserving' and 'undeserving' poor coloured approaches to beggary. Begging and alms-giving were central features of the public discourse on the question of the poor of Ireland and their relief. This discourse was shaped by wider social and economic factors, and in line with these fluctuating forces societal perceptions and responses varied. The emergence of mendicity societies – charities with the specific purpose of suppressing public begging – in Irish and British towns and cities in the first half of the nineteenth century arose from middle-class concerns over the extent of mendicancy and the deleterious effects of urbanisation, while also reflecting the emerging associational culture of middle-class life.

Contexts

Public discourse on Ireland in the early nineteenth century was almost invariably concerned with the pervasive impoverishment of the population. Increasing inquiry into the condition of the lower classes was not unique to Ireland, and social reformers and commentators who held forth on the unremitting problem of Irish penury drew upon parallel debates and initiatives regarding poor relief in Britain, continental Europe and throughout the Atlantic world. Numerous reports and social surveys were undertaken by private individuals, corporate bodies and parliamentary committees, unanimously agreeing on the exceptional extent of Ireland's poverty and the prevalence of beggary in a society lacking a statutory system of poor relief.

The century after 1750 witnessed significant levels of population growth throughout Europe, but the rate of increase in Ireland (quadrupling from *c*.2 million to more than 8 million) was unparalleled. This demographic growth was heavily weighted at the lower end of the social ladder, particularly among the labouring classes of rural Ireland. Furthermore, this population surge had regional patterns, being concentrated in the relatively impoverished western seaboard counties.[1] Declining access to a limited supply of land for a growing population entrenched Ireland's structural poverty, driving many into either habitual or occasional beggary. The half century or so before the Great Famine was a period marked by immeasurable levels of mobility among the Irish population, both within and beyond the island. For large numbers of the poor in pre-Famine Ireland, mobility was a central part of their subsistence, and this was true of both the rural and urban poor. An estimated 1.5 million people emigrated permanently to Britain, Canada and America between 1815 and 1845, a scale unprecedented until that point.[2] Among the factors facilitating this emigration were the cessation of the French Wars, which opened up continental Europe for travel, and also the advent of steam ships providing cheaper, quicker access to movement across the Irish Sea. By the 1830s, tickets to Britain could be purchased for as little as 5*d*. or 6*d*., opening up cross-channel travel to large swathes of the poorer classes.[3] Seasonal migration to Britain for harvest work formed a significant part of the yearly cycle and household income for countless numbers of landless or semi-landless agricultural labourers (*spailpíní*), and during their

---

1　Cormac Ó Gráda, *Ireland before and after the Famine: explorations in economic history, 1800–1925* (2nd edn, Manchester, 1993), p. 7.

2　Cormac Ó Gráda, 'Malthus and the pre-Famine economy' in *Hermathena*, no. 135 (Winter 1983), p. 88.

3　David Fitzpatrick, '"A peculiar tramping people": the Irish in Britain, 1801–70' in W.E. Vaughan (ed.), *A new history of Ireland*, vol. 5, *Ireland under the Union, I, 1801–70* (Oxford, 1989), p. 626.

absence their wives and children wandered the Irish countryside, supporting themselves through begging. Decades before the unprecedented levels of emigration that were witnessed during the Great Famine Irish paupers constituted large proportions of the destitute classes of British towns and cities, forming an estimated one-third of London's beggars in the 1820s.[4]

Countless multitudes of non-local poor also flocked to Irish urban centres in search of work, relief or an emigrant's ticket abroad. In a sermon in aid of the Belfast House of Industry in 1814, Presbyterian minister Rev. Henry Cooke observed that 'To every commercial town there is a great influx of strangers and their families, seeking employment. When calamity overtakes them, they have no friend to whom they can look for comfort or relief'.[5] Port towns and cities were magnets for rural migrants, both poor and otherwise. The lax implementation of anti-vagrancy laws in Dublin, in comparison with other towns and cities, led many people to look upon the city as a sort of 'haven' for the idle and vagrant. A report for the year 1818 of the Association for the Suppression of Mendicity in Dublin[6] claims that 'persons with large families have stated that they were induced to come to town from distant parts of the country, having heard of the good treatment which the poor received in this city and that they had ever since supported themselves by begging'.[7] A civic report from 1837 notes that 'there is no other place where the needy, or the famishing, will be sustained', so that 'nearly the whole tide of wretchedness and want must of necessity pour in upon Dublin'; to one charity official, the city was 'the derrier resort of those reduced to the lowest ebb of poverty'.[8] This influx of non-local poor was reflected in the fact that 56 per cent of the paupers in the city's House of Industry in 1837 were not natives of Dublin city or county; in the mendicity asylum, this figure was smaller but still

---

4 London Mendicity Society minute book, 29 Apr. 1820 (BL, Add. MS 50136); ibid., 27 Feb. 1822, 26 Feb. 1823; Copy of letter, W.H. Bodkin, London Mendicity Society secretary, to the Mayor of Cork, 10 May 1822 (TNA, Home Office Correspondence, HO 44/11, f. 183); *Report from committee on the state of mendicity in the metropolis*, pp. 6–7, H.C. 1814–15 (473), iii, 236–7.

5 Henry Cooke, *A sermon, preached in the meeting-house of the Third Presbyterian Congregation, Belfast, on Sunday, the 18th December, 1814, in aid of the funds of the House of Industry* (3rd edn, Belfast, 1815), pp. 21–2.

6 Hereafter referred to as the Dublin Mendicity Society.

7 *[First] Report of the Association for the Suppression of Mendicity in Dublin. For the year 1818* (Dublin, 1819), p. 2.

8 Quoted in Jacinta Prunty, *Dublin slums, 1800–1925: a study in urban geography* (Dublin, 1998), p. 211; Thomas Wright to Lord Melville, 29 Oct. 1830 (National Records of Scotland, Dundas family (Viscounts Melville) papers, GD51/9/498). See also *Second report of Geo. Nicholls, Esq., to Her Majesty's Principal Secretary of State for the Home Department, on Poor Laws, Ireland*, p. 17, H.C. 1837–8 [C 104], xxxviii, 673. For Cork, see Gerard O'Brien, 'The new Poor Law in pre-Famine Ireland: a case history' in *Irish Economic and Social History*, xii (1985), pp. 43–4.

significant at 35 per cent.[9] Town-dwellers experienced high levels of mobility and upheaval in their daily lives, owing to the uncertainty of their tenures. Throughout Europe many slum dwellers subsisted on short leases, oftentimes renting their lodgings by the week or even by the day.[10] The uncertainty of tenancy is reflected in the regular change of addresses of poor persons, with women and children being particularly vulnerable to domiciliary upheaval. An examination of a relief register of the Dublin Strangers' Friend Society for the 1790s reveals high levels of changes of address by poor persons.[11] In both rural and urban areas lax rental arrangements were frequently aggravated by uncertain and limited employment opportunities, and in this regard women were acutely vulnerable. For such individuals begging was a natural resort as a feasible survival strategy.

Economic trends in pre-Famine Ireland stood in stark contrast to those in rapidly industrialising Britain. Large-scale manufacturing was only successfully introduced into Belfast and its hinterland, while most of the island remained largely agricultural. The decline in the Irish domestic industry sector from the 1810s was aggravated by the economic downturn of the mid-1820s, when British manufacturers 'dumped' their superfluous goods onto the Irish market, undercutting Ireland's already-struggling cottage industry manufacturers. Many artisans and their families, categorised by contemporaries as the industrious poor, found themselves unemployed and with little alternative but to resort to beggary, a shift reflected in the increasing proportion of former textile workers among the mendicants of Irish cities from the mid-1820s onwards. Localised downturns also impacted on rates of poverty and mendicancy. In 1809, a manufacturing collapse in Belfast and its hinterland, where 2,000 calico looms 'were struck idle in five weeks', led directly to the establishment of a House of Industry, a voluntarily funded charitable society designed to suppress street begging.[12] As will be discussed in Chapter 5, most of the Ulster mendicity societies were founded in the mid- to late 1820s, arising from the impact of the manufacturing decline on foot of the depression of 1825–6. The downturn, which disproportionately impacted on the textile industries, led to increased

9 *Second report of Geo. Nicholls, Poor Laws, Ireland*, pp. 40–1.

10 Prunty, *Dublin slums*, pp. 340–1; Prunty, 'Mobility among women in nineteenth-century Dublin' in David J. Siddle (ed.), *Migration, mobility and modernization* (Liverpool, 2000), p. 153; *Appendices B. to F. to the eighth annual report of the Poor Law Commissioners*, p. 185, H.C. 1842 [C 399], xix, 197; Robert Jütte, *Poverty and deviance in early modern Europe* (Cambridge, 2001), pp. 62, 66.

11 Strangers' Friend Society register of relief recipients, 1794–9 (Methodist Historical Society of Ireland Archives, Belfast, IrBe.MS.OS42.02).

12 John Dubourdieu, *Statistical survey of the county of Antrim, with observations on the means of improvement; drawn up for the consideration, and by direction of the Dublin Society* (Dublin, 1812), pp. 410–11.

levels of poverty among the labouring classes (both skilled and unskilled), with increased numbers, unable to emigrate or failing to find alternative employment, resorting to begging.

The system of landholding in rural Ireland was characterised by widespread landlord absenteeism, subdivision of land, uncertainty of tenure, and a lack of capital investment, trapping many of the rural labouring classes into subsistence agriculture, surviving on a few acres of land and utterly dependent on the potato. An estimated half of Ireland's population was either completely or largely dependent on this single crop. This dietary dependency, as well as other factors, exposed the poor to harvest failure and starvation, and famines (and accompanying disease epidemics) were relatively common in pre-Famine Ireland. A number of crises occurred in the eighteenth century, most devastatingly in the early 1740s and in the early 1780s, and nationwide and localised famines and epidemics struck in 1799–1801, 1822, 1826–7, 1830–1 and 1832–3.[13] The most significant nationwide crisis in this period was that of 1816–19, in which an estimated 65,000 people died. Of significance to this book is that this post-1815 crisis, which was part of a wider transnational 'perfect storm' of aggravating factors, drove many into destitution and swelled the numbers of beggars moving throughout Ireland, in search of employment or relief. This famine and epidemic witnessed a hardening in attitudes towards beggars by both corporate authorities and individuals and led directly to the rapid growth of the mendicity society movement in Ireland and Britain.

The question of Ireland's prevalent beggary was never far from the heart of the decades-long debates on Irish poverty, which by the 1830s constituted a major and contentious political issue in Ireland and Britain. This was driven by increased demands from Irish lobbyists that Irish landed proprietors be forced to contribute their fair share towards the relief of poverty, as well as British concerns over the influx into British towns and cities of impoverished Irish migrants and the apparently generous tax benefits enjoyed by Irish landowners and farmers. The political debate, centring on the question of whether a statutory, rates-based system of relief should be introduced into Ireland, exercised the leading political figures and social reformers of this period; as Peter Gray has observed, 'The question of poverty in Ireland ... was intensely politicized'.[14] With the replacement in 1834 of the

13 Peter Gray, *The Irish Famine* (London, 1995), pp. 16–33; Cormac Ó Gráda, *The Great Irish Famine* (Basingstoke, 1989), pp. 12–32; Timothy P. O'Neill, 'Poverty in Ireland 1815–45' in *Folk-Life*, xi (1973), pp. 22–33.
14 Peter Gray, *The making of the Irish Poor Law, 1815–1843* (Manchester, 2009), p. 6; Virginia Crossman and Peter Gray, 'Introduction: poverty and welfare in Ireland, 1838–1948' in Virginia Crossman and Peter Gray (eds), *Poverty and welfare in Ireland, 1838–1948* (Dublin, 2011), pp. 1–6.

Elizabethan-era system of parochial outdoor relief in England and Wales with the workhouse-centred 'New Poor Law', the debate shifted to the applicability of this system to the Irish context. Among the most significant developments in the prolonged Poor Law debates was the establishment in 1833 of the Royal Commission of Inquiry into the Condition of the Poorer Classes in Ireland (hereafter referred to as the Poor Inquiry), chaired by the Church of Ireland Archbishop of Dublin, Richard Whately. The Poor Inquiry examined approximately 1,500 witnesses in selected areas across Ireland on the social and economic conditions of their respective localities. The subsequent reports, totalling more than 5,000 pages, provide an unequalled insight into the lives of and societal attitudes towards the poor in Ireland in the years immediately prior to the establishment of the workhouse system, and a decade before the catastrophe of the Great Famine. Almost 800 pages of Appendix A of the inquiry's reports comprise verbatim, first-hand testimony from members of all social classes – from landlords, their agents, merchants and clergymen to farmers, shopkeepers, labourers and beggars – as to the social conditions in their locality. The topic of begging is considered in Appendix A under the heading 'Vagrancy' and comprises the largest single section in the Poor Inquiry's entire published output. As Niall Ó Ciosáin has observed, 'it is rare to be able to listen to the voices of people anywhere in the past with the clarity that this report allows and it is particularly rare for the "hidden Ireland" before the Famine'.[15]

'Deserving' and 'Undeserving'

Whether or not one was deemed 'deserving' or 'undeserving' of alms was based on the causes of their penury. Self-inflicted poverty, through idleness, drunkenness, profligacy or other immoral behaviours, regularly warranted a stern refusal of alms, whereas a more benign view was taken towards the traditional categories of worthy supplicants, such as the elderly, the sick, widows and children, and temporarily unemployed, yet typically industrious, workers. The application of categories of moral classification was common across all denominations and, as demonstrated by Ó Ciosáin, throughout all social classes.[16] Public concern regarding the extent and nature of poverty and mendicancy fluctuated according to wider social and economic

---

15 Niall Ó Ciosáin, 'Introduction' in Maureen Comber (ed.), *Poverty before the Famine, County Clare, 1835* (Ennis, 1996), p. iii.

16 Niall Ó Ciosáin, 'Boccoughs and God's poor: deserving and undeserving poor in Irish popular culture' in Tadhg Foley and Seán Ryder (eds), *Ideology and Ireland in the nineteenth century* (Dublin, 1998), pp. 93–9.

factors; as destitute beggars became more prevalent and increasingly mobile (thus, crucially, more visible), fears of the dangers of mendicancy became heightened. Those who publicly sought alms without shame in public places were distinguished from those who suffered silently in their wretched dwellings: the provision of assistance to the 'shamefaced poor' was a virtuous act, as it would not corrupt the recipient or the giver, while alms-giving to the idle 'common beggar' only served to encourage this practice. The bonds of community also informed how the poor were perceived: local paupers were known and more trustworthy than unknown, 'strange' beggars who 'could not but create suspicion'.[17] Dean of Clogher Richard Woodward's outline of his proposed scheme for poor relief in Ireland, which influenced the Houses of Industry legislation in 1772,[18] drew a distinction between the 'Poor ... who though willing to work, cannot subsist by Labour' and 'those idle Vagrants who are a Pest to Society'.[19] The virtue of honourable poverty was extolled by the mayor of Cork city John Besnard in 1833 in a letter to the Chief Secretary Edward Stanley. Writing to highlight the plight of the poor of Cork city, Besnard suggested that those who warranted most sympathy were:

> the lower orders of resident industrious tradesmen and labourers – persons who willingly use all their efforts to gain a livelihood, and submit to any privations, however great, rather than become beggars in our streets ... those who unceasingly devote their time, and unsparingly give their labour, for the maintenance of their families, and yet find their efforts unequal to the attainment of any thing like even moderate comfort.[20]

For some, beggars of all descriptions were 'undeserving' and were to be distinguished from the 'respectable' poor who did not beg. In a sermon in aid of the Protestant Colonisation Society in Dublin around 1840,[21] Rev. J.B. McCrea drew on the words of Moses: 'For the poor shall never cease out of the land: therefore I command thee, saying, Thou shalt open thine

---

17 Brian Pullan, 'Charity and poor relief in early modern Italy' in Martin Daunton (ed.), *Charity, self-interest and welfare in the English past* (London, 1996), pp. 66–7; Stuart Woolf, *The poor in western Europe in the eighteenth and nineteenth centuries* (London and New York, 1986), pp. 17–20.
18 11 & 12 Geo. III, c. 30 [Ire.] (2 June 1772).
19 Richard Woodward, *An argument in support of the right of the poor in the kingdom of Ireland, to a national provision ...* (Dublin, 1768), p. 11.
20 *Cork Constitution*, 28 Nov. 1833.
21 This society, founded in 1830, settled Protestant families on uncultivated land in the west of Ireland and engaged in scriptural teaching.

hand wide unto thy brother, to thy poor, and to thy needy, in thy land' (Deut. 15:11). To McCrea, the category of poor spoken of here was not 'the wretched, abject, and mendicant', whose support would merely encourage 'that evil which we understand by pauperism', but, instead, 'that portion of society which we call the working classes, or the industrious poor, whether pastoral, agricultural, and the manufacturing, the labour of whose hands is necessary to their maintenance and the comfort of their families ... and which are an essential part of every happy and prosperous nation'.[22] Poverty was an indispensable part of society, sanctified by God and ought to be assisted; beggary and pauperism, on the other hand, were evils which must be eradicated.

The application of this binary model shaped the perceptions of alms-givers, but it may be questioned as to the extent to which it influenced their judgement on whether or not to relieve a mendicant. Certainly, there are accounts of individuals ranking supplicants according to a hierarchy of merit, with the amount of relief given, whether in cash or in kind, depending on the specific circumstances of the begging party. In County Antrim, it was observed: 'The quantity usually given depends upon the compassion excited. The blind get most; widows and children and cripples rank next; the females with children, and then the aged. Single persons not incapable of work are not encouraged'.[23] Yet, the Poor Inquiry confirms that throughout Ireland indiscriminate alms-giving, without investigation into the character of beggars, was widespread, the practice being explained by the sheer number of paupers calling at dwellings and shops. Practicalities outweighed principle.

In speaking of the distinction between the 'deserving' and the 'undeserving' poor, it is important to note that these terms are not anachronisms imposed by historians in their retrospective analyses. Rather, the descriptions 'deserving', 'undeserving' and related derivatives were employed regularly by various commentators across all religious and political divides in their consideration of poverty and beggary.[24] The trope of the importunate street beggar was regularly contrasted with the silent suffering of the honest poor, resigned to their wretched abodes, out of sight, and the work of Brian Pullan on

---

22 J.B. McCrea, *Protestant poor a conservative element of society; being a sermon preached in Ebenezer Church, Dublin, for the Protestant Colonisation Society of Ireland* (Dublin, [c.1840]), p. 8.

23 *PI, Appendix A*, p. 715.

24 For a small sample of instances, see Thomas Dix Hincks, *A short account of the different charitable institutions of the city of Cork, with remarks* (Cork, 1802), p. 35; Last will and testament of Fr Paul Long, 14 July 1836 (DDA, DMP, 33/9/21); *Annual report for the year 1818, of the Benevolent or Strangers' Friend Society (originated in the year 1790)* (Dublin, 1819), p. 5.

poor relief in early modern Italy demonstrates that such frameworks, distinguishing the 'public poor' from the 'shamefaced poor', were pan-European in nature.[25] In 1811, the Belfast House of Industry contrasted what it termed 'the disgusting importunity of the habitual beggar' with 'the more affecting claims of silent unobtrusive distress',[26] while a decade later, the Roman Catholic bishop of Limerick, Charles Tuohy, praised the city's poor committee for their 'wise discrimination' between those poor who resisted the urge to solicit assistance and 'the common vagrant beggars, mendicant by profession, born so, and will live and die so'.[27]

For some, begging was their sole source of income, while for others begging was just one part of what Olwen Hufton termed the 'economy of makeshifts' – that is, the disparate survival strategies drawn upon by the poor. While Hufton centred her conceptual 'economy of makeshifts' around the practices of migration (for the sake of employment) and localised begging, subsequent historians have subsumed other strategies into this informal amalgamation of survival strategies, including petty theft, pawning, prostitution, resort to parochial or charitable relief, and kinship networks.[28] Hufton portrayed mendicancy as a life-skill taught in youth and drawn upon in times of acute distress:

> From early infancy, in fact, the children of the poor learnt to cadge a living, learnt about the viability of an economy of makeshifts, learnt the knack of presenting a cogent case, and the places and situations under which they would receive the most sympathy. This apprenticeship, for it was no less, occurred long before any other formal service as domestic servant, labourer, or textile worker. Should work run out, should they find themselves in later life between jobs or unable to support themselves on the proceeds of their labour, begging was their natural recourse.[29]

Hufton's concept has proved influential and lasting in capturing the desperate and disparate methods by which poor individuals and families scraped out a basic existence. It is a model which has shaped how social historians have approached the question of poverty and poor relief in

---

25 Pullan, 'Charity and poor relief in early modern Italy', pp. 66–7.
26 *BNL*, 8 Feb. 1811.
27 *Leinster Journal*, 15 June 1822.
28 Steven King and Alannah Tomkins, 'Introduction' in Steven King and Alannah Tomkins (eds), *The poor in England 1700–1850: an economy of makeshifts* (Manchester, 2003), pp. 1–38.
29 Olwen Hufton, *The poor of eighteenth-century France, 1750–1789* (Oxford, 1974), pp. 109–10.

Britain and, more recently, in Ireland.[30] Historiographical developments later focused attention on households as heterogeneous units, with family members playing different roles according to their respective stage in the life-cycle.[31] In more recent years, Rachel Fuchs has discerned the 'cultures of expediencies' of the poor, in response to the constant 'climate of calamities' in which the poor lived: '[they] sought creative and expedient ways to manage situations, adapting behaviour as they went along, usually within the larger cultural parameters of ethics, morality, economics, and the law'.[32] A common theme running through the present book is the fact that the poor in pre-Famine Ireland, including those who engaged in begging, deployed agency in their engagement with individuals and relief mechanisms. Paupers are not to be seen as powerless dupes but as individuals who weighed up consequences and made decisions, based on the most advantageous anticipated outcome.[33]

Nature of Charity

In an age of religious revival and restructuring among all the major denominations in Ireland, religious sentiment universally coloured acts of charity, whether carried out on an informal, individual basis or through corporate and organised means. Individual and communal concepts of poverty and charity were shaped by confessional teachings, drawing on a universal relevance of the life and example of Christ. Religion was significant 'both in terms of individual inspiration and organisational structures'.[34] Furthermore, the performance of public charity was coloured by confessional characteristics: inflamed sectarian tensions, especially from the 1820s onwards, infiltrated the realms of philanthropy and charity, with Virginia Crossman

30 Steven King, *Poverty and welfare in England, 1700–1850: a regional perspective* (Manchester, 2000); King and Tomkins, *The poor in England 1700–1850, passim*; Donnacha Seán Lucey, 'Poor relief in the west of Ireland, 1861–1911' in Crossman and Gray, *Poverty and welfare in Ireland*, pp. 37–51.

31 Laurence Fontaine and Jürgen Schlumbohm, 'Household strategies for survival: an introduction' in *International Review of Social History*, xlv (2000), pp. 1–17.

32 Rachel Fuchs, *Gender and poverty in nineteenth-century Europe* (Cambridge, 2005), p. 5.

33 Recent studies which consider how the poor exerted agency include King and Tomkins, *The poor in England 1700–1850*; Fuchs, *Gender and poverty*, pp. 1–19. For recent Irish angles to this question, see Georgina Laragy, 'Poor relief in the south of Ireland, 1850–1921' in Crossman and Gray, *Poverty and welfare in Ireland*, pp. 53–66; Virginia Crossman, *Poverty and the Poor Law in Ireland 1850–1914* (Liverpool, 2013), *passim*.

34 Maria Luddy, 'Religion, philanthropy and the state in late eighteenth- and early nineteenth-century Ireland' in Hugh Cunningham and Joanna Innes (eds), *Charity, philanthropy and reform from the 1690s to 1850* (Basingstoke, 1998), p. 154.

noting 'the almost totally segregated nature of philanthropy in Ireland'.[35] The potential that religious tensions held out for intra-denominational disharmony was most vividly seen in the charity work of women with poor children, particularly from the 1840s onwards.[36]

In an era marked by the prolonged debates and campaigns for or against a national Poor Law, in which doctrinal thinking and the personal zeal of clergymen and the laity were key influences, each of the main churches and religious societies in Ireland contributed to the discourse on beggary and alms-giving, with the nuances of each denomination's world view and organisational structure carrying through to the negotiation of mendicancy, despite the fact that moralising middle-class philanthropists of all denominations shared similar views and deployed an almost homogeneous language of condescending charity. A key consideration of this book will be whether Catholics and Protestants (of various denominations) perceived and responded to beggary and alms-giving in different or similar ways. Can Roman Catholic approaches, for example, be distinguished from those of Anglicans or Presbyterians? In considering this fundamental question, an important assertion from the pioneering social historian of nineteenth-century Ireland, Timothy P. O'Neill, warrants attention:

> To the Protestant moralist the effects on the recipient and the result of almsgiving on the economy and society were of the greatest importance and so all charity had to be carefully examined to ensure that it did not create a new class of beggars or endanger the economic framework. The Irish poor had different values and held different notions about charity. They regarded charity as a duty for the donor and all beggars were recognised as objects worthy of help.[37]

Here, O'Neill draws distinctions between Protestant and Catholic attitudes to labour, industry and poor relief in nineteenth-century Ireland. The reader is presented with the attitudes of what O'Neill describes as, on the one hand, 'the Protestant moralist' and on the other, 'the Irish poor'. While not explicitly stated, this latter category is implicitly pigeon-holed as being homogeneously Roman Catholic, an assumption which is problematic,

35 Crossman, *Poverty and the Poor Law in Ireland*, p. 21.
36 Maria Luddy, *Women and philanthropy in nineteenth-century Ireland* (Cambridge, 1995), pp. 68–96; Jacinta Prunty, 'Battle plans and battlegrounds: Protestant mission activity in the Dublin slums, 1840s–1880s' in Crawford Gribben and Andrew R. Holmes (eds), *Protestant millennialism, evangelicalism and Irish society, 1790–2005* (Basingstoke, 2006), pp. 119–43.
37 Timothy P. O'Neill, 'The Catholic Church and relief of the poor 1815–45' in *Archivium Hibernicum*, xxxi (1973), p. 133.

particularly if one is to consider the working-class Presbyterian poor in the towns of eastern Ulster or the substantial Church of Ireland distressed working classes of Dublin city.[38] In differing from O'Neill's argument, Seán Connolly has demonstrated that aversion to indiscriminate alms-giving was not unique to any one denomination, stating that 'in this, as in other matters, the real line of division was social class rather than religion'.[39] More recent contributions to this historiographical discussion by Maria Luddy, Margaret Preston and Virginia Crossman have stressed the importance of class, race and gender in understanding the dynamics of welfare provision in this period,[40] while Niall Ó Ciosáin has recently determined that, 'the distinction is not between denominations but between the clergy of all denominations and the representatives of the state on the one hand, and the laity of all denominations on the other'.[41] The later chapters of this book will ask of nineteenth-century Ireland what Brian Pullan has asked of early modern Europe: can certain traits of Catholic and Protestant theory and practice pertaining to poor relief be discerned as being distinct from each other? Religion, however, was not the only determinant in how charity was practised, and the giving and soliciting of alms was also influenced by gender and social class, while the peculiarities of rural and urban life also influenced the prevailing cultures of mendicancy.

While this study is largely concerned with the solicitation by beggars of individuals in a public place, what was arguably the most common avenue of relief resorted to by the destitute poor requires acknowledgement – namely, the networks of informal support provided by kin, neighbours and friends. The poor did not live in a social vacuum but resided, laboured and struggled within communities comprising multitudes of families living similar experiences. In a period prior to a statutory relief network and when corporate support, through parishes and charities, was largely ad hoc and

38 For studies of these significant urban Protestant working-class communities, see Jacqueline Hill, 'The Protestant response to repeal: the case of the Dublin working class' in F.S.L. Lyons and R.A.J. Hawkins (eds), *Ireland under the Union: varieties of tension. Essays in honour of T.W. Moody* (Oxford, 1980), pp. 35–68; Ronnie Munck, 'The formation of the working class in Belfast, 1788–1881' in *Saothar*, xi (1986), pp. 75–89.

39 S.J. Connolly, 'Religion, work-discipline and economic attitudes: the case of Ireland' in T.M. Devine and David Dickson (eds), *Ireland and Scotland 1600–1850: parallels and contrasts in economic and social development* (Edinburgh, 1983), p. 244 n. 4.

40 Luddy, *Women and philanthropy*; Margaret H. Preston, *Charitable words: women, philanthropy and the language of charity in nineteenth-century Dublin* (Westport, CT and London, 2004), pp. 41–65; Virginia Crossman, 'Middle-class attitudes to poverty and welfare in post-Famine Ireland' in Fintan Lane (ed.) *Politics, society and the middle class in modern Ireland* (Basingstoke, 2010), pp. 130–47.

41 Niall Ó Ciosáin, *Ireland in official print culture, 1800–1850: a new reading of the Poor Inquiry* (Oxford, 2014), p. 118.

subject to strict moralising from wealthy benefactors, seeking assistance from family and friends was the first avenue of choice for many poor people. Bishop James Doyle, in testimony to an 1830 parliamentary committee on the state of the poor in Ireland, gave evidence of this type of support: 'In visiting a poor creature in a hovel where distress and misery prevail, we find the creature surrounded by poor neighbours, one of whom brings him a little bread or meal, another a little meat, or prepares a little broth or soup, and they all comfort him with their conversation and society'.[42] Due to the scarcity of appropriate sources, this is an avenue of poor assistance which remains largely unexplored by Irish historians.[43] Some efforts have been made in recent years by historians of England, among whom Colin Jones has reasonably suggested that the provision of assistance through informal avenues was more common than through formal structures.[44] The fact, however, that the drawing upon of informal support remains largely irrecoverable for historians does not warrant the exclusion of this topic in any analysis of the experiences of the poor in this period. It was a support mechanism that, at the very least, merits acknowledgement in the absence of detailed analysis.

In examining the roles played by various parties in the giving and receiving of alms and assistance in Ireland, this book will focus on informal, private alms-giving, as well as the dynamics of welfare provision by non-state bodies, such as charitable societies and the main denominations. In doing so, this book is departing from the most common approach taken by historians of poverty and welfare in Ireland, whose works largely explore the 1838 Irish Poor Law Act, the Great Famine and the post-Famine decades: for instance, a recent edited

---

42 *Report of the select committee on the state of the poor in Ireland; being a summary of the first, second and third reports of evidence taken before that committee: together with an appendix of accounts and papers*, p. 33, H.C. 1830 (667), vii, 33.

43 To date, only brief references to the familial and neighbourly support have been presented by historians of Ireland: Mary Cullen, 'Breadwinners and providers: women in the household economy of labouring families, 1835–6' in Maria Luddy and Cliona Murphy (eds), *Women surviving* (Dublin, 1990), p. 107; Virginia Crossman, *The Poor Law in Ireland, 1838–1948* (Dundalk, 2006), p. 4. The informal and mutual support provided among prostitutes has been considered in Maria Luddy, *Prostitution and Irish society, 1800–1940* (Cambridge, 2007), pp. 61–70.

44 See for instance, Anne Digby, *British welfare policy: workhouse to workforce* (London, 1989), pp. 58–93; Heather Shore, 'Crime, criminal networks and the survival strategies of the poor in early eighteenth-century London' in King and Tomkins, *The poor in England, 1700–1850*, pp. 137–65; Sam Barrett, 'Kinship, poor relief and the welfare process in early modern England' in King and Tomkins, *The poor in England, 1700–1850*, pp. 199–227; Richard Dyson, 'Welfare provision in Oxford during the latter stages of the Old Poor Law, 1800–1834' in *Historical Journal*, lii, no. 4 (2009), pp. 958–9; Colin Jones, 'Some recent trends in the history of charity' in Daunton, *Charity, self-interest and welfare*, pp. 51–63.

collection of articles exploring poverty and relief mechanisms commences with the passing of the Poor Law Act.[45] The cataclysmic impact that the Famine exerted on Irish society was such that historians' emphasis on this event and its legacy is understandable. By comparison, the pre-Famine decades remain relatively neglected. Moreover, the specific topics of begging and alms-giving, ubiquitous throughout pre-Famine Ireland, have been largely overlooked. The institutional shadow of the workhouse looms large over the historiography of this period.[46] However, the role of the main churches and religious societies in framing how individuals perceived and responded to poverty, begging and alms-giving remains largely omitted from historians' studies.

Crucial to understanding how contemporaries addressed begging and alms-giving is an analysis of the wider debates on poverty, the poor and welfare initiatives. The most significant contribution to the historiography of nineteenth-century Irish poverty is Peter Gray's *The making of the Poor Law*, which examines the long and fraught ideological debates and campaigns which preceded the 1838 Irish Poor Law Act. Gray demonstrates that mendicancy, vagrancy and alms-giving were never too far from the centre of the discourse on the condition of the Irish poor. Fresh outbreaks of distress, such as those of the late 1810s and the mid-1820s, 'created new classes of paupers who were neither 'casual' nor 'professional' but structural'.[47] These periods of crisis witnessed renewed zeal among Irish and British elites to address the problem of Irish poverty. The cultural nuances that shaped the practices of mendicancy and alms-giving are the subject of important studies by Laurence M. Geary and Niall Ó Ciosáin.[48] Drawing on the voluminous testimony recorded in the mid-1830s by the Poor Inquiry, both Geary and Ó Ciosáin concluded that distinctions between the 'deserving' and 'undeserving' poor were not limited to moralising middle-class philanthropists and commentators but were also to be found among the lower classes of Irish society. Their work correctly argues that approaches to beggary were inherently complex, with perceptions being coloured by religion, social class and gender.

The corporate bodies which were most active in responding to beggary were parish vestries, the historiography of which has been largely confined

45 Crossman and Gray, *Poverty and welfare in Ireland*.
46 John O'Connor, *The workhouses of Ireland: the fate of Ireland's poor* (Dublin, 1995); Helen Burke, *The people and the Poor Law in nineteenth-century Ireland* (Littlehampton, 1987); Crossman, *Poverty and the Poor Law in Ireland*.
47 Gray, *Making of the Irish Poor Law*, p. 17.
48 Laurence M. Geary, '"The whole country was in motion": mendicancy and vagrancy in pre-Famine Ireland' in Jacqueline Hill and Colm Lennon (eds), *Luxury and austerity*, Historical Studies XXI (Dublin, 1999), pp. 121–36; Ó Ciosáin, 'Boccoughs and God's poor', pp. 93–9; Ó Ciosáin, *Ireland in official print culture*, pp. 73–107.

to their seventeenth- and eighteenth-century incarnations. In his search for the 'old Irish Poor Law', David Dickson placed the parish vestry at the centre of corporate initiatives to alleviate poverty prior to the introduction of the Poor Law and workhouse system in the late 1830s.[49] Yet, the records of parish vestries, especially the vestry minute books which are rich in social history, remain unexplored by historians of poverty in nineteenth-century Ireland, and this book will attempt to fill that lacuna, placing the parish's evolving role in welfare provision in the post-Poor Law period into the context of the declining civil role for parishes in Irish society. The multiplication of charitable societies across Ireland and Britain from the late eighteenth century forms a crucial context for this book's analysis of begging and alms-giving. James Kelly has stressed the importance of the emerging associational culture among the rising middle classes to the growth of charities in this period, while noting features peculiar to the Irish context, especially the lack of any national state system of poor assistance. Kelly also makes the important point that contrary to parish bodies, charities founded in the late eighteenth century targeted their resources at specific categories of the distressed poor, and 'were more selective both in the numbers they targeted and in the assistance they provided'.[50] In his study on British voluntary societies, Robert Morris argues that these bodies, of which charities formed a substantial proportion, shared three distinct traits: they were urban-based, were formed and driven by the elites of the middle classes, mainly from the professional and commercial classes, and their goal was to improve the condition of the labouring classes with minimal state assistance or interference.[51] Adopting Kelly's argument about selectivity and discrimination in voluntary charity provision, this book will present a case study of the mendicity society movement which flourished across Ireland and Britain in the first half of the nineteenth century. Mendicity societies were voluntarily funded charities founded in cities and towns with the primary purpose of suppressing street begging. To date, the historiography of Irish mendicity societies has been limited. Brief case studies of the Dublin, Galway, Drogheda and Belfast societies are

---

49 David Dickson, 'In search of the old Irish Poor Law' in Rosalind Mitchison and Peter Roebuck (eds), *Economy and society in Scotland and Ireland, 1500–1939* (Edinburgh, 1988), pp. 149–59.

50 James Kelly, 'Charitable societies: their genesis and development, 1720–1800' in James Kelly and Martyn J. Powell (eds), *Clubs and societies in eighteenth-century Ireland* (Dublin, 2010), p. 103. For more on this associational culture, see Colm Lennon (ed.), *Confraternities and sodalities in Ireland: charity, devotion and sociability* (Dublin, 2012), and R.V. Comerford and Jennifer Kelly (eds), *Associational culture in Ireland and abroad* (Dublin, 2010).

51 R.J. Morris, 'Voluntary societies and British urban elites, 1780–1850: an analysis' in *Historical Journal*, xxvi, no. 1 (Mar. 1983), pp. 95–118.

provided in the works of Jacinta Prunty, John Cunningham, Ned McHugh and Alison Jordan.[52] These accounts all stress the financial embarrassment which underpinned these institutions' (almost invariably brief) existence and their eventual supplanting by the Poor Law union workhouses, yet the stark concentration of these societies in relatively small towns in Ulster has gone without analysis. Audrey Woods's administrative history of the Dublin Mendicity Society is admirable in its extensive use of source material but fails sufficiently to locate this important charity within the context of wider voluntary charitable provision in Dublin city and also in the context of the international mendicity society movement.[53]

Human Element

The historian of poverty in pre-Famine Ireland is inevitably left frustrated by the dearth of accounts from the poor themselves – this is more so with studies of those who engaged in begging, either habitually or on occasion. While a detailed analysis of the lives, backgrounds, motivations, emotions and decisions of individual beggars is desirable, it largely remains aspirational; as such, beggars and vagrants are given 'at best, walk-on parts in Irish social history'.[54] Whereas historians of eighteenth- and nineteenth-century Britain are well served by collections of paupers' or beggars' letters to parochial authorities[55] – since 1601, the parish performed a statutory function in welfare provision in England and Wales – there are no bodies of similar sources for Ireland. The available source material for Ireland simply precludes any such analysis; as social historians of any country in any period appreciate, accounts of poverty and the poor most often come to us from the viewpoints of wealthier members of society. Published reports of parliamentary committees inquiring into poverty and distress, the memoirs of middle-class social campaigners, the registers and minute books of charitable societies, preachers' sermons and the records of church relief initiatives give insights into the experiences of poverty; however, when the poor appear in

---

52 Prunty, *Dublin slums*, pp. 205–9; John Cunningham, *'A town tormented by the sea': Galway, 1790–1914* (Dublin, 2004), pp. 47–54; Ned McHugh, *Drogheda before the Famine: urban poverty in the shadow of privilege, 1826–45* (Dublin, 1998), pp. 46–51; Alison Jordan, *Who cared? Charity in Victorian and Edwardian Belfast* (Belfast, [1992]), pp. 20–4.

53 Audrey Woods, *Dublin outsiders: a history of the Mendicity Institution, 1818–1998* (Dublin, 1998).

54 Caitriona Clear, 'Homelessness, crime, punishment and poor relief in Galway, 1850–1914: an introduction' in *Journal of the Galway Archaeological and Historical Society*, 1 (1998), p. 118.

55 For instance, see Thomas Sokoll (ed.), *Essex pauper letters, 1731–1837* (Oxford, 2001).

such records, they are generally observed at a remove. As Rachel Fuchs has stated, 'the poor often become visible to historians only when they meet the literate middle classes in the workplace or public arenas. As a result, historians have largely observed the lives of the underprivileged through middle-class eyes that viewed them from a safe distance through lenses distorted by fear, distrust, and disgust'.[56] In a similar vein, Niall Ó Ciosáin has commented that 'most of the archives and material objects which survive were produced by rich and powerful minorities, and deal with their immediate concerns. When the majority are described, it is usually by hostile or uncomprehending observers'.[57] An effort has been made in this book to mitigate this unevenly weighted base of primary sources, by presenting the perspectives of a broad range of individuals, both rural and urban, from all social classes, and also by examining the experiences of women, as both the givers and receivers of alms. Each chapter begins with a vignette, depicting the attitudes and experiences of different people in the giver/receiver exchange and in some instances these words are those of mendicants in pre-Famine Ireland. Virginia Crossman, writing of post-Famine Poor Law records, reminds us that 'The voices of the poor are faint, but they are not absent',[58] yet within our earlier period such voices are only audible through the voluminous transcriptions of testimonies to the Poor Inquiry.

Outline

The book is divided into three sections. Section I (encompassing Chapters 1–3) examines the issue of mendicancy, noting the significance of location, visibility, gender and employment opportunities in framing explanations of what was begging and who engaged in this practice. Chapter 2 will move this discussion of beggary from definition to measurement, analysing the importance to many contemporaries of calculating estimates of the amount of beggars, on either a national or local level, and the amount doled out in alms. Chapter 3 will explore the many ways in which begging was perceived in the early nineteenth century. Mendicancy was seen as a threat on many levels and a number of these perceived threats will be analysed as case studies. Due consideration will also be given to perceptions of begging as a natural right of the poor, while the common association of mendicants with superstitions in popular folk culture will be explored. In the second and third

---

56 Fuchs, *Gender and poverty*, p. 154.
57 Niall Ó Ciosáin, *Print and popular culture in Ireland 1750–1850* (new edn, Dublin, 2010), p. 1.
58 Crossman, *Poverty and the Poor Law in Ireland*, p. 9.

sections of the book, comprising Chapters 4–7, the focus will shift towards the responses of charities, vestries and the major churches and religious societies in pre-Famine Ireland to begging. The evolving role of parish vestries in managing local responses to fluctuating levels of mendicancy throughout Ireland is the subject of Chapter 4, which will place the vestries' declining position in welfare provision in the second quarter of the century into the context of a wider diminution of parishes' civil functions. Chapter 5 presents a case study of the mendicity society movement, which flourished across Ireland and Britain in the first half of the nineteenth century, and will contrast the mendicity societies with the earlier Houses of Industry, which also had a remit of suppressing mendicancy, before concluding with an analysis of the rapid decline of these charities in the late 1830s. Chapter 6 considers Roman Catholic perceptions and responses, commencing with an analysis of Catholic teaching pertaining to good works and alms-giving, as spelled out in contemporary catechisms. The apparent flaws found in these teachings by numerous Protestant polemicists will be considered alongside the refutation of such polemical utterings by senior Catholic clerics. The views of the long-neglected figure of Archbishop of Dublin, Daniel Murray (1768–1852), will be closely analysed, as will those of Mary Aikenhead (1787–1858), foundress of the Religious Sisters of Charity. As a counterpoint to the study of Catholic approaches, Chapter 7 analyses Protestant discourses on and responses to beggary in Ireland. The impact of evangelicalism in shaping perceptions of mendicancy and the influence of clergymen-cum-political economists, such as Richard Whately and Thomas Chalmers, will be explored, as will the disparate internal mechanisms by which Protestant denominations responded to beggary.

I Begging and Alms-Giving: Framing the Issues

1

Defining Begging and Alms-Giving

From what [weaver Edward] McNally has stated of his neighbourhood, it must be difficult to draw a distinction and institute between the beggar and the labourer, for, as he has already stated, there are labourers or persons willing to labour, holding a patch of ground, whose families beg on all occasions, on which their provisions run short, and this occurs so frequently that McNally has already counted them among beggars. There are others who hold a larger portion of land, and whose families beg only in summer; others holding more land and cheaper are still labourers, and work for hire, but are never reduced to beggary; among the two former cases it is hard to distinguish, for the purpose of comparison where the beggar begins and the labourer ends.

Poor Inquiry report for Aughavale, County Mayo, 1835[1]

Introduction

For the people who lived in pre-Famine Ireland, and subsequently for historians, perhaps the single greatest challenge when considering mendicancy and its extent is defining just who and what is being discussed. This challenge was not unique to nineteenth-century Irish society. Paul Slack's study of vagrancy in seventeenth-century England considers whether 'vagrants' and 'vagabonds' – which he rightly describes as 'emotive, elastic terms' – were wandering pedlars or minstrels, the archetypal 'able-bodied professional beggars of the criminal underworld' or

1 *PI, Appendix A*, p. 494.

'simply unskilled migrant labourers and paupers'?[2] Differentiating between begging and casual employment regularly proved difficult, as reflected in the quotation above from the mid-1830s Poor Inquiry. In some instances, begging was carried out without resort to other survival strategies, while perhaps in most cases alms-seeking was a practice that individuals resorted to occasionally and in accordance with their fluctuating economic circumstances. Experiences of begging in early to mid-nineteenth-century Ireland were never homogeneous. In Drogheda, the Poor Inquiry commissioners observed that the 'distinction between the less industrious, honest, frugal, and independent families of the working class, and the *mendicants* or *vagrants*, is not very broadly marked, as, in times of sickness or want of employment, having no savings to fall back upon, and being unable to obtain credit, their only resource is to pray for alms'.[3] The circumstances which motivated an individual to go out into the roads and streets and seek alms differed from person to person. Some commentators crudely lumped all beggars and vagrants together and categorised them as the lazy, idle poor who preferred the mendicant life to one of industry; the historian ought to avoid such crude categorisations. If one was, for the sake of argument, to embrace Henry Mayhew's famous threefold breakdown of the poor of London into those who will work, those who cannot work and those who will not work – into the third of which Mayhew clumsily massed beggars, thieves and prostitutes[4] – it would be evident that street beggars in nineteenth-century Ireland transcended all three groupings.

What Was Begging?

Negotiating the Terminology of Mendicancy
The terms 'beggar' and 'mendicant', as well as their derivatives 'begging' and 'mendicancy', were used interchangeably in the pre-Famine period when referring to individuals engaged in the solicitation of alms. Impoverished people were spoken of as being 'in want', 'in distress' and, in more extreme cases, 'living in destitution'. These poor persons had numerous survival options open to them, one of which was begging/mendicancy, and for different individuals, households and families, their resort to this strategy varied from regular begging to rare instances. On the other hand, a person

---

2 Paul Slack, 'Vagrants and vagrancy in England, 1598–1664' in *Economic History Review*, xxvii, no. 3 (Aug. 1974), p. 362.
3 *PI, Appendix C, Part I*, p. 49.
4 Gertrude Himmelfarb, 'Mayhew's poor: a problem of identity' in *Victorian Studies*, xiv, no. 3 (Mar. 1971), p. 309.

or family could be regarded as being poor and living in destitution but not engaged in mendicancy. An area in which this distinction arises is in the language of charity, which championed the silent suffering of the 'honest', 'deserving' poor (the 'shamefaced poor'),[5] in stark contrast to the idle 'undeserving'. For instance, an 1840s report for the Dublin Strangers' Friend Society advised its readers (existing and prospective subscribers and donors) that:

> [the] worst forms of distress and destitution are not those which are presented on the streets. In the retired and depressed portions of the city, they are to be found, as well as in its dark and narrow lanes, where every house is inhabited by an almost incredible number of families, and every thing congenial to disease and misery is found to exist.[6]

Here, the charitable society was clearly distinguishing between the 'distress and destitution' of the 'deserving' in contrast to the solicitations of 'undeserving' street beggars.

The term 'vagabond' is mostly of early modern usage and outside its appearance in the 1770s Houses of Industry legislation[7] the term rarely appears in nineteenth-century sources for Ireland, while the word 'tramp' did not become common until the late nineteenth century.[8] The case is rather different, however, regarding the terms 'vagrant' and 'vagrancy'. In sources pertaining to pre-Famine Ireland, and this is also the case with Britain, the labels 'vagrant' and 'vagrancy' pertained to the criminal acts of wandering, being without the means to support oneself and, in certain scenarios, public begging (criminal acts which were subjected to revised definition in line with the evolution of legislation). Instances of vagrancy were among the most common cases that came before local magistrates at the petty sessions, and magistrates' manuals for the period usually included substantial sections on the existing vagrancy legislation, listing the relevant statutes, the various categories of persons who could be tried under the

---

5 Woolf, *The poor in western Europe*; Brian Pullan, 'Catholics and the poor in early modern Europe' in *Transactions of the Royal Historical Society*, 5th series, xxvi (1976), pp. 15–34; Sandra Cavallo, *Charity and power in early modern Italy: benefactors and their motives in Turin, 1541–1789* (Cambridge, 1995), pp. 12, 15. See also Preston, *Charitable words*, pp. 41–65.

6 *Annual report of the Strangers' Friend Society (founded in 1790) for visiting and relieving distressed strangers and the resident sick poor, in Dublin and its vicinity; with an account of some of the cases relieved, and list of subscribers for 1842* (Dublin, 1843), p. 7.

7 11 & 12 Geo. III, c. 11, s. 13 [Ire.] (2 June 1772); 11 & 12 Geo. III, c. 30, s. 8 [Ire.] (2 June 1772); 13 & 14 Geo. III, c. 46, s. 5 [Ire.] (2 June 1774); 15 & 16 Geo. III, c. 35, s. 1 [Ire.] (4 Apr. 1776).

8 Crossman, *Poverty and the Poor Law in Ireland*, pp. 198–203.

vagrancy laws and the requisite punishment.[9] Typically, the defining characteristics of 'vagrants' were that they were non-local, work-shy and carried
'the aura of criminality'.[10] Since the sixteenth century, the term 'vagrancy'
was used as a catch-all term for the various categories of the mobile poor
throughout Europe. Robert Jütte has discerned 'a new concept of collective
crime which is usually summarized under the heading "vagrancy"', similar
to Beier's description of early modern vagrants representing 'a new social
problem … in being a large landless element with no firm roots and few
prospects'.[11] 'The implication was that vagrants were no ordinary criminals;
they were regarded as a major threat to society, and therefore pursued by all
authorities and stigmatized as deviants'.[12]

Beggars, Begging and the Law
Laws curtailing mendicancy and vagrancy in Ireland dated back to 1542,[13] and
in the following centuries numerous acts were passed by Irish and English
parliaments dividing the poor between the 'deserving' and 'undeserving',
whose resort to begging was to be regulated and punished respectively.[14] In
the mid-1630s, the Irish Parliament passed an act for the erection of houses
of correction, targeting 'rogues, vagabonds, sturdy beggars, and other idle
and disorderly persons'.[15] The lumping together of beggars and vagrants with
'tories' and robbers – illustrating the common association of beggary with
crime, sedition and outrage – influenced the passing of the 1703 act, which
provided for the transportation of such individuals to British plantations in

---

9 Leonard MacNally, *The justice of the peace for Ireland: containing the authorities and
   duties of that officer …* (2 vols, Dublin, 1808), ii, 354–74, 807–12; William Toone, *The
   magistrate's manual; or, a summary of the duties and powers of a justice of the peace,
   carefully compiled from the best authorities; with extracts from adjudged cases and the
   statutes to the 56th George III. 1816 …* (2nd edn, London, 1817), pp. 804–34.
10 D.J.V. Jones, '"A dead loss to the community": the criminal vagrant in mid-nineteenth-
   century Wales' in *Welsh History Review*, viii (1976–7), p. 314; Rosalind Mitchison,
   'Who were the poor in Scotland, 1690–1830?' in Rosalind Mitchison and Peter Roebuck
   (eds), *Economy and society in Scotland and Ireland 1500–1939* (Edinburgh, 1988), p. 143.
11 Jütte, *Poverty and deviance*, p. 6; A.L. Beier, *Masterless men: the vagrancy problem in
   England 1560–1640* (London and New York, 1985), p. xxi. For the emergence in the
   sixteenth century of the vagrant as the archetypal 'criminal stereotype', see J.A. Sharpe,
   Crime in early modern England, 1550–1750 (London and New York, 1984), pp. 99–103.
   Thomas Harman's *Caveat for common cursetors* (1567), an early example of rogue
   literature, lists 24 different types of vagrant.
12 Jütte, *Poverty and deviance*, p. 146.
13 This act, 33 Hen. VIII, c. 15 [Ire.] (1542) was based upon an earlier English statute, 22
   Hen. VIII, c. 12 [Eng.] (1530–1).
14 Comprehensive accounts of the history of Irish legislation in this field are given
   in George Nicholls, *A history of the Irish Poor Law* (London, 1856); Law Reform
   Commission, *Report on vagrancy and related matters* (Dublin, 1985).
15 10 & 11 Chas. 1, c. 4 [Ire.] (1635).

America,[16] and four years later this legislation was extended so as to include 'all loose, idle vagrants', defined as 'such as pretend to be Irish gentlemen and will not work or betake themselves to any honest trade or livelihood, but wander about demanding victuals, and coshering from house to house'.[17]

The most significant act pertaining to beggars, prior to the nineteenth century, was a statute of 1771–2 facilitating the establishment throughout Ireland of Houses of Industry, which were multi-faceted poorhouses that simultaneously served as refuges for the 'deserving' destitute poor and carceral facilities for idle, 'sturdy beggars'. The opening sentence of the 'Act for badging such poor as shall be found unable to support themselves by labour' stated that 'strolling beggars are very numerous in this kingdom', thus outlining the perceived urgency for this new statute's relief and punitive measures.[18] This act created a visual distinction between the 'deserving' and the 'undeserving' which went beyond perceptions. The attachment of a badge onto the garments of 'the helpless poor' identified them to prospective almsgivers as being worthy of charity.[19] This conveyed the inherent implication that those without such a 'licence to beg' were deemed, by the newly formed corporations on whom the powers of relief and punishment of the vagrant poor were bestowed, to be 'sturdy beggars and vagabonds'. Not only were they not deserving of charitable relief, but their supposed delinquency warranted marginalisation, punishment and institutional confinement.

Upon the establishment of the Dublin House of Industry, the punitive powers of the city poorhouse (founded in 1703–4) were transferred to the new institution. Within a few years, however, the system of granting begging licences was discontinued in Dublin, due in part to the overwhelming number of applicants but also because of 'the difficulty of discriminating

16 2 Ann., c. 12 [Ire.] (4 Mar. 1704). See Patrick Fitzgerald, 'A sentence to sail: the transportation of Irish convicts and vagrants to colonial America in the eighteenth century' in Patrick Fitzgerald and Steve Ickringill (eds), *Atlantic crossroads: historical connections between Scotland, Ulster and North America* (Newtownards, 2001), p. 116.

17 6 Ann., c. 12 (30 Oct. 1707), cited in James Kelly, 'Transportation from Ireland to North America, 1703–1789' in David Dickson and Cormac Ó Gráda (eds), *Refiguring Ireland: essays in honour of L.M. Cullen* (Dublin, 2003), p. 114.

18 11 & 12 Geo. III, c. 30 [Ire.] (2 June 1772); Mel Cousins, 'The Irish parliament and relief of the poor: the 1772 legislation establishing houses of industry' in *Eighteenth-Century Ireland*, xxviii (2013), pp. 95–115.

19 While the badging of parish paupers in Dublin dated back to the late seventeenth century, it appears that the practice had declined by the 1730s, when Jonathan Swift published his famous proposal for badging the city's poor: W.A. Seaby and T.G.F. Paterson, 'Ulster beggars' badges' in *Ulster Archaeological Journal*, 3rd series, xxxiii (1970), p. 96; Raymond Gillespie (ed.), *The vestry records of the parishes of St Catherine and St James, Dublin, 1657–1692* (Dublin, 2004), p. 151; [Jonathan Swift], *A proposal for giving badges to the beggars in all the parishes of Dublin* (London, 1737).

between the meritorious poor and the impostor', which 'demonstrated this method to be useless and impracticable', according to a later report.[20] Despite being empowered to curtail mendicancy, the governors of the House of Industry exerted these powers only occasionally, usually at times of crisis and in response to public outcry. Thus, in July 1801, in the midst of a prolonged period of inclement weather, food shortages and disease epidemics, the governors informed the public that as they 'intend in a short time to enforce the Laws against Vagrants, &c. they earnestly request that the Public will not give Alms to Beggars in the Streets, as such a practice must necessarily defeat all their endeavours for that purpose'.[21] The injection of new blood and administrative reform also renewed authorities' zeal in suppressing street begging. The accession of Major James Palmer to the governorship of the House of Industry in 1820 was cited by one newspaper as the cause of a renewed initiative to curtail mendicancy, stating that 'the former apathetical feeling no longer remains'. The provision of additional cells for 'sturdy beggars and disgusting objects' and increased vigilance by the police led to 'several of these sturdy fellows, who were the terror of respectable females when walking unattended' being apprehended and confined in the institution.[22]

Cultural representations of the mendicant classes at this time focused on the archetypal able-bodied, idle male vagrant, who represented a substantial threat to the social order. However, criminal records for Ireland reveal that by far the majority of people tried under the vagrancy laws were women. An examination of Irish prison registers for the period 1822–45 identifies 194 convictions for the crime of vagrancy, and amongst this number 130 convicts (67 per cent) were female.[23] Women also constituted the majority of persons sentenced to seven years' transportation for vagrancy offences between 1836 and 1868, with the 330 female convicts (62.5 per cent) far outnumbering the 198 males (37.5 per cent).[24] This research supports Audrey Eccles and David Hitchcock's recent work on vagrancy in seventeenth- and eighteenth-century England wherein the authors undermine the traditional assumption that early modern and modern vagrants were mostly men.[25] Women were more

---

20 *PI, Appendix C, Part II, Report upon vagrancy and mendicity in the City of Dublin*, p. 18a*.
21 *FJ*, 7 July 1801.
22 *FJ*, 21 Nov. 1820.
23 Irish Prison Registers 1790–1924, consulted at findmypast.ie (accessed 19 October 2017).
24 Australian transportation database, available at National Archives of Ireland www. nationalarchives.ie (accessed 2 Feb. 2012).
25 Audrey Eccles, *Vagrancy in law and practice under the Old Poor Law* (Farnham, 2012), pp. 87–103, 201–12; David Hitchcock, *Vagrancy in English culture and society, 1650–1750* (London, 2016), pp. 123–47.

vulnerable than men to economic distress and destitution, and took to the road in greater numbers, as 'out of place' domestic servants or, in the rural Irish case, as labourers' wives (and children) wandering the countryside, begging during the 'hungry months' while the husband/father was working on the harvest in the eastern regions or in Britain.

Throughout nineteenth-century Europe, social and public order legislation was at times vague and ill-defined, ultimately leaving the definition of crime to the discretion of the police. Writing of Victorian Britain, F.M.L. Thompson observed that some of the relatively minor laws dealing with public order 'were vague and generic, allowing in practice considerable discretion in their interpretation. Thus, the police could in effect decide what constituted a public nuisance, a disorder, or a threat to the public peace'.[26] English vagrancy laws infamously outlined a litany of deviant characters, typically defined by their occupations (if any), who constituted 'vagrants', and among this grouping 'beggars' (defined simply as those seeking alms) were invariably included. Philanthropist and social inquirer Frederic Eden's 1797 *State of the poor* noted the 'very dubious nature' of English vagrancy laws, which 'must frequently require nice legal acumen to distinguish whether a person incurs any, and what, penalty'.[27] However, vagueness in the composition of vagrancy legislation was not the reserve of English laws, and Hitchcock and Shoemaker's observation of eighteenth-century London – 'While constables and justices of the peace certainly believed they knew a vagrant when they saw one, the legal definition, while broad, was also obscure'[28] – was true of vagrancy laws in pre-Famine Ireland. A crucial difference between Irish and English vagrancy laws was that the latter were more complex given the centrality of settlement to the English Poor Laws since the early modern period.[29] The legislative pitfalls in terms of public begging in Ireland were highlighted by the 1830 parliamentary select committee on the poor in Ireland, which criticised the fact that the early eighteenth-century legislation facilitating the transportation of vagrants remained in force. Noting the need for continued vigilance in enforcing anti-begging laws, the committee stated that it 'cannot but think that a more constitutional and efficient system may be adopted than one which allows

26 F.M.L. Thompson, 'Social control in Victorian Britain' in *Economic History Review*, 2nd series, xxxiv, no. 2 (May 1981), p. 197.

27 Frederic Morton Eden, *The state of the poor: a history of the labouring classes in England, with parochial reports*, ed. A.G.L. Rogers (1797; repr. London, 1928), p. 55.

28 Tim Hitchcock and Robert Shoemaker, *London lives: poverty, crime and the making of the modern city, 1690–1800* (Cambridge, 2015), p. 238. See also Eccles, *Vagrancy in law and practice*, pp. 49–86; Hitchcock, *Vagrancy in English culture and society*, p. 5.

29 Under an English act of 1662, a person was required to possess 'settlement' in a parish (typically his/her native parish) in order to receive relief through the Poor Law.

the penalty of transportation to be inflicted upon the mere authority of the presentment of a grand jury, and this, not for an offence defined with precision, but, under contingencies extremely vague and uncertain'.[30] This view drew the support of Poor Law Commissioner George Nicholls[31] and such sentiment can also be found in the Poor Inquiry's report on vagrancy and mendicancy in Dublin, wherein the commissioners argued that 'the whole legal code respecting vagrancy is contradictory, uncertain and but little acted upon'.[32]

While legislation provided for the strengthening of previous provisions and new acts bestowed powers of arrest and detention to the police and certain welfare institutions (such as the Houses of Industry), it is clear that both before and during the nineteenth century the ambiguity surrounding terms such as 'vagrants' was used to the advantage of authorities, on behalf of the general public, and to the detriment of the vagrant under suspicion.[33] A late eighteenth-century statute added the proviso that a 'stranger' under suspicion could be detained for not satisfactorily explaining his presence in a particular location.[34] For instance, in Kilcullen, County Kildare in December 1821, local magistrate William Brownrigg detained to Naas Gaol 'four very suspicious persons as vagrants as they could not give a proper account of themselves'. In two of the cases, the arrested men claimed to be traders in tin ware and linen but had no such materials on their person. In each case, the magistrate commented that the vagrant 'could not give any satisfactory account of himself'.[35] It is clear that vague definitions of crimes such as 'vagrancy' were being used to detain and subsequently prosecute those deemed by the authorities to be suspicious or deviant. The Poor Inquiry concluded that the word 'vagrant':

is now held to apply to persons suspected of great crimes but against whom there is not sufficient legal evidence of such crimes, and who

---

30 *Report of the select committee on the state of the poor in Ireland; being a summary of the first, second and third reports of evidence taken before that committee: together with an appendix of accounts and papers*, p. 23, H.C. 1830 (667), vii, 23.

31 Nicholls, *A history of the Irish Poor Law*, p. 100.

32 *PI, Appendix C, Part II, Report upon vagrancy and mendicity in the City of Dublin*, p. 29a*.

33 For an analysis of this feature of the vagrancy laws in eighteenth-century Ireland, see Neal Garnham, 'The criminal law, 1692–1760: England and Ireland compared' in S.J. Connolly (ed.), *Kingdoms united? Great Britain and Ireland since 1500: integration and diversity* (Dublin, 1999), pp. 220–2.

34 36 Geo. III, c. 20, s. 15 [Ire.] (24 Mar. 1796). See also 35 Geo III, c. 36 [Ire.] (5 June 1795).

35 'Papers relating to the committal of four men to Naas jail, County Kildare, on charges of vagrancy', 1–22 Dec. 1821 (NAI, CSORP, CSO/RP/SC/1821/187).

have no ascertained mode of obtaining an honest livelihood, and who are, therefore, presumed to live by dishonest and illegal means.[36]

In Dublin city, individuals were occasionally arrested and confined on the suspicion that they *may* engage in begging. In 1824, the city's mendicity society directed its street inspectors, in co-operation with the police, to apprehend individuals 'whom they may find prowling about the streets, without any visible occupation, or means of subsistence, *whom they have reason to suspect are there for the purpose of begging, although not in the act of begging at the moment* [emphasis added]'.[37] That same year saw the passing of the influential 1824 Vagrancy Act, limited in its scope to England, which codified existing vagrancy legislation and legislatively cemented the rights of policemen 'pre-emptively' to arrest an individual on the suspicion that they may have the intention to commit an offence.[38]

The situation was not rectified by the passing of the 1838 Irish Poor Law, which omitted vagrancy clauses against the recommendation of Nicholls, the act's architect.[39] Under the 1838 act the newly established Poor Law Union Boards of Guardians were empowered to relieve the destitute poor who could not support themselves. This was carried out through the workhouse system and guardians were explicitly prevented from providing outdoor relief. Yet, against the wishes of Nicholls, the Whig government dropped plans to include vagrancy clauses in the act, leaving the question of beggary unresolved under the new Poor Law system. Wishing to address this defect, Lord Morpeth introduced an ultimately unsuccessful mendicity bill in March 1840, pointing to the failings of the present laws: 'that their definitions were obsolete and uncertain, or that they subjected the parties to such severe penalties as to defeat their own object; they gave the extreme punishment of transportation for vagrancy; and such was their severity, that, being repugnant to the feelings of the people, they could not be enforced'.[40] A similar want of clarification in the Scottish vagrancy laws was held in the 1840s to contribute to localised variations in implementation and, consequently, ineffectual methods for suppressing vagrancy and

---

36 *PI, Appendix C, Part II, Report upon vagrancy and mendicity in the City of Dublin*, p. 31a*.
37 Dublin Mendicity Society minute book, 23 Mar. 1824 (NLI, DMSP, MS 32,599/3).
38 Paul Lawrence, 'The Vagrancy Act (1824) and the persistence of pre-emptive policing in England since 1750' in *British Journal of Criminology*, lvii, no. 3 (2017), pp. 513–31. For an example of contemporary criticism of the 1824 act, on the grounds that it allegedly suppressed civil liberties, see 'A barrister', *The Vagrant Act, in relation to the liberty of the subject* (London, 1824).
39 1 & 2 Vict., c. 56 (31 July 1838).
40 Hansard 3, lii, 1251–4 (19 Mar. 1840). See Gray, *Making of the Irish Poor Law*, pp. 302–3.

mendicancy.[41] These ambiguities in the legislation were not confined to the vagrancy laws. The Medical Charities Act of 1851, which transferred responsibility for dispensaries to the Poor Law unions, established a system by which, according to the wording of the legislation, 'any poor person' was entitled to receive free medical treatment at their local dispensary.[42] The imprecise definition of just who qualified for free medical treatment led, in one historian's terms, to 'gross abuse' of the system in the post-Famine decades.[43] The inefficacy of the existing statutes pertaining to mendicancy in Ireland was also criticised by political economist Nassau Senior in a comprehensive article on Irish vagrancy laws. 'There are, indeed, such laws in the statute-book; but defects in their machinery, the severity of their punishments, and the absence in their enactments of any reference to a legal provision for the poor, have rendered them inefficient'.[44] These difficulties were finally addressed and legislated for at the height of the Great Famine with the passing of the 1847 Vagrancy Act, which criminalised public begging, encouraging a child to engage in begging or wandering from one Poor Law union to another for the sake of obtaining relief, crimes liable to one month's imprisonment with hard labour.[45]

Beggars, Begging and the 'Pauper Professions'
Begging in pre-Famine Ireland took on more forms than the mere solicitation of alms. At times, begging was cloaked under the guise of the sale of some trivial item, such as flowers or home-made devotional articles, or the provision of a service. A statute of 1774 included unlicensed street sellers within the confines of the definition of 'vagabond' and 'vagrant beggars', noting that this practice – 'hawking about small wares, whereby they cannot earn a subsistence' – constituted 'indirect begging'.[46] Encompassing peddling and street entertainment, charring and prostitution, shoe-blacking and tin mending, 'the beggarly professions came in an almost unlimited variety'.[47] In his work on eighteenth-century London street cultures, Tim Hitchcock has

---

41   *Report from Her Majesty's commissioners for inquiring into the administration and practical operation of the Poor Laws in Scotland*, p. lxii, H.C. 1844 [C 557], xx, 68.

42   14 & 15 Vict., c. 68, s. 9 (7 Aug. 1851).

43   Laurence M. Geary, *Medicine and charity in Ireland, 1718–1851* (Dublin, 2004), p. 211. For more on the 1851 act, see ibid., pp. 210–16.

44   [Nassau William Senior], 'Mendicancy in Ireland' in *Edinburgh Review*, lxxvii, no. 156 (Apr. 1843), p. 399.

45   10 & 11 Vict., c. 84 (22 July 1847). The 1847 Vagrancy Act remained the primary statute concerning public begging in Ireland until the passing of the Criminal Justice (Public Order) Act, 2011 (5/2011) (2 Feb. 2011).

46   13 & 14 Geo. III, c. 46, s. 6 [Ire.] (2 June 1774).

47   Tim Hitchcock, 'Begging on the streets of eighteenth-century London' in *Journal of British Studies*, xliv, no. 3 (July 2005), p. 491.

noted the importance that, first, these 'pauper professions' were unregulated and, secondly, these individuals made use of the public street as a space in which to pursue 'those innumerable tasks which combined begging and service'.[48] Largely operating outside the formal economy, individuals could enter and leave these 'professions' as they wished. Licences for hawking, peddling 'or other trading … going from place to place' could be bought but the price of £2 was beyond the means of most people engaged in this type of work.[49]

Authorities were prone to occasional bursts of anti-mendicancy sentiment, driven by perceived rises in the levels of beggary at times of social crisis and economic decline. For instance, in July 1832, when a cholera epidemic was spreading throughout Dublin, access to the Ormond Market on the city's north side was prohibited to 'Beggars, Hawkers, and disorderly persons within the precincts of the Market'.[50] Being subject to such proscriptions, street people were required to justify their presence in thoroughfares and public spaces. The notice banning undesirables from the Ormond Market further stated that 'we will allow no Basket-woman or Porter to loiter or continue within the Market *unless actually engaged* [emphasis added]'.[51] The Poor Inquiry of the mid-1830s observed that in Dublin some beggars 'carry or take some small article for sale as a pretence',[52] reflecting the advantage to the mendicant of being seen with some goods for sale, giving the impression of industry and self-sufficiency rather than idleness and dependency. Similarly, in rural Ireland, male labourers wandering the countryside in search of employment usually carried a tool, such as a spade or sickle, and enquiries as to the availability of work were usually accompanied by requests for alms, although the latter were oftentimes conducted by his wife and children.[53] In Ballydehob, labourer Bartholomew Brown told the Poor Inquiry: 'There was a good strong able-bodied man came to my cabin this morning; he said he wanted employment and could not get it; I gave him the little alms I could spare, two or three potatoes'.[54] Here, the act of seeking assistance was framed, by both the labourer/beggar and Mr Brown, within the wider narrative of seeking employment, implying industriousness and honesty.

---

48 Tim Hitchcock, *Down and out in eighteenth-century London* (London, 2004), pp. 49–51.
49 *Saunder's News-Letter*, 10 Apr. 1805. This licence covered 'any hawker, pedlar, or petty chapman, or other trading person going from place to place, carrying to sell or exposing to sale, any goods, wares, or merchandise; also to travelling tinkers, and casters of iron and metal, and to persons hawking about tea or coffee for sale'.
50 *FJ*, 6 July 1832.
51 Ibid.
52 PI, *Appendix C, Part II, Report upon vagrancy and mendicity in the City of Dublin*, p. 42a*.
53 PI, *Appendix A*, pp. 355, 485, 492, 504, 585, 658, 720.
54 Ibid., p. 667.

In his pioneering work on the poorer classes in mid-nineteenth-century London, Henry Mayhew observed the often-indistinct relationship between informal street trading and beggary, noting that:

> petty trading beggars [were] ... perhaps the most numerous class of beggars in London. Their trading in such articles as lucifers [friction matches], boot-laces, cabbage-nets, tapes, cottons, shirt-buttons, and the like, is in most cases a mere 'blind' to evade the law applying to mendicants and vagrants ... The box of matches, or the little deal box of cottons, is used simply as a passport to the resorts of the charitable. The police are obliged to respect the trader, though they know very well that under the disguise of the itinerant merchant there lurks a beggar.[55]

The sweeping of crossings on London's public streets was also widely considered to be 'a mere cloak for mendicity'.[56]

Among the evidence recorded by the Poor Inquiry in Dublin was a return showing the previous occupations of inmates at the Mendicity Society's asylum, which reveals a wide array of skilled, semi-skilled and, in particular, unskilled trades, wherein street-based professions were prominent. These included 'Shopkeepers, Pedlars, and Hucksters', 'Washerwomen', 'Fruit and Cake-sellers in the Streets', 'Egg-sellers', 'Fish-dealers', 'Newspaper and Pamphlet-sellers' and 'Scourers, Charwomen, &c.'[57] The close connection between street-selling and outright begging is reflected in Hugh Douglas Hamilton's drawings of mid-eighteenth-century Dublin, *Cries of Dublin*. Throughout the 66 prints, unparalleled in the realistic and sympathetic depiction of Dublin street characters and their daily lives, Hamilton presents the purveyors of a wide range of products and services, together with a number of real and well-known street beggars: sellers of fish, whey, peas, fruit, eggs, perukes and brooms are vividly represented, as are carmen, stocking menders, cobblers and chimney sweeps.[58] For providers of such services and goods, the ability to excite compassion and sympathy in

55 Peter Quennell (ed.), *Mayhew's London underworld* (London, 1987), p. 414.
56 *The first report of the society established in London for the suppression of mendicity* (London, 1819), pp. 20–1.
57 *PI, Appendix C, Part II, Report upon vagrancy and mendicity in the City of Dublin*, p. 25a*.
58 William Laffan (ed.), *The cries of Dublin &c: drawn from the life by Hugh Douglas Hamilton, 1760* (Dublin, 2003). For an analysis of Dublin's economy in this period, see T.C. Barnard, 'Hamilton's "Cries of Dublin": the society and economy of mid-eighteenth-century Dublin', ibid., pp. 26–37. See also *The Dublin cries. Or a representation of the various cries and callings throughout the streets, lanes and allies of the city and liberties of Dublin* ([c.1770s]), reproduced in Laffan, *Cries of Dublin*, p. 52.

prospective customers was as important as their salesmanship, thus blurring the lines between mendicancy and selling. The Poor Inquiry *Report upon vagrancy and mendicity in the city of Dublin* noted: 'At almost every door your alms are solicited in the shape of a purchase of some little article by a female, who urges on your attention the claims of a sick husband or children'.[59] Rural communities were also visited by travelling characters of all sorts, usually consisting of the same individuals or families, whose stay in a locality was short-lived. In rural as in urban places, beggary regularly accompanied, and was indistinguishable from, petty peddling and hawking. Hugh Dorian's account of life in a mid-century rural Donegal community recalled that the 'newcomers or yearly visitants consisted of tinkers, pedlars, pipers, fiddlers, show-men and beggars, and many otherwise idle with no profession'.[60] The entertainment provided by itinerant musicians and ballad-singers – the harper Turlough O'Carolan (1670–1738) and the poet Antaine Raiftearaí (1799–1835), both blinded by smallpox, being the best known examples – was regularly indistinguishable from outright begging; indeed, as early as the seventeenth century, anti-vagrancy legislation included vagrant musicians within its remit.[61]

One form of solicitation which does not appear to have been practised as much in Ireland as in Britain was the professional writing of begging-letters. These compositions, invariably claiming respectability, reduced circumstances and genuine distress, and pleading for monetary sums to be forwarded to a given address, were seen as the inventions of skilled impostors, preying on the benevolence of the charitable. The practice was so widespread that the London Mendicity Society established a Begging Letter Department to investigate the extent of the problem, while Henry Mayhew devoted a substantial section of his survey of London's poor to this category of beggar.[62] Among the cases investigated by this sub-committee of the London society was that of an 'impostor' writing from Dublin, who claimed to be the wife of a military man, shipwrecked abroad; in each begging letter sent to a London address, the note was accompanied by 'a forged certificate

---

59 *PI, Appendix C, Part II, Report upon vagrancy and mendicity in the City of Dublin*, p. 27a*.

60 Hugh Dorian, *The outer edge of Ulster: a memoir of social life in nineteenth-century Donegal*, ed. Breandán Mac Suibhne and David Dickson (Dublin, 2001), p. 212. For a later period, see also Mary Carberry, *The farm by Lough Gur: the story of Mary Fogarty (Sissy O'Brien)* (London, 1937), pp. 58–66.

61 10 and 11 Chas. I, c. 4 [Ire.] (1635).

62 London Mendicity Society minute book, 26 Feb. 1823; Notes regarding London Mendicity Society Begging Letter Department, 1838 (National Records of Scotland, Papers of the Dukes of Buccleuch, GD224/155/1); Quennell, *Mayhew's London underworld*, pp. 345–69.

headed with the royal arms'.[63] While this practice is well recorded in sources pertaining to Britain, there is little evidence that this occurred in Ireland. Yet, occasional Irish instances of this practice are recorded. Rev. Thomas Shore, a Church of Ireland clergyman in the Dublin parish of St Michan's, recalled the discovery 'in the house of a noted imposter upon the public charity a list of the most humane and opulent persons in Dublin, and a number of copies of a begging circular, which it was intended to send them, looking for relief for some imaginary distress'.[64] In Kilkee, non-local beggars were known to carry 'recommendations' and 'plenty of letters and documents' with them, but were identified as 'impostors' and largely ignored by the local population.[65] In the County Longford town of Ballymahon, a number of persons, supposedly from 'respectable families', were known by the parish priest to produce 'documents and recommendations [which] were forged'.[66]

Various Forms of Alms

Alms solicited or given could take a number of forms and here an important distinction between the provision of private charity in rural and urban contexts requires assertion. The Poor Inquiry evidence reveals that in urban areas cash played a greater part in people's daily lives and was, therefore, provided as alms more frequently. On the other hand, in rural areas alms were most commonly given in the form of potatoes or lodgings.[67] When doling out alms, people gave what they had to hand, and which would not be too burdensome to relinquish. For labourers and small farmers in rural areas, any cash raised during the year largely went towards the payment of rent and, as such, occasional rummages into the large stockpile of potatoes for passing vagrants were less likely to impact on the household budget. The potato was, according to the surgeon and statistician William Wilde, 'the circulating medium for the mendicant'.[68] R.J. Mansergh St George of Headford Castle told the Poor Inquiry in Headford, County Galway:

---

63 *Dublin Evening Packet and Correspondent*, 9 Aug. 1845. See also *Morning Post*, 13 Nov. 1846.

64 *Dublin Morning Register*, 12 Jan. 1837. For other instances, see *PI, Appendix A*, p. 691.

65 *PI, Appendix A*, p. 625.

66 Ibid., pp. 562–3.

67 *PI, Supplement to Appendix A*, pp. 2–409; Return of answers to queries from the Poor Inquiry, by Rev. William Walsh, Parishes of Clontarf, Coolock and Santry, Dublin, [*c*.1833], answer no. 30 (DDA, DMP, 32/3/44).

68 [William R. Wilde], 'The food of the Irish' in *Dublin University Magazine*, xliii, no. 154 (Feb. 1854), p. 133. See also Arthur Young, *A tour in Ireland: with general observations on the present state of the kingdom. Made in the years 1776, 1777, and 1778, and brought down to the end of 1779* (2 vols, Dublin, 1780), ii, Part II, p. 33.

'Farmers always prefer giving food, because there is no coin of so low a value as to represent a potatoe [*sic*], and because they always have plenty of potatoes, and often have no money; beggars always prefer money, for they take the raw potatoe [*sic*] only with the view of converting it into money'.[69] Many Poor Inquiry witnesses claimed that beggars preferred receiving alms in the form of money as they could spend it on luxuries, such as whiskey and tobacco, yet the practical reality that for transient individuals cash was easier to carry on their person than potatoes should not be overlooked. On his travels throughout Ireland in 1829, James Ebenezer Bicheno stopped and conversed with beggars, inquiring into 'how they obtained their living. I found many of them going as roundsmen, from cabin to cabin, sleeping in any place that they chose to select; and it seemed to me as if every house was open to a poor beggar; if he was in want, he had only to enter the cabin and relief was afforded him from the potato; the potato appeared to me to be almost a common food; as long as it lasts, it is for the benefit of every man who wants it'.[70] In rural Ireland, assistance was also given in the form of a night's lodging, either in the dwelling of a labourer or cottier, or in a farmer's shed or barn. The provision of lodgings for wandering beggars was an ingrained part of life in rural Ireland, such that in County Mayo, sleeping arrangements in a labouring family's cabin regularly accounted for the anticipated presence of mendicant visitors:

they [the family] lie down *decently*, and in order; the eldest daughter next the wall farthest from the door, then all the sisters, according to their ages; next the mother, father, and sons in succession, and then the strangers, whether the travelling pedlar, or tailor, or beggar; thus the strangers are kept aloof from the female part of the family, and if there be an apparent community there is great propriety of conduct.[71]

This account, from the pen of Church of Ireland clergyman and writer Rev. Caesar Otway, suggests that while 'strangers' could be welcomed into the dwellings of the poorer classes, they still remained suspicious characters, as evidenced by the need to separate them, as much as possible, from the female members of the family. The widespread practice by poor labourers and cottiers of providing shelter to mendicants contributed to the dissemination of diseases, such as typhus fever, and at times of epidemic, all too often in pre-Famine Ireland, this custom was identified and criticised by middle-class

---

69 *PI, Appendix A*, p. 476. See also ibid., p. 490.
70 *Second report of evidence from the Select Committee on the State of the Poor in Ireland. Minutes of evidence: 18 May–5 June*, p. 380, H.C. 1830 (654), vii, 556.
71 [Caesar Otway], *Sketches in Erris and Tyrawly* (Dublin, 1841), p. 32.

commentators, particularly medical practitioners.[72] A public notice issued in December 1817 informing the inhabitants of an unspecified Ulster town on the best means of preventing the spread of fever advised readers: 'Do not lodge Beggars, unless in an outhouse. Their cloathing and persons are almost always in a very filthy state, and infection is often conveyed in the Blankets they carry with them'.[73]

Where Did Beggars Beg?

As a survival strategy, begging must be visible to be successful. The unseen mendicant, by the very fact of him/her not being observed, is ignored by the prospective alms-giver and remains empty-handed. In nineteenth-century Ireland beggars could maximise their chances of receiving alms by increasing their visibility, whether through importunate solicitation or through frequenting well-travelled locations through which large amounts of people passed. In the 1850s, Caesar Otway recalled hearing the story that some years previously £100 was paid 'for a beggar's right to beg on Palmerstown Hill, near Chapelizod' outside Dublin city.[74] Whether or not £100 was ever paid, or to whom, for the right to beg on Palmerstown Hill is not of significance here; what is important is the perception, passed down orally, that beggars prized prime locations for plying their trade, where their visibility and access to prospective alms-givers were maximised – in this case, the prime patch was located on the main western road to and from Dublin city. Given the importance to mendicants of being seen, the visibility of the problem focused minds and mobilised public opinion. During the construction of Nelson's Pillar on a prominent site half-way up Dublin's Sackville Street, the city's main north-side thoroughfare, it was feared that the new memorial column was poorly sited and 'promises to be a rallying point for beggars and idlers to gather round, and choak [*sic*] up a very important opening in the confluence of four streets'.[75] A Mary H. from Rainsford Street in Dublin was known to the city's mendicity society for exposing her young children at 'their regular post' 'next the wall of the Royal Dublin Society's lawn in Merrion-Square'; another culprit, Mary M. of Vicar Street, sent out 'her three little children, the eldest a boy eight

72   Timothy P. O'Neill, 'Fever and public health in pre-Famine Ireland' in *Journal of the Royal Society of Antiquaries of Ireland*, ciii (1973), pp. 3–4; Report of Dr John Cheyne, physician attached to the Dublin House of Industry, on the fever epidemic in Ireland, 1819 (NAI, CSORP, CSO/RP/1819/229).

73   'Printed notice giving rules to observe for the avoidance of fever', 10 Dec. 1817 (PRONI, Abercorn papers, D623/A/131/3).

74   *Ninth annual report of the Commissioners for Administering the Laws for Relief of the Poor in Ireland, with appendices*, appendix A, no. 4, p. 54, H.C. 1856 [C 2105], xxviii, 468.

75   *Leinster Journal*, 14 May 1808.

years old. She has them placed sometimes near the Bank [at College Green], more frequently on Carlile-Bridge [adjoining Sackville Street].[76]

In towns and cities an arriving or departing carriage attracted interest, serving as a 'rallying point for beggars'.[77] Coaches were used primarily by the commercial and professional classes, who were the targets of the 'swarming' supplicants. In market and post towns throughout Ireland, carriages attracted supplicants soliciting assistance[78] and travellers' accounts from this period almost invariably cite instances of being 'surrounded' by groups of mendicants.[79] This practice was almost invariably described in negative terms; the traveller/writer usually perceived the gathering of mendicants as most bothersome and the congregated beggars were usually described as being among the most disagreeable category of poor. The beggars of Mullingar were noted as being particularly importunate in their 'attacks' upon coach passengers, while a group of as many as 40 beggars were known to 'obtain a great deal from passengers in coaches, cars, &c.' in Cork city: 'There are a regular set of them who attend the conveyances that start from this parish [Holy Trinity]; they are very numerous ... They are the most impudent, and annoy and pester the passengers ... they are the worst and most dissolute description of beggars, and are regular frequenters of the gin shops'.[80] In the view of one Dublin policeman, such beggars were 'exceedingly troublesome and importunate. I heard one a few days ago ask a lady in her carriage for a shilling'.[81] The German geographer Johann Georg Kohl recorded how in his 1842 travels in Ireland, his Bianconi car was 'constantly surrounded' on the roads between Limerick and Kilkenny, via Cork, by gangs of beggar children in pursuit and soliciting money. Kohl observed that the design of these conveyances, with passengers sitting unsheltered on the outside, lent itself to the annoyance of beggars' solicitations:

76 Quoted in Woods, *Dublin outsiders*, p. 101.
77 Asenath Nicholson, *Annals of the Famine in Ireland*, ed. Maureen Murphy (1851; Dublin, 1998), p. 142.
78 For Drogheda, see *PI, Appendix C, Part I*, p. 49; McHugh, *Drogheda before the Famine*, p. 46. For Killarney, see *PI, Appendix A*, p. 684.
79 John Gamble, *Sketches of history, politics, and manners in Dublin, and the north of Ireland, in 1810* (new edn, London, 1826), p. 91. See also Jonathan Binns, *The miseries and beauties of Ireland* (2 vols, London, 1837), ii, p. 23; [Mrs] S.C. Hall, *Tales of Irish life and character* (Edinburgh and London, 1910), p. 89; John Griscom, *A year in Europe, comprising a journal of observations in England, Scotland, Ireland, France, Switzerland, the north of Italy, and Holland, in 1818 and 1819* (2 vols, New York, 1823), ii, p. 456.
80 *PI, Appendix A*, p. 582; ibid., p. 649.
81 *PI, Appendix C, Part II, Report upon vagrancy and mendicity in the City of Dublin*, p. 41a*.

Bianconi's cars are so constructed as to be of great advantage to these beggars, for the passengers are placed in such a manner as to have them constantly before their eyes, and very close to them ... An alteration in the form of these carriages would, should it ever take place, therefore sensibly affect the poor mendicants of Ireland.[82]

The image of the child beggar in pursuit of a jaunting car, a primitive version of Bianconi's model of vehicle, is memorably depicted in Daniel Maclise's 'An outside jaunting car in a storm' (Figure 1.1), which accompanied John Barrow's *A tour round Ireland through the sea-coast counties in the autumn of 1835.*[83]

Large gatherings of people also acted as magnets for beggars. Fairs, markets, patterns and sporting events were common places for mendicants to ply their 'trade'; such events provided opportunities for the seeking of alms, trading, theft, the sale of stolen goods and, in the case of fairs, the hiring of farm labourers, as well as social engagement, entertainment and jovial celebrations.[84] These events were typically fixed points in the calendar, meaning that a day's begging could be planned in advance. According to one account from County Clare, 'They [beggars] are well acquainted with the days on which fairs are held, and portions of almanacks containing such information have not unfrequently been observed in their possession'.[85] The use of the contemporary description of this practice as a 'trade' is appropriate given that these public occasions tended to attract the fraudulent and professional 'fair beggars' rather than the more 'deserving' paupers. Among the most common stories was that of seeing impostors at fairs feigning injury or disability, while being later seen drawing on full physical faculties (usually in drunken brawling).[86] The Enniscorthy Races was known to attract crowds of 'Hawkers, beggars with every imaginable deformity, showmen, players, gingerbread women, ballad singers, and every specimen of the lowest of the human species'.[87] Sites of pilgrimage were popular places for beggars, due to the congregation of large numbers of prospective benefactors who, driven by a heightened sense of Christian devotion, regularly wished to demonstrate

---

82 Quoted in Constantia Maxwell, *The stranger in Ireland from the reign of Elizabeth to the Great Famine* (London, 1954), pp. 243–4.

83 A similar scene is depicted in William Turner de Lond's painting *The marketplace and court-house, Ennis, Co. Clare* (1820).

84 A.L. Beier, 'Vagrants and the social order in Elizabethan England' in *Past & Present*, lxiv (Aug. 1974), pp. 24–5.

85 *PI, Appendix A*, p. 620.

86 Ibid., pp. 476, 478–9, 483, 684, 692. For instances of beggars frequenting fairs, see ibid., pp. 486, 502, 588, 614.

87 *Wexford Independent*, 1 Oct. 1842.

Figure 1.1   Daniel Maclise, 'An outside jaunting car in a storm' from
John Barrow, *A tour round Ireland, through the sea-coast counties, in the autumn
of 1835* (London, 1836) (reproduced courtesy of National Library of Ireland)

their piety through charitable deeds. Beggars' attendance at pilgrimage
sites fluctuated according to seasonal trends and local feast days. William
Carleton's account of his high-season pilgrimage to St Patrick's Purgatory
at Lough Derg, albeit subject to fictional gloss, contains a cast of beggars,
cripples and a 'gipsy, fortune-teller … a tinker's widow',[88] while the earlier
account of his literary mentor Rev. Caesar Otway's off-season visit to the
same location is strikingly void of references to mendicants (or indeed any
'pilgrims' at all).[89] While only three paupers were believed to be resident in
Carne, County Wexford, the parish was 'abundantly supplied with itinerant
beggars from other parts of the kingdom, owing … to our being in the
neighbourhood of St. Mary's Island, commonly called the Lady's Island,
a place of great devotion and pilgrimage'.[90] The popularity of Kilkee as a

88 [William Carleton], 'A pilgrimage to Patrick's Purgatory' in *Christian Examiner and
    Church of Ireland Magazine*, vi, no. 34 (Apr. 1828), pp. 268–86 and ibid., vi, no. 35 (May
    1828), pp. 343–62.
89 [Caesar Otway], *Sketches in Ireland: descriptive of interesting, and hitherto unnoticed
    districts, in the north and south* (Dublin, 1827), pp. 129–200.
90 William Shaw Mason, *A statistical account or parochial survey of Ireland, drawn up from
    the communications of the clergy* (3 vols, Dublin, 1814–19), iii, p. 128.

bathing location in the summer months caused a parallel influx of beggars, who were said to 'follow ... the quality then'.[91]

Throughout Europe since the medieval period, rituals evolved around the practice of alms-giving, frequently centring on significant events in the life-cycle – births, marriages and deaths. The ritualistic regularity of this charitable work, frequently carried out at the local church, reflects, as Robert Jütte has observed, 'the awareness of the sacred nature of charity'.[92] In the Christian world, the doors and gates to churches and meeting houses long attracted the presence of mendicants, hoping to attract the sympathy and compassion of church-goers, and life-cycle events, such as weddings and funerals, also attracted mendicants as such occasions commonly included an opportunity for the distribution of alms, a practice mirrored in other countries, such as Scotland.[93] The appearance of ragged beggars outside the doors of chapels and churches evoked mixed reactions: to some, the church exterior was an inappropriate place for paupers to 'prey' upon respectable church-goers, while to others, it was a suitable site for God's poor to solicit assistance from their wealthier neighbours. Richard Browning, a Protestant employed to ward off beggars outside the Catholic chapel on Dublin's Camden Street, estimated that there were typically 30 or 40 mendicants at the chapel on Sundays, 'and about 50 on great festivals'.[94] In Galway, the yard of the parish church of St Nicholas's was bemoaned as a congregating place for 'idle and disorderly persons ... during the time of divine Service', a practice considered to be 'a discredit to the character of the Town, and highly offensive to such of its Inhabitants as attend the Worship of God in the Church'.[95]

Yet, the Poor Inquiry evidence suggests regional variations in the practice of begging and alms-giving at church doors. Throughout Leinster, Munster and Connaught, witnesses testified that while the practice was largely discouraged, a small number of mendicants received alms (2*d.* or 3*d.*) every Sunday, typically at the Catholic chapel. For example, in Newmarket-on-Fergus, four beggars had been relieved at the chapel door the previous Sunday but none were assisted at the Anglican church, as 'the congregation always put their subscriptions into the poor-box'; in Macroom, there were 'about 20 beggars who attend the chapel on Sundays; they may get 1*d.* or 2*d.* each; they are generally aged or infirm women resident in the parish'.[96] These instances,

---

91 *PI, Appendix A*, p. 624.
92 Jütte, *Poverty and deviance*, p. 125.
93 *PI, Appendix A*, p. 671; Rosalind Mitchison and Leah Leneman, *Sexuality and social control: Scotland 1660–1760* (Oxford, 1989), pp. 36–7.
94 *PI, Appendix C, Part II, Report upon vagrancy and mendicity in the City of Dublin*, p. 43a*.
95 *Galway Weekly Advertiser*, 27 Sept. 1823.
96 *PI, Appendix A*, pp. 644, 661. See also ibid., p. 480.

reflective of wider patterns, suggest that Sunday begging at Catholic places of worship was tolerated to a certain degree. However, in Ulster, especially in the north-east of the province, witnesses' testimony was more assertive in stating that begging at Protestant church-doors was not countenanced.[97] Claims that 'None are assisted on Sundays at places of worship' (Ahoghill) and 'The practice of giving money to mendicants at the doors of places of worship does not exist here' (Ballymoney) are representative.[98] In Carrickfergus, it was stated that 'Mendicants are driven away from the places of religious worship, if they go there to solicit alms'.[99] The parish vestry of Keady, County Armagh issued begging badges to local paupers in 1818, allowing them to solicit alms in public, on the condition that 'No person to beg on Sundays'.[100] In seeking to explain this regional pattern, one may be tempted to attribute it to a stereotypical Protestant antipathy towards beggary – such an assertion is simply too difficult to prove or disprove. Alternatively, this regional trend may be explained with reference to the influence of (largely Protestant) Sabbatarian sentiment in the north-east, emerging from Protestant evangelicalism. Sabbatarians may have viewed begging as an inappropriate practice on the Sabbath, particularly at a place of worship, and this explanation may be supported by the fact that the two instances recorded by the Poor Inquiry in County Antrim where begging was tolerated at a place of worship was at two Catholic chapels (in Ballymena and Rasharkin).[101] What may also have driven this regional pattern is the fact that in most of the locations in County Antrim where witnesses claimed that no Sunday begging took place, there was a mendicity society in operation in the town or within a ten-mile radius – that is, within one day's walking distance. Furthermore, Protestant services, such as the liturgy for the Anglican service, included a poor collection (see below, Chapter 7), thus avoiding the need for congregants to dole out private alms outside the church or meeting house: all local 'deserving' cases were to be alleviated through the poor box.

The arrival and departure of well-known public figures also occasioned the distribution of alms. Upon departing Kilkenny city in October 1819, after her successful and acclaimed performance in *Othello*, the actress Eliza O'Neill distributed 'a large parcel of silver among the beggars who had collected around [her carriage]'.[102] The arrival of Denis O'Conor Don, MP for Roscommon, at his home in the county town 'brought immense

---

97 This trend has also been identified in Kathryn Tumilty, 'The Church of Ireland and the Famine in Ulster, 1845–52' (PhD thesis, Queen's University Belfast, 2009), p. 96.
98 PI, *Appendix A*, pp. 702, 706.
99 Ibid., p. 710. See also pp. 708, 712, 714, 725, 729.
100 Seaby and Paterson, 'Ulster beggars' badges', p. 106.
101 PI, *Appendix A*, pp. 717, 727.
102 *Leinster Journal*, 27 Oct. 1819.

throngs of beggars to the door', with the 'news of his arrival ... spread[ing] like wildfire'. The congregation of mendicants was further swelled 'by the intelligence ... that his servant was flinging money amongst the people from a bag. Each shower of copper was hailed with shouts from men, women, and children, which echoed from one end of the town to the other; and the distribution continued for a considerable time'.[103]

Who Begged and Why?

By far the majority of mendicants in pre-Famine Ireland were women, reflecting patterns in Europe and Britain.[104] The Poor Inquiry's report on vagrancy and mendicancy in Dublin city in the mid-1830s stated:

> if you frequent the more public and fashionable streets, at every corner your eyes alight upon some young widow; or the deserted wife, with two or three helpless children ... At almost every door your alms are solicited in the shape of a purchase of some little article by a female, who urges on your attention the claims of a sick husband or children.[105]

An 1809 report into charitable institutions in Dublin estimated that 'four-fifths of those who subsist by begging are females'.[106] The reasons for this are manifold but the most important factors in explaining this universal trend is that women and children constituted more sympathetic figures than men and were more vulnerable to destitution than adult men. The 'classic' categories of the 'deserving' poor included widows, deserted women and young children, as well as the elderly (of both sexes). By the early nineteenth century, many beggars were women and children of military men who had either died, absconded or were serving abroad, and the concentration of these 'followers' of regiments was a feature of life in barracks and garrison towns throughout Ireland and Britain.[107] In Athlone, which boasted a large barracks

---

103 Isaac Weld, *Statistical survey of the county of Roscommon, drawn up under the direction of the Royal Dublin Society* (Dublin, 1832), p. 407.
104 Hufton, *The poor of eighteenth-century France*, pp. 114–15; Matthew Martin, *Letter to the Right Hon. Lord Pelham, on the state of mendicity in the Metropolis* (London, 1803). For Martin's claim that up to 90 per cent of London's beggars were women, see 'Summary of 2,000 cases of paupers' towards the end of his *Letter*.
105 *PI, Appendix C, Part II, Report upon vagrancy and mendicity in the City of Dublin,* p. 27a*.
106 *A report upon certain establishments in the city of Dublin, which receive aid from parliament* (Dublin, 1809), p. 20.
107 See, for instance, Shaw Mason, *Statistical account of parochial survey of Ireland*, iii, p. 67; Prunty, 'Mobility among women'.

accommodating approximately 2,000 men, it was recorded that 'a number of soldiers' wives (and their children) who are left by their husbands when ordered on foreign service, as well as the widows of those who died in the garrison, serve to render that class of the [mendicant] community still more numerous'.[108]

The proliferation of women among the country's mendicant classes also arose due to women's relatively more limited employment opportunities than men, with more women resorting to habitual or occasional begging. These workforce constraints were most acutely felt in rural society, where women's income was mostly limited to spinning, husbandry and begging. In urban areas, a whole array of service- and street-based employments were available to women. Thirdly, men were more likely than women to feel ashamed of resorting to begging.[109] For many, such a resort signified personal failure and emasculation. Novelist William Carleton captured this sense of male shame, in his depiction of an exchange between Owen McCarthy, an industrious and honest labourer, and his wife Kathleen, whose family is driven to destitution and beggary during the economic downturn of the post-1815 period:

Beg: that u'd go hard wid me, Kathleen. I'd work – I'd live on next to nothing all year round; but to see the crathurs that wor decently bred up brought to that, I couldn't bear it, – Kathleen 'twould break the heart widin me. Poor as they are, they have the blood of kings in their veins; and, besides, to see a McCarthy beggin' his bread in the country where his name was once great – The McCarthy More, that was their title – no acushla; I love them as I do the blood in my own veins; but I'd rather see them in the arms of God in heaven ... than have it cast up to them, or have it said, that ever a McCarthy was seen beggin' on the highway.[110]

To assert that men were more ashamed than women to ask for alms is not to undermine the latter's experiences of poverty, charity and mendicancy. Rather, as Laurence Geary rightly asserts, 'women were no less aware of the social taint, but the responsibility for putting food in their children's bellies devolved ultimately on them'.[111]

---

108 Shaw Mason, *Statistical account of parochial survey of Ireland*, iii, p. 78. For more on 'soldiers' wives and followers, with their children' in Athlone, see Weld, *Statistical survey, county Roscommon*, p. 550.
109 Ó Ciosáin, *Ireland in official print culture*, p. 75.
110 William Carleton, 'Tubber derg; or, the red well' in William Carleton, *Traits and stories of the Irish peasantry* (1844; 2 vols, repr. Gerrards Cross and Savage, MD, 1990), ii, p. 374.
111 Geary, '"The whole country was in motion"', p. 124.

For mendicant families wandering the roads, however, an appreciation of the gendered roles that shaped cultures of mendicancy helped maximise their potential of successfully soliciting assistance. The reality was that a woman with children was more likely to receive sympathy, and, therefore, alms than if an able-bodied man was accompanying them. Being aware of the greater compassion which a woman and her children could inherently excite, poor families wandering the country regularly travelled separately. Men separated from their families and remained out of sight, while their wives and children entered a town or approached a homestead to engage in direct begging. In Longford town, it was noted 'that though able-bodied men are rarely found begging the streets themselves, yet they may frequently be found loitering outside towns, waiting for their families who are begging in them, and to whom their presence would be a disadvantage, since they represent themselves generally as widows and orphans'.[112] In the County Sligo town of Ballymoat, it was stated that 'the man takes his spade and the woman a bag, and they go along the road. If he can get employment, he will work, if not, his wife goes up to the farmers' houses to beg, while he loiters behind on the road'.[113] The deliberate absence of the father/husband in alms-seeking was as much a part of the mendicants' script as the family's fitting into the guise of the classical 'deserving' poor.

Gendered roles also shaped the survival strategies of agricultural labourers and their families from year to year. Many of those labelled as vagrants were able-bodied agricultural labourers (*spailpíní* or *spailpíní fanach*), traversing the country in search of short-term employment. After planting their potato crop male labourers, particularly those living in the west and south of Ireland, left their homesteads for the spring and summer months and migrated, sometimes elsewhere in Ireland but commonly across to England and Scotland for seasonal harvest work (made easier from 1815 by the advent of steamships). These labourers were typically seen as the deserving, honest, working poor, yet in the event that they could not obtain casual work in rural areas often resorted to begging: Connaught labourers were to be found throughout the island, Carlow labourers would 'beg their way' to port towns such as Dublin and Waterford and the north-eastern county of Antrim attracted large numbers of beggars from the western regions of Ulster.[114] This custom continued, certainly among Connaught labourers, into the post-famine period.[115] In the labourers' absence, their wives and children spent these months begging and this alms-seeking was carried out

---

112 *PI, Appendix A*, p. 573.
113 Ibid., p. 526.
114 Ibid., pp. 475, 544, 702.
115 *Ninth annual report, Poor Law Commissioners*, pp. 50–1.

at considerable distance from the home-place and for weeks and months at a time. Mayo labourers' wives and children, for example, were known to beg in parts of Leinster.[116]

The preponderance of women among the country's mendicants can also be seen in the level of institutional engagement by female beggars. In the 1770s, most of the inmates of the House of Industry in Dublin were female, while half a century later, addressing its members in its second annual report, the Dublin Mendicity Society reported that it was to the female sex that 'the great portion of your poor belong'.[117] Of the 2,823 admissions into the Mendicity Society's institution during 1824, 1,687 (59.8 per cent) were adult women, while the 457 adult males made up just 16.2 per cent of admissions. The remaining 679 (24 per cent) were children.[118] More stark ratios were seen in the Clonmel Mendicity Asylum, where there were only five men among 100 paupers.[119] The proportionately higher level of female engagement with charities and institutions in the early decades of the nineteenth century was not witnessed in the Poor Law workhouse system, where, in some workhouses for which admission records survive, the numbers of men and women in the workhouses were roughly equal in the pre-Famine period, although women became more numerous during the height of the Famine crisis. Analysis by Cormac Ó Gráda demonstrates that women were more common among those inmates aged between 15 and 49 years, while men predominated among those aged 50 years and older, suggesting 'that the gender gap in earnings and material comforts shifted over the life-cycle'.[120]

---

116 *PI, Appendix A*, p. 492. For the wider practice of seasonal migration and begging among this social class, see *First report from the select committee on the state of disease and condition of the labouring poor, in Ireland*, p. 19, H.C. 1819 (314), viii, 383; Dr Galway to Dr Cheyne, Aug. 1817 (NAI, CSORP, CSO/RP/1819/229); *PI, Appendix A*, p. 475 (Headford, County Galway); ibid., p. 488 (Tuam, County Galway); ibid., pp. 491–2 (Aughavale, County Mayo); ibid., p. 678 (Cahir (Caher), County Kerry); ibid., p. 762 (Coleraine, County Londonderry); Jonathan Bardon, *A history of Ulster* (Belfast, 1992), pp. 276–7. For Irish migration to England in this period, see Frank Neal, 'The English Poor Law, the Irish migrant and the laws of settlement and removal, 1819–1879' in D. George Boyce and Roger Swift (eds), *Problems and perspectives in Irish history since 1800: essays in honour of Patrick Buckland* (Dublin, 2004), pp. 95–116.

117 *Observations on the state and condition of the poor, under the institution, for their relief, in the city of Dublin; together with the state of the fund, &c. published by order of the Corporation instituted for the Relief of the Poor and for Punishing Vagabonds and Sturdy Beggars, in the County of the City of Dublin, March 25th, 1775* (Dublin, 1775), p. 19; *Second report of the Association for the Suppression of Mendicity in Dublin, 1819* (Dublin, 1820), p. 5.

118 Dublin Mendicity Society minute book, 19 Apr. 1825.

119 *Clare Journal, and Ennis Advertiser*, 24 Nov. 1836.

120 Cormac Ó Gráda, *Ireland: a new economic history 1780–1939* (Oxford, 1994), pp. 99–104.

Child Mendicants

Social commentators in the early nineteenth century were increasingly concerned about the number of children engaged in street begging. Invariably the children of the poor, young mendicants represented the rising generation of the labouring classes who had been, or were in danger of being, lost to lives of idleness, vice, intemperance and crime. Begging was seen as a stepping stone in a criminal's career, leading invariably to thievery and prostitution for boys and girls respectively. As well as being seen as a deplorable nuisance, and constituting in certain circumstances a criminal offence in its own right, street begging represented a stage in the descent of a poor child into delinquency and vice.[121] The concept of there being a rung on the social (and moral) ladder lower than mendicancy was embraced by the Poor Inquiry commissioners in Dublin, who referred in stark terms to those who were born and reared into a life of mendicancy, noting that of these individuals, 'few now pursue the same course of life. They have descended a step lower! – their daughters have become prostitutes, and their sons thieves; they are outcasts even from the "boccough's" dwelling'.[122] In the mid-1830s, a Mr McCarthy, chief constable of Drogheda, opined that some of the town's prostitutes 'are the children of mendicants, who have never pursued any course of industry ... and appear to be separated by a marked line from even the lowest of the labouring population'.[123] A contributor to the *Christian Examiner*, an evangelical Church of Ireland magazine, presented a similar picture in 1831 of the lower orders of the poor, stating that 'it is a common practice for the ruined labourer to commit some minor crime, in order to get into gaol, while his wife and infants set out to beg, and the elder children become thieves or prostitutes'.[124] For many observers, begging was the start

---

121 *PI, Appendix C, Part II, Report upon vagrancy and mendicity in the City of Dublin*, p. 27a*; J.J. Tobias, *Crime and industrial society in the nineteenth century* (Harmondsworth, 1972), pp. 88–92.

122 *PI, Appendix C, Part II, Report upon vagrancy and mendicity in the City of Dublin*, p. 27a*. For this common gendered dichotomy (poor boys became thieves and poor girls became prostitutes), see *PI, Appendix C, Part I*, p. 31; *PI, Appendix C, Part II, Report upon vagrancy and mendicity in the City of Dublin*, p. 41a*. For instances outside of Ireland, see *Report of the committee for investigating the causes of the alarming increase of juvenile delinquency in the metropolis* (London, 1816), p. 10; Heather Shore, *Artful dodgers: youth crime in early-nineteenth-century London* (Woodbridge, 2002), p. 10. According to the governor of the prisons of Glasgow, 'juvenile begging ... almost invariably, on the part of the girls, leads to juvenile prostitution': quoted in William Logan, *An exposure, from personal observation, of female prostitution in London, Leeds and Rochdale, and especially in the city of Glasgow, with remarks on the cause, extent, results and remedy of the evil* (2nd edn, Glasgow, 1843), p. 36.

123 *PI, Appendix C, Part I*, p. 50.

124 'Hibernicus', 'On the Poor Laws' in *Christian Examiner*, xi, no. 74 (Aug. 1831), p. 590.

of a 'downward spiral' leading to theft and robbery.[125] An editorial carried in the Dublin-based *Correspondent* in 1818 reflected the views of a large portion of contemporary opinion, which tended to source a range of social evils to the prevailing system of street begging:

[Mendicancy] instructs the young thief to steal from his thoughtless benefactor, and rears the young robber to the perpetration of dexterous burglaries, by means of which the mature villain enters and plunders. It is hardly possible to point out any of the prevalent street-crimes of this metropolis, or any thing foul, filthy, or infectious, which has not its roots in the enormous mendicity, which we shamefully suffer to lay us under all manner of exactions and contributions.[126]

The pernicious influences to which poor children were vulnerable derived not solely from inanimate sources, such as the environment in which they lived, but also from hardened, criminalised individuals preying on these juveniles. Reports of children being mutilated or impregnated for the sake of exciting compassion in passers-by were common.[127] Under the influence of such persons, invariably older youths or adults, the street child was 'initiated into vice'.[128] This process is captured in Charles Dickens's portrayal of Fagin initiating Oliver Twist into a gang of thieves through making a 'very curious and uncommon game' of pick-pocketing.[129] While the unknowing and naive Oliver merely enjoys what he considers to be a game, the reader is left in no doubt that Fagin is, in modern parlance, 'grooming' Oliver for a life of thievery – that is, preying on the child's vulnerability from an adult's position of power and influence. While the terminology was different in the nineteenth century, fears of such individuals and their practices influenced

125 Prunty, *Dublin slums*, p. 196.
126 *Correspondent*, 13 Jan. 1818.
127 Arthur Dobbs, *An essay on the trade and improvement of Ireland* (2 parts, Dublin, 1729–31), ii, p. 45; *FJ*, 26–9 Mar., 26–30 Apr. 1768, cited in Joseph Robins, *The lost children: a study of charity children in Ireland, 1700–1900* (Dublin, 1980), p. 103 n. 6; Richard Woodward, *An address to the public, on the expediency of a regular plan for the maintenance and government of the poor ...* (Dublin, 1775), p. 10; Richard Whately, *Christ's example, an instruction as to the best modes of dispensing charity. A sermon delivered for the benefit of the Relief and Clothing Fund, in Doctor Steevens' Hospital* (Dublin, 1835), p. 21. A particularly harrowing case of cruelty is recorded in *Full and true account of the trial of two most barbarous and cruel beggar-women, Sarah Mullholland & Maria Burke, who were found guilty of strangling a child, for the purpose of extorting charity!!! Together with various particulars concerning the impostures of other street beggars* (n.p. [Dublin?], [c.1830]), broadside held in the RIA library, Dublin (SR 3 B 53–56(561)).
128 *Report on juvenile delinquency in the metropolis*, p. 32.
129 Charles Dickens, *The adventures of Oliver Twist* (1839; Oxford, 1987), p. 61.

middle-class perceptions of poor juveniles. Later in *Oliver Twist*, this corruptive process is vividly narrated:

> In short, the wily old Jew had the boy in his toils; and, having prepared his mind, by solicitude and gloom, to prefer any society to the companionship of his own sad thoughts in such a dreary place, was now slowly instilling into his soul the poison which he hoped would blacken it, and change its hue for ever.[130]

In the pages of the *Belfast News-Letter* in 1851 is to be found evidence of Dickens's most infamous villain resounding in the popular mind, when the paper referred to boys and girls who engaged in organised theft being 'regularly hired or supported by "Fagins" of the lowest grade'.[131] In his examination of the alleys and courts which harboured deviants in mid-nineteenth-century Belfast, Unitarian minister William Murphy O'Hanlon asserted that 'unwary youth[s]' were 'entrapped and drawn into these places as flies into a spider's web', where they were corrupted, ruined and primed 'to plunge headlong on in their career of vice and degradation'.[132] A specific example which illustrates the reality of such 'grooming' by vagrant mendicants in an Irish context is that of Mary Quin, 'an itinerant beggarwoman' who was convicted in September 1840 of kidnapping four children from Belfast. Quin wandered through County Antrim pretending to be the widowed mother of the children, 'whom she treated most unmercifully while training them to the various tricks resorted to by pauper children to impose on the humane'. Quin was also known to have induced girls 'of very tender years' to leave their parents 'and, by introducing them to houses of ill-fame, brought them to a course of prostitution'.[133] Cases such as Quin's reminded the public that characters like Fagin were not confined to the pages of fiction.

Beggars' Previous Occupations: A Dublin Case Study
A return depicting the stated previous occupations of 2,099 inmates at the Dublin Mendicity Society's asylum during 1826 illuminates the study of the backgrounds and experiences of Ireland's beggars in the pre-Famine

---

130 Ibid., p. 134. Fagin later advises his colleagues: 'Once let him feel that he is one of us – once fill his mind with the idea that he has been a thief – and he's ours. Ours for his life!', ibid., p. 141.
131 *BNL*, 16 June 1851, quoted in Brian Griffin, *The Bulkies: police and crime in Belfast, 1800–1865* (Dublin, 1998), p. 75.
132 W.M. O'Hanlon, *Walks among the poor of Belfast, and suggestions for their improvement* (Belfast, 1853), pp. 21–2.
133 *BNL*, 11 Sept. 1840.

period.[134] Unlike most other charitable societies which shunned street beggars, the Mendicity Society catered explicitly for that class of poor; as such, the paupers who passed through its doors were those most likely to engage in mendicancy. Of course, the records of a single institution do not provide a comprehensive picture of the experiences of a largely marginalised, heterogeneous class of people, yet, this source proves illustrative. The return divides the 2,099 mendicants into 69 different occupations. To represent this information visually, the eight most common occupations (representing 72 per cent of the total) have been extracted and presented in Table 1.1 and Figure 1.2 as individual categories. The remaining 28 per cent (consisting of 61 different occupations) have, in the interest of clarity, been amalgamated and presented as 'Others'. Examining solely the eight most common occupations, it will be seen that these can be split between (largely female) unskilled labourers – scourers, charwomen, washerwomen and day labourers – and (largely male) unemployed textile workers. For many persons in these occupations there was little if any security in their regular income, and at times of under- or unemployment begging was an instinctive resort as a survival strategy in the 'economy of makeshifts'. Criminal records for the middle of the century support the return's evidence that scourers and charwomen regularly engaged in direct begging, for which they could be (and in some cases were) convicted and imprisoned. In 1850, Ellen Fullerton was described by respectable householders who petitioned on her behalf as a 'most industrious poor woman, constantly working for charring'; Catherine Maher (60 years old) was also described as a charwoman, as was 74-year-old Anne Farrell, who 'always earned her bread by charring'.[135] In each of these cases of imprisonment on foot of a conviction for public begging, the intervention of respectable inhabitants, typically shopkeepers and merchants, led to the remission of the 14- or 15-day sentence and the early release of the prisoner. The evidence for Dublin supports the findings of Tim Hitchcock, whose work on street begging in eighteenth-century London found that charwomen were not only the most numerous 'working mendicants' but also 'the group who most effectively confused the division between pauper employments and outright beggary'. Charwomen's pleas for work, as they knocked on the doors of city inhabitants, were frequently indistinguishable from pleas for material assistance (alms). According to Hitchcock, 'in the end, it is clear

---

134 PI, Appendix C, Part II, Report upon vagrancy and mendicity in the City of Dublin, p. 25a*.

135 Criminal Index File of Ellen Fullerton, Jan. 1850 (NAI, Criminal Index Files, CIF/1850/F/4); Criminal Index File of Catherine Maher, Aug. 1854 (ibid., CIF/1854/M/25); Criminal Index File of Anne Farrell, Dec. 1856 (ibid., CIF/1856/F/27).

that charring made foggy and indistinct the boundary between begging and service'.[136]

While Figure 1.2 is helpful in identifying the typical occupations undertaken by some of Dublin's mendicants, some problems arise as to the extent to which the statistics are representative. First, it appears that the 69 occupations exclude those of children. This is quite a substantial omission, given that a large proportion of street beggars in nineteenth-century towns and cities were children. Juveniles' engagement in mendicancy ranged from outright solicitations of alms to the offering of some trivial paid labour. According to a German traveller to Dublin in 1828, 'the streets are crowded with beggar-boys, who buzz around one like flies, incessantly offering their services'.[137] Secondly, it is not recorded how the information on the paupers' previous occupations was ascertained and it may only be assumed that this was through face-to-face inquiry of the mendicants upon their admission to the Dublin Mendicity Society's asylum. As such, the questions of whether such information is reliable and whether the paupers had an interest in misrepresenting their previous economic activities have to be asked. Thirdly, beggars were admitted into the mendicity asylum on a voluntary basis and the source, therefore, excludes those mendicants who declined to engage with the charity.

Fourthly, and most importantly, in considering the prominence of textile workers in this sample, the subject year (1826) is significant. Late 1825 and 1826 witnessed a severe economic downturn in Britain and Ireland, caused by a British monetary crisis. British manufacturers dumped their goods onto the Irish market, undercutting small Irish manufacturers, which led to the collapse of many woollen, silk and cotton businesses and consequential mass unemployment. In Dublin city, the south-western quarter known as the Liberties, where the city's textile trade was concentrated, suffered enormous distress, compounded by a typhus fever epidemic. One estimate put the number of destitute at 20,000 in this quarter alone.[138] Given the impact of this economic downturn and accompanying fever epidemic, it may be suggested that the proportion of textile workers on the books of the

136 Hitchcock, 'Begging on the streets of eighteenth-century London', pp. 489–90.
137 [Hermann von Pückler-Muskau], *Tour in England, Ireland, and France, in the years 1826, 1827, 1828, and 1829, with remarks on the manners and customs of the inhabitants, and anecdotes of distinguished public characters. In a series of letters* (Philadelphia, 1833), p. 326.
138 Timothy P. O'Neill, 'A bad year in the Liberties' in Elgy Gillespie (ed.), *The Liberties of Dublin* (2nd edn, Dublin, 1974), p. 79; *The census of Ireland for the year 1851. Part v. Table of deaths.* vol. 1, p. 200, H.C. 1856 [C 2087-I], xxix, 464. For the social impact of this crisis in Dublin city, see David O'Toole, 'The employment crisis of 1826' in David Dickson (ed.), *The gorgeous mask: Dublin 1700–1850* (Dublin, 1987), pp. 157–71.

Table 1.1 Previous occupations of inmates of the Dublin Mendicity Society, 1826

Description of previous occupation	Number of cases	Percentage of total
Servants	476	22.7%
Scourers, charwomen, etc.	377	18.0%
Silk weavers and throwsters	188	8.9%
Cotton weavers and spinners	182	8.7%
Dressmakers, lacemakers, bonnet-makers and plain workers	99	4.7%
Day labourers	74	3.5%
Washerwomen	63	3.0%
Worsted weavers and stuff-makers	53	2.5%
Others	587	28.0%
Totals	**2,099**	**100%**

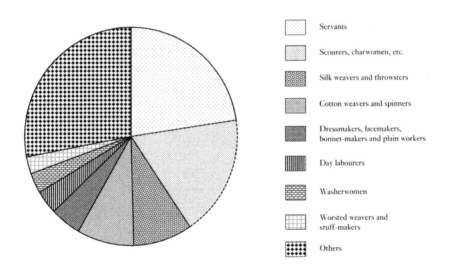

Figure 1.2 Chart showing previous occupations of inmates of the Dublin Mendicity Society, 1826

Source: Poor Inquiry, Appendix C, Part II, Report upon vagrancy and mendicity in the City of Dublin, p. 25a*.

city's mendicity society increased beyond its usual rate, as newly unemployed
individuals and their dependants sought charitable assistance. In 1826, the
annual report of the Dublin Mendicity Society noted that unemployed
factory workers were 'the most common and alarming group of beggars' in
the city.[139] The following year, the society reported that the more than 2,000
people on its books included 'the unprecedented number of 736 tradespeople
(including their families)'.[140] The occupational analysis above may, then,
be considered to be somewhat skewed in how it depicts the momentary
prominence of textile workers among the inmates of the Mendicity Society.
On the other hand, the downturn of the mid-1820s dealt a fatal blow to
textile industries in the Liberties, as well as to other Irish urban centres.
Thousands of artisans never returned to this line of employment, and
many emigrated, found alternative employment or took to street begging.[141]
The above figure, therefore, may be interpreted not as over-representing
textile workers among the beggars of 1820s-Dublin in the short-term but
as reflecting the beginning of a long-term shift in the demographics of the
city's mendicant classes, among whom former textile artisans were *now* more
prominent. The Poor Inquiry evidence supports the latter argument that,
from the mid-1820s, unemployed and formerly independent textile workers
formed a substantial group from which street beggars in large Irish urban
centres derived. According to the Assistant Commissioners who carried out
examinations in Cork city in the mid-1830s, 'the majority of the distressed
persons in the parish are persons reduced; many, from the decay of the
woollen and cotton manufacturers, scarcely any whose parents had been
beggars'.[142] The inquiry in Dublin city was told by Richard Browning, the
Protestant 'bangbeggar', that most mendicants he encountered 'were women,
widows whose husbands had been weavers, or in different branches of trade
connected with weaving; they were mostly elderly'.[143]

Despite these instances of typically industrious individuals resorting
to beggary in circumstances of distress, there was evidently an underclass
of professional beggars who refused to work and who survived predominantly through begging. The language of social description in later

---

139 Woods, *Dublin outsiders*, p. 51.
140 *Tenth report of the general committee of the Association for the Suppression of Mendicity
     in Dublin. For the year 1827* (Dublin, 1828), p. 44.
141 O'Neill, 'A bad year in the Liberties', p. 81.
142 *PI, Appendix A*, p. 672. For destitution among Cork city's former artisan class, see
     Maura Cronin (née Murphy), 'The economic and social structure of nineteenth-
     century Cork' in David Harkness and Mary O'Dowd (eds), *The town in Ireland*,
     Historical Studies XIII (Belfast, 1981), p. 146.
143 *PI, Appendix C, Part II, Report upon vagrancy and mendicity in the City of Dublin*,
     p. 43a*.

nineteenth-century Britain referred to a 'residuum', that is a morally toxic layer existing beneath the respectable working class.[144] This mass of unskilled urban poor offended the sensitivities and challenged the expectations of middle-class society regarding the virtues of industry, providence, sobriety and religious piety; the former's lifestyles and values were ones of moral degradation. This 'residuum' corresponds to Karl Marx's 'lumpenprole-tariat', which he described as 'a recruiting ground for thieves and criminals of all kinds, living on the crumbs of society, people without a definite trade, vagabonds, people without a hearth or home'.[145] For one English Poor Law commissioner, this class of persons constituted 'the refuse of society',[146] reflecting their marginalisation from 'respectable' society. An Irish insight into this 'residuum' can be gleaned from the autobiography of novelist William Carleton. Having left his rural County Tyrone home around 1817, Carleton travelled south through Ireland before reaching Dublin some time the following year. Among the most striking images of his autobiography is the account of his one night's stay in an underground lodging place occupied by multitudes of professional beggars:

> There were there the lame, the blind, the dumb, and all who suffered from actual and natural infirmity; but in addition to these, there was every variety of impostor about me – most of them stripped of their mechanical accessories of deceit, but by no means all … Crutches, wooden legs, artificial cancers, scrofulous necks, artificial wens, sore legs, and a vast variety of similar complaints were hung up upon the walls of the cellars, and made me reflect upon the degree of perverted talent and ingenuity that must have been necessary to sustain such a mighty mass of imposture.[147]

Carleton's account presents a traditional dichotomous portrayal of the city's poor, 'deserving' living alongside 'undeserving', the latter comprising a relatively significant element of the poorer classes and characterised by dishonesty, 'perverted talent and ingenuity'. An 1840s account of a low lodging house in Ashton-under-Lyne, a Lancaster town to the east of Manchester, recorded a similar scene to that witnessed by Carleton, noting

144 Geoffrey Crossick, 'From gentlemen to the residuum: languages of social description in Victorian Britain' in Penelope J. Corfield (ed.), *Language, history and class* (Oxford and Cambridge, MA, 1991), pp. 162–4.

145 David McLellan, *The thought of Karl Marx: an introduction* (3rd edn, London, 1995), p. 185.

146 *Reports and communications on vagrancy*, p. 2, H.C. 1847–8 [C 987], liii, 240.

147 William Carleton, *The autobiography of William Carleton* (1896; repr. London, 1968), pp. 164–5.

the 'hawkers' baskets, pedlars' boxes, musical instruments, and beggars' crutches' to be found within.[148]

Carleton's memorable description of the cellar scene throws light on the reality that most beggars in this period had dwellings of some kind.[149] In Irish towns or cities, these were rented lodgings, in tenements and in wretched abodes in back streets, alleys, lanes and courts. Many of the street beggars who received relief from the Dublin Mendicity Society had dwellings, and throughout its early history the Mendicity Society proudly advertised the fact that its paupers did not reside on its premises, but were put to work for the day, provided with food (and the children with rudimentary education) and sent 'home' in the evening: the parents and children 'met again in the evening, and retired together in the evening – not to the ward of an hospital, or a prison, but to their common home, which, humble as it was, served to keep up the social bond of communion between the parent and the infant'.[150] James Whitelaw's famous survey of Dublin in 1798 described parts of the Liberties as being, 'with their numerous lanes and alleys ... occupied by working manufacturers, by petty shopkeepers, the labouring poor, and beggars, crowded together, to a degree distressing to humanity'.[151] Indeed, the Poor Inquiry commissioners visited the dwellings of known beggars in the Liberties, and recorded their detailed and grim descriptions of the wretchedness of these tenement dwellings. The commissioners visited a tenement room occupied by four family units (mothers and daughters and elderly, single women) in Fordham's Alley, a street formerly occupied by industrious artisans; but now only six families out of 700 individuals supported themselves.[152]

While much of the begging in rural Ireland was undertaken by migrant labourers who had left their home dwelling (a small cabin), as discussed above, most rural parishes had their own local and known beggars – individuals who lived locally on a permanent basis and whose survival relied on the regular solicitation of assistance from neighbours; local beggars were guaranteed – or at least, were more confident of receiving – alms from neighbours and parishioners to whom they were familiar. Typical of this 'home-grown' mendicant was Terence Loughlin, a 'beggar' who testified

148 Raphael Samuel, 'Comers and goers' in H.J. Dyos and Michael Wolff (eds), *The Victorian city: images and realities*, vol. 1, *Past and present, and numbers of people* (London, 1976), p. 128.
149 Hufton, *The poor of eighteenth-century France*, pp. 48–50.
150 *FJ*, 25 May 1826. See also ibid., 10 Jan. 1843.
151 James Whitelaw, *An essay on population of Dublin, being the result of an actual survey taken in 1798 ...* (Dublin, 1805), p. 50.
152 *PI, Appendix C, Part II, Report upon vagrancy and mendicity in the City of Dublin*, p. 27a*.

before the Whately Poor Inquiry commissioners in Kilchreest parish, County Galway:

> I am 73 years of age; I was able to work a little three years ago; I was a labourer and was middling well off, for I had work almost every day. I live in town, and have a cabin and half-a-quarter [acre] of ground from Mr Pearse, for which he charges me no rent … I go amongst my neighbours to get a sup of milk or a lock of potatoes; I carry a bag, and always get from two to three stone at a time; I'd get more than another because I am an old neighbour; I was never refused by any of them yet that I went to … I don't go far from home.[153]

Loughlin's account of his own resort to mendicancy as a survival strategy framed himself as being amongst the 'deserving' poor: he opened his account by asserting that he was formerly an industrious labourer with regular work and income, and his dependency on the charity of his neighbours was occasioned solely through his infirmity through old age. His subsistence through mendicancy was supported by local people who provided their 'old neighbour' with a rent-free plot of land, milk and potatoes.

Beggars' Denominational Background
To plot a denominational breakdown of beggars in Ireland accurately is next to impossible, and what figures that survive are varied and unreliable. What can be asserted with confidence is that most beggars were from a Roman Catholic background. In the first two years after the opening of the Dublin House of Industry (1773–5), an institution founded 'for the relief of the poor, and for punishing vagabonds and sturdy beggars', Catholics comprised 69.8 per cent of inmates.[154] Of the 388 paupers at the Limerick House of Industry between 1774 and 1793 whose occupation was listed as 'beggar' or 'stroller', only 24 (6.2 per cent) were Protestants; in the 1830s, it was reported that there were 40 Protestants among the 460 inmates (8.7 per cent).[155] Historian Donal McCartney provides the statistic – regrettably unreferenced – that 1 per cent of vagrants in nineteenth-century Ireland belonged to the Church of Ireland.[156] Henry Inglis stated that upon his visit to the Dublin Mendicity Society's asylum in 1834, 200 of the 2,145 paupers

153 *PI, Appendix A*, p. 479.
154 *Observations on the state and condition of the poor, 1775*, p. 19.
155 David Fleming and John Logan (eds), *Pauper Limerick: the register of the Limerick House of Industry 1774–1793* (IMC, Dublin, 2011); G.F.G. M[athison], *Journal of a tour in Ireland during the months of October and November 1835* (London, 1836), p. 138.
156 Donal McCartney, *The dawning of democracy: Ireland 1800–1870* (Dublin, 1987), p. 27.

(9.3 per cent) were Protestants,[157] while of the 5,322 convicted vagrants imprisoned at the Richmond Bridewell during 1849, 244 (4.6 per cent) were members of the Church of Ireland and none was a Dissenter.[158] A return for the parish of Urney, County Tyrone submitted to the Poor Inquiry estimated that 14 per cent of the parish's beggars (that is, 16 out of a total of 116 mendicants) belonged to the Church of Ireland, while the remaining paupers were Catholic and Presbyterian, although the precise breakdown is not provided.[159]

Who Gave Alms and Why?

Beggars calling at the houses of the wealthier inhabitants of a town or city were usually dealt with by domestic servants, who were frequently criticised in public pronouncements for giving alms, mostly in the form of leftover food ('broken meat'), to street beggars.[160] An inhabitant of Mountjoy Square, Dublin was rebuked by the city's mendicity society because 'his servants are in the constant habit of giving broken meat to mendicants' and he was urged 'to stop a practice so injurious to the objects of this association'.[161] The Galway Mendicity Society attributed the continued presence of beggars on the streets to 'the relief that is still given by servants and other mistaken persons, at the doors, and is certainly the greatest abuse of charity that can be conceived'.[162] In Waterford, it was claimed that the work of the mendicity asylum was undermined by 'the servants retaining them [provisions] for the strolling beggars', a practice which encouraged street mendicancy.[163] Similar sentiments were expressed in Edinburgh, where servants were blamed for assisting beggars at their employers' homes, 'bestowing what is, properly speaking, not their own'.[164] In her advice manual to female servants, the

157 Henry D. Inglis, *Ireland in 1834. A journey through Ireland, during the spring, summer, and autumn of 1834* (2nd edn, 2 vols, London, 1835), i, pp. 16–17.

158 *Prisons of Ireland. Twenty-eighth report of the Inspectors-General on the general state of the prisons of Ireland, 1849; with appendices*, p. 26, H.C. 1850 [C 1229], xxix, 346. These figures do not allow for cases of recidivism.

159 *PI, Supplement to Appendix A*, p. 409.

160 *FJ*, 21 Sept. 1826; *An address to the mechanics, workmen, and servants, in the city of Dublin* (Dublin, 1828) in DDA, DMP, 30/11/17; Dublin Mendicity Society minute book, 17 Dec. 1822 (NLI, DMSP, MS 32,599/2).

161 Dublin Mendicity Society minute book, 22 June 1824 (NLI, DMSP, 32,599/3).

162 *Galway Weekly Advertiser*, 1 Jan. 1825.

163 Report on the state of the poor in Waterford city and on the charitable institutions of that city, 5 Apr. 1834 (NLI, MS 3288, f. 28ʳ).

164 Quoted in Andrew J. Dalgleish, 'Voluntary associations and the middle class in Edinburgh, 1780–1820' (PhD thesis, University of Edinburgh, 1991), p. 112.

prolific English writer Eliza Haywood (*c.*1693–1756), who spent some time in Dublin as an actress, warned that 'tho' Charity and Compassion for the Wants of our Fellow creatures are very amiable Virtues', servants ought not to give leftover food to beggars without the permission of their masters.[165] She further advised her readers not to give alms to mendicants on the streets.[166] An important point to be made is that the majority of domestic servants in Ireland – perhaps as much as 80 per cent, according to the 1841 census[167] – were female, suggesting that most of the alms-giving from this particular source was carried out by women. Servants came from social backgrounds closer to those of the persons they relieved than did their employers and this undoubtedly evoked empathy and sympathy and influenced servants' willingness to proffer alms.

Accounts of landed proprietors personally giving alms to beggars further reveal the gendered nature of alms-giving; such 'Big House' benefactors were almost invariably women. A Mrs Johnston, the proprietor of Glynn parish in County Antrim, personally doled out alms to beggars calling at her home every Friday and also granted 'a free house ... to each of 6 helpless old people'.[168] In Dublin, a Mrs P___ was so well known to give silver to beggars that, according to one Poor Inquiry witness,

all her movements are watched, and are well known. One morning, when it was known that she was going out of town, I passed her house, and saw upwards of 50 beggars at her door; and at one glance down the street you may, at any time, know whether she is in town according as there may be a crowd of beggars in the street or not.[169]

This Irish situation resembled the gendered dynamics in the provision of assistance to the poor was also evident in eighteenth-century Breton society, where female members of noble families acted as godmothers to local pauper children and provided them with references for domestic positions in urban centres.[170]

In provincial towns and large cities shopkeepers were among the most regular providers of alms. On the one hand, shopkeepers were most likely

---

165 [Eliza Haywood], *A present for a servant-maid. Or, the sure means of gaining love and esteem* (Dublin, 1744), p. 29.
166 Ibid., pp. 44–5.
167 *Report of the commissioners appointed to take the census of Ireland. For the year 1841*, p. 440, H.C. 1843 [C 504], xxiv, 552.
168 *OSM*, xxvi, pp. 22, 13.
169 *PI, Appendix C, Part II, Report upon vagrancy and mendicity in the City of Dublin*, p. 43a*.
170 Hufton, *The poor of eighteenth-century France*, p. 114.

to have disposable income or leftover food items to dole out as charity; on the other hand, for the trading community, the prevalence of hordes of mendicants posed a constant threat to business, a theme analysed in detail in Chapter 3. Street beggars caused a nuisance to passers-by, importunately pushing out a soliciting hand (or, in many instances, a famished infant) to excite compassion. Furthermore, persons having intercourse with such individuals ran the risk of contracting a potentially fatal disease. Business owners feared that their clientele, frustrated with being imposed upon by alms-seekers, would take their custom elsewhere. To avoid this nuisance, shopkeepers frequently gave a regular allowance to mendicants, on the understanding that the latter would not loiter at the former's premises. In the 1770s, Church of Ireland bishop Richard Woodward referred to the common practice of shopkeepers providing a weekly subvention to beggars 'on condition of their not molesting their doors, and interrupting their business'.[171] A similar weekly 'allowance' was also provided by shopkeepers in the market town of Naas, County Kildare to approximately 100 local beggars in the 1830s. The stated justification for such charity was that the shopkeepers 'prefer a regular weekly allowance to being annoyed daily'.[172] In Cork city, it was commented that 'the respectable shopkeepers often give to get rid of a teazing [sic] beggar'.[173] While some shopkeepers opted to give money directly to mendicants, others subscribed (individually or collectively) to mendicity charities, in the hope that their financial support for these initiatives would mitigate the nuisance of street begging and impact positively on the footfall in their shops. For instance, in 1838, the bakers of Dublin contributed £122 to the city's Mendicity Society.[174]

Alms-Givers in Rural Ireland
Turning to rural Ireland, it can be seen that most of the alms-giving was carried out by the families of poorer farmers, cottiers and labourers, whose precarious subsistence left them not far removed from the threat of destitution. It was the inevitable conclusion of social investigators and foreign travellers to Ireland that it was, largely, the poor who supported the poor.[175] There were a number of reasons why the relief of mendicants fell so hard on the shoulders on the poor. Traditional attitudes of charity and reciprocity among the lower

---

171 Woodward, *Address to the public, regular plan for the poor*, p. 25.
172 *PI, Appendix A*, p. 556.
173 Ibid., p. 673. The Poor Inquiry also identified this practice in County Antrim (ibid., pp. 703, 707) and Mullingar, County Westmeath (ibid., pp. 590–1).
174 *Clare Journal, and Ennis Advertiser*, 30 Sept. 1839.
175 *Third report of the commissioners for inquiring into the condition of the poorer classes in Ireland*, p. 25, H.C. 1836 [C 43], xxx, 1; *Second report of Geo. Nicholls, Poor Laws, Ireland*, p. 24.

social groups coloured responses to poverty and beggary and these beliefs derived from a traditional Christian framework wherein the poor were seen as virtuous beings whose relief could result in elysian rewards.[176] Furthermore, the fact that so many of Ireland's poor lived on the brink of destitution – which could be brought about through a family illness or a poor harvest – undoubtedly developed in them greater sympathy towards mendicants, thus making them more likely to dole out assistance. In addition to these factors, wealthier landowners, by the sheer extent and design of their farms and estates, were spatially removed from beggars, who did not have access to the former's residences: 'the small farmer or cottier is more exposed than the large proprietor to the application of these vagrants, as he has no means of keeping them off, whereas the houses of the rich are usually guarded by an approach through which mendicants do not so easily penetrate'.[177] In Ballymahon, County Longford, the Poor Inquiry was told that 'The gates and sometimes the dogs of the wealthy secure them against the intrusion of the beggar'.[178] When the commissioners in Kilchreest, County Galway were told that the gates of the gentry were often shut so as to keep out itinerant mendicants, they asked whether anything was left at the gate for the paupers. They were told: 'Yes, the order to shut them out is left for them'.[179]

Much of the alms-giving in rural homes was the domain of the female members of a household. In Milltown Malbay, in County Clare, the 'duty of giving alms almost always falls to the share of the woman of the house or her daughters, and their feelings are in favour of those who have families of young children'.[180] In Kildysart, in the same county, the Poor Inquiry was told by a shopkeeper that the farmers, who preferred the prevailing system of casual alms-giving to a rates system, 'really do not know how much goes out of their houses in charity. If they were to stay at home one long day in summer and watch all that their wives give away, they would soon alter their way of thinking'.[181] Cottier John Casey in Abbeyshrule parish remarked: 'Many a time a man has to check his wife for having too free a hand, and I am often bad enough to do it myself as well as another'.[182] In larger farms, female servants undertook this role of dealing with beggars and some farmers were known to complain of the 'constant interruption to which their women servants were liable from beggars'.[183] This gendered practice was reflected

176 Ó Ciosáin, *Ireland in official print culture*, pp. 79–90.
177 *PI, Appendix C, Part I*, p. 49.
178 *PI, Appendix A*, p. 564.
179 Ibid., p. 479.
180 Ibid., p. 619; also p. 636.
181 Ibid., p. 232.
182 Ibid., p. 564.
183 Ibid., p. 616.

Figure 1.3   'The first alms-begging' from William Carleton, 'Tubber derg: or, the red well' (1852) (reproduced courtesy of National Library of Ireland)

in the alms-giving exchange illustrated in William Carleton's 'Tubber derg: or, the red well', a short story about a once-industrious and proud labouring family whose eviction as a result of the post-Waterloo economic and agrarian downturn reduces them to destitution and, ultimately, mendicancy: it is the mother/wife of the newly mendicant family who pleads for assistance at the farmer's cabin door, ensuring her benefactor that this is 'our first day to be upon the world', and she is received by the woman of the house, who instinctively approaches the begging family with a double handful of meal (*gabhpán*) even before a word is uttered in supplication (see Figure 1.3).

The father/husband of the beggarly family is depicted as slumped over the host family's table, head in his hands, and overcome with the shame of their reduced station. In John and Michael Banim's *Father Connell* (1842), the female 'potatoe beggars' are noted as interacting with 'farmers' wives ... in pursuit of their calling'.[184] While being regular providers of alms, women did not necessarily distribute alms indiscriminately and were known to form judgements on the moral character and deservedness of the mendicant before them. According to Timothy Gorman, a County Clare small farmer with about twelve acres:

> I saw my wife refuse alms to a woman yesterday; and I asked her why she refused on a Monday (a thing we consider unlucky for the rest of the week); she said the woman had been coming to her for the last three days, and that she had a stout able-bodied son who would not work, but preferred living on the sale of what his mother collected.[185]

The gendering of this role may be due to the traditional female caregiver model (whereby womanhood is associated with compassionate and welfare-based duties), but may also be attributable to the more practical fact that women were more likely than men to be in the house when beggars called to the door, a point illustrated in the words of Pat Curtis in Killaloe, a 'decent small farmer' of three and a half acres, who explained that 'I am not much at home, but the old woman gives a handful to everybody that calls'.[186]

Conclusion

It is worth revisiting the Dublin Mendicity Society's direction to its street inspectors in 1824, to apprehend individuals 'whom they may find prowling about the streets, without any visible occupation, or means of subsistence, whom they have reason to suspect are there for the purpose of begging, although not in the act of begging at the moment'.[187] Leaving aside the fundamental point this order raises concerning the civil liberties of the poor, it points to a question pertinent to this chapter – namely, what constituted begging and who constituted a beggar? This particular resolution from the capital's most prominent charitable society tackling the social problems

---

184 O'Hara Family [John and Michael Banim], *Father Connell* (3 vols, London, 1842), i, pp. 125–6.
185 *PI, Appendix A*, p. 613.
186 Ibid., p. 623. See Ó Ciosáin on this point in *Ireland in official print culture*, p. 75.
187 Dublin Mendicity Society minute book, 23 Mar. 1824.

connected with poverty focuses its attention on those engaged in, or believed likely to engage in, what we may term outright begging. Such individuals were to be identified by the absence of any visible means of earning a living. However, as demonstrated in this chapter, the reality of mendicancy and the experiences of mendicants in pre-Famine Ireland were more complex than this. Beggary regularly overlapped with the sale of a good or service, the offering of which was essential for justifying one's presence in a public thoroughfare, more so in urban than rural areas. Beggars knew which locations, situations, categories of passers-by and stories of distress maximised their chances of receiving sympathy and alms. The 'swarming' of carriages by mendicants is a ubiquitous trope to be found in travellers' accounts of pre-Famine Ireland, while pilgrimages, life-cycle events and sporting occasions also attracted supplicants, reflecting some level of seasonality, regularity and mobility to patterns of mendicancy. Regional variations in the toleration (or not) of church-door begging has been explained by reference to Sabbatarian sentiment among Irish Protestants at this time, while the facts that northern towns and villages were relatively well serviced by mendicity societies and Protestant contributions to poor collections inside their church or meeting house negated the need, for many, to also give alms to beggars.

In answering the question of who were the beggars of pre-Famine Ireland, it has been demonstrated that they were mostly women and children, owing to a mixture of social, cultural and economic factors, all of which were shaped by the gendering of roles within the poor's 'economy of makeshifts'. Women and children predominated among supplicants of both formal and informal charity. Destitute or near-destitute independent male labourers were more likely to be guided by their shame of begging, but more significant than this was that women's vulnerability to spousal desertion and their relatively limited employment opportunities also contributed to this gendered imbalance. Furthermore, the fact that it was women who faced the challenge of feeding their children suggests that pragmatism and urgency overtook any possible sense of female shame. In the Dublin Mendicity Society in the mid-1820s, most inmates – all habitual mendicants – were unskilled labourers or unemployed textile workers, but critical analysis of this particular source suggests that only a skewed picture of the institution's inmates is possible. What is certain is that large numbers of habitually independent artisans lived perilously close to destitution, and when illness or an economic downturn struck, the resort to alms-seeking, once unfathomable, became a necessary survival strategy – albeit one only for certain members of the family unit. In parts of rural Ireland, begging was a seasonal practice undertaken by many among the labouring classes, but in such instances, also, gendered norms dictated that it was women and children who tramped the roads seeking alms, while the father/husband migrated for seasonal work. The reason why people begged differed from person to person. For some, beggary was an attempt to relieve short-term distress; for other, alms-seeking was a regular source of income and could be considered as something of an occupation. Beggary carried a varied significance in people's own 'economy of makeshifts'.

The solicitation of alms was a dual-role encounter, involving the soliciting mendicant and the solicited (prospective) alms-giver. Just as with the former, the demographic make-up of the latter category reflected prevalent social roles governed by cultural, economic and gender factors. In villages, towns and cities, alms-givers were frequently shopkeepers (and their families) and domestic servants. This is not to ignore the frequency of casual alms-giving on streets by passers-by, a form of alms-giving regrettably beyond analysis. In rural areas, female members of a family typically oversaw the distribution of alms to itinerant beggars. Urban/rural patterns can also be discerned in the nature of alms given: money was most common in towns and cities (while servants commonly doled out leftover food) and potatoes constituted the currency of mendicancy in rural Ireland. The labourer and cottier class also lodged vagrants in their dwellings, representing in many cases the only means of assistance that could be offered by people with little in the way of material possessions, and this custom appears to have been utterly absent from the urban context.

Defining begging, beggars and alms-giving in a pre-Famine Ireland requires a cautious and measured approach, and this chapter has analysed a wide range of inherent complexities which arise from numerous factors in defining the acts of begging and alms-giving, and those people who engaged in these practices: the fluid nature of the poor person's resort to beggary; the multifaceted day-to-day dynamics of alms-seeking; the various forms in which alms were bestowed; and the disparate experiences of men, women and children as street beggars. Chapter 2 will discuss and analyse how contemporaries attempted to measure the problem of beggary and its monetary cost in pre-Famine Ireland.

2

Measuring Begging and Alms-Giving

Introduction

Among the witnesses who gave evidence to the Whately Poor Inquiry in Dublin city were two policemen: Chief Constables Michael Farrell and Henry Gilbert Goodison. Both were senior and experienced officers, Farrell having served in that position for the previous 26 years, while Goodison had been based in the College Street police division for more than a decade.[1] When asked to provide estimates as to the number of mendicants in Dublin city, however, these two men gave strikingly disparate figures. Farrell divided the beggars into four categories: approximately 100, excluding their children, who resorted to begging from genuine destitution, 'whose very manner of begging, look and dress bespeak them at once to be objects of real charity, so that he [Farrell] cannot himself refrain from giving them alms in the streets'; 500 regular beggars, including children; 500 who lived on the outskirts of the city and begged in surrounding villages; and 100 who were 'strangers passing through'.[2] Farrell's figures gave a total of 1,200 mendicants in Dublin city. Goodison's estimate, however, put the figure at closer to 8,000 'beggars ... using the word in its widest significance, including men, women, their children, and orphans'.[3] The significance here lies in the gap – a sixfold variance – in estimates. We may assume the two senior officers shared an intimate knowledge of the city's streets and a first-hand appreciation of the extent of visible poverty and mendicancy. The disparity in their estimates, therefore, must be explained by these two individuals' different definitions of what constituted a 'beggar', the term used by both men. Farrell drew upon some manner of rudimentary categorisation,

---

1 *PI, Appendix C, Part II, Report upon vagrancy and mendicity in the City of Dublin*, p. 41a*; *Dublin Evening Mail*, 27 Aug. 1824.
2 *PI, Appendix C, Part II, Report upon vagrancy and mendicity in the City of Dublin*, p. 41a*.
3 Ibid.

while Goodison decided to interpret the word 'beggar' in broader terms. This example illuminates an inherent challenge when discussing beggars and begging. As already discussed, definitions of what constituted begging and beggars were never precise, with outright solicitation constituting just one of the 'pauper professions' which prevailed in the 'economy of makeshifts'. The Poor Inquiry commissioners in Macroom, County Cork observed that 'It is scarcely possible to form anything like an accurate notion of the number of persons who beg. There are some who live entirely by begging, and some beg only at particular seasons'.[4] The difficulty in defining begging and beggars shaped contemporary attempts to measure the extent of the problem, a significant feature of the discourse surrounding poverty and the Poor Laws in pre-Famine Ireland.

Matthew Martin, whose 1790s investigation into beggary in London pioneered statistics-based inquiry into this field, earning him the sobriquet 'Mendicity Martin',[5] spoke of the need to ascertain the true extent of street begging, 'both in respect to the average number of London beggars, and the gross amount of the sums annually extorted from the public by their importunities'.[6] In proposing measures to curtail street begging in the city, Martin asserted his aim as being to reduce the expense to the public of managing the poor.[7] To develop this study, it is necessary to examine attempts to undertake in Ireland what Martin did in London, by exploring how contemporaries tried to establish the number of beggars (at national and local levels) and the amount of money doled out in alms to mendicants. The significance of these questions, and the heightened urgency in the 1830s to resolve them, will be set in the context of the developing Poor Law debates in Ireland and Britain in that decade, wherein the monetary cost to ratepayers of new (as in Ireland and Scotland) or reformed Poor Law systems (in the case of England and Wales) proved crucial.

Emergence of Statistical Inquiry

The first half of the nineteenth century witnessed the emergence of statistics as a scientific discipline. The popularity of the 'statistical revolution' was

4 *PI, Appendix A*, p. 660.
5 Francis Place's account of the 1815–16 Mendicity Committee, 1825 (BL, Place papers, Add. MS 35145, ff. 70–78); Anon. (rev. Anita McConnell), 'Martin, Matthew' in *ODNB*, xxxvi, pp. 966–7.
6 Matthew Martin, *Substance of a letter, dated Poet's Corner, Westminster, 3d March, 1803, to the Right Hon. Lord Pelham, on the state of mendicity in the Metropolis* (London, 1811), p. 12.
7 Ibid., pp. 14, 21.

closely linked to prevailing concerns in educated, elite circles for the moral and spiritual condition of the population at large, but particularly the lower classes. The compilation of vast quantities of figures, which were collected in a scientific manner, allowed researchers and social campaigners to argue from a higher moral platform than would otherwise be the case. Statistics allowed for the testing of subjective theories and opinions through the use of cold, objective facts. The pioneers in statistical inquiry saw their endeavours as being part of a wider movement that was abounding in excitement, intellectual stimulation and promise, which could be achieved through the development and refinement of new methodologies.[8] These individuals sought to affect great change throughout society, with the ultimate goal of 'improvement', which was 'one of the guiding ideas of social thinkers in this period'.[9]

In a paper to the Dublin Statistical Society in the late 1840s, founding member James Anthony Lawson reflected on, first, his contemporaries' attempts to define the new discipline of statistics and, secondly, the objectives of the society. Lawson stated: 'Upon the best consideration I can give it, I think Statistics may be defined as "the collecting of facts which relate to man's social conditions"'.[10] The Statistical Society of London defined statistics in its maiden publication as the collection of 'facts which are calculated to illustrate the condition and prospects of society' and the purpose of statistical science was 'to consider the results which they produce, with the view to determine those principles upon which the well-being of society depends'.[11]

Early statistical inquiries focused on what Scottish essayist Thomas Carlyle termed 'the Condition-of-England question'[12] – namely, the state of the working and domestic lives of the labouring classes. The founding members of the statistical society in Manchester, a city whose economic and demographic expansion in the opening decades of the century epitomised the modern city,[13] defined their aim as being 'to assist in promoting the progress of social improvement in the manufacturing population by which

  8 Prunty, *Dublin slums*, p. 5; M.J. Cullen, *The statistical movement in early Victorian Britain: the foundations of empirical social research* (Hassocks and New York, 1975).
  9 Ó Ciosáin, *Ireland in official print culture*, p. 44. For the use of social statistics in 1840s France, see Joan Wallach Scott, 'A statistical representation of work: *La statistique de l'industrie à Paris, 1847–1848*' in Joan Wallach Scott, *Gender and the politics of history* (New York, 1988), pp. 113–38.
  10 James A. Lawson, 'On the connexion between statistics and political economy' in *Transactions of the Dublin Statistical Society*, i, session 1 (1847–8), p. 3.
  11 'Introduction' in *Journal of the Statistical Society of London*, i, no. 1 (May 1838), p. 1.
  12 Thomas Carlyle, *Chartism* (London, 1840), p. 1.
  13 Tristram Hunt, *Building Jerusalem: the rise and fall of the Victorian city* (London, 2005), *passim*.

they are surrounded'.[14] At a time of increasing industrialisation and urbanisation, the condition of the urban labouring classes and the slums in which
they resided not only worried but threatened the middle and upper classes, in
both Ireland and Britain. In a century that was ravaged by numerous disease
epidemics, comprehensive statistics on mortality rates and their connection
to housing and sanitary conditions was considered of utmost importance to
the common good. Jacinta Prunty has observed that:

> On investigation all aspects of poverty were found to be inter-connected:
> high mortality, poor sanitary provision, overcrowded and substandard
> housing, 'immorality', vagrancy and casual work, drunkenness and
> the dispiritedness due to unemployment, criminality and the mixing
> of all sorts in the 'rookeries' of the back streets; illiteracy, prosti-
> tution, irreligion, the disintegration of the family unit, and indeed
> the degeneration of the 'urban' race. The spiralling nature of poverty,
> where children born into such circumstances were unable to escape,
> was especially worrying.[15]

As Bulmer *et al.* have noted, these early statisticians were 'working in a time
receptive to the statistical approach', while the spirit of the age has also been
captured by G.M. Young, who observed that 'it was the business of the
[1830s] to transfer the treatment of affairs from a polemical to a statistical
basis, from Humbug to Humdrum … Statistical inquiry … was a passion
of the times'.[16]

Statisticians' Interest in the Problem of Mendicancy

From the earliest days of the statistical movement the issues of poverty and
mendicancy attracted the interest of the pioneers of this new discipline.
Many of the founding members of the Dublin Statistical Society were leading
contributors to the Irish Poor Law debate. Archbishop Richard Whately
(president of the society) chaired a royal commission of inquiry into this topic,
and devoted much time and energy to the question of poverty, both in Ireland
and during his early career in England; Mountiford Longfield (vice-president)

14 T.S. Ashton, *Economic and social investigations in Manchester, 1833–1933: a centenary
    history of the Manchester Statistical Society* (1934; repr. Brighton, 1977), p. 13.
15 Prunty, *Dublin slums*, p. 1.
16 Martin Bulmer, Kevin Bales and Kathryn Kish Sklar, 'The social survey in historical
    perspective' in Martin Bulmer, Kevin Bales and Kathryn Kish Sklar (eds), *The
    social survey in historical perspective, 1880–1940* (Cambridge, 1991), p. 8; G.M. Young,
    Portrait of an age: Victorian England (annotated edn, London, 1977), pp. 48–9.

delivered a number of lectures (subsequently published) on the question of the Poor Laws; James Haughton (council member), as well as Whately, were active members of the city's mendicity association for many years.[17] Other founding members, such as Thomas Larcom, John K. Ingram and William Neilson Hancock, became leading Poor Law commentators in the post-Famine period.[18] Just months before the foundation of the Manchester Statistical Society, its main instigator, William Langton, founded a Manchester branch of the Provident Society, which had the stated objective of encouraging 'frugality and forethought, the suppression of mendicity and imposture, and the occasional relief of sickness and unavoidable misfortune amongst the poor'.[19] Founding members of the London Statistical Society also paid much attention to the Poor Law question: Thomas Spring Rice, MP chaired the 1830 parliamentary inquiry into Irish poverty,[20] historian Henry Hallam was an early member of the London Mendicity Society's board of management,[21] and an early vice-president of the statistical society was MP and Poor Law reformer William Sturges Bourne.[22]

Measuring Mendicancy

Attempts to gauge the level of mendicancy in a particular area at any one time were inherently beset with challenges. First, as reflected in the policemen's estimates at the beginning of this chapter, definitions of what constituted begging and who could be classed as beggars could be vague, and frequently varied from person to person. Secondly, the sheer extent of mendicancy in pre-Famine Ireland, in both rural and urban areas, also prevented a reliable enumeration of this body of people. Furthermore,

---

17 The best account of the Whately commission is Gray, *Making of the Irish Poor Law*, pp. 92–129. See Mountiford Longfield, *Four lectures on Poor Laws, delivered in Trinity term, 1834* (Dublin, 1834). For Haughton's involvement in the society, see *FJ*, 15 Apr. 1839; *The Advocate; or, Irish Industrial Journal*, 1 Mar. 1856. For his wider interest in poverty and poor relief, see Samuel Haughton, *Memoir of James Haughton, with extracts from his private and published letters* (Dublin, 1877), pp. 42–3; James Haughton, 'What is doing for the people in Dublin?' in *People's Journal* (London), ii (1846), pp. 232–6.
18 Peter Gray, 'Irish social thought and the relief of poverty, 1847–1880' in *Transactions of the Royal Historical Society*, xx (2010), pp. 141–56.
19 Ashton, *Economic and social investigations in Manchester*, p. 4.
20 *Gentleman's Magazine*, i (Apr. 1834), p. 422.
21 Ibid.; *The first report of the society established in London for the suppression of mendicity* (London, 1819), p. 6.
22 'Proceedings of statistical societies' in *Journal of the Statistical Society of London*, i, no. 1 (May 1838), p. 51; David Eastwood, 'Bourne, William Sturges' in *ODNB*, vi, pp. 863–4.

transience was a regular part of life for such individuals, with seasonality shaping the cultures of mendicancy, especially among the rural poor. The blurred line between work and beggary is reflected in a police report of June 1817, which described a group of 'sixteen men, apparently country men' who arrived in Dublin city seeking employment or alms. 'There are groups only of a Monday, in consequence of going to Dunleary expecting to commence a week's work, and not being able to procure it, they beg their way back to their respective parishes', the report stated.[23] While this sole report contained a specific estimate of the number of people identified, this was not possible in most cases. The transiency of large portions of the population was captured in one Limerick gentleman's striking, yet exaggerated, assertion that 'the whole country appeared to be in motion'.[24] The above factors – difficulties in negotiating vague definitions, large amounts of people and a transient population – are encapsulated in the account of the Poor Inquiry testimony of Rev. Vaughan, a Catholic priest in Killaloe:

Inquiries were first made as to the number of paupers subsisting on charity in the town of Killaloe, and it was estimated that they amounted to about 16. 'But,' says the Rev. Mr. Vaughan, 'the beggars are for the most part strangers; but it is my opinion that there are in the whole parish about 100 families, or about 1,000 persons who are occasionally obliged to beg; and I do not think I know the face of more than one in twenty that I see in the streets.'[25]

In large urban areas, most notably in Dublin, indigenous and 'strange' poor people increasingly 'swarmed' into the teeming tenements and slums, subsisting out of sight in city back streets which were perceived and spoken of by elites as unchartered territories. Social surveys of this period reflected the otherworldliness of these hidden parts of the city where, as Prunty has observed, 'the "natives" were depicted as "denizens" and "poor creatures", despite the proximity of the slums to the wealthy districts'.[26] When combined, the above factors explain the difficulties in enumerating the extent of an inherently marginalised and mobile part of the population at a time when modern state-driven census-taking was in its infancy. The difficulties in

23 Police report on country beggars in Dublin, 17 June 1817 (NAI, State of the Country papers, SOC 1825/6).
24 F[rancis]. Barker and J[ohn]. Cheyne, *An account of the rise, progress, and decline of the fever lately epidemic in Ireland, together with communications from physicians in the provinces, and various official documents* (2 vols, Dublin, 1821), i, p. 40.
25 *PI, Appendix A*, p. 629.
26 Prunty, *Dublin slums*, p. 18. For the international context, see Fuchs, *Gender and poverty in nineteenth-century Europe*, pp. 114–15.

quantifying beggars were known to contemporary commentators and were
described by antiquary John Peter Boileau, in a paper to the Statistical
Section of the British Association in Swansea in August 1848. Boileau, who
was among the vice-presidents of the London Mendicity Society,[27] stated:

> The statistics of mendicancy in the united empire, if they could
> be correctly collected and compiled, would be a valuable addition
> to our knowledge, and lead to many important conclusions for the
> management and employment of our poor, enabling us more correctly
> to appreciate the large funds devoted to these purposes. I fear, however,
> that no means at present exist for this general object.[28]

One anonymous writer, seemingly associated with Dublin's House of
Industry, commented that 'accuracy in the first attempt [at measuring
indigence in the city] ought not to be expected',[29] while the problem of
quantifying the number of those reduced to utter destitution persisted into
the late nineteenth century, when Charles Booth, in his famous survey of the
labouring classes in London, commented that 'the lowest class of occasional
labourers, loafers and semi-criminals ... are beyond enumeration'.[30]
Anna Maria Hall, whilst eager to describe the habits of some beggars she
encountered upon entering Wexford town, experienced similar difficulties in
gauging the number of mendicants, given their sheer ubiquity: 'You cannot
walk out in a country town without meeting at every turn a population of
poverty. I have attempted to count the beggars – I found it impossible; the
barefooted creatures were beyond number'.[31] Hall's remarks are revealing
in highlighting the sheer extent of beggary as well as many contemporaries'
attempts – rudimentary or otherwise – to gauge the level of poverty and
mendicancy. For many, including Mrs Hall, the problem of beggary was
simply beyond quantification.

27 *The thirty-second report of the Society for Suppression of Mendicity, established in
    London, 1818* (London, 1850), p. v.
28 John P. Boileau, 'Statistics of mendicancy' in *Journal of the Statistical Society of
    London*, xii, no. 1 (Feb. 1849), p. 43.
29 *Observations on the House of Industry, Dublin; and on the plans of the association for
    suppressing mendicity in that city* (Dublin, 1818), p. 23.
30 Charles Booth, *Life and labour of the people in London* (12 vols, London, 1892), i, cited
    in Eric J. Evans (ed.), *Social policy, 1830–1914: individualism, collectivism and the
    origins of the Welfare State* (London and Boston, 1978), p. 158.
31 Hall, *Tales of Irish life and character*, p. 95.

Why Count Beggars?

The desire to quantify beggary on both a local and a national scale was grounded in the urge to understand Ireland's seemingly singular extent of poverty and misery. Travellers to Ireland invariably commented on the prevalence of impoverishment and misery, and beggars and beggary were arguably the most visible manifestation of the country's endemic poverty. The French traveller Gustave de Beaumount's oft-quoted assertion, following his visit to the country in 1835, reflects this sense of Ireland's omnipresent, overwhelming poverty:

> Misery, naked and famishing, that misery which is vagrant, idle, and mendicant, covers the entire country; it shows itself everywhere, and at every hour of the day; it is the first thing you see when you land on the Irish coast, and from that moment it ceases not to be present to your view; sometimes under the aspect of the diseases displaying his sores, sometimes under the form of the pauper scarcely covered by his rags; it follows you everywhere, and besieges you incessantly; you hear its groans and cries in the distance; and if the voice does not excite profound pity, it importunes and terrifies you.[32]

To outsiders, among the distinguishing features of Irish society, in contrast to neighbouring countries, was the extent of beggary.[33] Poor people were (and are) to be found in every society but the sheer numbers in Ireland who were engaged in mendicancy, a practice worthy of curiosity, observation and comment by reason of its persistent visibility, ensured that Ireland's unique experience and culture of mendicancy was prominent in any public discourse (involving politicians, clergymen, social commentators and other members of the elite) on the question of poverty.

The need to count Ireland's beggars also arose from the wealthier classes' concern for the monetary cost of poor relief and alms-giving; people wished to know how much money beggary was collectively costing them. In a period when the suitability of a statutory rate-based Poor Law for Ireland was being vehemently debated, the cost of such a scheme required contrast with the prevailing situation of voluntary assistance, either private or organisational. Calculations of the level of mendicancy were frequently accompanied by estimated costs of alms-giving and commentators invariably concluded that the prevailing system of casual alms-giving was more expensive than any rate-based relief system. To George Nicholls,

---

32 Quoted in Gray, *Making of the Irish Poor Law*, p. 1.
33 Ó Ciosáin, *Ireland in official print culture*, pp. 122, 168–9.

the designer of the New Poor Law, begging was 'the most expensive and the most demoralising' 'mode of relief'.[34] The cost of poor relief was a significant part of the prolonged Poor Law discourse in Ireland, which was closely linked to parallel debates in Britain and from the 1790s the rising costs of relief took centre stage in the Poor Law debate in England and Wales, arising from the Speenhamland system of allowances for the able-bodied poor (from 1795) and societal awareness of the rising population, whose growth was concentrated along the bottom rungs of the social ladder. Ratepayers were aggrieved that more money was being spent to relieve the distressed through the Poor Law system, yet the number of paupers was rising significantly.

But, in Ireland, the Poor Inquiry evidence reveals a level of hesitancy among the poorer classes to quantify the number of mendicants and the alms given to such individuals.[35] For numerous witnesses from humble social backgrounds, any such attempt would result in a measurement in tangible terms of their charity, an endeavour they found to be inappropriate and unnatural. In County Clare, it was observed: 'There appeared to be much reluctance on the part of all the witnesses present to compute how much they were in the habit of giving away in alms; they did not wish to measure what they bestowed for the honour of God; and it was mentioned that it was a common saying, "that what was given away in charity never diminished a man's substance, and that his crops were often increased by it"'.[36] Another explanation would be that some people perhaps felt uncomfortable discussing in public, in full view of their neighbours and local community, the amount of alms (if any) they doled out to mendicants.

Counting Ireland's Beggars: National Estimates
Estimates of the extent of mendicancy throughout Ireland are available from as early as the first half of the eighteenth century. In 1731, Arthur Dobbs provided the strikingly particular estimate of 34,425 'stroling Beggars' in the country, 'of which there are not 1 in 10 real Objects', a calculation arrived at by estimating the presence of 15 beggars (a figure warranting suspicion) in each of the kingdom's 2,295 parishes; ten years later, Philip Skelton recorded contemporary estimates of up to 50,000 'strolling beggars ... rambling from place to place'.[37] Three decades later, Richard Woodward's influential scheme for a national provision focused on 'deserving' persons 'who occasionally may

---

34 *Second report of Geo. Nicholls, Poor Laws, Ireland*, p. 18.
35 This is discussed in Ó Ciosáin, *Ireland in official print culture*, pp. 79–84.
36 *PI, Appendix A*, p. 610.
37 Dobbs, *Essay on the trade and improvement*, ii, p. 46; Philip Skelton, *The necessity of tillage and granaries. In a letter to a member of parliament living in the county of ____* (Dublin, 1741), pp. 43–4.

want Assistance'. Woodward estimated this class to comprise 3 per cent of the population, certainly a significant underestimate, although he added that another 63 per cent subsisted on 'only absolute Necessaries'. Habitual beggars and vagrants were omitted from his figures.[38]

The utilisation of statistical data in calculating the extent of beggary nationwide appears not to have been adopted by Mallow banker and former high sheriff Robert de la Cour in his testimony to the 1825 select committee on the state of the country, when he asserted that of the approximately 7 million people then living in Ireland, 'I think I under-rate the number of those who procure the means of their subsistence by beggary and plunder at 1,000,000 including men, women and children; I think that is as low an estimate as can be taken'.[39] De la Cour offered no indication as to how he arrived at this calculation, yet echoed other commentators in claiming that a national system of poor relief would be considerably less expensive than the current system of casual and indiscriminate alms-giving, a question that is considered later in this chapter.

Societal understanding of Irish poverty, and the extent of beggary and beggars, was put on a new footing in the 1830s with the investigations and subsequent publications of the Poor Inquiry. In one of the most extensive analyses into the condition of the poor anywhere in nineteenth-century Europe, Whately's commission drew upon three years of investigations, numerous public sittings (at many of which members of all social classes, from landlords to beggars, gave testimony) and thousands of completed and returned questionnaires from parishes throughout the country, to produce reports totalling more than 5,000 pages, which provide unparalleled information on social and economic conditions in pre-Famine Ireland. In their final report, the Poor Inquiry commissioners concluded that of the approximately 8 million people living in Ireland, 585,000 were 'out of work and in distress during thirty weeks of the year'; taken together with their 1.8 million dependants, these 2,385,000 people constituted 30 per cent of the population, a proportion which by its very scale proved, in the commissioners' view, the futility of a rates-funded workhouse-based Poor Law.[40] In this light, as Peter Gray has observed, 'This statement of numbers was crucial'.[41] The inquiry's secretary John Revans, however, dissented from this estimate and in a pamphlet criticising the final recommendations, suggested

38 Woodward, *Argument in support of the poor*, p. 53.
39 *Minutes of evidence taken before the select committee of the House of Lords, appointed to inquire into the state of Ireland, more particularly with reference to the circumstances which may have led to the disturbances in that part of the United Kingdom. 24 March–22 June, 1825*, p. 558, H.C. 1825 (521), ix, 558.
40 *PI, third report*, p. 5.
41 Gray, *Making of the Irish Poor Law*, p. 118.

that the number of persons who would be likely to avail themselves of a Poor Law was considerably less.[42]

Among the most illuminating elements of the commission's vast inquiry was a template questionnaire (Supplement to Appendix A) that was distributed to local elites, mainly clergymen and landowners. The completed forms (3,100 of the 7,600 circulated sets were returned from a total of 1,100 parishes) covered parishes throughout the country and 1,636 were included in the published supplement, across more than 400 pages. The nine questions on the form focus on gauging the extent of various social phenomena, such as the number of 'bastard' children, the number of widows and children and the number of infirm elderly people. Included among these questions were enquiries into the extent of mendicancy in the respondents' locality: 'What number of persons in your parish subsist by begging? and are alms usually given in money or provisions? What number of householders are in the habit of letting lodgings for strolling beggars, and what is the price usually paid for a night's lodging?'[43] The questions sought to identify definite and measurable quantities, yet the responses were largely subjective and impressionistic, displaying great variety and a lack of consensus on many matters.[44] An interesting feature of the responses to these questions is the stark difference between respondents' perceptions of begging and beggars in their locality. Almost invariably, rural respondents gave some indication of the extent of beggary in their parish and drew distinctions between local, 'native' paupers and 'strange' mendicants from other counties: in Modreeny, County Tipperary, Rev. William Homan's assertion that 'There are very few paupers of the parish begging, but immense numbers come from the surrounding parishes, and particularly at the period that the Irish go to England to labour' is representative of the wider trend.[45] In large urban centres on the other hand, respondents were almost universal in leaving these questions unanswered and the appropriate column blank; this was the case in the cities of Dublin, Kilkenny, Waterford, Cork and Limerick, as well as in Belfast, Drogheda, Athlone and Tralee. It suggests that for inhabitants of larger urban centres, the task of enumerating the number of mendicants was beyond their ability, due to the sheer scale of beggary and the associated difficulty in distinguishing between local and non-local mendicants.

In 1837, Poor Law Commissioner George Nicholls, who had been appointed the previous year to draw up a report on the suitability of the new

---

42   John Revans, *Evils of the state of Ireland; their causes and their remedy – a Poor Law* (London, [*c*.1836]), p. 95.
43   *PI, Supplement to Appendix A*, p. 2.
44   Ó Ciosáin, *Ireland in official print culture*, pp. 30–50.
45   *PI, Supplement to Appendix A*, p. 259.

English Poor Law system to Ireland, following the government's rejection of the Poor Inquiry's recommendations, presented a picture of unrestrained and uncontrollable beggary throughout the Irish countryside. For Nicholls, this 'almost universal prevalence of mendicancy' was such that 'mendicancy and wretchedness have become too common to be disgraceful'. For the readers of his report the impression of Ireland was of a beggar-ridden country: 'A mass of filth, nakedness, and misery, is constantly moving about, entering every house, addressing itself to every eye, and soliciting from every hand'.[46] The number of beggars was 'very great' and indeed so great that 'they are therefore of some importance as a class'.[47] Nicholls did not view the problem of mendicancy as a mere nuisance and inconvenience; instead, he insisted that legislative measures aimed at suppressing mendicancy ought to be an indispensable part of his proposed Poor Law scheme. The passing of vagrancy laws was required 'in unison with the Poor Law, for without such a harmony of action, both laws would be in a great measure ineffective'.[48] The extent, as Nicholls saw it, of Ireland's mendicancy problem and the unquestionable need for anti-mendicancy legislation required his readers, particularly members of Russell's Whig government, to appreciate the seriousness of the problem and it is in this light that his assertions are to be read and understood.

Aside from these generalised comments on the prevalence of misery and mendicancy in Ireland, Nicholls provided specific estimates as to the precise extent of destitution and these warrant some discussion. In designing his workhouse system for Ireland, Nicholls estimated that (indoor) workhouse accommodation for the relief of the destitute poor ought to be provided for 1 per cent of the population of circa 8 million – that is, 80,000 persons. In arriving at this figure of 1 per cent, Nicholls drew upon recent precedents from four 'highly pauperised' English counties, where approximately 1 per cent of the population was catered for in workhouses.[49] Strikingly, the source of these figures, a report of the English Poor Law Commissioners, reveals that the number of recipients of outdoor relief (a welfare provision excluded from Nicholls's scheme for Ireland) totalled in some areas ten times the number of indoor recipients.[50] When this omitted category is included and these revised figures are applied to the returns for the aforementioned four 'highly pauperised' counties, the proportion of paupers to the total population rises from 1 per cent to approximately 7.7 per cent. If Nicholls had applied

46 *Report of Geo. Nicholls, Esq., to His Majesty's Principal Secretary of State for the Home Department, on Poor Laws, Ireland*, p. 5, H.C. 1837 [C 69], li, 207.
47 *Report of Geo. Nicholls, Poor Laws, Ireland*, p. 27.
48 *Second report of Geo. Nicholls, Poor Laws, Ireland*, p. 29.
49 *Report of Geo. Nicholls, Poor Laws, Ireland*, p. 37.
50 *Second annual report of the Poor Law Commissioners for England and Wales; together with appendices A. B. C. D.*, p. 32, H.C. 1836 (595), xxix, 32.

this figure to the Irish context as crudely as with his eventual calculation, his estimated total of Irish paupers would have risen from 80,000 to around 616,000. Here, Nicholls's methodology deserves rebuke for, first, distorting the picture of Irish poverty and, secondly, for crudely assuming similar cultures of welfare in Ireland, and England and Wales.[51] Despite widespread scepticism of Nicholls's figures upon the publication of his report, his calculations were supported by the findings of Dublin statistician William Stanley, who estimated the destitute of Ireland to be 82,806 (1.1 per cent), defining the term 'destitute' to mean 'only those persons who, without the aid of local charities, and the resource of mendicancy, must necessarily starve, if they obey the law against theft'.[52] Stanley echoed Nicholls's attack on the Whately inquiry for allegedly exaggerating the extent of Irish destitution; however, the crudeness of Stanley's methodology left most critics unconvinced.[53]

Area-Specific Estimates of Mendicancy

The prevalence of poverty and beggary in Ireland was subject to national, and indeed international, factors, yet localised patterns of mendicancy were shaped by area-specific influences. The rise in the number of beggars in Belfast in 1809–10 was due to the closure of a number of factories in the town and 300 'beggars [engaged] in the daily practice of seeking alms' were said to stalk the streets of Belfast. However, the anonymous author who provided this figure excluded these beggars' families, as well as an estimated 200 'poor room-keepers', presumably too respectable to resort to street begging.[54] The significant rise in mendicancy in Wexford in the early 1830s, where the number of 'vagrants' in the town of approximately 10,000 inhabitants was said to total 600, tripling in the previous quarter of a century, was attributed to a mixture of national and local factors – namely, 'the operation of the [1826] Subletting Act [which facilitated increased evictions], and the total failure of the oyster fishery'.[55] In the mid-1830s the Poor Inquiry commissioners estimated that of 87,000 people living in Cork city, 22,000 could be considered as living in 'distressed' conditions – that is, being 'only able to obtain about half employment, [and] who are living, therefore, from hand to mouth'. Of these 22,000 people, approximately 6,000 were estimated as being 'destitute, their chief support being from begging: they live in crowded hovels, sleeping on straw with merely their day rags for covering'.[56] However, this figure of

---

51 For Nicholls's defence of his figures, see *Second report of Geo. Nicholls, Poor Laws, Ireland*, p. 24.
52 Ibid., pp. 50–1.
53 Gray, *Making of the Irish Poor Law*, p. 194.
54 Dubourdieu, *Statistical survey, county Antrim*, pp. 410–11; *BNL*, 1 June 1810.
55 *PI, Appendix A*, p. 597.
56 *PI, Appendix C, Part I*, p. 44.

6,000 habitual mendicants ought to be considered an overestimate, as there is no evidence, nor is it likely, that there were 6,000 mendicants soliciting alms on the streets of Cork at any one time.

As the capital city of Ireland, the largest urban centre on the island and a port town, Dublin always attracted countless scores of non-local vagrant poor; furthermore, there were numerous and frequent attempts (however rudimentary) to measure the extent of mendicancy and destitution in the city, far more than for other areas throughout Ireland. The most famous demographic survey of this period was that undertaken in Dublin city in the summer of 1798 by Rev. James Whitelaw, whose report is significant for its description of the hovels which constituted the homes of so many of the city's poorer classes, who formed 'the great mass of the population of this city'.[57] His was the first Irish study into the interlinked problems of overcrowding, poor sanitary conditions and epidemic disease that characterised nineteenth-century slums. Yet, the social backgrounds of the city's population were crudely categorised by Whitelaw as 'Upper and middle class', 'Servants of ditto' and 'Lower class', whose breakdown among the population was calculated as 37,305 (21.8 per cent), 18,315 (10.7 per cent) and 115,174 (67.4 per cent) respectively.[58] Whitelaw's report regrettably did not offer an estimate of the begging poor in the metropolis, an element of the population who would have been included within Whitelaw's category of 'Lower class'. According to Rev. Thomas R. Shore, curate in the Church of Ireland parish of St Michan's,[59] out of an estimated population of 212,000 living in the city in the mid-1830s, there were '40,000 or 50,000 so destitute in Dublin who know not in the morning how they will obtain support in the day'.[60] This represented approximately 21 per cent of the capital's population. However, a divisional president for the Sick and Indigent Roomkeepers' Society, Charles Sharpe, gave a significantly lower total of between 12,000 and 15,000 'persons now in Dublin who do not know where they will get a breakfast to-morrow'. In addition to this figure, Sharpe estimated that in the city there were 'about 70,000 or 80,000 [persons] who would take alms, and would seek them if they thought they could get them, and have the means of supporting themselves'.[61]

---

57 Whitelaw, *Essay on the population of Dublin*, p. 4.

58 Ibid., fold-out table facing p. 14. These figures do not include the north-eastern suburb of Spring Garden or a number of institutions (such as army barracks and prisons).

59 For the identification of Rev. Shore as being based in St Michan's, see St Michan's parish, Dublin, vestry minute book, 23 Dec. 1828 (RCBL, St Michan's parish, Dublin, vestry minute books, P 276.05.5); ibid., 27 Mar. 1837; Dublin Mendicity Society minute book, 4 May 1830 (NLI, DMSP, MS 32,599/4).

60 *PI, Appendix C, Part II, Report upon vagrancy and mendicity in the City of Dublin*, p. 32a*.

61 Ibid., p. 4.

While the scale of the latter estimate is impossible to prove or disprove, it does reflect the common perception that large portions of the poorer classes were so immoral and work-shy as to consider seeking alms while being able-bodied.

Mobility was a regular feature of life among the poor of Dublin, both for those migrating into the city from rural areas and among those already resident there. Mobility fluctuated in line with wider social and economic conditions, invariably increasing to alarming levels at times of recession, epidemic and crop failure. Estimates as to the extent of mendicancy, therefore, ought to be considered in the context of the constant flow of (poor) people into and out of the city. William Stanley's figures for Dublin city, wherein he estimated that 5,646 of the city's 284,000 population (2 per cent) were destitute, claimed a higher prevalence of poverty than the rest of the country, a finding he explained by reference to the great numbers of rural poor who descended on the capital for work or relief. Of these 5,646 destitute poor, 960 were designated by Stanley as 'street mendicants' who were distinct from those individuals receiving relief in institutions such as the House of Industry and the Mendicity Society.[62] Stanley was, therefore, estimating that in Dublin city there were almost 1,000 habitual beggars who, for unknown reasons, were not 'on the books' of the two main institutions with responsibilities for dealing with mendicants. This corresponds with the assertion of the Mendicity Society that there was a cohort of habitual street beggars who never applied to the organisation for relief,[63] presumably preferring the freedom of a vagrant life to institutional enclosure, supervision, regulation and hard labour.

According to a pamphlet published in 1818 as part of the campaign to establish a mendicity society in Dublin, 'it may be safely stated that there are not less than 5,000 begging poor in and about this city'.[64] If this figure is to be believed and taking the city's population to be just less than 180,000 (according to the 1821 census),[65] it can be estimated that 2.8 per cent of the city's people were engaged in begging. The reader is not enlightened as to how this figure of 5,000 was arrived at, but besides this fact other considerations must be taken into account. This estimate was made during a severe typhus fever epidemic, economic downturn and food shortage throughout Ireland, and at a time when many rural poor descended on the capital seeking succour; one Dublin physician asserted that 'Mendicants in unusual number were to be seen in every quarter; and many wretched country labourers, sometimes followed by wives and children, their pallid and emaciated countenance testifying

---

62 *Second report of Geo. Nicholls, Poor Laws, Ireland*, pp. 50–1.
63 *Second report, Dublin Mendicity Society, 1819*, p. 21.
64 Anon., *Arguments in proof of the necessity of suppressing street begging*, p. 7.
65 W.E. Vaughan and A.J. Fitzpatrick (eds), *Irish historical statistics: population, 1821–1971* (Dublin, 1978), p. 5.

the reality of their wants, resorted to the streets of the city in expectation of obtaining employment and escaping from the horrors of want'.[66] Regardless of whether or not the estimate of 5,000 mendicants was accurate, we can be sure that the number of 'begging poor in and about' the city was at that time beyond all 'normal' levels; as such, any estimate must be interpreted as being unrepresentative. Furthermore, the fact that this estimate originated from a campaign aimed explicitly at gaining public support for the suppression of mendicancy raises further questions about the reliability of this claim; the social reformers who recorded this figure had an interest in embellishing the extent of mendicancy, so as to maximise public support for their campaign. The challenges inherent in negotiating estimates of beggary are illustrated in three authorities' disparate opinions on the mendicity campaign's calculation of 5,000 street beggars: Warburton *et al.*, in their contemporaneous history of Dublin city, accepted the figure as being accurate; an anonymous writer, seemingly associated with Dublin's House of Industry, which experienced tense relations with the mendicity society campaign, rejected the estimate of 5,000 beggars, lowering the figure significantly to 2,000; while the Poor Inquiry *Report on vagrancy and mendicity in the city of Dublin* concluded that '5,000 is very considerably below the real number'.[67]

Private citizens were known to offer their own estimates as to the number of mendicants in their localities. Pastry-cook and confectioner W. Mitchell of No. 10 Grafton Street in Dublin, one of a number of traders who employed a street inspector to ward off beggars outside their premises, estimated that there were no fewer than 15,000 beggars in the city, of whom 'not less than 40 or 50 pass my door every day'.[68] Two of the street inspectors employed by traders and property owners – namely, Edward Ost and William Flinn – each claimed to encounter between 40 and 50 beggars on their respective 'beats' every day but they did not speculate as to the extent of mendicancy throughout the city.[69] Disparities arose in Clifden, County Galway as to

66 F[rancis]. Barker, *Medical report of the house of recovery and fever-hospital, in Cork-street, Dublin* (Dublin, 1818), p. 7.

67 J. Warburton, J. Whitelaw and Robert Walsh, *History of the city of Dublin, from the earliest accounts to the present time* ... (2 vols, London, 1818), ii, p. 1346; *Observations on the House of Industry, Dublin*, p. 25; *PI, Appendix C, Part II, Report on vagrancy and mendicity in the City of Dublin*, p. 22a*.

68 *PI, Appendix C, Part II, Report upon vagrancy and mendicity in the City of Dublin*, p. 44a*.

69 Edward Ost was 'appointed and paid by the inhabitants of the five houses in Dawson-street nearest to Nassau-street' and his duty was to 'walk backwards and forwards, opposite to those houses, for the purpose of keeping beggars from importuning persons who frequent the street', while William Flinn was employed by a 'few of the inhabitants of Grafton Street' to do the same: *PI, Appendix C, Part II, Report upon vagrancy and mendicity in the City of Dublin*, p. 42a*.

the extent of mendicancy in the locality. The town's founder and landlord
John D'Arcy expressed his belief to a public sitting of the Poor Inquiry that
not more than three or four people in the town lived exclusively through
begging, while a Catholic priest put this number at 'fifteen and upwards'.
Most interestingly, a group of five men, comprising a builder, two masons,
a weaver and a freeholder, contradicted the local landlord and asserted:
'There are more than fifty persons, this day resident in Clifden, who are
supported entirely by begging'.[70] The men then proceeded to name each of
the approximately 50 persons included in this estimate. The question arises
whether D'Arcy, who founded Clifden in 1815 as a regional commercial
centre, publicly played down the true extent of poverty and mendicancy in
his town in the interest of presenting his relatively new development as a
hub of industry. Another possible explanation for the disparity in estimates
is that D'Arcy was opposed to a proposed compulsory poor rate, of which,
as a landlord, he would be a principal contributor. This explanation would
correspond with Niall Ó Ciosáin's assertion that it 'could be in the landlords'
interest, therefore, to play down the extent and growth of poverty'.[71] Yet, on
the other hand, manipulated figures may have been presented for unknown
reasons by the priest or the group of five men and it must be considered that
these deponents and D'Arcy, divided by social class and probably religion,
most likely possessed different interpretations of what constituted begging.
Estimates of the number of beggars in an area could be loaded assertions,
serving a particular individual or party purpose. A similar disagreement
arose in the County Longford parish of Abbeyshrule, incorporating the
town of Ballymahon. Two Anglican clergymen estimated the number of
mendicants in the town and its immediate hinterland at around 30. After
being challenged by a local merchant, who mentioned 'the names of sixty
persons who had no other mode of subsistence than begging', the clergymen
accepted the higher figure, but insisted that the local priest's estimate of up
to 250 beggars was excessive. In defending his estimate, the Catholic priest
claimed that he spoke 'not from calculation, but from actual observation, of
the numbers residing in the different parts of the parish', which can be read
as an implicit criticism of the Anglican clergymen, alleging that he possessed
a deeper understanding of social conditions in the largely Catholic locality
than the clergymen of a minority denomination.[72]

It may be suggested that such estimates as have been discussed above
reveal, first, the difficulties faced by contemporaries who attempted to describe
and categorise the multi-layered social substrata who constituted 'the poor';

70 *PI, Appendix A*, p. 485.
71 Ó Ciosáin, *Ireland in official print culture*, p. 43.
72 *PI, Appendix A*, p. 560.

secondly, the fact that begging was a common-sense and somewhat dependable survival strategy open to many people; and, thirdly, the impact that the visibility of public street beggars had on contemporaries, to the extent that the highly visible practice of public mendicancy was viewed as being considerably more prevalent than was truly the case.[73] Many mendicants were mobile, strangers in the areas where they begged and engaged in 'face to face' encounters with the public, and, as such, 'these conditions of their existence undoubtedly made them appear to be more numerous than they were'.[74] While some of the aforementioned statistics of mendicancy are questionable in their accuracy and contradictory, they can serve a use for historians. These figures make clear that there were large, albeit not determinable, numbers of mendicants in pre-Famine Ireland, a fact which influenced the prominent place that public beggary played in the prolonged discourse about Irish poverty. Historians of poverty, welfare and mendicancy in Britain and Europe have also grappled with the difficult question of how to negotiate contemporary statistics for beggars in a given jurisdiction. Stuart Woolf has demonstrated how the statistics published by the *Comité de mendicité*, which detail the numbers of poor and the extent of poor relief in early revolutionary France, are questionable owing to the manner in which the figures were recorded and collected (an oversupply of figures rounded to the nearest ten and 'suspiciously neat returns' betraying the unscientific method of data collection), local authorities' 'different interpretations of the term "beggars"' and evidence of bureaucratic altering of figures for unknown reasons.[75] In Beier's study of vagrancy in Tudor and Stuart England, he outlines the complexities inherent in 'the numbers issue', given that 'contemporaries' estimates of vagrant numbers are nearly useless'; for Beier, surviving records for criminal proceedings against alleged vagrants are limited, raising the question of how representative those sources are of wider national patterns.[76] While the impossibility for historians satisfactorily to enumerate beggars in the past must be acknowledged, contemporary exercises in information-gathering can serve as a means to reach broader understandings of the nature of poverty and mendicancy. For instance, Tim Hitchcock utilises Matthew Martin's information regarding beggars in late 1790s London and concentrates his focus not on the number of people begging on the metropolis's streets but, rather, on the fact that these figures suggest that 'many people,

---

73 For a case-study discussion of the interplay between the visibility and scale of begging in England, see Richard Dyson and Steven King, '"The streets are paved with idle beggars": experiences and perceptions of beggars in nineteenth-century Oxford' in Beate Altahammer (ed.), *Bettler in der europäischen Stadt der Moderne: Zwischen Barmherzigkeit, Repression und Sozialreform* (Frankfurt am Main, 2007), pp. 59–89.

74 Beier, *Masterless men*, p. 15.

75 Woolf, *The poor in western Europe*, pp. 118–27.

76 Beier, *Masterless men*, pp. 14–15. See also Slack, 'Vagrants and vagrancy in England'.

particularly women, could preserve a begging life without being significantly troubled by constables and watchmen, and without becoming subject to the carceral ambitions of the state'.[77]

Statistics of Arrest

The most common figures utilised by historians when examining begging and beggars are the statistics of arrest and prosecution for vagrancy offences. Throughout early modern Europe the range of activities and behaviours that fell within the remit of 'vagrancy' widened considerably, such that ever-larger proportions of the poor – especially the mobile poor – could be arrested and confined as deviants. Statistics arising from these arrests are widely available to historians of poverty in Europe, given the eagerness with which local and national governments kept records pertaining to the preservation of civil peace. However, these records are notoriously problematic: they only tell us what was recorded, reflecting the wider problems inherent in the relationship between recorded crime and actual crime. Fluctuations in arrests for begging and related vagrancy offences did not necessarily reflect ebbs and flows in the levels of beggary but, rather, frequently represented changes in law-enforcement agencies' fervour in enforcing the laws pertaining to these social problems. Increases in vagrancy arrests could also reflect seasonal movements of people (agricultural labourers migrating in the summer), a post-conflict demobilisation of soldiers and a movement of persons owing to temporary unemployment or a poor harvest.[78]

A consultation of statistics for the arrest, prosecution and confinement of individuals under Irish vagrancy laws reveals that such sources are utterly inadequate as a means to gauge the extent of mendicancy. Between 1805 and 1810, the increase in the number of offenders committed to Irish gaols awaiting trial for alleged vagrancy offences rose from ten to 77, a significant rise proportionally but still remaining a relatively miniscule number among the total population;[79] this small number of cases pertained to more serious offences under the vagrancy statutes, carrying high tariffs such as transportation, while most instances of criminal beggary were likely to have been discharged at the petty sessions.[80]

Figures for convictions for vagrancy reveal a relatively low rate of prosecution and the utter unsuitability of statistics of vagrancy convictions as

---

77 Hitchcock, 'Begging on the streets of eighteenth-century London', p. 481.
78 Jütte, *Poverty and deviance*, pp. 148–9; Sharpe, *Crime in early modern England*, pp. 1–20, 99–103.
79 *A statement of the number of offenders committed to the several gaols in Ireland, for trial at the different assizes, commissions, and quarter sessions, in the years 1805, 1806, 1807, 1808, 1809 & 1810 ...* p. 2, H.C. 1812 (246), v, 1006.
80 Garnham, 'The criminal law', p. 222.

Table 2.1   Numbers convicted of vagrancy in Ireland, 1805–31[1]

Date	Numbers convicted of vagrancy
1805	6
1806	2
1807	6
1808	13
1809	6
1810	3
1811	40
1812	19
1814	12
1822	285
1823/1823[2]	73/239
1824	186
1825	134
1826	115
1827	137
1828	85
1830	57
1831	36

1 *Poor Inquiry, Appendix C, Part II, Report upon vagrancy and mendicity in the City of Dublin*, p. 30a*. See also *Prisons of Ireland. Thirteenth report of Inspectors General of Prisons, Ireland: 1835*, pp. 56–9, H.C. 1835 (114), xxxvi, 436–9.
2 It appears that the discrepancy for the year 1823 is owing to the fact that the first figure (73) was compiled from the returns of clerks of assizes and the second figure (239) arose from returns submitted by the Inspector-General of Prisons.

a means of measuring beggary in Ireland is demonstrated in Table 2.1, which records the numbers convicted for vagrancy in select years between 1805 and 1831. Of these 1,454 convictions, 257 (17.7 per cent) resulted in transportation for seven years, with two cases of transportation 'for life', sentences which were not handed down for mere begging. The upsurge in vagrancy convictions between 1814 and the mid-1820s can probably be explained by the prolonged social and economic crisis of 1816–22 (encompassing poor harvests, famine conditions and disease outbreaks), coupled with the Rockite agrarian disturbances of 1821–4, both of which drove many poor persons across the countryside and heightened fears amongst the wealthier classes of the poor.

Throughout this period, criminal statistics record prosecutions of vagrancy cases but not of instances of criminal beggary, as reflected in J.M. Wilson's 1850s guide to Irish criminal statistics, which includes vagrancy within the category of low-tariff offences but makes no specific mention of beggary.[81]

How Much Was Given in Alms?

Intrinsically linked to the question of how many beggars were in the country, or in a locality, was the consideration of how much was given to beggars, in cash or in kind. Those who contributed to the discourse on poverty and mendicancy wished to put meat on the bones of their arguments through the use of statistical methods and the deployment of hard figures. Calculating how much was doled out to mendicants served to emphasise the monetary burden that beggars placed on the general public, and the calculation and utilisation of such statistics strengthened throughout the 1830s, reflecting wider developments in the Poor Law debates throughout Ireland and Britain. These efforts also sought to reflect the significance of the perceived moral danger which mendicancy and associated activities posed to the citizenry; English magistrate and police reformer Patrick Colquhoun, who was also a prominent officer in the Society for Bettering the Condition and Increasing the Comforts of the Poor, stressed that in 'contemplating the state of the indigent, there is perhaps more to be dreaded from the increasing depravity of manners than from the great expense incurred in supporting them, enormous as it certainly is'.[82]

Dublin barrister James Butler Bryan claimed in his evidence to the 1830 Select Committee on the State of the Poor that, based on rather crude calculations, approximately £1 million worth of potatoes was given by rural householders to beggars every year.[83] Addressing the same parliamentary investigation, Catholic bishop of Kildare and Leighlin, James Doyle, put this figure at £1.5 to £2 million.[84] The Whately Poor Inquiry arrived at similar conclusions, estimating that between £1m and £2m was

---

81 James Moncrieff Wilson, *Statistics of crime in Ireland, 1842 to 1856. A paper read before the section of Economic Science and Statistics of the British Association. At Dublin, on Saturday, 29th of August, 1857* (Dublin, 1857), p. 45.

82 Patrick Colquhoun, *A treatise on indigence; exhibiting a general view of the natural resources for productive labour; with propositions for ameliorating the condition of the poor ...* (London, 1806), p. 35.; M.J.D. Roberts, *Making English morals: voluntary association and moral reform in England, 1787–1886* (Cambridge, 2004), pp. 59–142.

83 *First report of evidence from the select committee on the state of the poor in Ireland. Minutes of evidence: 24 March–14 May*, p. 46, H.C. 1830 (589), vii, 218.

84 *Report (summary) of Poor Committee, 1830*, p. 33.

given annually in 'spontaneous alms', chiefly by 'the smaller farmers and cottiers'. This alms-giving was carried out 'without system, or without inquiry, to the good and the bad' and, as a result, 'the really destitute and the pretenders to destitution receive alike their maintenance out of the earnings of the industrious, to their great impoverishment, and to the great injury of the morals and good order of the kingdom'.[85] While the most prominent contributors to the mendicancy discourse focused on the national scale, others were more concerned with the level of alms-giving in their localities. According to a letter-writer to the *Belfast News-Letter*, the town's estimated 300 beggars (excluding their families) received £5,200 annually from inhabitants in private alms given on the streets,[86] while one report claimed that £100,000 was given annually to street beggars in Dublin alone.[87]

In considering how much was given to beggars in casual alms the most illuminating source is the collection of Poor Inquiry testimony from the mid-1830s. Numerous witnesses throughout the country offered estimates of the amount of alms that local farmers and shopkeepers typically gave, on a daily, weekly or annual basis, to mendicants. While most calculations were impressionistic and not grounded in scientific methodology, the range of such estimates from a wide array of witnesses throughout the country justifies the use of these figures as a means to explore the level of alms-giving, although the following exercise holds out no pretention as to comprehensiveness. As with many aspects of the mendicant problem, a rural/urban distinction must be made. In rural areas, nearly all alms-giving was carried out by farmers and labourers (and their families), and mostly in the form of potatoes. Solicitations at the cabin door resulted in the provision of a handful of potatoes, varying according to the number of beggars and the perceived worthiness of the case – a woman with children received the largest amount. In villages, towns and cities, however, cash played a greater part in the giver/receiver exchange, and sums of money were typically doled out to mendicants. In many towns, alms were provided to mendicants on specific days of the week: in the Donegal towns of Lifford and Letterkenny,

85 *Poor Inquiry (Ireland), Appendix (H) – Part I. containing reasons for recommending voluntary associations for the relief of the poor; and reasons for dissenting from the principle of raising funds for the relief of the poor by the voluntary system, as recommended in the report. Also, Tables No. I, II, II, referred to in Third Report*, p. 3, H.C. 1836 [41], xxxiv, 645.

86 *BNL*, 1 June 1810.

87 Anon., *Arguments in proof of the necessity of suppressing street begging, Dublin*, p. 8. This figure of £100,000 appears to have been accepted by other commentators on social conditions in Dublin: Whitley Stokes, *Observations on contagion* (2nd edn, Dublin, 1818), p. 55.

this occurred on Monday and Saturday respectively; in Stranorlar and Ballybofey, the 'helping-days' were Wednesday and Friday respectively, the shopkeepers giving 'money, food, bits of soap and bits of tobacco'; in Kilbrogan, County Cork, beggars calling on Fridays received ½d. each.[88] Bucking this trend, no weekly allowances were provided in Ennistymon, 'for every day is helping day', the Poor Inquiry commissioners were told.[89] Beggars in Cork city were said to receive between 3s. and 5s. each week in casual alms, namely 'fragments and halfpence'.[90]

Forty-seven instances have been identified in the Poor Inquiry report where specific estimates were provided as to how much money the average local shopkeeper doled out to mendicants, either daily, weekly or annually, and these are represented in Table 2.2. The average sums provided were greater in large towns and cities than in smaller locations, presumably owing to greater levels of disposable income among larger shopkeepers in bigger towns, as well as the greater number of mendicants in receipt of alms. In the towns of Gorey and Wexford, as well as in Cork city, the average sums totalled between 3s. and 4s. per week; between 2s. and 3s. was given weekly in other large urban centres, such as Carlow, Naas, Granard, Longford, Kinsale, Derry, Coleraine and Carrickfergus. Smaller average sums were given in smaller villages in Counties Antrim and Donegal. In Tuam, the Church of Ireland archbishop Power Le Poer Trench estimated that shopkeepers gave 2½d. daily to beggars, totalling £3 16s. per year, although Trench qualified his estimate by acknowledging that the amount given depended on factors such as the number of people in the mendicant family.[91] In Ballina, County Mayo, the amount given by shopkeepers was estimated at £5 per annum (3¼d. per day), while in Ballymahon, County Longford, shopkeepers were estimated to give on average 1s. each per week.[92] In Carlow town, 'malster and brewer ... a respectable shopkeeper' John Coffey (or Coffee) stated that he distributed 4s. to beggars on a weekly basis, totalling £10 8s. per annum. With his property valued at £50, the inquiry noted that Coffee 'is actually charging himself with a poor rate of 4s. in the pound', that is, 20 per cent. Smaller shopkeepers in the town were known to give 3d. or 4d. per day.[93] In the parish of Dunleekney, just north of Bagnelstown in County Carlow, eight shopkeepers each gave 2d. to mendicants daily, totalling £3 0s. 10d. per annum each or £24 6s. 8d. cumulatively.[94]

88   *PI, Appendix A*, pp. 734, 736, 757, 653; Ó Ciosáin, *Ireland in official print culture*, p. 79.
89   *PI, Appendix A*, p. 638.
90   Ibid., pp. 671, 649.
91   Ibid., p. 488.
92   Ibid., pp. 496, 564.
93   Ibid., p. 539.
94   Ibid., p. 543.

Table 2.2 Estimated amounts given by individual shopkeepers in alms to beggars in 1830s Ireland

Town / parish	County	Daily	Weekly	Annually	PI, Appendix A	Comments
Tuam	Galway	2½d.	1s. 5½d.	£3 16s. ½d.	p. 488	Average
Aughavale	Mayo	2½d.	1s. 4½d.[1]	£3 11s. 6d.	p. 494	Average
Ballina	Mayo	3¼d.	1s. 11d.	£5 0s. 0d.	p. 496	Average
Athlone	Roscommon / Westmeath	1¾d.	1s. 0d.	£2 12s. 0d.	p. 521	Average (20 shopkeepers)
Carlow	Carlow	3d.–4d.	1s. 9d.–2s. 4d.	£4 11s. 0d.–£6 1s. 4d.	p. 539	Average
Dunleekney	Carlow	2d.	1s. 2d.	£3 0s. 8d.	p. 543	Average (8 shopkeepers)
Wells	Carlow	2d.	1s. 2d.	£3 0s. 8d.	p. 543	Average (45 shopkeepers)
Tullow	Carlow	2d.	1s. 2d.	£3 0s. 8d.	p. 547	Average
Castledermot	Kildare	2d.	1s. 2d.	£3 0s. 8d.	p. 552	Average
Kilcock	Kildare	3d.	1s. 9d.	£4 11s. 0d.	p. 555	Average (60 shopkeepers)
Naas	Kildare	3d.[2]	1s. 9d.	£4 11s. 0d.	p. 558	Average (sixty shopkeepers)
Rathangan	Kildare	1¾d.	1s. 0d.	£2 12s. 0d.	p. 560	Average (45 shopkeepers)
Ballymahon	Longford	1¾d.	1s. 0d.	£2 12s. 0d.	p. 564	Average
Granard	Longford	2d.–6½d.	1s. 2d.–3s. 10d.	£3 0s. 0d.–£10 0s. 0d.	p. 569	30 of 50 shopkeepers gave within this range

Town / parish	County	Daily	Weekly	Annually	PI, Appendix A	Comments
Longford	Longford	4¾d.	2s. 9d. 'and broken food'	£7 3s. 0d.	pp. 574–5	Average of 2 cases (a merchant and a baker)
Mullingar	Westmeath	8½d.	5s.	£13 0s. 0d.	p. 590	One instance (Mort Mahon, shopkeeper)
Multyfarnham	Westmeath	2d.	1s. 2d.	£3 0s.8d.	p. 592	Average
Gorey	Wexford	6d.	3s. 6d.	£9 2s. 0d.	p. 596	Average given by 'small shopkeeper[s]… in food or money'
Wexford	Wexford	6d.	3s. 6d	£9 2s. 0d.	p. 598	Average
Enniscorthy	Wexford	1¾d.–2½d.	1s. 0d.–1s. 6d.	£2 5s. 7½d.–£4 0s. 0d.	p. 600	Average
Kildysart	Clare	2d.	1s. 2d.	£3 0s.8d.	p. 617	Average given, 'in food and money'
Miltown Malbay	Clare	2d.–3d.	1s. 2d.–1s. 9d.	£3 0s.8d.–£4 11s. 0d.	p. 623	Average
Killaloe	Clare	½d.–¾d.	4d.–5d.	17s. 4d.–£1 1s. 8d.	p. 632	Average
Newmarket-on-Fergus	Clare	2d.–3d.	1s. 2d.–1s. 9d.	£3 0s.8d.–£4 11s. 0d.	p. 646	Average
Holy Trinity parish	Cork city	6d.–8d.	3s. 6d.–4s. 8d.	£9 2s. 0d.–£12 3s. 4d.	p. 649	Average
Macroom	Cork	< 1½d.	< 1s.	< £2 12s. 0d.	p. 662	Average in most cases
Kinsale	Cork		2d.³		p. 674	Average

Town / parish	County	Daily	Weekly	Annually	PI, Appendix A	Comments
Clonmel	Tipperary	½d.	4½d.	£1 0s. 0d.	p. 701	£1 'in meat' given by shopkeepers with annual incomes of £400–£500, in addition to contributions to charities
Ahoghill	Antrim	>1½d.	1s.	<£2 10s.	p. 703	Average
Ballymoney	Antrim	2d.	1s. 2d.	£3 0s. 0d.	p. 707	Average
Billy	Antrim	<½d.– >1½d.	2½d.– <1s.	10s.– £2 10s.	p. 709	Average
Carrickfergus	Antrim	4¼d.	2s. 6d.	£6 10s.	p. 711	Average
Rasharkin	Antrim	1d.	7d.	£1 10s.	p. 728	Average
Glenarm	Antrim	½d.–1d.	3½d.–6d.	15s.–£1 5s. 0d.	p. 730	Average; shopkeepers in the town 'are not wealthy'
Glenavy	Antrim	1d.	7d.	£1 10s.	p. 715	Average, 'in food or in money'
Larne	Antrim	3¼d.	2s. 0d.	£5 0s. 0d.	p. 720	Average, in alms and contributions to mendicity society
Layde	Antrim	½d.–2½d.	4½d.–1s. 6d.	£1 0s. 0d.–£4 0s. 0d.	p. 722	Average
Buncrana	Donegal	1¾d.	1s.	£2 12s. 0d.	p. 744	Average
Letterkenny	Donegal	1¾d.	1s.	£2 12s. 0d.	p. 737	Average
Moville	Donegal	1¾d.	1s.	£2 12s. 0d.	p. 755	Average

Town / parish	County	Daily	Weekly	Annually	PI, Appendix A	Comments
Coleraine	Londonderry	>4½d.	>2s. 8d.	>£7 0s. 0d.	p. 763	Average
Newtown Limavady	Londonderry	>1½d.–2½d.	1s.–1s. 6d.	£2 10s. 0d.–£4 0s. 0d.	p. 770	Average
Dungiven and Banagher	Londonderry	3½d.–5d.	**2s. 1d.–2s. 11d.**	£5 8s. 4d.–£7 11s. 8d.	p. 773	Weekly distribution of ½d. to 50–70 beggars
Kilrea	Londonderry	1d.	7½d.	**£1 12s. 6d.**	p. 780	Average; distributed among around 30 people
Maghera	Londonderry	2d.–2½d.	**1s. 2d.–1s. 6d.**	£3 0s. 8d.–£3 18s. 0d.	p. 784	Average
Magherafelt	Londonderry	1d.	**7d.**	**£1 10s. 0d.**	p. 786	Average (minimum estimate)
Derry	Londonderry	3¼d.	2s. 0d.	**£5 0s. 0d.**	p. 791	Average of 'higher classes' of shopkeepers

Note. The table lists instances in the *PI, Appendix A* where specific estimates, or a range of estimates, for the amount of alms provided by local shopkeepers are recorded. In the 'Daily', 'Weekly' and 'Annually' columns, the figures in bold illustrate the specific estimate that was provided; the other two figures for that instance have been extrapolated from the base figure. For the ease of the reader, these extrapolated calculations have frequently been rounded and are to be interpreted as rough rather than precise calculations.

1 Calculated as follows: 40 shopkeepers who gave 2s. 6d. weekly, as well as another 60 who gave between 3d. and 1s. (the average of this latter group taken as 7½d.).

2 The average daily assistance provided by ten shopkeepers giving 8d. and 50 giving 2d.

3 As 2d. per week appears like an unusually small sum in a large town, this figure may be an error in the primary source. If 2s. per week is correct, it would correspond to daily and annual contributions of 3½d. and £5 4s. 0d. respectively.

The Poor Inquiry evidence reveals that in many instances shopkeepers' alms to beggars were provided due to the lack of an alternative relief mechanism for these individuals. In towns where mendicity societies and poorhouses were established shopkeepers typically ceased or severely curtailed their indiscriminate alms-giving, preferring instead to subscribe or donate to the local charity. Crucially, the average subscription to a local mendicity society was considerably lower than the amount doled out in casual alms, thus relieving shopkeepers of both the nuisance and the monetary burden of beggary. In Carrickfergus and Coleraine, shopkeepers' habit of giving weekly allowances ceased following the opening of the towns' respective mendicity asylums; in the latter case, some shopkeepers' burden was said to have been relieved by a total of 5s. weekly, equivalent to £13 per annum.[95] That more was given in casual alms than in subscriptions to charities was evident in Ballymena, where subscribers to the town's mendicity society reported that their subscriptions totalled 'half the amount of what they formerly gave', while in Derry, 'since the establishment of the Mendicity, the custom of helping-days has ceased', with one man reporting local shopkeepers as saying 'that 1l. [i.e.. £1] to the Mendicity saved 5l. [£5] to the beggars'.[96] In Ballymoney, shopkeepers were said to have been much relieved by the establishment of the mendicity society, removing from them the burden of doling out on average £3 per annum to beggars;[97] the average contribution to the Ballymoney society, based on a listing of 95 named subscribers and their contributions, was 10s. 9d.[98] The average subscription to the Ballyshannon Mendicity Society in 1834 was £1 17s. 6d. but this figure may have been skewed by a small number of disproportionately large subscriptions by members of the local gentry.[99] In Sligo town, shopkeepers were noted as giving very little to beggars by the mid-1830s, instead subscribing to the town's Mendicity Society, as they 'consider it a great advantage to their trade, as the beggars are kept out of the streets'.[100] George Nicholls concurred with the view that more was given in casual alms than would be paid through organised means, stating that, from his investigations, 'the shopkeepers too and manufacturers and dealers generally ... [would] be gainers at the end of the year, whatever might be the amount legally assessed upon them; for that they could neither close their doors, nor turn their backs upon the wretched objects who were constantly applying

---

95 Ibid., pp. 711, 763.
96 Ibid., pp. 718, 791.
97 Ibid., p. 707.
98 *OSM*, xvi, pp. 16–17. The average is based on omitting three large subscriptions, which would have distorted the calculation.
99 *PI, Appendix A*, p. 749.
100 Ibid., p. 535.

to them for aid'.[101] Table 2.2 presents supporting evidence for Nicholls's assertion: in 38 of the 47 cases recorded, the average sum given in casual alms on an annual basis was greater than £2 5s., considerably more than the typical subscription to a mendicity society. These figures point to a driving motivation among Ireland's middle classes, particularly merchants and shopkeepers, to establish charities for suppressing street begging – namely, the provision of institutional assistance that cost significantly less than the prevailing system of private and largely indiscriminate alms-giving.

With the establishment of the Poor Law system in the late 1830s and early 1840s, financed through locally specified rates on owners and occupiers of land, the provision of assistance for the destitute poor was put onto a statutory footing. There was now, in Ireland, a formal structure, framed by legislation and overseen by a centralised authority (the Poor Law Commission), for the relief of those categories of the poor who formally had resort to mendicancy. The survival of a small number of poor rate books allows us to identify the amount levied on individuals in given locations and contrast these figures with the aforementioned estimates of casual alms-giving by shopkeepers and subscriptions to mendicity societies. Regrettably, it is difficult to source information on individual payments of poor rates for areas that correlate to locations where information exists as to the extent of private alms-giving and subscribing to mendicity societies. Nonetheless, some informed suggestions can be made.

A poor rate book for Castleblaney Poor Law Union in County Monaghan for 1847 shows that in the rural townland of Toome, the average holding by the 28 tenants measured approximately nine acres, for which the average annual poor rate was 9s. 4½d.[102] Caution must be applied in this case, as this level of rating dates from the autumn of 1847, when the destructive impacts of the Great Famine were particularly acute. A more accurate reflection of levels of payable rates from non-crisis times can be found in the rate books for the Thurles Poor Law Union from the early to mid-1840s. In the town of Thurles, where there were 171 ratepayers listed with addresses on Main Street, the commercial hub of the town where property valuations and, subsequently, rates were highest, the average annual poor rate paid in 1845 was 8s. 6½d. Individuals who paid in and around this average rate were typically food retailers: for instance, baker Patrick Fanning and grocer Valentine Mara (O'Meara) paid 6s. 8d. and 8s. 4d. respectively, while professionals (as occupiers of typically more valuable properties) were liable to higher rates, with medical practitioner Thomas (O')Sullivan and bank

101 *Report of Geo. Nicholls, Poor Laws, Ireland*, p. 10.
102 P. Mac Doinnléibhe, 'Castleblaney Poor Law rate book (1847)' in *Clogher Record*, v, no. 1 (1963), pp. 131–48.

manager Michael Bird paying £1 1s. 8d. and £1 11s. 8d. respectively.[103] The
properties occupied by ratepayers living and trading on smaller streets in the
town were valued at a lower rate, leading to lesser levies. In less significant
towns, comparatively reduced property valuations led to smaller levies: the
155 ratepaying occupiers of property on Francis Street (now Main Street)
in Templemore paid on average 3s. 1d. in 1842.[104] In the rural district of
Inch, where approximately half of the holdings measured ten acres or less,
the average levy (charged at a rate of 5d. in the pound) paid in 1842 was 6s.
9¾d.[105] In the same year, ratepayers in Ballycahill, another rural Tipperary
parish, were levied with an average payment of 5s. 1d.[106] These figures
demonstrate that, as with subscriptions to charitable societies, amounts paid
in poor rates were significantly less than those doled out in casual alms
to beggars: in monetary terms, indiscriminate alms-giving was without
question the most expensive form of charity – at least for those who decided
to dole out alms in this manner.

Conclusion

Estimates as to the extent of mendicancy and the amount doled out in alms
to beggars formed a crucial part of the Irish Poor Law debates in the first
half of the nineteenth century. The main contributors to this discourse, such
as the Whately commissioners and George Nicholls, presented calculations
of the extent of the problem in Ireland and there were good reasons for
attempting to quantify beggary. The wealthier classes, who faced being
the principal ratepayers under any new statutory Poor Law scheme, had
an economic interest in identifying the cost of maintaining the prevailing
system of voluntary charity in contrast to the proposed new rates-based
system. Efforts to quantify mendicancy were also part of a wider effort to
employ statistical analysis and supposedly objective methodologies in the
'improvement' of the moral condition of the lower classes. Such calculations
rarely reflected a consensus and a number of reasons have been suggested

103 Thurles E.D. rate book, Dec. 1845 (Thurles Library, Thurles Poor Law Union records,
    BG151/N/26/1). The ratepayers on Main Street are listed at numbers 542–638 and
    959, 961–1034. The named individuals' occupations were identified in *Slater's national
    commercial directory of Ireland* ... (Manchester and London, 1846), pp. 315–17.
104 Templemore E.D. rate book, Jan. 1842 (Thurles Library, Thurles Poor Law Union
    records, BG151/N24/2). The ratepayers on Francis Street are listed at numbers
    560–714.
105 Inch E.D. rate book, Jan. 1842 (Thurles Library, Thurles Poor Law Union records,
    BG151/N/11/1).
106 Ballycahill E.D. rate book, Jan. 1842 (Thurles Library, Thurles Poor Law Union
    records, BG151/N/1/1).

for disparities, the prime explanation being the dissimilar definitions held by different individuals and parties of who and what constituted beggars and begging. The mobility of large numbers of persons, a distinguishing feature of the poorer classes in pre-Famine Ireland, compounded the difficulty. Analysis of the Whately Commission reports suggests that rural dwellers had a firm understanding of the extent of mendicancy in their locality through the greater likelihood of their being acquainted with 'local' paupers and able to distinguish them from 'strangers'. To urban dwellers, greater proportions of their poorer neighbours, whether 'local' or 'strange', were unknown to them.

Even in cases where some form of statistical methodology was utilised, both the perceptions of the extent of beggary and the resulting estimates were highly impressionistic: as Laurence Geary has correctly observed, 'it is easier to qualify than quantify begging in pre-Famine Ireland'.[107] Statistical methodologies could produce detailed calculations of beggary and alms-giving but, as demonstrated for both national and local estimates, figures varied. The example of the Dublin mendicity campaign's estimate of 5,000 beggars in the city points to complexities in the experiences and perceptions of poverty. One topic on which consensus was reached was that casual alms-giving was more costly, in material terms, than subscribing to a local charity such as a mendicity society. The establishment of a mendicity society served to provide an immediate solution to the nuisance of mendicancy – by removing street beggars and accommodating them in an industrious environment – as well as, crucially, reducing the monetary burden on traders. It is no surprise, then, that shopkeepers and merchants were at the forefront of efforts to establish mendicity societies in towns and cities throughout Ireland. However, the desire to quantify mendicancy did not transcend social barriers and was not felt necessary by the poor themselves. For the large numbers of the poor, mendicancy was a practice neither to be subjected to considerations of statistical analysis nor to be thought of in material terms, thus marking out definite variations in how the problem was perceived across the social spectrum.

---

107 Geary, "'The whole country was in motion'", p. 127.

3

Begging and Alms-Giving: Perceptions and Motivations

Introduction

The English novelist William Makepeace Thackeray was among the numerous visitors to Ireland who commented on the prevalence of beggary and their own personal encounters with Irish mendicants. Thackeray's description of beggars in Ballinasloe is illustrative in this regard:

> I think the beggars were more plenteous and more loathsome here than almost anywhere. To one hideous wretch I was obliged to give money to go away, which he did for a moment, only to obtrude his horrible face directly afterwards half eaten away with disease ... and as for the rest of the beggars, what pen or pencil could describe their hideous leering flattery, their cringing, swindling humour![1]

This short piece from Thackerary usefully highlights many of the perceptions of beggary which ran through public discourse on the question of the poor: the author mentioned the extent and unpleasantness of the town's beggars; he felt compelled to give alms merely to be rid of this nuisance; one mendicant is presented as being disease-ridden and 'as for the rest of the beggars', who utilised skills of the trade ('hideous leering flattery, their cringing swindling humour') to procure alms, they were simply beyond description. As a counterpoint, more benign portrayals of Irish beggars and the practice of mendicancy were provided by the Presbyterian army surgeon John Gamble, who travelled around Ireland throughout the 1810s. Many of Gamble's references to soliciting mendicants note the 'poetical and animated' address of Irish beggars, in contrast to their English counterparts, while the number

---

1 William Makepeace Thackeray, *The Irish sketchbook of 1842* (1843; repr. Dublin, 2005), p. 215.

of beggars in Dublin proved not the extent of poverty in the city but the abundance of benevolence and charity among its inhabitants.[2] Thackeray's beggars were disease-ridden nuisances while Gamble's were characters who evoked curiosity and compassion.

Gauging perceptions of mendicancy in early nineteenth-century Irish society is far from a simple task. Attitudes towards beggars and beggary varied greatly, yet most accounts portrayed mendicancy and its practitioners in a negative light. Beggars propagated disease, sedition and all manner of moral evils in a community. However, mendicants could also be viewed with sympathy and as 'deserving' persons; their fellow men pitied the plight of the poor and looked upon their woes as an opportunity to follow Christ's example in relieving the sick and the distressed. Meanwhile, for some, beggars could be merely ubiquitous figures, always part of the physical and social landscape, and whose presence was not necessarily benign nor malevolent but merely constant.

This analysis will first consider contemporary arguments that begging was a natural resort for people in distress, with some commentators speaking of an innate right to beg and the harmonious social relations which were fostered by the solicitation and giving of alms. The analysis will then shift to consider how, like many other social problems such as prostitution and juvenile delinquency, beggary was largely deemed to be a threatening presence due in large part to its visibility. In urban centres, authorities and various interested parties went to great lengths to shield the citizenry from the unsightly spectacle of mendicancy. But, those same 'respectable' middle classes also came to appreciate and use the visibility of beggary in campaigns to promote charitable initiatives. Many commentators spewed out a litany of threats that beggars posed to communities and this chapter will concern itself with two of these dangers: begging as a means of spreading disease and as a threat to economic activity. In the former case, a case study will be presented of the 1816–19 typhus fever epidemic in Ireland, during which disease was spread throughout the country by itinerant mendicants, resulting in localised systems of expulsion, parliamentary legislation and the emergence of the Irish mendicity society movement. In the latter case, the prominence of shopkeepers in efforts to curtail – or at the very least, to manage – mendicancy will be studied in the context of this group's particular vulnerability to nuisance and inconvenience caused by beggars. On a more popular level, attitudes towards begging and beggars were widely influenced by superstition, which, together with the figure of the 'boccough', facilitated among the lower classes a system of judgement as to the deservedness of mendicants.

2 Gamble, *Sketches of history, politics, and manners*, pp. 48, 90.

The Right to Beg

The act of begging was considered by some to constitute an unquestionable right; the solicitation of assistance from one's fellow man was seen as a natural resort for those in distressed circumstances. In early 1826, a gentleman was walking across Carlisle (now O'Connell) Bridge in Dublin city when he observed a woman being dragged away by two watchmen for public begging. The woman had an infant and two other 'half-starved' children with her. In the eyes of the gentleman, the woman constituted a truly deserving case and had a legitimate reason to beg. Writing a letter to a Dublin newspaper the man commented bitterly: 'Now, Sir, is it not heart-rending to think, that a poor mother who sees her children starving at home, and steals out in the dark of the evening to implore some sustenance for their support, is to be thrust into a dungeon with the vilest characters that the guardians of the night arrest'.[3] Yet, the question ought to be asked as to whether the writer was offended by the removal of a beggar from the street or the apparently heavy-handed removal of a woman with young children. If the watchmen had dragged away an able-bodied male mendicant, would the observer have been sufficiently disgusted and exercised to write his public letter?

In an 1830 pamphlet addressing the proposed establishment of a Poor Law system in Ireland, the author, a Henry Flood,[4] championed an individual's right publicly to seek alms. 'There is no right more clearly recognised by God and nature, than the right of sueing for the sympathy of our fellow-creatures', Flood asserted. 'We have peculiar tones of voice, and our features particular muscles, to give expression, as in a universal language, to our wants; ... an appeal in public, decent and modest, should not, however frequent, be denied'. His argument was not unqualified, however, and carried the stipulation that 'such beggars as offend, by violent importunity, or by infectious and disgusting exhibitions, should be removed'. Flood did not deny that some beggars were undeserving of assistance. In his opinion, begging and alms-giving benefited both the supplicant and the solicited passer-by. For the former, the exchange exposed them to individuals whom they should aspire to emulate – the sober, the clean, the industrious, the charitable: 'The mind of the sufferer, by enjoying the light of heaven, even by the view of others in health and spirits, and by the hopes of receiving alms, acquires a train of cheerful thoughts which cannot exist in workhouses, or in the society of wretches like himself'.[5]

---

3 Cited in *Cork Mercantile Chronicle*, 27 Feb. 1826.
4 The author is not to be confused with the well-known late eighteenth-century parliamentarian Henry Flood.
5 Henry Flood, *Poor Laws: arguments against a provision for paupers, if it be parochial or perpetual* (Dublin, 1830), p. 15.

The ability of charitable deeds to foster harmonious relations between the different social classes was a common theme in the moralising language of charity in this period. For example, to James Digges La Touche, of the famous Dublin Huguenot banking family, a Sunday School education for the poor promoted many beneficial effects for all classes in society: 'it brings them in contact together, and tends considerably to harmonise the different ranks of society'.[6] On the other side of the exchange, beggars reminded the givers of charity of their Christian duty to the poor, whose penury was regularly hidden away in slums which wealthier citizens rarely witnessed. Flood asserted:

> If misery exists, it ought to be known and to be seen; the presence of the poor, at the entrance of places of worship, disposes our minds to God, who has exempted us from the sufferings we see inflicted on others, perhaps more meritorious, perhaps our former companions and friends. The presence of the poor in the thoroughfares of pleasure or businesses, are living lessons of prudence and moderation to the young and the presumptuous.[7]

This view depicted mendicancy as a binary, reciprocal exchange, in which both the alms-seeker and the alms-giver performed social and moral roles. Each party reminded the other of their responsibilities and their expected conduct. Near Monaghan town John Gamble met an elderly beggar woman who sought alms from him. Satisfied with the woman's 'judicious' appeal for assistance, Gamble gave her some money and they parted company 'mutually satisfied with each other'.[8]

This perception of the alms-giving transaction was succinctly expressed in the first report of the Edinburgh Mendicity Society, which asserted that in removing importunate beggars from the city streets it did not wish 'to interfere with the exercise of private charity. They have no intention of robbing the benevolent of this highest privilege which affluence can give; who, in relieving the wants of virtuous and unobtrusive poverty, will find abundance of room for gratifying the best feelings of the human heart'.[9] The language here was similar to that used by the Dublin Mendicity Society five years later, when it expounded on the act of alms-giving, but, crucially, noted the flawed logic inherent in an act of indiscriminate assistance:

6　*First report of the commissioners on education in Ireland*, p. 65, H.C. 1825 (400), xii, 69.
7　Flood, *Poor Laws*, p. 15.
8　Gamble, *Sketches of history, politics, and manners*, pp. 184–5.
9　*The first report of the society, instituted in Edinburgh on 25th January 1813, for the suppression of beggars, for the relief of occasional distress, and for the encouragement of industry among the poor. With an account of receipts and disbursements from 27th February to 1st November 1813* (Edinburgh, 1814), p. 15.

It is indeed a custom founded on a prejudice hard to overcome. The benevolent mind will naturally follow the ready impulse; the heart, perhaps, is warmed with the idea of extending relief to apparent misery, and waits not for the slow and needful process of inquiry which can alone insure its right application: but, be it remembered, this is not charity.[10]

Here, the mendicity society implicitly advertised and extolled its own system of enquiry into and clarification of paupers' true condition before assistance was provided – if provided at all. Criticism of 'mistaken benevolence' ran through numerous reports and studies on the problem of street begging, exposing the folly of indiscriminate alms-giving.[11]

In recording apparently verbatim testimonies by members of all social classes, the reports of the Poor Inquiry shed light on the immeasurable sense of Christian charity, solidarity, and sociability among the poorer classes which was utterly distinct from, in Ó Ciosáin's words, the 'instrumentalist principles which had dominated discussions of poor relief within the elite for a century or two before the 1830s'.[12] This 'older view of charity', which can be associated with the pre-Famine period, is typified in testimony recorded in Inishannon, County Cork, wherein one witness (seemingly, an innkeeper) asserted that he would rather continue giving alms directly to beggars at his door than pay less in monetary terms in a poor tax: 'We would much rather give as we do at present; we do not feel it going; ... if I was forced to pay it as a tax, it would not be charity, it would not be my own act; ... I would not feel the pleasure of relieving a poor creature with my own hand'.[13] Throughout all ranks of society – from County Cork innkeepers to the middle-class philanthropists of the Dublin and Edinburgh mendicity societies – people placed significant importance on the personal encounter between the giver and receiver of charity. In Headford parish, in County Galway, a William King spoke at length on why he gave alms to mendicants:

I consider that I would be in greater want if I gave none away than if I gave a great deal away, for I think charity never shortens the quantity ... If a meal was going on, and a beggar called, you would never miss

10 *Report, Dublin Mendicity Society, 1818,* p. 17.
11 *Report of the general committee of the Association for the Suppression of Mendicity in Dublin. For the year 1820* (Dublin, 1821), p. 25; *The fifth report of the general committee of the Mendicity Association, instituted in Londonderry, 13th May, 1825; with a statement of the accounts, and a list of the subscribers for the last year* (Derry, 1830), p. 7; Report on the state of the poor in Waterford, 1834, f. 28ʳ.
12 Ó Ciosáin, *Ireland in official print culture,* p. 83.
13 Cited ibid.

what you would give away. I gave away, myself, part of the cake made of a quart of meal to a beggarman, and at the time I had no more victuals in my house, nor the hope of getting it to earn the next day; but I hoped that as God gave it to me that day he would some more the next day ... When I give I do so for the good of my soul, the honour of God, and for their benefit.[14]

Elsewhere in Galway, Kilchreest schoolmaster Patrick Cassidy (most likely a Catholic) explained:

When I give alms I am actuated by a sense of gratitude towards my Saviour, who gave his life as a ransom for my soul, not vainly hoping that I am performing a meritorious deed for 'man's righteousness is but as filthy as rags,' and the inspired Apostle writes, 'though I give all my goods to feed the poor, and have not charity, it profiteth me nothing'.[15]

It was important for people not to be seen as being niggardly in their alms-giving. According to Rev. Thomas O'Connor, Catholic priest in Tracton, County Cork, 'A farmer will not let a beggar go from his door, because he does not like it should be said of him that he is unlike his neighbours; that he does not treat the poor like other people'.[16]

The Ubiquitous Beggar

Mendicants were ubiquitous figures in pre-Famine Irish towns and cities, as well as in rural areas. The biblical teachings, 'The poor shall never cease out of the land' (Deut. 15:11) and 'For ye have the poor always with you' (Matt. 26:11) were taken to heart by contemporaries, and regularly cited by polemicists, social commentators, preachers and charitable societies.[17] Some, though, drew distinctions between the poor and beggars: the former were to be tolerated, the latter suppressed. Similarly, poverty was distinguished

---

14 *PI, Appendix A*, p. 477.
15 Ibid., p. 479.
16 Ibid., p. 677.
17 *Annual report of the Strangers' Friend Society; (founded in 1790) for visiting and relieving distressed strangers, and the resident sick poor, at their habitations, in Dublin and its vicinity: with an account of some of the cases relieved, and a list of subscribers, for 1823* (Dublin, 1824), p. 5; *Report, Dublin Mendicity Society, 1820*, p. 9; Michael Fitzgerald, *Wickedness and nullity of human laws against mendicancy, and the anti-Christian character of the Irish Poor-law, proved from the consideration of alms-giving, mendicancy, and Poor-laws, on Christian and Catholic principles ...* (Dublin, 1843), p. 17.

Figure 3.1
James
Malton,
'View from
Capel Street,
looking over
Essex Bridge,
Dublin' (1797)
(reproduced
courtesy of
National
Library of
Ireland)

from pauperism, which were seen respectively as the result of misfortune and depravity.[18] Referring to the passage quoted above from Deuteronomy, Catholic priest Rev. Thaddeus O'Malley asserted: 'But that blessed Providence, as benevolent as it is wise, has nowhere decreed that amongst those poor there shall be a class of beggars without any other security for the morsel that sustains life in them than the chance pity of the passer-by'.[19] O'Malley drew on this biblical passage in his argument in favour of a statutory Poor Law, which, he believed, while not extinguishing poverty, ought to curtail habitual mendicancy.

While most accounts depicted the beggar as a deviant figure, mendicants were treated by some commentators as merely ubiquitous characters, a constant part of daily life and in such accounts the description of beggars reflected a desire neither to denigrate nor to romanticise these individuals but merely to acknowledge and record the fact that they were an ever-present part of society. According to Tim Hitchcock, beggars were 'a normal part of every street scene'.[20] James Malton's 1797 painting, 'View from Capel Street, looking over Essex Bridge, Dublin' (Figure 3.1) captures this sense of the ubiquity of mendicancy. The painting, part of a set published in the 1790s, was intended to showcase the grandeur of late eighteenth-century Dublin, particularly the Georgian architecture framing Parliament Street and drawing the eye as far as the Royal Exchange, two recently completed civic developments. Included in Malton's depiction, however, is a ragged, seemingly indigent beggar, cap in hand and soliciting alms from a gentleman on horseback. Even within the splendour of pre-Union Dublin and in this sanitised representation of the streetscape, the beggar was a ubiquitous part of life.[21] According to William Laffan, 'topographical artists patronised by the Dublin elite and middling classes deliberately ignored this marked contrast between splendour and poverty. Consistently in the visual tradition, beggars, and indeed the majority of the city's more unsightly inhabitants, were either excluded from show or else rendered generically picturesque and hence acceptable for inclusion in depictions of the city'.[22]

---

18 Boyd Hilton, *The age of atonement: the influence of evangelicalism on social and economic thought, 1795–1865* (Oxford, 1988), p. 122.
19 Thaddeus O'Malley, *Poor Laws – Ireland. An idea of a Poor Law for Ireland* (2nd edn, London, 1837), p. 1.
20 Hitchcock, 'Begging on the streets of eighteenth-century London', p. 493.
21 A beggar is also portrayed as an inconspicuous character in Malton's *The west front of St Patrick's Cathedral, Dublin* (1793).
22 William Laffan, 'Behind the gorgeous mask: Hugh Douglas Hamilton's "Cries of Dublin" rediscovered' in William Laffan, *The cries of Dublin*, p. 10.

The Visibility of Begging

The visibility of ragged and dirty mendicants offended the sensitivities of the middle classes who increasingly esteemed and expected respectability in one's conduct and appearance. The removal of these eyesores from public spaces frequented by the respectable classes was an important motivating factor behind initiatives to suppress street begging; writing of contemporary welfare cultures in Oxford, Dyson and King have observed that 'the nineteenth century was to see both an increased awareness of beggars and a determination to do something about them'.[23] As Jacinta Prunty has observed, 'it was the visibility of such persons that led to public concern',[24] while, addressing the related urban problem of prostitution, Maria Luddy has argued that the 'most common concern ... was its visibility'.[25] In the first report of the Londonderry Mendicity Society, the public was reminded of 'how great has been the improvement effected by the removal of so many miserable objects from public view'.[26] However, for some commentators, initiatives to remove the visibility of poverty and beggary were overzealous and unjustified. One anonymous author went so far as implicitly to criticise legislative attempts to suppress the visibility of mendicancy as mere measures to protect the interests of the urban commercial classes. Referring to the beggars and vagrants who were criminalised under the 1847 Vagrancy Act, the author, aiming his acerbic comments at the supporters of the statute, wrote: 'They [beggars] may crawl along the by-ways or through the fields – they may pine in the prison – they may die in their desolate homes – but they must not drag their gaunt frames and ghastly visages into "The marts where merchants most do congregate"'.[27]

The ability of beggary to shock the wealthier classes partially drove opposition to the relocation of the Dublin Mendicity Society's premises from Copper Alley in the city centre to Usher's Island on the capital's western outskirts. Householders from St Audeon's parish, where the institution was

---

23 Dyson and King, '"The streets are paved with beggars"', p. 62.

24 Prunty, *Dublin slums*, p. 196.

25 Maria Luddy, '"Abandoned women and bad characters": prostitution in nineteenth-century Ireland' in *Women's History Review*, vi, no. 4 (1997), p. 491. One commentator in Athlone complained of the visibility of the town's prostitutes, a 'vice not hiding its deeds in darkness, but boldly stalking abroad in open day': Weld, *Statistical survey, county Roscommon*, p. 551.

26 *The first report of the general committee of the Mendicity Association, instituted in Londonderry, 13th May, 1825; with a statement of the accounts, and a list of the subscribers for the last year* (Derry, 1826), pp. 6–7.

27 Anon., 'Tenant right, repeal and Poor Laws: dangers and duties of the Conservative Party and landed interest in Ireland' in *Dublin University Magazine*, xxxi, no. 181 (Jan. 1848), pp. 142–3. The final phrase in this quote is from William Shakespeare's *The Merchant of Venice*.

to be relocated, complained that Usher's Island was 'the principal entrance to the City from the West of Ireland' and feared the concentration of 'such a mass of pauperism & wretchedness' at this prominent location.[28] To allay these worries the society assured the parishioners that access to the institution from Usher's Island, which fronted onto the quays and the main thoroughfare:

> will only be made use of by the gentlemen of the Committee and the Visitors of the Institution, and in that respect it will not at all differ from a private house. The entrance for the poor will be altogether from Island Street [a back lane to the rear of the property] and so cannot in the least degree be a nuisance to any one.[29]

A later minute explicitly stated that the purpose of erecting a 'proper wall' at the front of the premises was 'so as to prevent the Mendicants being seen at work from the quay'.[30] These arrangements ensured that the beggars' access to and egress from the institution would be kept out of sight of the main thoroughfare.

The importance of the spectacle of mendicancy is evident in the Dublin Mendicity Society's decision in September 1818, and again in September 1828 and August 1839, to parade beggars through the streets of the city.[31] The motivation behind these bizarre exhibitions, usually held at times of diminished income due to falling subscriptions and donations, was to exert pressure on those 'most callous and thoughtless' inhabitants of Dublin who refused, yet had the means, to contribute financially to the society.[32] The initiative also implicitly threatened inhabitants with the consequences of the institution's failure if sufficient public support was not

28 Dublin Mendicity Society minute book, 18 June 1822.
29 Ibid., 25 June 1822.
30 Ibid., 28 Oct. 1823; ibid., 23 Dec., 30 Dec. 1823.
31 Woods, *Dublin outsiders*, pp. 21, 84, 116. See also *FJ*, 21 Sept. 1826. A similar instance of an unidentified mendicity society 'of a commercial town' parading paupers to the houses of non-subscribers is cited by an anonymous pamphleteer, but it is not clear whether the author was referring to the Dublin society and one of the aforementioned instances: Anon., *A letter to the Right Hon. Lord Goderich, on the deplorable condition of the helpless poor in Ireland, with a plan of relief, as at present partly in operation in several districts of the province of Ulster. By a member of a parochial poor relief committee* (Dublin, 1827), p. 21.
32 *Twenty-second annual report of the managing committee of the Association for the Suppression of Mendicity in Dublin. For the year 1839* (Dublin, 1840), p. 8. The parading of beggars was discussed in the summer of 1836, at a time of 'alarming emergency' for the society, but postponed: Dublin Mendicity Society minute book, 13 June 1836 (NLI, DMSP, MS 32,599/5); ibid., 14 June, 14 July 1836.

forthcoming. Householders were subjected to verbal aggression and 'shout[s] of execration'.[33] A newspaper report claimed that the mendicity society 'sent the starving paupers to besiege the houses of non-subscribers, with incessant applications for assistance, and the consequence was, that their funds for the ensuing year were amply sufficient for the demands that were made upon them'. Such a policy was justified, and indeed encouraged, by the paper's editor, who argued that 'itinerant beggars should be allowed to infest the doors of such characters as these', who absconded from their duty in contributing to the suppression of mendicancy in their city.[34] With crowds of mendicants congregating and shouting outside their home, the besieged householders undoubtedly felt much pressure and intimidation to financially support the institution in future. The Dublin parish of St James's also experimented with this unorthodox practice, arranging for a procession of the parish's 'starving poor' from the city to the southern suburb of Stillorgan, in the hope of intimidating a householder into parting with overdue rates.[35] The Coleraine Mendicity Society deployed a different tactic, in threatening to publish the names of those who did not subscribe to the charity.[36] The Dublin society came under pressure in 1830 to cancel its proposed parade of beggars due to the 'determined opposition' of the Lord Mayor and the government, although the reason for this opposition is not recorded. Through gritted teeth the charity consented to the request but not without expressing its belief that previous parades had proved 'both harmless & beneficial'.[37]

The Threatening Beggar

Beggars and the Spread of Disease

The association between mendicancy and disease pre-dates any scientific understanding of the latter. Disease, while being no discriminator between different social classes, nonetheless impacts the poor disproportionately. Consequences of poverty, such as an insufficient diet and wretched living conditions, increase one's susceptibility to infection, and in pre-Famine Ireland, the onslaught of illness could rapidly propel a once-industrious and independent family into a life of dependency and even destitution.

---

33 John Douglas, *Observations on the necessity of a legal provision for the Irish poor, as the means of improving the condition of the Irish people, and protecting the British landlord, farmer and labourer* (London, 1828), p. 24.
34 *BNL*, 10 Jan. 1832.
35 *FJ*, 9 Oct. 1838.
36 *OSM*, xxxiii, p. 73. For the Belfast House of Industry, see *BNL*, 16 Nov. 1810.
37 Dublin Mendicity Society minute book, 14 Sept., 12 Oct. 1830.

The connection between beggars and the dissemination of plague was appreciated by societies in medieval and early modern Europe when stigmatisation and expulsion of the vagrant poor was common.[38] In Ireland in the same period similar associations can be identified. The enforcement of punitive measures against vagrants and beggars intensified at times of plague: 'The beggar was not merely a nuisance, an idler and an annoyance; he was a definite source of danger to the community, from whom the shadow of plague was never very far distant'.[39] The spread of fever during the 1739–41 famine led to increased punitive measures against vagrants and beggars,[40] while throughout the nineteenth century beggars were blamed for introducing and disseminating disease – most commonly typhus fever, cholera and smallpox – to both rural and urban areas across Ireland.[41] Indeed, the very language deployed in public discourse on the topic of mendicancy was grounded in the imagery of disease and pestilence, with areas being commonly described as being 'infested' with 'swarms' of beggars.[42]

While the identification and understanding of the distinct diseases of typhus, typhoid and relapsing fever dates from the mid-nineteenth century, the Irish population had for generations appreciated the contagiousness of fever. According to Laurence Geary, 'the exposure of the Irish people to centuries of fever left them with an unrivalled knowledge of the symptoms and consequences of the disease'.[43] Lice-ridden rags worn by the wandering beggars of the pre-Famine period were ideal vehicles for the safe breeding of febrile organisms, while the insanitary habits, overcrowded dwellings and transient lifestyle of such individuals ensured the spread of the disease. The *Freeman's Journal*, in September 1817, echoed these views, stating that 'it is ascertained that contagious infection is retained a long time in the foul rags of these miserable outcasts, and has been too frequently scattered by

---

38 Jütte, *Poverty and deviance*, pp. 22–3.
39 Colm Lennon, '*Dives* and Lazarus in sixteenth-century Ireland' in Hill and Lennon, *Luxury and austerity*, pp. 56–7; Joseph Robins, *The miasma: epidemic and panic in nineteenth-century Ireland* (Dublin, 1995), pp. 27–8; Thomas King Moylan, 'Vagabonds and sturdy beggars, I: poverty, pigs and pestilence in medieval Dublin' in *Dublin Historical Record*, i, no. 1 (Mar. 1938), p. 12.
40 David Dickson, *Arctic Ireland: the extraordinary story of the great frost and forgotten famine of 1740–41* (Belfast, 1998), p. 56.
41 In the case of typhus, see Barker and Cheyne, *Account of the rise, progress, and decline of the fever epidemic in Ireland*, i, pp. 66, 141. For cholera in 1832, see *PI, Appendix A*, p. 560; Robins, *The miasma*, p. 76. For smallpox in the 1880s, see J.P. Murray, *Galway: a medico-social history* (Galway, [c.1993]), p. 107.
42 Examples of the use of such language throughout this period include: *Leinster Journal*, 17 July 1819; Cooke, *Sermon preached in aid of the Belfast House of Industry*, p. 24; Binns, *Miseries and beauties of Ireland*, ii, p. 323.
43 Laurence M. Geary, *Medicine and charity in Ireland, 1718–1851* (Dublin, 2004), p. 75.

them through the country, with general and baleful effects'.[44] The first report of the Dublin Mendicity Society, founded in 1818 at the height of a fever epidemic, asserted that 'crowds of unfortunate and clamorous beggars' frequently carried about 'in their persons and garments the seeds of contagious diseases'.[45] In a similar vein, Dr Francis Barker of the Cork Street Fever Hospital, Dublin asserted that 'fever and mendicity, like many other evils, are reciprocally productive, and the suppression of either must tend to that of both'.[46] Through the spread of disease, the mendicant's nomadic habits led to increasing demands on the limited resources of the country's medical institutions and charities. In a report of a sub-committee of the Kilkenny House of Industry, it was stated that the claims on the funds of the city's fever hospital and dispensary 'must diminish when the beggar is prevented from strolling about, and spreading where he goes the seeds of contagion'.[47]

Case Study: Beggars and the 1816–19 Fever Epidemic in Ireland
The end of the Napoleonic Wars in June 1815, just weeks after an unprecedented meteorological disaster, ushered in what John D. Post famously termed 'the last great subsistence crisis in the western world'.[48] Throughout Europe, hundreds of thousands of demobilised men returned home to societies shaken by a post-war economic downturn, agrarian distress, a prolonged period of inclement weather (owing to the worldwide distribution of ash from the eruption of the Tambora volcano in Indonesia) and consecutive bad harvests. Social disorder also prevailed and in parts of north-western Europe food riots and popular disturbances developed into large-scale acts of rebellion.[49] Added to this distress was a severe typhus fever epidemic that proved particularly destructive in Ireland, always 'a fever-ridden country' (serious epidemics were also recorded in the Hapsburg lands south of the Alps, Italy and Switzerland),[50] and the widespread migration of poor persons in search of food, employment and other survival options. The ranks of beggars swelled accordingly and throughout the continent 1817 became known as 'the year of the beggars'.[51] The extent of mendicancy in Ireland during this

44 *FJ*, 10 Sept. 1817.
45 *Report, Dublin Mendicity Society, 1818*, p. 2.
46 Barker, *Medical report, Cork-street Fever Hospital, Dublin*, pp. 43–4.
47 *Leinster Journal*, 19 Apr. 1820.
48 John D. Post, *The last great subsistence crisis in the western world* (Baltimore, MD and London, 1977); Gillen D'Arcy Wood, *Tambora: the eruption that changed the world* (Princeton, NJ, 2015).
49 Post, *Last great subsistence crisis*, pp. 75–86.
50 O'Neill, 'Fever and public health, p. 1; Post, *Last great subsistence crisis*, p. 127.
51 Post, *Last great subsistence crisis*, p. 86.

crisis resembled parts of pre-industrial Europe, such as eastern France and central Europe, owing to the lower levels of economic development and less rationalised administrations. On the other hand, while Britain in the mid- to late 1810s was affected by a flooded labour market, demographic dislocation and increasing levels of unemployment and poor relief, the country was not subjected to the extraordinary levels of mendicancy that marked Ireland, Switzerland, south-western Germany, Italy, the Habsburg Empire and the Balkan peninsula in these years.[52] A notable exception to this pattern was London, which as an urban centre and port town attracted large numbers of mobile poor from the provinces, and the swelled numbers of beggars in the metropolis influenced the establishment of a parliamentary committee (1815–16) on mendicancy in the city and also of the London Mendicity Society in January 1818.[53]

In Dublin, another factor, singular to the city, contributed to the deepening of the demographic, social and medical crisis. In 1816, the city's House of Industry, a state-funded institution which for more than 40 years had been the main place of confinement for street beggars, ceased admitting mendicants through compulsion into its premises in the north city, upon the orders of the Chief Secretary, Robert Peel. Instead, the House of Industry's resources were to be focused on relieving various categories of the sick poor, whom Peel described as 'the proper objects of admission into the House of Industry'.[54] The continued admission of 'vagrant and refractory beggars, constituting that class which is called the compelled' would, it was believed, stretch the institution's resources beyond its capacity.[55] In this light, Jacinta Prunty has perceived the decision, taken following overcrowding crises in 1815 and 1816 and the 'anarchy' involved in indiscriminate admissions of the vagrant poor, as revealing the institution determining 'to wash its hands of the troublesome classes'.[56] Ironically, while the House of Industry governors could proudly assert in their annual report for 1818 that the 'aged and infirm now fill the places formerly preoccupied by the vagrant and healthy' resulting in 'more health, cleanliness, sobriety and order' inside the institution,[57] they

52 E.L. Jones, 'The agricultural labour market in England, 1793–1872' in *Economic History Review*, new series, xvii, no. 2 (1964), p. 325; Post, *Last great subsistence crisis*, pp. 86–8.

53 *Report from committee on the state of mendicity in the metropolis*, H.C. 1814–15 (473), iii, 231; M.J.D. Roberts, 'Reshaping the gift relationship: the London Mendicity Society and the suppression of begging in England 1818–1869' in *International Review of Social History*, xxxvi (1991), pp. 201–31.

54 Copy of letter (original dated 14 Sept. 1816) from Robert Peel to the House of Industry governors, n.d. (NAI, CSORP, CSO/RP/1820/688).

55 Ibid.

56 Prunty, *Dublin slums*, p. 203.

57 Quoted ibid.

appeared to have ignored the fact that on the city streets outside the walls of the House of Industry the consequences of their actions were to be seen in horrific reality. Large parts of the Dublin outside those walls, the Dublin of 1818, were anything but healthy, clean, sober and orderly.

The fever epidemic raged in Ireland for three years and the most reliable contemporary estimate placed the total number of fatalities at up to 65,000, while 1.5 million people were believed to have been afflicted with disease at some point during the outbreak.[58] While other factors contributed to the spread of the disease, the significance of beggary in this regard was such that the government (belatedly) passed a fever act in May 1819 empowering local authorities to confine, wash and clean, or remove beggars from a parish.[59] As various national and local authorities struggled, and in many cases failed, to cope with the level of distress, attempts were made by well-placed observers to identify the causes of the epidemic. A number of histories of the outbreak were published in the decade or so after its demise and all highlighted the role that mendicants played in spreading the disease. In their comprehensive history of Dublin, Warburton *et al.* stated that 'through Dublin it [typhus] was supposed to be propagated by 5,000 beggars who conveyed the contagion in their clothes from street to street and from house to house'.[60] The authors echoed the widely held view that contagion was introduced into the city by wandering mendicants from rural areas and once the epidemic established a footing amongst Dublin's population its progress through the overcrowded, unsanitary dwellings of the city's poorer classes was unrelenting. Medical practitioners were the most prominent commentators blaming the epidemic's dissemination on vagrant beggars. Doctors Francis Barker and John Cheyne, physicians in the Cork Street Fever Hospital and House of Industry respectively, attributed the spread of contagion to wandering mendicants and their 'filthy and neglected clothing', while the custom among the poor, particularly in rural areas, of providing lodging to strange beggars was seen as contributing to 'this evil'.[61] The physicians of the Cork Street Fever Hospital claimed confidently in January 1818 that they were 'satisfied by accounts received from every part of the Country that Beggars have contributed greatly to extend infection'.[62]

---

58 Barker and Cheyne, *Account of the rise, progress, and decline of the fever epidemic in Ireland*, i, pp. 145, 62.

59 59 Geo. III, c. 41, s. 9 (14 June 1819).

60 Warburton *et al.*, *History of the city of Dublin*, ii, p. 1346.

61 Barker and Cheyne, *Account of the rise, progress, and decline of the fever epidemic in Ireland*, i, p. 141; 'A table of the population of Church and Barrack Street', [*c.*late 1817] (NAI, CSOOP, CSO/OP474/8).

62 St Catherine's parish, Dublin, vestry minute book, 24 Jan. 1818 (RCBL, St Catherine's parish vestry minute books, P 117.05.7).

In a separate, self-penned report, Dr Cheyne expanded on this matter and placed the blame for the spread of disease squarely at the feet of Ireland's wandering mendicants. While noting the role played by other social factors, such as the holding of wakes and gatherings at fairs and chapels, Cheyne continued by stating:

> it is probably not known to what extent the vagrant habits of many of the poor and the migratory movements of the beggars prove injurious by disseminating contagion. These are chiefly observable in the South and West of Ireland, but the North is not altogether exempt from the evil; indeed it is generally thought that the beggars were the great carriers of contagion during the late epidemic, and that to them it was owing that the disease spread so rapidly all over Ireland.[63]

Cheyne based his analysis on correspondence with medical practitioners from across Ireland and his notes attest to the strength with which the association between beggars and disease was held by medical men at this time. Table 3.1 reveals the locations where doctors, in correspondence with Cheyne, attributed the spread of disease to the wandering habits of mendicants. This table is not comprehensive and not every county is represented. However, the table *does* demonstrate that across Ireland, indeed in each of the four provinces, the introduction of typhus fever into a particular area was attributed by local experts, especially medical men, to wandering beggars. The findings are supported by a similar but independent contemporary report by Dr William Harty, physician to the King's Hospital in Dublin, based on accounts from each of the thirty-two counties.[64]

In the first-hand accounts of authorities throughout Ireland, the dangers inherent in the mobility of large numbers of fever-stricken, poor people figure prominently. A Dr Galway, writing from Mallow, observed that his locality had witnessed an increase in migrating mendicants from County Kerry, and claimed that 'every farmer's pig sty and out hovel was occupied by groups of squalid creatures, who were still seen crawling ... [and] begging alms, in all lapses of typhus fever'. At the far end of the country, in Ballyshannon, a local gentleman commented that 'fever has been kept up and widely spread by the hospitality of the people allowing lodgings to mendicants and poor travellers'. In the east, a Dr Johnston in Athy stated

---

63 Report of Dr John Cheyne, physician attached to the Dublin House of Industry, on the fever epidemic in Ireland, 1819 (NAI, CSORP, CSO/RP/1819/229).

64 William Harty, *Historic sketch of the causes, extent, and mortality of contagious fever, epidemic in Ireland in 1741, and during 1817, 1818, and 1819: together with a review of the causes, medical and statistical productive of epidemic fever in Ireland* (Dublin, [1820]), unpaginated, see tables at rear of text.

Table 3.1   **Reports from medical practitioners across Ireland, in which the spread of disease was attributed to beggars, 1817**[1]

County	Town	Date of report	Reference to beggars
Cavan	Cavan	19 September 1817	Disease spread by 'beggars'; 'beggars expelled [from the town]'
Donegal	Ballyshannon	17 September 1817	'spread by beggars'
Down	Downpatrick	3 September 1817	Outbreak 'preceded by smallpox which was introduced by vagrant beggars'
Fermanagh	Enniskillen	18 September 1817	'propagated by beggars'
Tyrone	Omagh	18 September 1817	'propagated by beggars'
Carlow	Bagnelstown	18 September 1817	'spread by mendicants'
King's County (Offaly)	Tullamore	12 September 1817	'contagion introduced by stranger beggars'
King's County	Parsonstown (Birr)	15 September 1817	'disease introduced by beggars'
Kilkenny	Durrow[2]	21 September 1817	'caused by misery of every kind – despondency, idleness, but particularly by contagion carried about by beggars from house to house'
Longford	n/a	17 September 1817	'communicated by mendicants'
Wicklow	n/a	1 September 1817	'many cases of fever were traced to strolling mendicants, who were taken in from motives of charity'
Cork	Mallow	20 September 1817	'disease spread by migrating beggars'
Galway	Loughrea	undated	'infection from poor beggars who came from Galway'
Roscommon	Elphin	12 September 1817	'contagion spread by beggars'

County	Town	Date of report	Reference to beggars
Roscommon	Roscommon	22 September 1817	'In May, disorder formidably spread by legions of beggars, who traversed the whole face of the country'.

1 'Four provincial reports by Drs Perceval and Cheyne on the state of the public health in Ireland', 1817 (NAI, CSOOP, CSO/OP474/22). While other factors, such as the poor quality of food, chronic poverty and poor lodgings, were also presented as factors determining the virulence of the epidemic, this table identifies those reports where mendicants were cited as the propagators of contagion.

2 This townland is not to be confused with the large post-town of Durrow in Queen's County (Laois).

that 'fever was brought into this neighbourhood by itinerant beggars and labourers. The inhabitants of the cabins where they lodged all took the fever'.[65] While mendicants were held to be carriers of contagion, it was only through their interaction with other people that disease could be disseminated through the population. Intercourse between the general population and beggars was strongly discouraged, a most difficult proposition given the widespread practice in rural areas of admitting wandering vagrants into one's home, where food or a place to sleep would be offered.[66] In Galway city, members of the 'lower orders' were advised to be 'particular in the admission of strange beggars to their houses', while a printed notice from 1817, for an unspecified Ulster location, advised the public: 'do not lodge Beggars, unless in an outhouse'.[67] In counties Wicklow and Wexford, the practice of giving shelter to mendicants was admonished from the altar by several priests.[68]

Fears of the introduction of disease into localities became heightened in response to the increased migration of large numbers of the mendicant

65 Report of Dr John Cheyne on the fever epidemic in Ireland, [c.1819].

66 Evidence of this practice is to be found in *First report from the select committee on the state of disease and condition of the labouring poor, in Ireland*, p. 42 (County Galway); ibid., p. 70 (Wexford town); ibid., p. 74 (Ballitore, County Kildare). In 1826, a public notice issued in Roscrea, County Tipperary advised householders: 'Don't let strolling Beggars enter your homes as they frequently carry infection from one house to another': Poster entitled 'To the public!! Advice to prevent fever', 1826 (NAI, CSORP, CSO/RP/1826/15206).

67 *Connaught Journal*, 15 Sept. 1817, quoted in Cunningham, *'A town tormented by the sea'*, p. 57; 'Printed notice giving rules to observe for the avoidance of fever', 10 Dec. 1817.

68 *First report from the select committee on the state of disease and condition of the labouring poor, in Ireland*, p. 71.

poor, escaping localised outbreaks of disease and in search of relief.
Contemporary reports invariably commented on the significant movement
of poor people during this crisis: in Limerick, it was observed that 'the whole
country appeared to be in motion', while the travel writer John Gamble
wrote of Strabane:

> Hords [sic] of wandering beggars, impelled by the cravings of hunger,
> carried the distemper from door to door; and, from their wretched
> habiliments, wafted contagion far and wide. Almost the entire mountain
> population, literally speaking, took up their beds and walked; and, with
> their diseased blankets wrapped round them, sought, in the low lands,
> the succour which charity could not give, but at the hazard of life.[69]

Systems of expulsion were enforced, thus reviving a practice which had
operated across Europe since medieval times.[70] Authorities in Vienna
expelled outsiders, while non-native vagrants in Bavaria were whipped and
confined in compulsory workhouses (with a tiered system of punishments for
repeat offenders); other authorities passed ordinances that prohibited public
begging.[71] In a number of locations in Ireland, guards were stationed at the
perimeters of the town, with strict orders to prevent mendicants entering. In
Tullamore, 'sickly itinerants' were intercepted by guards and were prevented
from entering the town, which shut down trade and other interactions with
neighbouring areas and was described as being 'thus in a state of blockade'.[72]
Similar measures were adopted in Roscommon town, while in Coleraine
public notices were issued which urged 'that all foreign Beggars should, if
possible, be put out of town'.[73] This policy of expulsion and prohibition was
praised by the *Freeman's Journal* as being as 'justifiable as that first law, or
self-preserving duty, that allows the depriving a fellow creature of life, if it
shall become indispensably necessary for the protection of our own'.[74] The
warding off of beggars was seen as a matter of self-defence, justified by
resort to natural law. An appreciation that itinerant beggars were spreading

69 Barker and Cheyne, *Account of the rise, progress, and decline of the fever epidemic in
   Ireland*, i, p. 40; John Gamble, *Views of society and manners in the north of Ireland, in a
   series of letters written in the year 1818* (London, 1819), p. 155.
70 For a consideration of what Robert Jütte has termed 'the ancient remedy of expulsion',
   see Jütte, *Poverty and deviance*, pp. 165–9.
71 Post, *Last great subsistence crisis*, pp. 88–91.
72 Barker and Cheyne, *Account of the rise, progress, and decline of the fever epidemic in
   Ireland*, i, p. 60.
73 *First report from the select committee on the state of disease and condition of the labouring
   poor, in Ireland*, p. 46; Notice regarding fever epidemic in Strabane, 18 Dec. 1817
   (PRONI, Abercorn papers, D623/A/131/4).
74 *FJ*, 10 Sept. 1817.

disease was not limited to authorities and wealthier members of society; the poor also made connections between the movement of vagrant paupers and the dissemination of contagion and responded accordingly. 'So convinced were the poor of the disease being infectious that their conduct in many places towards itinerants, and in particular itinerant beggars, from being kind and hospitable, had become stern and repulsive; they drove all beggars from their doors, charging them with being the authors of their greatest misfortunes, by spreading disease through the country'.[75]

Beggars and Shopkeepers

For the trading community in towns and cities the prevalence of hordes of mendicants threatened their businesses. Having 'frequently observed [customers] ... go to other Shops, rather than suffer such a Persecution' in 1730s Dublin city, Jonathan Swift described shopkeepers as 'the greatest Complainers' of street mendicancy.[76] The first report of the Waterford Mendicity Society complained of the doors of shops being crowded 'by persons whose clamours impeded the transaction of business, and often obliged the intending purchaser to make a precipitate retreat to some other place, where he vainly expected to experience less annoyance'.[77] An 1820s guide to Dublin recalled that just a few years previously 'whenever a well-dressed person entered a shop to purchase any thing, the door was beset by beggars, awaiting his egress'.[78] As noted in Chapter 1, a common response by shopkeepers was to provide regular alms ('allowances') to mendicants, either to be rid of the immediate nuisance or as part of an understanding that the traders' customers would not subsequently be solicited.

Traders' fears were reflected in the first two annual reports of the Dublin Mendicity Society, which carried on their title pages the Spectator's assertion of a century earlier that 'Of all men living we Merchants, who live by buying and selling ought never to encourage Beggars'.[79] The prominence given to this quote in the founding literature of the mendicity society signifies that the commercial classes were the main economic grouping that constituted the membership of the organisation, and also that this cohort of

---

75 First report from the select committee on the state of disease and condition of the labouring poor, in Ireland, p. 76.

76 [Swift], Proposal for giving badges to the beggars, p. 13.

77 First annual report, of the Association for the Suppression of Mendicity in the City of Waterford (Waterford, 1822), p. 4.

78 G.N. Wright, An historical guide to the city of Dublin, illustrated by engravings, and a plan of the city (2nd edn, London, 1825), p. 125. For nineteenth-century Oxford, see Dyson and King, '"The streets are paved with beggars"', p. 86.

79 This assertion is from The Spectator, no. 232 (26 Nov. 1711), quoted on the title pages of Report, Dublin Mendicity Society, 1818 and Second report, Dublin Mendicity Society, 1819.

merchants perceived themselves and their economic interests to be acutely vulnerable to the 'evil' of beggary. The first report of the Dublin Mendicity Society bemoaned the fact that 'the doors of carriages and shops, to the interruption of business, were beset by crowds of unfortunate and clamorous beggars, exhibiting misery and decrepitude in a variety of forms',[80] while the *Freeman's Journal*, commenting that the capital was 'already overcrowded with groupes [*sic*] of mendicants', editorialised at the commencement of the 1816–19 fever epidemic: 'one can't stop in the streets for a moment without being encircled and obtruded on by them; all the markets are dreadfully infested with beggars; and most of the shop doors are completely stopped up by them'.[81] As Jacinta Prunty has observed, 'because of the proximity of the city slums to the wealthy residential districts and the commercial heart of the city, the scandal of the famished and desperate readily spilled over to the very hall-doors and shop-fronts of respectable society, even at times of apparent "normality"'.[82] For the inhabitants of Dublin city at this time, mendicants were a ubiquitous presence on the streets where they lived, worked, shopped and worshipped.

The plight of Dublin's shopkeepers and merchants was raised with the authorities in Dublin Castle by Dr Robert Perceval of the Hardwicke Fever Hospital in December 1817, when the post-war typhus fever epidemic was raging through the city. In a letter to Chief Secretary Robert Peel, Dr Perceval stated that 'trading people must be aware of the loss they sustain by the desertion of their shops (from apprehension of infection from Beggars) and by the regulations of quarantine'.[83] Two months later, Perceval returned to the subject of the threat posed by disease-ridden mendicants to the business community, in a proposal to check the progress of contagion in the city primarily by suppressing street begging. The plan centred on, first, proposals to establish an office where beggars, once their claims of destitution were confirmed, could attend and have their clothes washed, and, secondly, a public declaration calling on the citizenry not to give alms in the street. Perceval referred to 'the interest which shopkeepers must feel in keeping their doors clear of filthy mendicants, who it is well known deter their customers from frequenting their shops'.[84] In presenting his plan to

---

80 *Report, Dublin Mendicity Society, 1818*, p. 2.

81 *FJ*, 10 Sept. 1817.

82 Prunty, *Dublin slums*, p. 201.

83 Robert Perceval to Robert Peel, 12 Dec. 1817 (NAI, CSOOP, CSO/OP474/44). The text within the brackets is contained in a hand-written footnote, inserted by Perceval into the manuscript letter.

84 'Plan for the cooperation of the health subcommittee in preventing the causes of disease & checking the progress of contagion in the city, by Robert Perceval', 19 Feb. 1818 (NAI, CSOOP, CSO/OP474/56).

Dublin Castle, Perceval was acutely aware of how sensitive the commercial classes were to the threat posed by street begging and also their power in mobilising public opinion against this practice.

By the 1830s, frustrated by the failure of the state to curtail street begging through the police, the magistrates and the House of Industry, the Dublin business community and private householders resolved to take the matter into their own hands and employed extra-legal street inspectors for the sole purpose of removing mendicants from outside their respective shops and premises. These inspectors possessed no legal powers and appear to have been enabled in their endeavours by the street beggars' ignorance of the inspectors' powerlessness. The employment of street inspectors was undertaken by merchants and traders who combined into small collectives, and the average cost to a business owner was between £4 and £5 a year.[85] The principal areas where these inspectors were deployed were Westmoreland Street, Castle Street, Dame Street, Sackville Street, College Green, Parliament Street, High Street, Christchurch Place and Wellington Quay.[86] These streets, located in either the medieval city core or the later eastern area of development, represented the largest commercial thoroughfares in the city.

Among the Dublin shopkeepers who employed extra-legal street inspectors was W. Mitchell of No. 10 Grafton Street. Mitchell, a pastry cook and confectioner, told the Poor Inquiry that he and some neighbours employed 'at our own expense, a street-inspector, who parades all day up and down on one side of the street, from Nassau-street to No. 16, a distance of about 12 or 14 doors'. For this service, which had operated for the previous two years, Mitchell paid 1s. 6d. a week, which totalled £3 18s. 0d. annually. Before he combined with his neighbours, Mitchell employed a person, 'solely at my own expense, to keep my own shop-door clear [of beggars]'. The trader's frankness regarding the extra-legal nature of the practice is striking:

> These inspectors are not constables, nor are they authorized to apprehend beggars, they are only instructed to remove beggars as much as they can from the doors of shops, and keep them from besetting carriages. This plan has operated beneficially, the beggars generally not being aware that the inspectors are not constables, and have not legal powers.[87]

---

85   *PI, Appendix C, Part II, Report upon vagrancy and mendicity in the City of Dublin*, p. 29a*. For more on this practice, see *Sixth report of the general committee of the Association of Mendicity in Dublin. For the year 1823* (Dublin, 1824), p. 21.

86   *PI, Appendix C, Part II, Report upon vagrancy and mendicity in the City of Dublin*, p. 42a*.

87   Ibid., p. 44a*.

In assessing the merits of this initiative, one must consider the context of this undertaking. The city's shopkeepers' resort to such a draconian measure is to be seen in light of the fact that no satisfactory initiative was forthcoming from the civil authorities for the suppression of mendicancy. Traders thus felt obliged to implement this unique strategy for dealing with an alarming social problem which threatened their economic survival.

These fears on the part of the commercial classes of urban areas were not confined to the capital. In a charity sermon in 1811 for the benefit of the Belfast House of Industry, which was established two years previously for the purpose of suppressing street begging, the town's inhabitants were reminded of 'the numerous groups of beggars which beset their shops' prior to the activities of the charity.[88] One week later, complaining of what he considered to be the meagre £140 raised at this charity sermon, a 'Paddy Driscol' wrote a letter to the editor of the *Belfast News-Letter*, criticising the citizens of Belfast for their alleged 'apathy'. His first targets were members of the town's business community: 'Are the shopkeepers unwilling to pay a small contribution towards preventing their shops being crowded with beggars, to the great annoyance of themselves and their customers?'[89] In Drogheda, it was observed that the most common form of begging was 'for the mendicants to go from door to door, chiefly to the shops, as these are open, and the tradesman when engaged in serving a customer will often give something to a beggar in order to be rid of his importunity'.[90] For traders, the short-term solution of giving alms superseded any consideration of the long-term impact of the pernicious practice of indiscriminate alms-giving; economic survival trumped moral principle. In late 1823, the *Connaught Journal* called for the establishment of a mendicity society in Galway by members of the city's commercial classes, 'whose shops are beset, and whose profits must be considerably diminished by the droves of beggars that haunt every part of this Town'.[91] One year later, and some months after the establishment of a mendicity society in the western city, another paper, the *Galway Weekly Advertiser*, elatedly reported: 'our doors that used to be infested by a horde of vagrants were left unmolested, and strangers could pass in and out of our shops, and make their purchases, without having their eyes offended by the squalid filth, or the ears shocked by the horrid imprecations of mendicants of the worst description'.[92] The impact in this regard of the Galway Mendicity

---

88 *BNL*, 12 Feb. 1811.

89 *BNL*, 19 Feb. 1811.

90 *PI, Appendix C, Part I*, p. 49. See also *Drogheda Journal*, 4 Sept. 1840, cited in McHugh, *Drogheda before the Famine*, p. 46 n. 30.

91 *Connaught Journal*, 6 Oct. 1823, cited in Cunningham, '*A town tormented by the sea*', p. 48.

92 *Galway Weekly Advertiser*, 13 Nov. 1824.

Society was 'immediate and palpable'.[93] This perception of shopkeepers being subjected to irrepressible waves of mendicants was conveyed by Dr John Milner Barry of the Cork House of Recovery, who claimed that 'swarms of beggars, which infested our streets … stormed every door and shop'.[94] Another Cork gentlemen described the southern city as being 'inundated with them', adding: 'They blocked up the doors of the principal shops, or attended the public conveyances at their arrival and departure, cursing or praying with equal fervour, as their application was granted or refused'.[95]

Superstitious Beliefs and the Beggar's Curse

Superstition pervaded daily life among the labouring classes in pre-Famine Ireland. The persistence into the nineteenth century of belief in fairies, magic, changelings and witches, operating outside the realms of official religion, is well recorded.[96] Beggars were among the ubiquitous characters of pre-Famine life that were frequently associated with the Christian and non-Christian supernatural. Many mendicants claimed to possess supernatural powers, and practices such as fortune-telling were practised by such individuals.[97] Legislation associating fortune-telling and palmistry with vagabondage dated back at least to the 1630s and continued into the nineteenth century.[98] Associations between wandering mendicants and the supernatural appear also in nineteenth-century literary sources. In William Carleton's 'Phelim O'Toole's courtship' a 'poor mendicant', also described as a 'boccagh', provides advice to a childless couple on a folkloric cure to their 'great affliction'.[99] The advice offered by the mendicant is to visit a particular holy well on the appropriate pattern day, kiss a 'Lucky Stone' while saying the Rosary, and circle the well nine times, before leaving behind a piece of material and then departing.[100] The prescribed method demonstrates the frequent intermixture of folk practices – such as lucky

---

93 Ibid.
94 Barry, *Report of the House of Recovery and Fever Hospital of the city of Cork, 1817*, p. 21.
95 Denis Charles O'Connor, *Seventeen years' experience of workhouse life: with suggestions for reforming the Poor Law and its administration* (Dublin, 1861), pp. 9–10.
96 W[illiam]. R. Wilde, *Irish popular superstitions* (Dublin, [1852]); S.J. Connolly, *Priests and people in pre-Famine Ireland, 1780–1845* (Dublin, 1985), pp. 100–20.
97 *PI, Appendix A*, p. 549.
98 10 & 11 Chas I, c. 4 [Ire.] (1635), cited in George Nicholls, *A history of the Irish Poor Law, in connexion with the condition of the People* (London, 1856), p. 30; William Alex Breakey, *Handbook for magistrates, clerks of petty sessions, solicitors, coroners, &c., being a comprehensive index and synopsis of the common and statute law in Ireland.* (Dublin, 1895), p. 275.
99 William Carleton, 'Phelim O'Toole's courtship' in William Carleton, *Traits and stories* (repr. 1990), pp. 191, 188.
100 Ibid., p. 191.

charms – with Christian traditions, as demonstrated by the holy well and the pattern day.

There are also numerous references in the pre-Famine period to a fear of the 'beggar's curse'. Author and Poor Law commentator James Ebenezer Bicheno, who served on the Poor Inquiry, recorded that Irish peasants believed 'that a curse will be upon him who turns a beggar from his door',[101] while Poor Law Commissioner George Nicholls asserted that 'there is a superstitious dread of bringing down the beggar's curse, and thus mendicancy is sustained in the midst of poverty'.[102] These assertions, however, require deeper consideration. First, references to belief in the 'beggar's curse' almost invariably arise in rural areas. For example, in a letter to a Dublin physician in May 1822, a County Cork clergyman expressed his opinion that many poor people gave alms to beggars to prevent some disaster falling on the household and noted that 'these abuses originate in superstition'. He continued: 'I have often known them to say when a cow has died, that was such a beggar's curse'.[103] An anonymous Anglican clergyman in the south of Ireland identified a similar practice in the mid-1820s: 'The farmers, universally, dread the curse of the beggar; and, therefore, seldom deny a few potatoes'.[104] The proliferation of these instances in rural areas and the contrasting scarcity of references to the beggar's curse in urban centres points to the wider prevalence of superstitious beliefs among rural peasant communities, yet rare examples of the existence of belief in the 'beggar's curse' in an urban setting do arise. One such instance is provided by the Dublin Mendicity Society's street inspector, George Rogers, who told the Poor Inquiry that 'many persons are induced to give from a fear of the "poor man's curse"'.[105] The same inquiry heard that servants in Carrickfergus frequently gave assistance to vagrants for fear of the beggar's curse.[106]

Secondly, the work of Niall Ó Ciosáin demonstrates that in many parishes people did not heed a beggar's curse, on the grounds that a virtuous person would not issue a curse; a beggar's prayer, on the other hand, was

---

101 J.E. Bicheno, *Ireland, and its economy; being the result of observations made in a tour through the country in the autumn of 1829* (London, 1830), p. 251.

102 Nicholls, *History of the Irish Poor Law*, p. 206.

103 'Letter from Reverend Richard Woodward, Glanworth Glebe, Fermoy, County Cork to Dr William Disney, regarding relief of local poor', 27 May 1822 (NAI, CSORP, CSO/RP/1822/441/2).

104 Anon, *The real grievance of the Irish peasantry, as immediately felt and complained of among themselves, a fruitful source of beggary and idleness, and the main support of the Rock system …* (London, 1825), p. 39.

105 *PI, Appendix C, Part II, Report upon vagrancy and mendicity in the City of Dublin*, p. 42a*.

106 *PI, Appendix A*, p. 711.

widely regarded and cherished.[107] Such viewpoints served as a means of distinguishing between 'deserving' and 'undeserving' claimants of alms. As a counterpoint to the malevolence of the 'beggar's curse', wandering mendicants also promised to say prayers for the givers of alms and this was a regular trade for some beggars. Prayers could be offered for the living or the dead, a practice frequently carried out by a 'voteen', one who swapped prayers for alms.[108] An anonymous contributor to the *Dublin Penny Journal* in 1833, possibly William Carleton, presented to his readers the character of Darby Guiry, 'the Ballyvoorny beggarman' who 'took care to leave his best benefactor beads, which if not made of the true wood of the cross, were, at least, of the same species of timber, crucifixes procured at Lough-derg'.[109] In his early published writings, William Carleton railed against the ignorance of the Catholic lower orders – his former co-religionists – whose belief in the virtue of indiscriminate alms-giving was such that 'a man who may have committed a murder overnight, will the next day endeavour to wipe away his guilt by alms given for the purpose of getting the benefit of "the poor man's prayer"'.[110] In the parish of Moore, County Roscommon, the Poor Inquiry was told by a weaver, J. McNamara, about the manner in which one local beggar carried out this transaction:

[There is] a very old man, who is called 'Forty bags'; he has been begging since he left his service, 15 years ago. His plan is to say prayers for the people of each house he comes to; he repeats them in Irish, and it generally takes him a full quarter of an hour to go through them. The woman of the house can never understand the half of what he says, and I think they are mostly his own invention; and as to the quality of them, at least they are good for him.[111]

Arriving in the town of Castleblaney, County Monaghan, John Gamble was bestowed with 'a world of blessings' in return for 'some trifling change'. He added:

Ireland is the best country in the world for an economical man to be charitable in; for he always gets the full value of his money in praises,

107 Ó Ciosáin, *Ireland in official print culture*, pp. 85–6.
108 *PI, Appendix A*, p. 486.
109 E.W., 'The beggarman's tale' in *Dublin Penny Journal*, i, no. 51 (15 June 1833), p. 406. Lough Derg (St Patrick's Purgatory) in County Donegal has since the medieval period been among the most prominent sites of penitential pilgrimage in Ireland, where St Patrick is reputed to have fastened to expel demons.
110 Carleton, 'Tubber derg', p. 386.
111 *PI, Appendix A*, p. 521.

to say nothing of the prayers put up for his future happiness: whether or no[t] the people have more religion in the heart, they certainly have more on the tongue, than any other people in the universe.[112]

Physician Denis Charles O'Connor, writing in 1861, recalled the regular inflow of beggars offering prayers two decades previously in Cork city. 'Another class, chiefly from the country, walked from door to door in the outskirts, giving prayers in return for potatoes, both parties thinking they had got a fair equivalent for what was given'.[113] The giving of alms in return for prayers was seen by many as a truly equitable transaction. In this exchange, the beggar's prayer was an intangible commodity available for purchase, and one which was highly valued.

'Boccoughs'

Just as the topic of beggars' curses and prayers served as a means of distinguishing between 'deserving' and 'undeserving' claimants of alms at a popular level, the figure of the 'boccough' can also be considered in this light. Beggars known as 'boccoughs' or 'bacachs' represented the archetypal class of imposters, who resorted to fraud and intimidation to solicit alms from the public. Boccoughs, also known as 'fair beggars' or 'trading beggars', were professional mendicants.[114] Originally referring to a crippled beggar (*bac* being the Irish word for lame), the term boccough had evolved by the 1830s to carry connotations of dishonesty and imposture. One account presented boccoughs as belonging to a 'mysterious brotherhood' and a 'Bacach tribe', with its own language, marriage customs and initiation practices, and which was unchristian, insular and somewhat organised.[115] According to the 1851 census, the third largest category of occupation among the 'lame and decrepit' in Ireland, after labourers and servants, were mendicants.[116] The prominence of the lame poor among mendicants can also be seen in a sample study of physical disabilities among beggars in early modern Europe, which demonstrates that the lame constituted the largest category among identifiable cases.[117] In Ireland, the term boccough was

---

112 Gamble, *Sketches of history, politics, and manners*, pp. 165–6.
113 O'Connor, *Seventeen years' experience of workhouse life*, p. 10.
114 Geary, "'The whole country was in motion'", p. 123.
115 William Hackett, 'The Irish bacach, or professional beggar, viewed archaeologically' in *Ulster Journal of Archaeology*, 1st series, ix (1861–2), pp. 262, 265.
116 *The census of Ireland for the year 1851. Part III. Report on the status of disease*, p. 68, H.C. 1854 [C 1765], lviii, 72. The census report also lists others' versions of the term, such as *bacach* or *losg* denoting lameness; *bacaighe* meaning a hindrance; *clarineach* meaning 'going on stools', ibid., pp. 69, 113.
117 Jütte, *Poverty and deviance*, p. 25.

applied 'to sturdy, wandering beggars who feigned disease or deformity or who mutilated or impregnated their children in order to excite compassion', Geary has observed.[118] The use of this term seems to have been limited to western Ireland and by far the majority of references contained in the Poor Inquiry reports were by individuals from counties Roscommon, Sligo and predominantly Clare.[119] The popularity of this categorisation of a certain class of beggar extended into south Munster and was evident in County Cork in the 1830s, where the Poor Inquiry's assistant commissioners noted that 'there was a sort of beggars called "boccoughs", who used to make themselves appear lame, but there are very few of them now'.[120] In Clonakilty, County Cork, the inquiry officials heard that 'boccoughs, who are or were guilty of various knavish tricks ... are becoming comparatively scarce, except at fairs ... they constitute quite a distinct class of mendicants'.[121] Rev. Patrick Mullins, a Catholic priest in Kilchreest parish in County Galway, told the Poor Inquiry that 'they frequently assume the appearance of being crippled or maimed for the purpose of exciting pity; none do it but the fair beggars'.[122]

Occasional references to the boccough were recorded in urban centres. The assistant commissioners who carried out examinations in St Finbar's parish in Cork city noted the former prevalence of boccoughs who made 'a regular trade of begging', 'attended fairs and weddings, where they got a great deal of money, but were sometimes detected in their false sores and lamenesses'.[123] Another use of the term outside the rural, western region is the recollection of writer Anna Maria Hall (1800–81) of witnessing a crowd of beggars surrounding her carriage upon entering Wexford town, wherein she makes reference to 'a *bocher*, or lame man [who] succeeded in clearing a space that he might give my honour a dance'.[124] The boccough also appeared in the travel writings of a mid-century French writer, who noted the similarity between this Irish figure and the character Edie Ochiltree in Walter Scott's *The antiquary*.[125]

The image of the boccough was not unique to Ireland but must be seen in an international context. 'As a representation, the boccough shares many aspects of the classic image of the undeserving poor in early modern

---

118 Geary, '"The whole country was in motion"', p. 123.
119 *PI, Appendix A*, pp. 510, 527, 608, 618, 621, 636. See also Ó Ciosáin, 'Boccoughs and God's poor', p. 95.
120 *PI, Appendix A*, p. 652.
121 Ibid., p. 655.
122 Ibid., p. 478.
123 Ibid., p. 671.
124 Hall, *Tales of Irish life and character*, p. 92.
125 Amédee Pichot, *L'Irlande et Le Pays de Galles, esquisses de voyages, d'économie politique, d'histoire, de biographie, de littérature, etc., etc., etc.* (2 vols, Paris, 1850), i, pp. 379–81.

Europe'.[126] In the works of novelists such as Carleton and the Banim Brothers, travel writers such as Thomas Croften Croker and ethnographers such as John Windele, boccoughs make frequent appearances but are rarely quoted directly. Irish people had voluminous information about the boccoughs but, seemingly, very few people had ever met one. Niall Ó Ciosáin has suggested that by the mid-nineteenth century the boccough constituted 'very much a figure of speech', a trope created and utilised, in the case of folklorists, to salvage some aspect of that disappearing society of pre-Famine Ireland. Furthermore, the image of the boccough validated prevailing notions of charity and reciprocity among the Irish lower classes which complicated distinctions between the 'deserving' and 'undeserving' poor. 'Instead of stigmatizing informal charity, however, this image functions within the evidence as a reinforcement of the virtue of almsgiving. There were certainly beggars, organized and fraudulent, to whom one should under no circumstances give anything, but they were always somewhere else'.[127]

Conclusion

There is no doubting the complex nature of begging and alms-giving in pre-Famine Ireland. Attitudes towards begging and beggars varied greatly, and these perceptions were subject to variation, depending on wider social and economic conditions. Most givers of alms to mendicants were poor, but during the typhus fever epidemic of 1816–19, many among the labouring classes refused to provide lodgings to itinerant beggars for fear of contracting disease. Beggars' curses and prayers were part of the vocabulary of rural Ireland and these oral interactions were used by the poor as a means of judging who was or was not deserving of alms. The figure of the boccough also served as a lightning rod for judgements of the undeserving poor, yet by the 1830s appears to have evolved into a cultural trope, a category of pauper rarely if ever seen, yet constantly present in popular culture.

Mendicants exerted a ubiquitous and very visible presence in pre-Famine Irish society: they were inevitable (and at times indispensable) figures within travel narratives and were also useful props in contemporary paintings of both urban and rural locations. Some commentators spoke of the natural right of those in distress publicly to solicit alms and framed this practice as a necessary survival strategy in a Christian land; others developed this sentiment and emphasised the fundamental inviolability of the relationship between the giver and receiver of alms, a cherished exchange with defined

126 Ó Ciosáin, *Ireland in official print culture*, p. 95.
127 Ibid., p. 107.

roles and behaviours, and one which was worth preserving in the face of civic anti-begging initiatives. Yet, it is clear that for many in this society beggars posed a real threat: they spread disease throughout the country, aggravated at times of crisis when mobility among this class of persons increased, and they intimidated customers away from the doors of shopkeepers and merchants. Trading communities perceived themselves to be acutely vulnerable to this threat and resorted to various initiatives to mitigate the problem, whether through employing street inspectors, as in Dublin, or the establishment of mendicity societies, as evinced throughout the country (and indeed western Europe and the Atlantic world). Having so far focused on defining, on the measurement and on the disparate perceptions of the issue of mendicancy in pre-Famine Ireland, attention will now turn to the responses to this social phenomenon from civil parishes, charities and the main churches and religious societies.

II Responses I: Cross-Denominational Approaches

4

Civil Parishes' Responses to Begging

Introduction

In his 1737 tract on the need to badge 'foreign beggars' in Dublin city, Jonathan Swift betrayed a surprising ignorance of the role of Irish parishes in assisting the poor and curtailing mendicancy. Swift incorrectly asserted that in Ireland, as in England, 'every Parish is [legally] bound to maintain its own Poor'.[1] His mistake lay in the fact that whereas in England Elizabethan Poor Laws had identified the parish as the institutional driving force for the implementation of the statutory Poor Law system, one in which the poor were conferred with an entitlement to support from their native parish, Irish parishes possessed no such significance. While a mid-seventeenth-century act bestowed powers on a Dublin parish to levy a rate to support a localised poor scheme, Irish parishes on a nationwide level were devoid of any critical legal standing in this respect. His inaccuracy notwithstanding, Swift's intervention in the ongoing Poor Law debates of the 1720s and 1730s reflects the reality that the parish stood at the centre of corporate efforts to relieve 'deserving' distress and punish 'undeserving' idleness.

An assembly of male householders in a given parish, which met at least once a year – typically Easter Monday or Tuesday – to levy a local rate (cess) on parishioners to fund the provision of ecclesiastical and civil services within the parish, the vestry was, from the mid-seventeenth century, a unit of local government, overseeing road maintenance, fire-fighting, public lighting and street cleaning. The extent to which the vestry exerted those civil functions varied from place to place, with vestries in Ulster and in large urban centres being most active as it was in these locations that there was a greater concentration of members of the Established Church.[2] Many

---

1 [Swift], *Proposal for giving badges to the beggars*, p. 6.
2 The most comprehensive analysis of the evolving functions of Irish parishes remains Rowena Dudley, 'Dublin parishes 1660–1729: the Church of Ireland parishes and their

corporate bodies had their roles to play in responding to beggary and poverty: municipal authorities, the central state, the charitable sector and the various churches and religious societies. Parish vestries constitute a particularly interesting case, not only given their relative historiographical neglect, at least regarding their nineteenth-century incarnations, but also because of the technical complexities inherent in the nature of their association. Parish vestries exerted ecclesiastical functions according to their status within the Established Church. But, they also carried out civil duties, such as suppressing street begging and relieving poverty, the operation of which were approved at meetings open to parishioners of all denominations. These initiatives, such as the badging of mendicants and the employment of parochial officers of health to remove 'nuisances' and filth-ridden beggars, may be seen, then, not as the institutional responses of the Church of Ireland to social questions such as poverty and beggary but as the responses of the wider civil community.

'It Is a Temporal Matter': Ecclesiastical and Civil Parish Vestries

At the 1838 Easter meeting of the St Paul's select parish vestry in Dublin city, a Catholic parishioner, Mr Brenan, demanded to be allowed to speak on the matter of the election of churchwardens. Brenan acknowledged that, as a Roman Catholic, he was not entitled to vote at the select vestry, but wished, at the very least, for his suggestion – that a 'liberal Protestant' named Mr Atkinson be nominated – to be heard. Brenan, who served the parish as an officer of health, was criticised by Anglican parishioners, being told that they did not disturb proceedings at the Catholic chapel: 'You are only allowed to attend here as a matter of courtesy, and you cannot interfere in the proceedings'. To this, Brenan replied: 'You say you never interfered with us in our chapels. I say we never interfered with you in your churches. I think a vestry meeting is a different thing altogether. It is a temporal matter. We are in the majority of the ratepayers of the parish, and we have a right to interfere'. The newspaper report of this incident noted that upon the conclusion of this initial vestry meeting, a second meeting commenced, 'which was open to all the inhabitants of the parish'.[3]

This instance points to an important feature of the structure of parish vestries in nineteenth-century Ireland, arising from the complex coexistence

---

role in the civic administration of the city' (PhD thesis, 2 vols, University of Dublin, 1995). See also Donald Harman Akenson, *The Church of Ireland: ecclesiastical reform and revolution, 1800–1885* (New Haven, CT and London, 1971), pp. 52–5; Maighréad Ní Mhurchadha, 'Introduction' in Maighréad Ní Mhurchadha (ed.), *The vestry records of the united parishes of Finglas, St Margaret's, Artane and the Ward, 1657–1758* (Dublin, 2007), pp. 18–21.

3   *FJ*, 17 Apr. 1838. See also Bob Cullen, *Thomas L. Synnott: the career of a Dublin Catholic 1830–1870* (Dublin, 1997), pp. 18–21.

of ecclesiastical and civil parishes from the late medieval/early modern period. The above account from the St Paul's parish vestry demonstrates the existence of select and general vestries in nineteenth-century Irish parishes and the evolving role of these bodies within their own local communities. It also reveals how interdenominational tensions, particularly in areas where Protestants comprised a relatively large proportion of the population, such as in urban centres, remained close to the surface at this level of local government.[4] The language used at the St Paul's vestry by those quoted above draws on notions of communal allegiances and rivalries: Catholic and Protestant contributors used the group terms 'you' and 'your' (in the plural sense), as well as 'we', 'us' and 'our'. This example, reflective of wider trends, supports Raymond Gillespie's assertion that the 'wider scope of its civil functions ensured that the parish formed one of the key building blocks of local community identity'.[5]

Under an act of 1726,[6] reasserted by an 1826 statute,[7] Roman Catholics were allowed to attend vestry meetings but could not vote on church-related matters, such as 'providing Things necessary for the Celebration of Divine Service', election of churchwardens, setting the salary of the parish clerk or sexton, or any expenses for the repair of the church building.[8] An act of 1774 removed dissenters' right to vote at vestry,[9] which was the cause of great grievance and subsequent protest by Irish Presbyterians.[10] Petitions were sent to parliament in late 1775, in the main by Ulster Presbyterians, and the act was subsequently repealed the following year.[11] As these legal

---

4 John Crawford, *The Church of Ireland in Victorian Dublin* (Dublin, 2005), pp. 151–76. A similar instance was reported in *Constitution; or Cork Advertiser*, 13 Apr. 1830.
5 Raymond Gillespie, 'Introduction' in Raymond Gillespie (ed.), *The vestry records of the parishes of St Catherine and St James, Dublin, 1657–1692* (Dublin, 2004), p. 9.
6 12 Geo. I, c. 9 [Ire.] (8 Mar. 1726).
7 7 Geo. IV, c. 72 (31 May 1826).
8 7 Geo. IV, c. 72, s. 2.
9 13 & 14 Geo. III, c. 10 [Ire.] (session 1773–74) (4 May 1774). It stipulated (s. 1) that at vestry meetings, 'it shall and may be lawful for the Parishioners thus assembled, that are of the Communion of the Church of Ireland by Lawe established, or the major Part of them, to vote for, and assess on the Parishioners at large, of each Parish-Union and Chappelry respectively, such Sum and Sums of Money yearly, as to them shall seem necessary and proper for the Repairs and Preservation of the Church or Chappel respectively belonging to such Parish, Union, or Chappelry'.
10 Clarke H. Irwin, *A history of Presbyterianism in Dublin and the south and west of Ireland* (London, 1890), p. 72. I am grateful to Prof. David Hayton for bringing this matter to my attention.
11 Transcripts of Dissenters' petitions, 1775 (PRONI, Groves manuscripts, T808/15307), available at PRONI website https://www.nidirect.gov.uk/information-and-services/public-record-office-northern-ireland-proni-search-archives-online (accessed 1 June 2018); Extract from Dissenters' petitions, Dunmurry parish, County Antrim 1775–6 (PRONI, Census return and testamentary documents, T715/9); *The journals of the*

provisions lent themselves to disorderly and contentious meetings, the usual protocol in many parishes was for the holding of two vestry meetings: the select vestry and the general vestry. First, the select vestry assembled for its annual Easter meeting, for the election of two churchwardens (the most important parochial offices and almost invariably confined to Anglicans) and the confirmation of parish rates to fund ecclesiastical services for the coming year; votes on these matters were confined to members of the Church of Ireland. Upon the conclusion of the select vestry meeting, a second, 'general' vestry commenced, at which parochial ratepayers of all denominations could attend and vote on secular matters affecting inhabitants of the parish.[12] The general vestry was oftentimes held immediately after the conclusion of the select meeting but was also known to have taken place a number of days or weeks after the first meeting. For example, the select vestry held in St Bride's (Bridget's) parish in Dublin in April 1830 was one at which there were 'Roman Catholics present, but excluded from voting on this day'; the assessments on ratepaying parishioners on that day were limited to the celebration of Divine Service, and the maintenance and repair of the church building. More than two weeks later, the general vestry – 'Roman Catholics present, and entitled to vote at this vestry' – was held.[13] In the Dublin parish of St Andrew's, Catholics were entitled to vote on expenditure on 'deserted children', 'medicines for the poor of the parish' and 'coffins for the poor', but were restricted from voting for 'Bread and wine for the Communion' and a salary for the organist.[14] Returns for parishes in Cork city reveal similar distinctions between the separate vestries for members of the Church of Ireland congregation, and those for the entire community. At Easter 1830, the 'First or Protestant Vestry' of St Nicholas's parish made assessments on parishioners for items of expenditure such as salaries for the sexton and sextoness, 'bread and wine', 'bell-ringing', 'church linen' and 'candles for lighting the church'. At the 'Second or General Vestry' the items of expenditure included the fire-engine keeper's salary, 'coffins for the poor who are unable to provide coffins', 'support of foundlings' and a

---

House of Commons of the Kingdom of Ireland (19 vols, Dublin, 1796–1800), ix, pp. 176–7, 179, 181, 183–5; W.H. Crawford and B. Trainor (eds), *Aspects of Irish social history* (Belfast, 1969), pp. 156–65. The amending act was 15 & 16 Geo. III, c. 14 [Ire.] (7 Mar. 1776).

12 Raymond Gillespie has suggested the existence of select vestries in Dublin parishes as early as the seventeenth century: Raymond Gillespie (ed.), *The vestry records of the parish of St John the Evangelist, Dublin 1595–1658* (Dublin, 2002), p. 12.

13 *Dublin vestries. Returns of the several sums of money assessed in the several parishes in the city of Dublin, by vestries holden during Easter week, in the year 1830 ...* p. 5, H.C. 1830 (523), xxxi, 303.

14 Ibid., p. 2.

'parish nurse'.[15] A fascinating feature of the St Nicholas's return is that the clerk John Coyle received two separate salaries from the parish: a salary of £20 for his role as 'parish clerk' provided through the select vestry, and a salary of £15 as 'vestry clerk' as approved by the general vestry, suggesting a strict distinction in the ecclesiastical and civil functions of the clerk's role.[16] There were regional variations in the efficacy in how parish vestries carried out their civil functions, with the most active vestries being located in the north-east and east, especially in towns and cities; David Dickson has suggested that an Anglican community constituting a critical minimum of 15 per cent to 20 per cent of the local population was required for a parish to carry out its civil functions effectively, while Oliver MacDonagh portrayed Irish parishes as being largely unable to operate self-sufficiently, in contrast to English parishes, owing to a lack of manpower and resources.[17] In the north-east, Presbyterians played a greater role in the management of (civil) parish life; it was observed in Bangor, County Down that the 'Body of the Inhabitants of the Parish are Dissenters from the Established Church, and are mostly of the Church of Scotland, who form the great Majority at all Vestries'.[18] The Presbyterian system of kirk sessions also operated alongside parish vestries, exerting ecclesiastical, social and philanthropic functions, and deploying similar nomenclature, with kirk sessions occasionally referred to in congregational records as vestries.[19]

The operation of the parish at this level of local government was linked to the fact that from the early modern period the Anglican church building acted not only as an ecclesiastical space, for worship and prayer, but as a civil space, open to parishioners of all denominations. In some Church of Ireland churches since the sixteenth century, leases and contracts were drawn up in the porch.[20] Control of the vestry, however, remained in the hands of

---

15 *Cork vestries. Returns of the several sums of money assessed in the several parishes in the city of Cork, by the vestries holden during Easter week, in the year 1830 ...* p. 4, H.C. 1830 (525), xxxi, 296. See also, for St Peter's parish, ibid., pp. 6–7 and for St Finbar's (also Fin Barre's) parish Easter vestry in Cork city, see *Constitution; or Cork Advertiser*, 15 Apr. 1830.

16 *Cork vestries, 1830*, p. 4.

17 Dickson, 'In search of the old Irish Poor Law', p. 157; Oliver MacDonagh, *Ireland: the Union and its aftermath* (rev. edn, London, 1977), pp. 34–5.

18 *Ireland. An account of all sums of money levied in the several parishes of Ireland, by authority of vestry... Part I* (n.p., [c.1824]), p. 340, consulted at NLI (Ref. Ir274108i1).

19 Mary's Abbey vestry (session) book (Abbey Presbyterian Church, Mary's Abbey congregation records, books no. 9 and 14).

20 See, for instance, Raymond Gillespie, 'The coming of reform, 1500–58' in Kenneth Milne (ed.), *Christ Church Cathedral, Dublin: a history* (Dublin, 2000), p. 159; 'Will of Richard Lloyd, 1820' in Eilish Ellis and P. Beryl Eustace (eds), *Registry of deeds, Dublin: abstracts of wills* (3 vols, IMC, Dublin, 1984), vol. 3, *1785–1832*, p. 337. For

the Anglican members, mainly through the prohibition on Catholics and Dissenters to fill influential vestry offices, notably that of churchwarden. Vestry meetings served as civil forums, where parishioners – regardless of religion – could engage in discussion and debate; they were public assemblies, open to all parishioners (and to members of the press) and, in John Crawford's words, 'proved something of a forum for the expression of grievances'.[21] Heightened tensions among parishioners, especially in 1830s and 1840s Dublin, occasionally resulted in riot and affray breaking out at Easter vestry meetings, requiring the intervention of the police.[22] Of course, such incidents were the exception.

What is significant about these bodies and the manner in which they assembled is that when parish vestries in pre-Famine Ireland debated and voted on matters pertaining to the social conditions of the geographical parish (such as the support of foundlings, the provision of coffins for the poor and, most relevant to this study, the management of mendicancy), this was carried out in a cross-denominational forum. Protestants, Catholics and Dissenters could contribute to the discussion and all were entitled to vote on such measures.[23] Furthermore, the funding of these initiatives was generated through the applotment of a parish cess on all ratepaying parishioners – Anglicans and non-Anglicans alike. (The assessment of non-Anglicans for expenditure singular to the Church of Ireland community bred much resentment before being prohibited under the 1833 Church Temporalities Act.)[24] Therefore, the actions of parishes in responding to the threat posed by mendicancy – curtailing the movements of 'strange' beggars, badging local mendicants and employing officers tasked with warding off or detaining idlers – were not those of the Church of Ireland ecclesiastical congregation but, rather, the responses of a wider community (regardless of confessional allegiance) to fluctuations in the level of beggary in the locality.

Social Functions
In addition to its ecclesiastical and wider civil functions, the parish vestry acted as a welfare body which distributed alms to the poor, most commonly

evidence of this practice in early modern England, see William Brown (ed.), *Yorkshire Deeds*, Yorkshire Archaeological Society Record Series (10 vols, n.p., 1922), iii, p. 26.

21 Crawford, *The Church of Ireland in Victorian Dublin*, p. 153.

22 See, for instance, the vestry meetings in St Paul's parish, Dublin: *FJ*, 2 Apr.1839; St Peter's parish, Dublin: *FJ*, 22 Apr. 1862, 7 Apr. 1863. Also Crawford, *The Church of Ireland in Victorian Dublin*, pp. 153–4, 163–8.

23 Maighréad Ní Mhurchadha, 'Introduction' in Maighréad Ní Mhurchadha (ed.), *The vestry records of the united parishes of Finglas, St Margaret's, Artane and the Ward, 1657–1758* (Dublin, 2007), pp. 12–13.

24 3 & 4 Will. IV, c. 37, s. 73 (14 Aug. 1833); [John Newport], *A slight peep into the Church vestry system in Ireland* (London, [c.1825]).

in the form of money, food, fuel and clothes. Some parishes established and maintained an alms house for those paupers entered on its poor list,[25] while coffins were regularly provided for the local poor.[26] Relief, however, was not distributed on an unqualified basis, and in adherence to the traditional distinctions between the meritorious and unworthy poor parishes limited relief to selected groups, usually the local and 'deserving' poor.[27] Writing of eighteenth-century Ireland, Rowena Dudley has commented that relief was given to 'strange' beggars at times, 'but with the intention of encouraging the beneficiary to leave the parish'.[28] According to Toby Barnard, 'there was a universal reluctance to take responsibility for strangers, unless to return them to their places of origin or – in extreme cases – to bury them at the public charge'.[29] The welfare of the local poor was paramount. While a parish-based Poor Law had operated in England and Wales since 1601,[30] Ireland remained without a statutory provision until the Poor Law Act of 1838. Therefore, when parish vestries undertook the relief of the poor in their locality, this was done without statutory authority and at the discretion of the parish officers. An exception to this was the inclusion of a clause in an act of 1665 empowering the churchwardens of St Andrew's parish in Dublin to assess parishioners 'for the relief of the poor'.[31] In some instances, parishes co-operated with local urban corporations to oversee measures for suppressing mendicancy, such as systemised badging, the management of bequests, care of orphans and confinement of vagrants.[32]

---

25 St Peter's parish, Drogheda, vestry minute book, 28 Sept. 1772 (RCBL, St Peter's parish, Drogheda, vestry minute books, P 854.5.1); St Paul's parish, Cork, vestry minute book, 19 Oct. 1818 (RCBL, St Paul's parish, Cork, vestry minute books, P 349.5.1); St Catherine's parish, Dublin, vestry minute book, 27 Feb. 1805 (RCBL, St Catherine's parish, Dublin, vestry minute books, P 117.5.5).

26 Lisburn parish, County Antrim, vestry minute book, 5 Apr. 1779 (PRONI, Lisburn parish, County Antrim, vestry minute books, MIC1/4, microfilm); St Paul's parish, Cork, vestry minute book, 24 Mar. 1818; St Thomas's parish, Dublin, vestry minute book, 8 Apr. 1825 (RCBL, St Thomas's parish, Dublin, vestry minute books, P 80.5.2); Naas parish, County Kildare, vestry minute book, 24 Apr. 1832 (RCBL, Naas parish, County Kildare, vestry minute books, P 487.5.1).

27 Toby Barnard, *A new anatomy of Ireland: the Irish protestants, 1649–1770* (New Haven, CT and London, 2003), p. 287.

28 Dudley, 'The Dublin parishes and the poor', p. 87.

29 Toby Barnard, *The kingdom of Ireland, 1641–1760* (Basingstoke, 2004), p. 138.

30 John Broad, 'Parish economies of welfare, 1650–1834' in *Historical Journal*, xliv, no. 4 (1999), pp. 985–1006.

31 For a discussion of this act (17 & 18 Chas. II, c. 7 [Ire.]), see Dudley, 'The Dublin parishes and the poor', pp. 81–4.

32 Dickson, 'In search of the old Irish Poor Law', p. 150; Raymond Gillespie, 'Making Belfast, 1600–1750' in S.J. Connolly (ed.), *Belfast 400: people, place and history* (Liverpool, 2012), pp. 140–2.

Parish Vestries and the Badging of Beggars

The need visibly to identify those deemed to be worthy of alms was always stressed and many parishes distributed begging badges to 'deserving' cases among their own poor. Badges were signs of authentication. As beggary was long associated with imposture and fraud, such legitimatisation was a means to, first, discourage the fraudulent pleas of the sturdy beggar, secondly, protect the 'honest', 'deserving' and local mendicant in his pursuit of alms, and, thirdly, prevent the provider of charity from unknowingly misdirecting his benevolence. Badges were typically made from tin, copper and pewter, and were attached to the beggar's garments in such a way as to be clearly visible to others. These licences to beg were issued by the local minister and the churchwardens. The practice of badging the local parochial poor dated back, in Ireland, at least to 1634, when the parish of St John the Evangelist in Dublin licensed its beggars.[33] The enthusiasm for badging continued throughout the seventeenth century and into the eighteenth, with fluctuations in accordance with wider economic and social conditions.[34] During the 1700s, there is evidence of parochially organised badging, for example, in Dublin city,[35] Cork city,[36] Kells, County Meath, Ardee, County Louth and across Ulster.[37] A longer tradition of licensing the 'deserving' poor through badging had existed in many parts of Europe since the medieval period, although on the continent secular authorities largely exerted these powers.[38] English parishes oversaw badging regimes, operating in some locations since at least the early sixteenth century, but becoming increasingly popular on foot of the 1697 act for badging the poor; these powers were repealed by

---

33 Gillespie, *The vestry records of the parish of St John the Evangelist, Dublin*, p. 94. See also ibid., p. 167.

34 Seaby and Paterson, 'Ulster beggars' badges', p. 96; W.J.R. Wallace (ed.), *The vestry records of the parishes of St Bride, St Michael le Pole and St Stephen, Dublin, 1662–1742* (Dublin, 2011), pp. 98–9; Raymond Gillespie, 'Rev. Dr John Yarner's notebook: religion in Restoration Dublin' in *Archivium Hibernicum*, lii (1998), p. 30.

35 Barnard, *A new anatomy of Ireland*, p. 287; S.C. Hughes, *The church of S. Werburgh, Dublin* (Dublin, 1889), p. 44.

36 Dudley, 'The Dublin parish, 1660–1730', p. 293; St Finbar's parish, Cork, vestry minute book, 15 May 1773 (RCBL, St Finbar's parish, Cork, vestry minute books, P 497.5.1).

37 'Extract from vestry minute book of the parish of Inver [Larne], County Antrim' in Crawford and Trainor, *Aspects of Irish social history*, p. 132; Seaby and Paterson, 'Ulster beggars' badges', pp. 99, 101–6; Myrtle Hill, 'Expressions of faith: Protestantism in nineteenth-century Tyrone' in Charles Dillon and Henry A. Jeffries (eds), *Tyrone: history and society* (Dublin, 2000), p. 639; Ardtrea parish, County Tyrone, vestry minute book, 26 May 1729 (PRONI, Ardtrea parish, County Tyrone, vestry minute books, MIC1/319/1, microfilm); ibid., 7 May 1784.

38 Cavallo, *Charity and power*, pp. 25–6.

statue in 1810.[39] Badging was complemented by the provision of blue gowns for parochial pensioners in Scottish parishes in the seventeenth and early eighteenth centuries, with both forms of visual discrimination identifying the wearers as legitimate objects of charity.[40]

Badging in the Nineteenth Century

The practice of badging beggars appears to have declined in Ireland in the late eighteenth century but was retained in some areas into the nineteenth. Badging was most prevalent at times of acute crisis, as represented in Seaby and Paterson's listing of recordings of the badging of beggars by Ulster parishes, wherein badges were most commonly issued during famines and epidemics, such as the early 1740s, the early 1770s, 1799–1801, 1818–19 and the early 1820s.[41] Steve Hindle's extensive work with English parish records similarly concludes that badging was most stringently enforced when ratepayers felt most burdened, especially at times of high food prices.[42] In pre-Famine Ireland, parochial revival of badging was most noticeable during the economic downturn which followed the end of the Napoleonic Wars. In Ballymoney, County Antrim in 1817, the sum of 10s. was spent by the vestry on 'Printing Handbills relating to Beggars', while the following year parochial expenditure included £1 for 'printing Lists of badged and other Poor'.[43] In the same county, in Dunluce parish, £1 6s. 8d. was expended on 'Badges for the Poor of this Parish' in 1817.[44] The post-war upsurge in parochial badging was evident throughout Ireland. In 1818, the vestry of St Canice's parish in Kilkenny city met to ascertain 'the number of native poor to be Badged in the parish', while two years later the sum of £2 5s. was applotted for 'Badges for the poor of the Town' in St Nicholas' parish in Galway city.[45] Smaller town parishes also found it necessary to reinforce this

39 Steve Hindle, *On the parish? The micro-politics of poor relief in rural England* c.*1550–1750* (Oxford, 2004), pp. 434–43; Steve Hindle, 'Dependency, shame and belonging: badging the deserving poor, *c.*1550–1750' in *Cultural and Social History*, i, no. 1 (2004), pp. 6–35.

40 Rosalind Mitchison, *The Old Poor Law in Scotland: the experience of poverty, 1574–1845* (Edinburgh, 2000), p. 98.

41 Seaby and Paterson, 'Ulster beggars' badges', pp. 101–6. This is also reflected in Edward Dupré Atkinson, *An Ulster parish: being a history of Donaghcloney (Waringstown)* (Dublin, 1898), pp. 93–4.

42 Hindle, *On the parish*, p. 443.

43 *Ireland. An account of all sums of money levied in the several parishes*, p. 354.

44 Ibid., p. 377.

45 St Canice's parish, Kilkenny vestry minute book, 26 Oct. 1818 (RCBL, St Canice's parish, Kilkenny vestry minute books, P 622.5.1); St Nicholas's parish, Galway, vestry minute book, 2 May 1820 (RCBL, St Nicholas's parish, Galway, vestry minute books, P 519.5.1). See also St Mary's parish, Kilkenny vestry minute book, 26 Oct. 1818 (RCBL, St Mary's parish, Kilkenny, vestry minute books, P 792.5.2). The provision of tin badges was approved by the Mayor of Galway in 1817 'for the use of the poor of

practice. In 1815, the Mullingar vestry resolved that the town was 'infested with Sturdy Beggars from other parishes, Countys and even provinces, to the great annoyance of the publick and injury to the real objects of Charity in the parish', so 'in order to remove these inconveniences, the poor and meritorious objects of Charity belonging to the parish shall be badged and licensed to beg'.[46]

An account of the licensing of the poor persisting in a rural area in the early nineteenth century is provided in the writings of physician Lombe Atthill (1827–1910), whose posthumously published autobiography presents a medical practitioner's retrospective but first-hand insight into pre-Famine Ireland. Atthill recorded that his father, a Church of Ireland rector in Doncavey parish in north-western Fermanagh, 'had to issue a kind of ticket, which he distributed to those who were supposed to reside inside the bounds of his parish. They were supposed not to be relieved at his house without producing this'. The purpose of this ticketing system was to police the 'regular trade' of mendicancy, at a time when beggars were 'met on every road and seen at every door'.[47] The vestry minute book for the parish supports Atthill's account, with the vestry resolving in February 1801 'that the poor of the foresaid parish shall be forthwith badged, and that no person shall be allowed to receive a badge except such as shall produce two respectable parishioners to vouch for them upon oath'.[48]

The issuing of parish badges in Dublin and Belfast had declined by the early nineteenth century, most probably due to the opening of large poorhouses in these two urban centres – the House of Industry in Dublin (opened 1773) and the Belfast Charitable Society's Poor House (1774). These two institutions were independently established, yet they mirrored each other's *raison d'être* and manner of operating: they were both designed for the reception of the mendicant poor and a crucial part of the localised system of dealing with mendicancy was the issuing of badges to local 'deserving' beggars. With these two large bodies providing begging badges, local parishes were relieved of the burden of overseeing their own systems of licensing the mendicant poor. Upon its opening, the Belfast

the town and county of the town alone … as strangers will be exempted': *FJ*, 29 Sept. 1817. Badges were also issued in Tuam in 1818: W.J.V. Comerford, 'Some notes on the borough of Tuam and its records, 1817–1822' in *Journal of the Galway Archaeological and Historical Society*, xv, no. 3 (1931), p. 110.

46 Mullingar parish vestry minute book, 15 Nov. 1815 (RCBL, Mullingar parish vestry minute books, P 336.5.1).

47 Lombe Atthill, *Recollections of an Irish doctor* (1911; repr. Whitegate, 2007), p. 22.

48 'Notes on the old minute book of the vestry of Doncavey parish church, edited by Wilson Guy of Fintona in the year 1932', p. 33 (PRONI, Fintona papers, D1048/4). Atthill's father is identified as the parish rector, ibid., pp. 30, 31, 33.

poor house issued 'Badges and Licences to Beg for a limited time ... to the Beggars with Children, and to the Infirm Husband or Wife'.[49] The institution's zeal for the provision of badges fluctuated according to wider economic and social conditions, and the appetite among the town's citizenry for relieving mendicants, with the badging system being withdrawn and revived at various points in the poor house's history.[50] The governors of the Dublin House of Industry were empowered to issue begging badges and licences to designated mendicants, which served 'to distinguish real Objects of Charity from Vagrants and sturdy Beggars' and which were seen as the 'legal Credentials of their [the beggars'] Poverty and Inability'.[51] Upon its opening, the House of Industry issued 1,800 such badges to the city's mendicants.[52] A total of twelve Houses of Industry were established across Ireland under the 1772 act (excluding the Belfast Poor House, whose managing committee was incorporated by a separate statute) and the badging of beggars was carried out by these institutions in their respective localities.[53] It is important to note, however, that responsibility for relieving or punishing mendicants was not completely removed from the parishes. Instead, Dublin vestries co-operated with the city's House of Industry in apprehending unlicensed beggars and vagabonds, who were subsequently detained in the House of Industry. In July 1793, the vestry of St Andrew's parish resolved that it would implore its parishioners to 'discontinue giving alms to public Beggars', before committing that:

we will Individually and collectively co-operate with the Corporation for the Relief of the Poor &c in the city of Dublin [*i.e., the governors of the House of Industry*] in their laudable endeavours to free the streets of this Metropolis from beggars – That we will for that purpose point out to their Beadles such Impostures and public Beggars as may come

---

49 Quoted in R.W.M. Strain, *Belfast and its Charitable Society: a story of urban social development* (London, 1961), p. 57.

50 Strain, *Belfast and its Charitable Society*, pp. 59–61, 279.

51 *An account of the proceedings and state of the fund of the Corporation instituted for the Relief of the Poor, and for Punishing Vagabonds and Sturdy Beggars in the County of the City of Dublin, published by order of the corporation, March 22d, 1774* (Dublin, 1774), pp. 8–9.

52 *Nineteenth annual report of the managing committee of the Association for the Suppression of Mendicity in Dublin. For the year 1836: with resolutions upon the subject of the Poor Laws* (Dublin, 1837), p. 11.

53 Fleming and Logan, *Pauper Limerick*, pp. xii–xiii. For Kilkenny, see *(Finn's) Leinster Journal*, 11–14 Oct. 1775. Interestingly, while the Kilkenny corporation for relieving the poor was founded soon after the passing of the 1772 act, it would be another four decades before the city's House of Industry was to open: *Moderator*, 15 Jan., 2 Apr., 28 Apr. 1814; Fleming and Logan, *Pauper Limerick*, p. xii.

within our knowledge and That we will to the utmost of our power protect their officers from Violence in the execution of their duty.[54]

Other Dublin parishes – St Catherine's, St Werburgh's and St Mary's – passed similar resolutions in the same month, committing themselves to co-operating with the House of Industry in apprehending street beggars and protecting the latter institution's officers in the exercise of their duties.[55] This instance serves as an important indication of cross-institutional co-operation between various bodies with responsibility for the relief of the poor and suppression of mendicancy. The practice of badging beggars had all but disappeared by the middle of the nineteenth century, owing to the growth of voluntary charities and, more significantly, from the early 1840s, of the Poor Law union workhouses. A later instance of the brief revival of badging arose in Waterford city in 1851; of significance in this instance was the fact that it was not the parish vestry that reintroduced the practice but the Poor Law union Board of Guardians, who had succeeded parochial officials as the primary custodians of corporate relief measures in the locality.[56]

Parish Vestries, Public Health and the Suppression of Beggary
Crucial to the maintenance of civil order at this time was the protection of the public from epidemic disease and parish vestries also exerted responsibility in this respect. In July 1819, at the tail-end of the devastating typhus fever epidemic of 1816–19, parliament passed the Fever Act, which empowered vestries to elect unpaid officers of health who had the authority to direct that tenements, lanes and streets be cleaned, and that nuisances be removed from the streets. These officers were also empowered to apprehend and dismiss from the parish 'all idle poor Persons, Men, Women, or Children, and all Persons who may be found begging or seeking Relief' in the interest of 'preventing the Danger of Contagion and other Evils'.[57] In some instances, parishioners who were qualified medical practitioners were elected to these positions, such as David Brereton MD, in St Michan's in 1831.[58] In St Thomas's parish in 1828, the ten elected officers of health

---

54 St Andrew's parish, Dublin, vestry minute book, 4 July 1793 (RCBL, St Andrew's parish, Dublin, vestry minute books, P 59.5.1).

55 St Catherine's parish, Dublin, vestry minute book, 6 July 1791 (P 117.5.5); St Werburgh's parish, Dublin, vestry minute book, 12 July 1791 (RCBL, St Werburgh's parish, Dublin, vestry minute books, P 326.5.2); St Mary's parish, Dublin, vestry minute book, 29 July 1791 (RCBL, St Mary's parish, Dublin, vestry minute books, P 277.7.4).

56 *Waterford Chronicle*, 24 May 1851.

57 59 Geo. III, c. 41 (14 June 1819).

58 St Michan's parish, Dublin, vestry minute book, 23 Nov. 1831 (RCBL, St Michan's parish, Dublin, vestry minute books, P 276.5.5).

included three physicians and a surgeon.[59] These positions were invariably filled by respectable parishioners, driven by a sense of civic duty and the social prominence attached to parochial service; such individuals typically also served as churchwardens, sidesmen and overseers.[60] Toby Barnard has argued that 'as in England, so in Protestant Ireland, a willingness regularly to assume the burdens of parochial office may have helped the middling sort to define and so distinguish themselves from the lower ranks'.[61]

Throughout the 1820s, officers of health were not annual appointments in most vestries; instead, they were appointed in response to short-term crises. When the emergency abated these appointments were then rescinded.[62] A letter-writer to the *Cork Constitution* in 1828 criticised the southern city's parishes for failing to appoint officers of health, especially given the extensive array of powers available under the provisions of the 1819 act. Despite being of a 'most salutary character' and offering the opportunity concurrently to tackle a number of critical social problems, the act in Cork city was a 'dead letter', the writer asserted.[63] On the eve of the Great Famine, the *Hue and Cry*, the gazette of the Irish Constabulary, published without comment an excerpt from the 1819 Fever Act, singling out the provisions pertaining to the removal of street beggars and illustrating a perceived need to draw public attention towards these neglected powers.[64]

At times of crisis, parishes were not always proactive in appointing officers of health. This procrastination was evident in the autumn of 1826, when Chief Secretary Henry Goulburn wrote to the Dublin vestries alerting them to the fact that 'fever is now extending itself among the Poor of this City' and reminding them of their powers under the 1819 act.[65] The St Michan's vestry promptly elected five Officers of Health.[66] However, by this time, epidemic fever had been raging throughout the city for around

---

59 St Thomas's parish, Dublin, vestry minute book, 7 Apr. 1828.
60 Among the officers of health in St Michan's parish in the 1830s were Mark Flower of Old Church Street and merchant William Hill of 47 Pill Lane, who also served together as sidesmen and overseers of licensed houses: St Michan's parish, Dublin, vestry minute book, 7 Apr., 23 Dec. 1828, 9 Apr. 1832, 20 Apr. 1835. Hill also served as churchwarden: ibid., 4 Apr. 1836.
61 Barnard, *A new anatomy of Ireland*, p. 242.
62 This assertion, evidenced by examination of numerous vestry minute books, is supported by Francis White, *Report and observations on the state of the poor of Dublin* (Dublin, 1833), p. 22.
63 *Cork Constitution*, 17 Apr. 1828.
64 Quoted in *Londonderry Sentinel*, 16 Aug. 1845.
65 St Michan's parish, Dublin, vestry minute book, 5 Sept. 1826 (RCBL, St Michan's parish, Dublin, vestry minute books, P 276.5.4); St Catherine's parish, Dublin, vestry minute book, 29 Aug. 1826.
66 St Michan's parish, Dublin, vestry minute book, 5 Sept. 1826.

four months.[67] A public meeting of the parishioners of St George's parish on 31 August 1826 heard that officers of health had not yet been appointed, despite the claims of one parishioner – a medical practitioner named Dr. Reddy – that fever was prevailing extensively in the parish.[68] This epidemic waned in 1827 and it was not until late 1831 that officers of health once again became standard appointments at parish vestries, not just in Dublin but in urban centres across Ireland. The crisis that revived the appointment of parish officers of health was the onslaught of cholera, which eventually reached Ireland in early 1832. While typhus fever was endemic in Ireland, cholera was an unknown malady across western Europe. St Paul's parish vestry in Cork city later referred to 'the alarming period when that new and destructive Plague the cholera made its appearance in this City, and this Parish was first visited by its deadly Ravages', further labelling the disease a 'hitherto unknown Pestilence'.[69] Wandering beggars were blamed as being among the most serious causes for the spread of cholera,[70] with one authority referring to the 'fertile source of contagion, originating in vagrancy and mendicity'.[71] In Dublin, the Mendicity Society publicly drew the attention of parochial officers of health to lanes and houses where beggars were known to congregate, with particular emphasis being paid to the danger of the dissemination of disease.[72] St George's parish was active in utilising its powers under the 1819 Fever Act to wash and clean the clothes and persons of beggars who had 'an insuperable antipathy to cleanliness'; this procedure proved 'so disagreeable to them that they avoided subjecting themselves to it a second time'.[73] In Ballymena, parochial officers of health were active in keeping 'wandering beggars and vagrants from infesting the town'; in one instance, an individual was prosecuted before the town's magistrates for obstructing an officer 'in the execution of his duty', with the resulting fine of 7s. 6d. being allocated for the officer's work.[74] In April 1832, in Queen's County, 19-year-old Mary Carrol was apprehended by a local officer of health and tried for 'vagrancy', serving a 24-hour sentence.[75] It is important to note that the parish vestries were not the only corporate entity which had duties in responding to this epidemic. The state-run Central Board

---

67 *FJ*, 17 July 1826.
68 Reddy's claims were challenged by others at this meeting, including a fellow medical practitioner: *FJ*, 1 Sept. 1826.
69 St Paul's parish, Cork city, vestry minute book, 17 June 1833.
70 *BNL*, 17 Feb. 1832; Robins, *The miasma*, pp. 66, 76.
71 *BNL*, 8 Nov. 1831.
72 *Saunder's News-Letter*, 26 Apr. 1832.
73 Ibid., 8 May 1832.
74 *Belfast Commercial Chronicle*, 25 Aug. 1832.
75 Maryborough Prison general register, 17 Apr. 1832 (1/55/25), accessed at FindMyPast under 'Irish Prison Registers 1790–1924' (www.findmypast.ie) (accessed 13 Sept. 2017).

of Health established following the 1816–19 fever epidemic and which had retreated into administrative hibernation during the 1820s, was revived in late 1831. The Board offered advice to local bodies on how to prevent contagion and how to respond when cholera cases were identified, and oversaw the establishment of local hospitals.

Some parishes continued to appoint officers of health throughout the 1830s and into the 1840s, but, mostly, parishes drew on their powers under the 1819 Fever Act only at times of crisis and epidemic. As late as 1851, however, the Lisburn vestry received a report from its officers of health whose sanitary activities included 'keeping the town clear of strolling beggars'.[76] At the following year's Easter vestry in Belfast parish, the health officers' employment of three constables specifically for taking up street beggars was criticised as being insufficient.[77] This interestingly suggests a desire for a strengthened provision of parochial officers for suppressing street begging at a time when the northern town was served by numerous charitable organisations, not to mention a Poor Law-funded workhouse. The powers of parish vestries to appoint officers of health was repealed by the 1866 Sanitary Act,[78] which extended earlier legislation for England to Ireland and was passed at the height of yet another cholera epidemic. In Dublin, the parishes' responsibilities were subsequently transferred to a new Public Health Committee, which operated under the auspices of Dublin Corporation.[79]

The Declining Role of Parish Constables and Beadles
From the early modern period right into the nineteenth century, one of the main duties of Irish parish vestries in towns and cities was the preservation of law and order within their jurisdiction. At a time before the establishment of a national police force, responsibility for maintaining the public peace in cities and towns lay with groups of paid night watchmen and beadles, supervised by unpaid constables who were appointed annually by the members of the vestry. This was typically the case in both Ireland and England.[80] The positions of watchmen and beadles were paid ones, filled by men from the lower classes, and these officers were regularly open to accusations of corruption and inefficiency. Jonathan Swift condemned

76 *BNL*, 28 Apr. 1851.
77 *BNL*, 14 Apr. 1852. See also 3 May 1854.
78 29 & 30 Vict., c. 90, s. 69 (7 Aug. 1866).
79 Prunty, *Dublin slums*, pp. 70–1.
80 Dudley, 'Dublin parishes 1660–1729', ii, pp. 213–46; Elizabeth Malcolm, *The Irish policeman, 1822–1922: a life* (Dublin, 2006), pp. 17–18; N.J.G. Pounds, *A history of the English parish: the culture of religion from Augustine to Victoria* (Cambridge, 2000), pp. 193–5.

instances of 'Foreign Beggars' bribing parish beadles in Dublin (presumably so as to avoid detention),[81] while the St Bride's beadle was accused in the 1830s of keeping 'an improper house'.[82] Constables, on the other hand, were typically 'respectable' male householders from the parish whose voluntary service in this role spoke to their sense of civic duty and social prominence.[83] Occasional examples blurred these lines of social demarcation: William Wilson of Old Church Street in Dublin received his beadle's salary of £10 per annum from St Michan's vestry while also serving voluntarily as a parish constable.[84]

The duties of beadles, constables and watchmen centred around maintaining peace and order in the parish, particularly around the church at times of service; in St Bride's, Dublin, the beadle was required not to permit the disruption of Divine Service 'by allowing Idle or disorderly persons to assemble or make a noise about the Church or Church yard'.[85] The beadle also served as the messenger of the parish vestry.[86] The apprehension of beggars and vagrants was among their most common duties, as it was for their London counterparts.[87] In the 1750s, a beadle was employed in Shankill parish in Belfast to prevent vagrants from entering the town,[88] while in July 1791, the vestry of St Mary's parish in Dublin appointed a parishioner 'to assist the Beadle of this Parish' in bringing about the apprehension and punishment of 'idle vagrants so offending any where about the Church'.[89] A mayoral proclamation of October 1769 urged all Dublin parishes to direct their beadles and constables to apprehend

81 [Swift], *Proposal for giving badges to the beggars*, p. 12. See also St Werburgh's parish, Dublin, vestry minute book, 20 Mar. 1783.

82 Upon hearing this accusation at a vestry meeting, the beadle leapt onto a table and made 'a series of pantomimic gestures expressive of his wish to exercise his fists in a pugilistic encounter on the faces' of his critics: newspaper clipping, incorrectly dated *FJ*, 8 Apr. 1838, inserted inside St Bride's parish vestry minute book (RCBL, 327.3.3).

83 Rowena Dudley, 'The Dublin parish, 1660–1730' in Elizabeth Fitzpatrick and Raymond Gillespie (eds), *The parish in medieval and early modern Ireland: community, territory and building* (Dublin, 2006), pp. 294–5.

84 St Michan's parish, Dublin vestry minute book, 5 May 1828 (P 276.5.5). Wilson later served as the parish fire-engine keeper: ibid., 2 Jan. 1829.

85 St Bride's parish, Dublin vestry minute book, 15 Oct. 1832 (P 327.3.3).

86 John Finlay, *The office and duty of church-warden and parish officer* (Dublin, 1824), p. 171.

87 Anon., *The constable's assistant: being a compendium of the duties and powers of constables, and other peace officers; chiefly as they relate to the apprehending of offenders, and the laying of information before magistrates* (3rd edn, London, 1818), pp. 36–41; Hitchcock, *Down and out in eighteenth-century London*, pp. 151–80.

88 *BNL*, 11 Oct. 1757, quoted in Raymond Gillespie and Alison O'Keeffe (eds), *Register of the parish of Shankill, Belfast, 1745–1761* (Dublin, 2006), p. 37.

89 St Mary's parish, Dublin, vestry minute book, 29 July 1791.

and present before a Justice of the Peace 'all such sturdy strolling Beggars and Vagrants', for their committal to the Bridewell.[90] In June 1785, twelve years after the opening of the city's House of Industry, a public meeting, held for the purpose of tackling the mendicant problem, heard that Dublin remained plagued by a 'great number of idle and disorderly vagabonds and sturdy beggars, who have for some time past infested the same, to the great annoyance of the inhabitants, and disgrace of the police of this city'.[91] That such a meeting was held to discuss the sole issue of the policing of mendicants and vagrants suggests that the long-standing problem with the mendicant poor was still considered urgent, the prevailing night watch system was insufficient and the impact of the House of Industry in forcing beggars from the streets was questionable.

The emergence of centralised, usually state-funded, police forces from the late eighteenth century led to the gradual decline of the parish system of policing.[92] References to beadles and constables being engaged in the warding off of mendicants are largely lacking in vestry records from the turn of the century onwards and this decline can be linked from the 1770s to the establishment of Houses of Industry and from 1809 onwards to mendicity societies, which employed their own beadles for the purposes of removing beggars from the streets. The pre-Famine decades witnessed a more general diminution in the role of parish beadles and constables. In the Dublin parish of St Thomas's, the Easter vestry meeting in 1832 was the first at which no constables were appointed, while in St Andrew's and St Werburgh's parishes, the election of constables appears to have ceased in 1833 and 1835 respectively.[93] This trend was by no means universal: St Michael's parish was still electing parish constables in 1841, while constables remained among the parochial officers to be elected annually in the parishes of St Bride and St John into the post-Famine period.[94] However, an 1841 newspaper report of a vestry meeting in St Bride's parish suggests that the importance of the position had diminished almost to the point of uselessness. Upon the election of three men as constables for the succeeding year in St Bride's, one parishioner enquired into the duties of the constables, to which another parishioner quipped, 'If you get your coat torn, the parish constable will

90 *FJ*, 2–4 Nov. 1769.
91 *FJ*, 14–16 June 1785.
92 Malcolm, *The Irish policeman*, pp. 18–24; Stanley H. Palmer, *Police and protest in England and Ireland 1780–1850* (Cambridge, 1988), pp. 117–62.
93 St Thomas's parish, Dublin vestry minute book, 23 Apr. 1832; St Andrew's parish, Dublin, vestry minute book, 8 Apr. 1833 (P 59.5.2); St Werburgh's parish, Dublin vestry minute book, 21 Apr. 1835.
94 *FJ*, 14 Apr. 1841; St Bride's parish, Dublin vestry minute book, 29 Mar. 1853 (P 327.3.3); *FJ*, 22 Apr. 1862.

replace it with a new one', which was met with laughter.[95] The increasing decline in regard for these parochial positions continued into the post-Famine period, with the positions of constable and beadle being dismissed by Dublin parishioners respectively as '[an] unnecessary functionary ... [which] should at once be abolished' and 'a useless officer in a cocked hat'.[96]

Conclusion

The decades immediately before the Great Famine witnessed a significant shift in the civil role of the parish vestry in Ireland and a related transformation in how communities managed beggary in their locality. From the seventeenth century, parishes fulfilled various secular roles and were the most regular corporate providers of relief throughout Ireland, although, as demonstrated, regional factors dictated that parishes in the east and north-east were more active than their counterparts in poorer regions. While records allow us to identify trends in badging practices, gauging the efficacy of parochial badging is significantly more difficult. Did badging succeed in warding off 'strange' beggars and limiting parishioners' benevolence and alms to the local, 'deserving' poor? Could mendicancy actually be controlled, or even mitigated, through this licensing system? David Dickson has expressed scepticism of the potential that parochial badging could offer, given the sheer volume of mendicants in this period, the unpopularity of the measure among the poorer classes and the ingrained vagrant nature of Irish mendicancy.[97] An influential report on Dublin's charitable institutions concluded that the House of Industry's system of badging was 'useless and impracticable' given 'the number of applicants [and] the difficulty of discriminating between the meritorious poor and the impostor', leading to the system's discontinuance.[98] However, this raises the question of whether parish-based systems, overseen by locally based residents, who were surely familiar with many of their local paupers, were better suited to implement such a system than the House of Industry, which may be regarded in its early decades as a national poorhouse with thousands of paupers (locals and 'strangers') on its books. It appears most likely that badging was not undertaken as a long-term solution to the mendicant problem but was commenced, terminated and reintroduced according to wider economic and social crises; the badging of beggars was seen as a useful, relatively inexpensive way to 'manage' fluctuating levels

95 *FJ*, 14 Apr. 1841.
96 *FJ*, 22 Mar. 1856, 22 Apr. 1862.
97 Dickon, 'In search of the old Irish Poor Law', p. 155.
98 *Report upon certain charitable establishments, Dublin*, p. 16.

of mendicancy at times of crisis. It may be suggested that badging worked best when the licensing of the local poor was complemented by vigilance in discouraging or preventing non-local mendicants from soliciting in the parish, through the employment of beadles and constables. Regrettably, the available sources do not provide explicit answers to this question.

This period also saw an overhaul in the role of the parish vestries in the life of their local communities. The civil duties of parishes, which had grown since the seventeenth century and had been defined and cemented through legislation, were gradually chipped away, as their powers (to control beggary, the police and to prevent the spread of contagious diseases in their parish) were devolved to other corporate bodies.[99] This process commenced in the 1830s with the Church Temporalities Act, by which parishes could no longer levy a church-related cess on non-Anglican parishioners.[100] This act was a landmark part of the evolution of the Irish parish from being both a religious and a civil entity to constituting solely an ecclesiastical unit, serving its congregants.[101] This process became entrenched with the 1864 Cess Abolition Act,[102] which, five years before the Disestablishment legislation, removed entirely the parishes' power to levy a compulsory rate, thus ending the civil role of the Irish parish vestries.

---

99 MacDonagh, *Ireland*, pp. 34–5.
100 3 & 4 Will. IV, c. 37, s. 73 (14 Aug. 1833).
101 Akenson, *The Church of Ireland*, p. 172.
102 27 Vict., c. 17 (13 May 1864).

5

The Mendicity Society Movement
and the Suppression of Begging

Of all the trades agoing now,
A begging it's the worst, Sir,
Tho' later it seemed in this good town,
To be the very first, Sir.
It throve so well in every street,
With other trades so blended,
That 'twas determined at the last,
The city should be mended.
      Oh no! Mendicity's the way to mend-a-city
      Oh no! Mendicity's the way, &c.

An Association then was formed,
Of Gentlemen of all ranks;
Who all the Beggars straightway warned,
That they should quit their old pranks.
They drove those objects from our streets,
To Rick Burke's stores they sent them;
Where they will keep them with good will,
As long as they can rent them,
      Oh no! Mendicity, &c.

The better part of all this scheme,
Is that the poor are well off;
They work all day, it is most true,
But when their work they sell off.
One half they get, with meat and drink,
In short they are quite frisky;

THE MENDICITY SOCIETY MOVEMENT

When in the evening home they hi[d]e,
To take their tea and whiskey
        Oh no! Mendicity, &c.

Pale typhus no longer stalks,
At early day or later,
Nor will you in our public walks
Infected beggar mee, Sir,
Your Ladies may a-shopping go,
And whilst they purchase ___ pity,
And in a box a shilling drop,
'Twill help to Mend-the-city.
        Oh no! Mendicity, &c.

It's now you'll meet in every street,
Good humour and the next Sir;
Whilst to effect good, so complete,
Your mite you won't refuse, Sir.
And all is done, you can't but see,
With an intent the best, Sir,
To make this town as it should be,
First city of the west, Sir.
        Oh no! Mendicity, &c.
                Galway Weekly Advertiser, 27 November 1824

Introduction

In March 1836, the Dublin Mendicity Society received two new applications for admission – Sarah Doody and her son James, and Biddy Loghlin and her five-month-old son, also named James. In both instances, the women's husbands had been tailors who left their employment due to a strike ('combination'). The minutes of the managing committee's meeting at which these applications were considered record that Sarah Doody's husband, Timothy, 'in consequence of combination ... has quit his work, of which he had enough, & went to England, where he remains', presumably in search of alternative employment, while Biddy Loghlin's husband, William, 'is gone to England & that there is a turn out [*i.e., a strike*] among the tailors'. The committee then resolved to refuse admission to both these women and their young children.[1] For the managing committee of the

---

1 Dublin Mendicity Society minute book, 22 Mar. 1836.

city's largest and most prominent charity, which catered for a category of paupers ('common street beggars') specifically excluded from the remit of other charities, some mendicants were still less deserving than others. The refusal of relief to these women and children arose from the actions of their husbands and reflected the biases of the members of the charity's managing committee, comprising members of the city's merchant and professional classes who had an economic interest in the suppression of industrial dissent and insubordination.[2] A later report of the same charity attacked the 'heart-hardening effects ... of this unjust system of interference with the rights of labour', calling for government intervention 'to confer a lasting benefit upon the trade and manufactures of Ireland'.[3] (The Methodist-run Strangers' Friend Society also excluded men whose distress was caused by 'combination' from the benefits of its relief.)[4] A historian of the Edinburgh Mendicity Society has similarly observed that its hierarchy of interests 'included the protection of property, the discriminate distribution of resources, commercial prosperity and stable social relationships. They were congruent with the interests of property-owners, tax-payers and employers'.[5]

The aforementioned Dublin instance illuminates the experiences of both those who used and those who operated Irish mendicity societies, charities that emerged in the early nineteenth century as voluntary organisations committed to the suppression of beggary. While the habitual recourse to beggary, regardless of the cause of such resort, usually sufficed as a requirement for admission to the mendicity asylums, the benevolence of managing committees did not extend to certain individuals whose distress was seen as being self-inflicted. This was seen most clearly in the cases of men who went on strike; as is evident in the case of Sarah Doody and Biddy Loghlin, the partners and children of such men also suffered.

---

2 Jacqueline Hill writes that 'combination' was 'the pejorative term used by employers and those hostile to the practice of journeymen combining to try to maintain or improve wage levels, or limit the number of apprentices': Jacqueline Hill, 'Artisans, sectarianism and politics in Dublin, 1829–48' in *Saothar*, vii (1981), p. 17. 'Combination' was prohibited in Ireland under a statute of 1803, which was repealed in 1824. A number of middle-class deponents, such as clergymen and merchants, expressed their suspicion of 'combination' to the Poor Inquiry: *PI, Appendix C, Part II*, pp. 115–16. For 'combination' in early nineteenth-century Belfast, see S.J. Connolly and Gillian McIntosh, 'Whose city? Belonging and exclusion in the nineteenth-century urban world' in Connolly, *Belfast 400*, pp. 239, 244. See also Kelly, 'Charitable societies', p. 95; 'Evidence on combination, taken in Dublin', *PI, Appendix C, Part II*, pp. 1c–45c.

3 *Nineteenth report, Dublin Mendicity Society, 1836*, p. 31.

4 *PI, Appendix C, Part II*, p. 18.

5 Dalgleish, 'Voluntary associations and the middle class in Edinburgh, 1780–1820', pp. 99–100.

The emergence of mendicity societies throughout Ireland and Britain in the first half of the nineteenth century was symptomatic of the increased public concern towards the threat posed by mendicancy. Arising mainly in the immediate post-war period and, later, during the economic crisis of the mid-1820s, mendicity societies reflected middle-class zeal to tackle the 'evil' of street begging, which threatened to spread disease, encourage moral licentiousness among the labouring classes, and undermine the incentive to be industrious. The fundamental purpose of the mendicity societies was to suppress begging in a given town or city. This was not to be done simply by removing beggars from the street and confining them in a custodial institution. Instead, the mendicant poor were to be put to work at useful employment, where they would learn basic skills and 'habits of industry' which would assist them to gain employment and become independent. Child beggars in these institutions were provided with a rudimentary education, but one which instilled the virtues of industry, cleanliness, order and religion.

Charitable Societies and Associational Culture

The *modus operandi* of mendicity societies reflected the more general shift towards specialisation and discrimination in the provision of charity which emerged in the second half of the eighteenth century: mendicity societies were dedicated to the suppression of street begging. These charities were founded, run and supported largely by middle-class men, mostly from the professional and commercial classes and who were prominent members of their communities. By voluntarily serving their local mendicity society these individuals emphasised the virtue of civic duty which contributed to the formation of middle-class identity, while also contributing to the protection of their community from disease, idleness, intemperance and other moral evils typically associated with the lower classes.[6] (Of course, it would be remiss not to acknowledge the role that self-interest played in philanthropy.)[7] The public was assured that in the hands of such 'respectable' pillars of the community, their subscriptions and donations would be applied to the most truly 'deserving' cases. The publishing of comprehensive reports, full accounts of income and expenditure, statistical tables of the number of paupers relieved, and occasional vignettes of individual cases 'provided the

6 Laurence M. Geary, '"The best relief the poor can receive is from themselves": the Society for Promoting the Comforts of the Poor' in Laurence M. Geary and Oonagh Walsh (eds), *Philanthropy in nineteenth-century Ireland* (Dublin, 2015), p. 40.
7 Geary, *Medicine and charity*, pp. 3–4; Kelly, 'Charitable societies', p. 95.

public with a distinct impression of effectively targeted relief'.[8] Contrary to
the workings of mendicity societies in the first half of the nineteenth century,
earlier charities in Irish urban centres specifically excluded common beggars
from the benefit of their benevolence, as these individuals were commonly
dismissed as the deviant, idle poor who were 'undeserving' of the limited
resources of charitable funds. Most charities in Ireland focused their efforts
on the industrious poor, such as distressed artisans and manufacturers.[9]
Sturdy and refractory beggars were not considered to be fit objects for
charity. In Dublin, the Charitable Association was formed in 1806, according
to one historical account, 'to afford relief to all but common beggars', while
it is evident from the title of the Society for the Relief of Industrious Poor, a
largely Quaker entity founded in 1813, that the idle poor were excluded from
its remit.[10]

Houses of Industry: Precursors to the Mendicity Societies

The publication in the 1760s of two influential pamphlets by the Church
of Ireland Dean of Clogher, Richard Woodward, influenced the passing of
legislation for the erection of Houses of Industry across Ireland, establishing
a system of licensed begging and a place of detention and industry for
unlicensed street beggars. The statute, described by R.B. McDowell as 'the
most important piece of social legislation enacted by the Irish parliament
in the eighteenth century',[11] empowered, but did not compel, grand juries
partially to fund these institutions, and additional income was to come
from church collections and charity sermons.[12] Twelve Houses of Industry
(excluding the existing Belfast Charitable Society's poor house) were
established under this legislation and were largely concentrated in south
Leinster/east Munster and Ulster.[13] The Dublin House of Industry opened
for the admission of beggars on 8 November 1773 and for nearly 50 years
maintained its founding principles of apprehending street beggars through
the employment of beadles and confining them in its premises off Channel

---

8   Kelly, 'Charitable societies', p. 105. See Morris, 'Voluntary societies' for a detailed
    discussion of some of these themes.
9   Kelly, 'Charitable societies'.
10 Warburton *et al.*, *History of the city of Dublin*, ii, p. 901.
11 R.B. McDowell, 'Ireland on the eve of famine' in R. Dudley Edwards and T. Desmond
    Williams (eds), *The Great Famine: studies in Irish history, 1845–52* (Dublin, 1956), p. 31.
12 11 & 12 Geo. III, c. 30 [Ire.] (2 June 1772).
13 Fleming and Logan, *Pauper Limerick*, p. xii; Mel Cousins, 'Philanthropy and poor
    relief before the Poor Law, 1801–30' in Geary and Walsh, *Philanthropy in nineteenth-
    century Ireland*, pp. 26–8.

Row (later North Brunswick Street) in the north-west of the city.[14] In the early years of the nineteenth century, however, the House of Industry started admitting increasing amounts of the sick poor and its focus gradually shifted in this direction. An 1809 report into Dublin charitable institutions in receipt of parliamentary assistance found that the House of Industry had achieved limited success in its original object of suppressing street begging. Instead, the institution's focus was on 'the relief of the aged and infirm, and of those who laboured under temporary distress from want of employment'.[15] This pattern crystallised in the 1816 direction from Chief Secretary Robert Peel, implementing a recommendation from the aforementioned 1809 report,[16] that the House of Industry cease admitting beggars and vagrants and, instead, concentrate its resources on relieving varying categories of the sick and infirm poor in its multi-faceted institutional campus.[17] The impact of Peel's decision was significant. At a time of considerable social and economic distress and dislocation, caused by the post-war downturn, demobilisation of large swathes of the armed forces, and the prevalence of a typhus fever epidemic, the main institution in Dublin city with legal powers for the apprehension and confinement of street beggars was effectively stripped of this responsibility. This measure gave rise to a public campaign throughout 1817 and 1818 through which the city's inhabitants demanded the formation of a new organisation for the suppression of street begging. In the absence of any action from the central state or the local grand jury, the initiative of local men, largely from the professional and merchant classes, came to the fore and resulted in the establishment of the Dublin Mendicity Society in January 1818, drawing on the precedent set by similar charitable societies in Hamburg, Munich, Bath, Belfast and Edinburgh, and aimed at suppressing 'the disgusting and baleful influence of mendicity'.[18] In London, too, the inaction of the state in enforcing anti-begging measures spurred

14 Prunty, *Dublin slums*, pp. 202–3.
15 *Report upon certain charitable establishments, Dublin*, p. 39.
16 For the House of Industry, see ibid., pp. 13–40. The recommendation is ibid., p. 40.
17 Copy of letter from Robert Peel to the House of Industry governors. The institutions of the House of Industry, which Thackeray described as 'a group of huge gloomy edifices', comprised penitentiaries, hospitals and a lunatic asylum: Thackeray, *Irish sketchbook of 1842*, p. 316; *(Ireland). Report of the commissioners appointed by the Lord Lieutenant of Ireland to inspect the House of Industry, and to report upon the management thereof, with a view to the introduction of such reforms and improvements, as would render it, not only less expensive, but more efficient for the purposes for which it was originally designed*, pp. 13–15, 19–21, H.C. 1820 (84), viii, 289–91, 295–7.
18 Quoted in Woods, *Dublin outsiders*, p. 193. Useful accounts of the immediate background to the establishment of this society are given in: Anon., *Arguments in proof of the necessity of suppressing street begging*; *Observations on the House of Industry, Dublin*; *Report, Dublin Mendicity Society, 1818*.

the middle-class founders of the city's mendicity society into action in 1818; similarly, in Edinburgh, the impetus for policing reforms were closely linked to citizens' desire for anti-begging measures, leading to the formation in 1813 of the city's Society for Suppressing Begging.[19]

The Emergence of the Mendicity Society Movement

The poverty, social distress and demographic dislocation that arose following the end of the Napoleonic Wars in 1815 were direct causes of the emergence of mendicity societies. With occasional exceptions, such as the Bath and Belfast societies founded in 1805 and 1809 respectively, the early mendicity societies were established in the years immediately following the end of hostilities, when vagrancy levels rose sharply throughout Ireland and Britain. The evidence for Ireland supports M.J.D. Roberts's research into the origins of the London Mendicity Society,[20] with accounts attributing the emergence of these early societies to the peacetime downturn, the large-scale demobilisation of men and the consequent upsurge in beggary. The first report of the Dublin Mendicity Society asserted that the extent of mendicancy in the city, while always considerable, 'was greatly increased by the effects of the termination of the war upon the trading and agricultural interests in this country – by the disbanding of large portions of the army and navy', as well as two years of famine and disease epidemics.[21]

The mid- to late 1810s was a period of 'almost unexampled scarcity'.[22] The post-war demobilisation, together with a decline in agricultural prices, poor potato crops and a two-year nationwide fever epidemic resulted not only in alarming levels of mendicancy throughout Ireland, but, according to one account, 'gave it a character, form, and virulence which appeared to place it beyond the reach of cure'. The same report, referring to Dublin, continued: 'every asylum in the City being full, begging appeared not only excuseable, but justifiable; every hand distributed alms, a great part of the disgrace of seeking charity being removed'.[23] An observer, writing in 1816, painted a grim picture of Dublin city:

---

19 Roberts, *Making English morals*, pp. 103–4; W.H. Bodkin to Robert Peel, 21 Nov. 1822 (TNA, Home Office Correspondence, HO 44/12, ff. 361–362); Dalgleish, 'Voluntary associations and the middle class in Edinburgh', pp. 99–138.

20 Roberts, 'Reshaping the gift relationship', pp. 202–3. See also *The first report of the society established in London for the suppression of mendicity* (London, 1819), p. 9; *Morning Chronicle*, 6 Jan. 1818.

21 *Report, Dublin Mendicity Society, 1818*, p. 1. See also *PI, Appendix C, Part II*, p. 37.

22 *Report, Dublin Mendicity Society, 1818*, p. 1.

23 Ibid.

The City presented a spectacle, at once afflicting and disgusting to the feelings of its inhabitants; the doors of carriages and shops, to the interruption of business, were beset by crowds of unfortunate and clamorous beggars, exhibiting misery and decrepitude in a variety of forms, and frequently carrying about in their persons and garments the seeds of contagious disease; themselves the victims of idleness, their children were taught to depend on Begging, as affording the only means of future subsistence; every artifice was resorted to by the practised Beggar to extort alms, and refusal was frequently followed by imprecations and threats. The benevolent were imposed upon – the modest shocked – the reflecting grieved – the timid alarmed. In short, so distressing was the whole scene, and so intolerable was the nuisance, that its suppression became a matter of *necessity*.[24]

It was in this context that in villages, towns and cities across Ireland and Britain middle-class men came together to form voluntary associations with the primary aim of suppressing street begging in their locality.

The first of these societies to state its aim specifically as the suppression of street begging was, in fact, a pre-1815 entity. The Bath Mendicity Society was formed in 1805 and by 1818 similar associations had been established in Oxford, Edinburgh, Chester, Birmingham, Salisbury, Bristol, Liverpool, Coventry, Kendal, Kingston and Colchester.[25] The Belfast House of Industry, formed in 1809, just weeks after an estimated 2,000 calico looms in the town 'were struck idle', was a mendicity society in all but name; it was a voluntarily funded charitable society whose founding principle was 'not merely to check the growth of mendicity at present, but to cut it up by the roots, to come at the very source and spring of the evil that rankles in the vitals of every large town', and, despite its name, is not to be confused with the twelve Houses of Industry established under the 1770s legislation.[26] Mendicity societies drew inspiration from an initiative of a Hamburg institution, founded in 1788, under which a committee was formed, the town was divided into districts, house-to-house collection of subscriptions was undertaken, the

---

24 Ibid., pp. 2–3.
25 *First report, London Mendicity Society*, p. 27; Roberts, 'Reshaping the gift relationship', pp. 206–7.
26 'Rules and regulations for the House of Industry, in Belfast, laid before a general meeting of the town for their approbation, and unanimously agreed to' in *Belfast Monthly Magazine*, iv, no. 21 (30 Apr. 1810), p. 263; *Second report of Geo. Nicholls, Poor Laws, Ireland*, p. 11; *PI, Appendix C, Part I*, p. 11. For an expansion of this point, see Ciarán McCabe, 'Begging and alms-giving in urban Ireland, 1815–1850' (PhD thesis, Maynooth University, 2015), pp. 157–9.

circumstances of the poor were investigated, and a spinning school was commenced for women and children.[27]

Of the Irish mendicity societies, 52 have been identified to date, as shown in the Table 5.1. In mapping the geographical distribution of these societies, a number of points are to be made (see Figure 5.1). First, the concentration of the charities in Ulster is striking. Thirty-two of the 52 societies were located in the northern province and 11 societies were to be found in Leinster, with seven and two in Munster and Connaught respectively. The reason for the singular concentration of mendicity societies in Ulster may be explained as an Irish manifestation of the Scottish model of voluntary approaches to poor assistance, particularly given the fact that 96 per cent of Irish Presbyterians, who shared many cultural identities, theological world views and ecclesiastical structures with the Calvinist Church of Scotland, lived in Ulster.[28] Just as Ulster Presbyterianism influenced social, cultural, political and economic practices in the northern province, so too did it shape poor relief initiatives.[29] Just under two-fifths of all of the Irish mendicity societies were located in the two counties of Antrim and Down, largely in locations where Presbyterians constituted 50 per cent to 80 per cent of the population. Mendicity societies in Ulster differed from those elsewhere in Ireland not only in their geographic concentration but also in the fact that in many locations they were founded in relatively small towns and villages. The 20 societies located in Leinster, Munster and Connaught were established mostly in towns and cities with populations of more than 10,000. Yet, of the 32 Ulster societies, 23 were to be found in towns with populations smaller than 5,000. Indeed, the Stillorgan, Moate and Portarlington societies were the only non-Ulster societies located in towns with populations under 5,000. Another factor which certainly led to the concentration of mendicity societies in the north-east was the fall-out from the 1825–6 industrial downturn and commercial crisis, which severely impacted on textile manufacturers, such as

---

27 The importance of the Hamburg institution as a model for the later mendicity societies is to be found at: *Account of the management of the poor in Hamburgh, since the year 1788. In a letter to some friends of the poor, in Great Britain* (Dublin, 1796); Anon., 'Management of the poor in Hamburg' in *Belfast Monthly Magazine*, iii, no. 13 (31 Aug. 1809), pp. 94–9; 'Extract from the report of the establishments at Hamburg, in 1799', ibid., pp. 99–101; Leaflet advertising forthcoming publication of 'an account of the management of the poor in Hamburg since the year 1788', 1 Sept. 1817 (NAI, CSOOP, CSO/OP483/31); *Observations on the House of Industry, Dublin*, pp. 3, 5; Hansard 1, xxxi, 689 (8 June 1815); Dalgleish, 'Voluntary associations and the middle class in Edinburgh', pp. 110–11. For the Hamburg institution's influence in the USA, see Blanche D. Coll, 'The Baltimore Society for the Prevention of Pauperism, 1820–1822' in *American Historical Review*, lxi, no. 1 (Oct. 1955), p. 80.

28 S.J. Connolly, *Religion and society in nineteenth-century Ireland* (Dundalk, 1994), p. 3.

29 Gray, *Making of the Irish Poor Law*, pp. 116, 119.

Table 5.1   Irish cities, towns and villages
where mendicity societies were founded, 1809–45
(arranged in descending order according to population)

Population	Location	County	Population in 1831 census[1]
> 20,000	Dublin	Dublin	232,362
	Cork	Cork	107,016
	Limerick	Limerick	66,554
	Belfast	Antrim	53,287
	Galway	Galway	33,120
	Waterford	Waterford	28,821
	Kilkenny	Kilkenny	23,741
10,000–20,000	Derry	Londonderry	19,620
	Drogheda	Louth	17,365
	Sligo	Sligo	15,152
	Clonmel	Tipperary	15,134
	Newry	Down	13,065
	Wexford	Wexford	10,673
	Dundalk	Louth	10,078
5,000–10,000	Armagh	Armagh	9,470
	Carlow	Carlow	9,114
	Carrickfergus	Antrim	8,706
	Ennis	Clare	7,711
	New Ross	Wexford	7,523
	Kinsale	Cork	7,312
	Parsonstown	King's County	6,594
	Bushmills	Antrim	6,869
	Enniskillen	Fermanagh	6,056
	Coleraine	Londonderry	5,668
	Roscrea	Tipperary	5,512
	Lisburn	Antrim	5,218
< 5,000	Downpatrick	Down	4,784
	Newtownards	Down	4,442
	Ballymena	Antrim	4,067
	Knockbreda	Down	3,900
	Monaghan	Monaghan	3,848

Population	Location	County	Population in 1831 census[1]
	Ballyshannon	Donegal	3,775
	Dungannnon	Tyrone	3,515
	Kirkinriola	Antrim	3,291
	Portarlington	Queen's County (Laois)	3,091
	Carrickmacross	Monaghan	2,979
	Lurgan	Armagh	2,842
	Bangor	Down	2,741
	Antrim	Antrim	2,655
	Larne	Antrim	2,616
	Ballymoney	Antrim	2,222
	Kilmood	Down	2,219
	Omagh	Tyrone	2,211
	Portaferry	Down	2,203
	Moate	Westmeath	1,785
	Ballycastle	Antrim	1,683
	Hillsborough	Down	1,453
	Hollywood	Down	1,288
	Caledon	Tyrone	1,079
	Saintfield	Down	1,056
	Kilmore	Armagh	937
	Stillorgan	Dublin	650

1 *Population, Ireland. Census of the population, 1831. Comparative abstract of the population in Ireland, as taken in 1821 and 1831*, H.C. 1833 (23), xxxix, 3.

the cotton weavers of Belfast and those engaged in the linen industry in rural Ulster.[30] The effects of this downturn were not limited to the north-east. In the Liberties of Dublin, the capital's textile hub lying to the south-west of the medieval city centre, it was estimated that as many as 20,000 people (newly unemployed workers and their dependants) were reduced to a state of near-starvation.[31]

---

30 Philip Ollerenshaw, 'Industry, 1820–1914' in Liam Kennedy and Philip Ollerenshaw (eds), *An economic history of Ulster, 1820–1940* (Manchester, 1985), pp. 67–8.
31 O'Neill, 'Bad year in the Liberties', p. 79; *Census of Ireland, 1851. Tables of deaths*, vol. 1, p. 200.

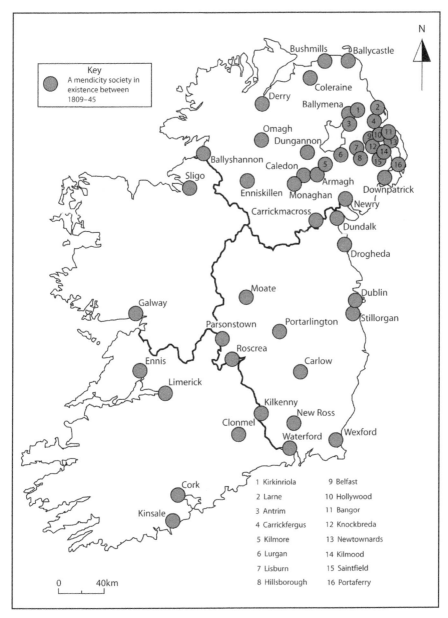

Figure 5.1   Map of mendicity societies in existence in Ireland, 1809–45

Compiled and drawn by Ciarán McCabe.

Just as the charitable fever hospital 'movement' spread through Britain and Ireland in the late eighteenth and early nineteenth centuries,[32] the contemporary proliferation of mendicity societies also represented a transnational 'movement', in that institutions with common objectives were formed under comparable conditions by persons from similar social backgrounds and driven by almost identical social and economic reasons. Furthermore, and crucially, these societies were not founded in an intellectual vacuum but in an environment where information regarding the work of like-minded charities was increasingly accessible and frequently exchanged. The founding literature of these charities, such as published statements and reports, typically made reference to earlier mendicity societies and the influence derived from these predecessors. Precedents established in Edinburgh and Gloucester influenced those who established the mendicity society in Belfast in 1809, while other Irish mendicity societies were also formed based on precedents set abroad.[33] The efforts of societies in Belfast, Edinburgh, Glasgow, Aberdeen, Munich and Hamburg, for instance, were known to the men who founded the Dublin Mendicity Society in January 1818 and who based their proposals for suppressing street begging on 'the result of actual practice, crowned, in more instances than one, with the most complete success'.[34] Similar language was used in a campaign to establish a mendicity asylum in Kilkenny, whose proponents consulted the published reports of earlier mendicity societies, 'those valuable associations on the Continent, in Great Britain, also in Ireland'. The public were told: 'The practicality of the measure has been proved by the best of all tests, experience, on the Continent and to different parts of the United Kingdom'.[35] In considering the financial viability of the Newry Mendicity Society, its managing committee contrasted its accounts with expenditure levels at the Dublin, Belfast, Derry and Edinburgh institutions.[36] Similarly, the 1821 report of the London Mendicity Society, founded three years earlier, noted that similar initiatives had been undertaken throughout England in the previous three years and commended 'the successful progress already made by many of these associations; and it has been observed, that upon the public roads

32 John V. Pickstone, 'Dearth, dirt and fever epidemics: rewriting the history of British "public health", 1780–1850' in Terence Ranger and Paul Slack (eds), *Epidemics and ideas: essays on the historical perception of pestilence* (Cambridge, 1999), pp. 132–3.

33 'Abolition of mendicity' in *Belfast Monthly Magazine*, ii, no. 11 (30 June 1809), pp. 437–8; Nicholls, *History of the Irish Poor Law*, p. 106.

34 Woods, *Dublin outsiders*, p. 12; *FJ*, 28 Jan. 1818; *Correspondent*, 28 Jan. 1818; *Arguments in proof of the necessity of suppressing street begging, passim*; *Report, Dublin Mendicity Society, 1818*, p. 26.

35 *Leinster Journal*, 19, 22 Apr. 1820.

36 *OSM*, iii, pp. 93–4.

contiguous to those towns which have Mendicity, or Vagrant Offices, not a beggar is to be seen'.[37] Baron Caspar von Voght, a founder of the precedent-setting Hamburg poor scheme, personified the transnational nature of this movement in the dissemination of his ideas across national borders – editions of his pamphlet promoting his Hamburg scheme were published in Dublin, London and Edinburgh[38] – and through his travels across Europe as part of the wave of 'philanthropic tourism'.[39]

Member societies of the movement were characterised as such by more than merely knowledge of the workings of similar bodies. Instances of co-operation between societies attest to the prevalence of a sense of belonging to a wider movement, wherein shared experiences informed the workings of individual organisations. Upon its establishment in 1821, the Waterford Mendicity Society forwarded its resolutions to the Dublin society for its consideration, thanking the latter for its co-operation and assisting in their labours.[40] The first report of the Waterford Mendicity Society made particular mention of the Dublin association, which furnished the southern city's body with 'every information in their power' and helped shape its 'original principles'. The Dublin members were also praised and thanked for being 'most earnest and assiduous in giving the instructions of their more enlarged practice to the friends of the Mendicant Asylum in Waterford'.[41] That same summer, a Rev. Price, secretary to the Waterford society, was elected an honorary associate of the Dublin committee.[42] Members of societies were also known to travel (sometimes long distances) to meet personally the founders of new bodies and offer advice first-hand. A Mr Hunt, among the founders of the Kinsale Mendicity Society, publicly offered to assist, through correspondence or in person, the foundation of a similar institution in Cork city,[43] while at an early meeting of the Cork Mendicity Society, 'a young Gentleman connected with the Dublin Association, Mr. Hudson, kindly attended, and gave to the Meeting information of a highly useful and interesting nature'.[44] The example

37 *The third report of the society for the suppression of mendicity, established in London, 1818* (London, 1821), p. 13.

38 [Caspar von Voght], *Account of the management of the poor in Hamburgh, since the year 1788: In a letter to some friends of the poor in Great Britain* (Dublin, 1796).

39 Caspar von Voght to James Edward Smith, 3 May 1795 (Linnean Society Archives, James Edward Smith papers, GB-110/JES/COR/10/57) accessed at Linnean Society of London http://linnean-online.org/62487/ (accessed 21 Jan. 2016); Joanna Innes and Arthur Burns, 'Introduction' in Arthur Burns and Joanna Innes (eds), *Rethinking the age of reform: Britain 1780–1850* (Cambridge, 2003), pp. 11–12.

40 Dublin Mendicity Society minute book, 22 May 1821.

41 *First annual report, Waterford Mendicity Society*, p. 11.

42 Dublin Mendicity Society minute book, 22 June 1821.

43 *Southern Reporter and Cork Commercial Courier*, 7 Nov. 1826.

44 *Cork Mercantile Chronicle*, 3 Nov. 1826.

of Irish mendicity societies supports Robert Morris's argument that voluntary societies were influenced and driven by 'the stimulus of action taken in other towns', yet his implication that the lack of an overarching central body prevented any meaningful connection between different charities is challenged by the example of some of the Irish mendicity societies.[45]

The proliferation of mendicity societies in Ireland at this time was such that in September 1820 the committee of the Dublin institution claimed in a memorial to the Lord Lieutenant that they had the satisfaction 'to observe that benevolent persons in remote parts of Ireland had succeeded in establishing similar institutions in several towns, and with the view to send up persons, in some instances, to be instructed in the system at their establishment in Dublin, where from the spacious accommodation hitherto possessed, the working of it could be shewn to advantage'.[46] The co-operation and exchange of information between the members of this movement transcended national boundaries, as seen in the London Mendicity Society's 1821 letter to the Dublin society, enclosing two of the former's reports and requesting any similar material published by the Dublin institution. In signing off, the London correspondent assured the Dublin committee of their guaranteed co-operation 'in the promotion of our mutual object'.[47] These instances support Jacinta Prunty's description of an 'urgent international debate', wherein the 'merits of Poor Law systems in Edinburgh, Bath, Hamburg, Munich, Amsterdam, Paris, New York and elsewhere [were] scrutinised and compared with the system proposed for or prevailing in Dublin'.[48] Within England, too, there were connections between mendicity societies, in terms of both philosophy and personnel. Among the founding resolutions of the London Mendicity Society in 1818 was 'to make application to the societies for the suppression of Mendicity already established in Edinburgh, Bath and other places for the purpose of obtaining their rules and regulations, and any other information likely to be useful to this Society'; the 1823 annual report noted that the society had corresponded with mendicity societies in at least 20 other locations throughout England.[49] Matthew Martin, who undertook an investigation into street begging in London in the 1790s and appeared as an expert witness to the 1815–16 London Mendicity Committee, was an early supporter of the Bath society as well as serving as an officer of the London association, while a Rev. Francis Randolph also served on both the Bath and London mendicity society committees.[50]

---

45 Morris, 'Voluntary societies and British urban elites', pp. 98, 103.
46 Dublin Mendicity Society minute book, 4 Sept. 1820 (NLI, DMSP, MS 32,599/1).
47 Dublin Mendicity Society minute book, 6 Feb. 1821.
48 Prunty, *Dublin slums*, p. 197.
49 London Mendicity Society minute book, 9 Jan., 25 Feb. 1818; ibid., 26 Feb. 1823.
50 Roberts, 'Reshaping the gift relationship', pp. 206–7, 209.

The Funding of Mendicity Societies

Mendicity societies resembled other charities in sourcing their income largely from voluntary sources, distinguishing them from the Houses of Industry. In 1831, the Coleraine Mendicity Society's income came from donations, subscriptions, cash received from the sale of broken stones (pulverised by male inmates), court fines and church collections.[51] Voluntary income consistently constituted around 90 per cent of the Derry society's total revenue, with other income coming from fines and the sale of sundry items.[52] Evidence for the societies in Dublin, Armagh, Drogheda, Sligo, Carrickfergus and Waterford, among others, confirms this trend of near or total dependency on voluntary contributions.[53] The Belfast House of Industry benefited on occasion from unorthodox sources of income: in 1817, £1 was donated by a group of travelling 'Indian Jugglers' who performed on the streets of Belfast, while in 1831 the institution received half of the proceeds of a ventriloquist show.[54] In 1839, the institution received 10s. from a donor, 'stopped from a servant's wages, for intemperance, and absenting herself without leave'.[55]

Financial uncertainty appears to have been the universal experience of mendicity societies, owing to their reliance on voluntary income. The charities were subject, therefore, to the shifting appetite of the public for addressing the problem of street begging. While the Galway mendicity asylum was described in 1825, shortly after its foundation, as 'the only institution of the kind that does not appear to be upon the verge of ruin'[56] – perhaps owing to initial enthusiasm for the institution being reflected in buoyant subscriptions – the asylum closed in 1829, due to indebtedness, and

51 'Historical notes compiled by Maxwell Given CE, Architect, Coleraine, for the History of Coleraine, vol. 7', 30 Mar. 1906, pp. 1707–10 (PRONI, Maxwell Given papers, D4164/A/7).

52 *First report, Londonderry Mendicity Society, p. 9; The second report of the general committee of the Mendicity Association, instituted in Londonderry, 13th May, 1825; with a statement of the accounts, and a list of the subscribers for the last year* (Derry, 1827), p. 12; *The thirteenth report of the general committee of the Mendicity Association, instituted in Londonderry, May 13, 1825; with a statement of the accounts, and a list of the subscribers for the year ending July 31, 1838* (Derry, 1838), p. 8.

53 *Third report of evidence from the Select Committee on the State of the Poor in Ireland. Minutes of evidence: 8 June–7 July. With an appendix of documents and papers, and likewise a general index*, p. 660, H.C. 1830 (665), vii, 840; ibid., pp. 669, 691, 698, 711.

54 BNL, 17 June 1817; P. Frederick Gallaher [*sic*] to William Cunningham, 30 Dec. 1831 (PRONI, Cunningham and Clarke papers, D1108/A/28A). For the identification of 'Gallaher' as a ventriloquist, see P. Frederick Gallaher to William Cunningham, 29 Jan. 1833 (PRONI, Cunningham and Clarke papers, D1108/A/28B).

55 *Belfast Commercial Chronicle*, 16 Feb. 1839.

56 *Galway Weekly Advertiser*, 25 June 1825.

between its re-opening in April 1830 and its permanent closure seven years later, the society was plagued by constant financial pressures and came to depend on income from the labour of the paupers for its survival.[57] In 1835, the Enniskillen society was required to be revived after its decline 'from the reduction in the contributions, of some of the subscribers, and the total withdrawal of others'.[58] Constant financial insecurity was also the experience of the Drogheda asylum, which operated between 1822 and 1838,[59] while the Limerick mendicity society saw its income drop from just more than £600 in 1823 to little over £200 six years later.[60] What is not clear is whether this sizeable decrease resulted from a waning of public support for the institution or the effects of the economic downturn of the mid-1820s, which would have negatively impacted on the society's subscribers and donors. An 1838 trade directory described the Limerick Mendicity Society as follows: 'Little can be said of this Society, as the charity is so badly supported that they cannot do much'.[61] The failure of the Ballycastle Mendicity Society in County Antrim was attributed to the farmers and shopkeepers who, in 'finding the mendicity [asylum] little or no relief, gave up their subscriptions for its support'.[62] The number of street beggars in Armagh city typically increased 'when the Mendicity Society [was] dissolved, which occasionally happens in consequence of funds being inadequate', according to the Church of Ireland Primate of Ireland, Lord John Beresford.[63] The main sources of income for the Caledon Mendicity Society, founded in 1829 by the Earl of Caledon and his wife for the purpose of giving relief to 'objects of real charity and to detect impostors and strangers, who have no claim to our assistance',[64] comprised an annual contribution of £100 from Lord Caledon and subscriptions averaging around £172 per annum.[65] The instance of Caledon is a unique example of an improving landlord – the earl erected stone-built houses and flour-mills in the town, and was described by Henry Inglis as being 'all that could be desired – a really good resident country gentleman'[66] – distributing relief to the poor of his community using the mendicity society model.

57 Cunningham, 'A town tormented by the sea', pp. 52–3.
58 Enniskillen Chronicle and Erne Packet, 10 Sept. 1835.
59 McHugh, Drogheda before the Famine, pp. 46–51.
60 PI, Appendix C, Part I, p. 95.
61 Deane's Limerick almanack, directory and advertiser, 1838, p. 37.
62 PI, Appendix A, p. 726.
63 PI, Supplement to Appendix A, p. 294.
64 'Account book of the Mendicity Society of Caledon, 1829–1869', 24 Jan. 1829, p. 9 (PRONI, Caledon papers, D2433/A/11/1).
65 Samuel Lewis, A topographical dictionary of Ireland ... (2 vols, London, 1837), i, pp. 243–4.
66 Inglis, Ireland in 1834, ii, p. 277. For Caledon's improving policies on his estate, see Lewis, Topographical dictionary, i, pp. 243–4; OSM, xx, pp. 1–4.

The funding of mendicity societies through subscriptions and donations was not the reserve of the wealthier classes. The Dublin society regularly received sums of money from 'tradesmen and labourers' as well as prominent citizens' servants, and these instances included either individual working men giving 10s. or a group of workers for a large company donating a cumulative sum. Employees at Guinness's brewery donated £38 15s. 7d. in 1840.[67] Given that the Guinness family had long connections with the mendicity society, it is to be wondered at how and why this particular charity was chosen for this communal donation. Were employees influenced, unduly or otherwise, by their employers' connections to the charity or were they being pragmatic in supporting a cause which attracted the benevolence of their paymaster? These considerations tie in with John Cunningham's analysis of the Galway Mendicity Society, which in 1824 expressed its 'peculiar satisfaction' at the donation of half a crown each by 46 of the town's weavers. Cunningham correctly asserts that this donation is better understood when one considers that these weavers, who were employed in 'the Hall of this town', were subject to a committee whose membership overlapped with that of the Mendicity Society.[68] Donating to the merchant-run charity may have been an act of self-interest by these working-class men, in terms of their future employment prospects, while the society's public advertisement of the weavers' collective donation also intended to embarrass wealthier inhabitants into contributing.

The Work of Mendicity Societies

Mendicity societies promised to citizens of Irish, British and European towns and cities, frustrated by the seemingly constant imposition of hordes of street beggars, a method of suppressing mendicancy which was relatively inexpensive and regulated by prominent members of the civil community. The key attraction of the societies was that they offered food and work for those who would probably resort to mendicancy for sustenance. These charities, therefore, removed the excuse for begging: with all the 'deserving' paupers receiving basic sustenance inside the mendicity asylum, those beggars who continued to solicit alms in the streets proved themselves to be 'undeserving' by the very fact of their public alms-seeking. Admission

---

67 *Twenty-third annual report of the managing committee of the Association for the Suppression of Mendicity in Dublin. For the year 1840* (Dublin, 1841), p. 44; *Twenty-second report, Dublin Mendicity Society, 1839,* p. 72; *An address to the mechanics, workmen, and servants, in the city of Dublin* (Dublin, 1828), p. 10.

68 Cunningham, *'A town tormented by the sea'*, p. 46.

to the mendicity asylum was not unqualified. In Sligo, proof of residence in the town for the three years prior to application was required.[69] In Dublin, a similar rule, requiring six months' residence, was in place but reportedly not strictly enforced.[70] The citizens of a given town or city were encouraged not to dole out alms to mendicants found begging in the streets but instead to refer alms-seekers to the mendicity society's premises where their claim to destitution would be assessed. This had the effect of ensuring that citizens were not 'double-taxed'.

The mendicity institutions differed from the Houses of Industry and the later Poor Law union workhouses in that paupers generally did not reside in the building.[71] Exceptions to this rule were the Sligo Mendicity Society, which in 1828 was providing accommodation for 43 of the 66 paupers on its books, and the Clonmel society, which lodged 50 paupers at its premises.[72] The general practice was that applicants were admitted in the morning, provided with food at stipulated times and discharged in the evening, when they returned to their places of residence or found shelter on the streets. During the day the able-bodied were put to labour, such as breaking stones or oyster shells, picking oakum and spinning, while the infirm and elderly were given succour and occasionally allocated basic work. The mendicity society in Derry raised income through the sale of items made by its paupers and among the articles for sale were 'Spangles of yarn, Herring net, Garden nets, Small tow nets, Flax nets, Hemp nets, Flax, Linen yarn socks'.[73] The Belfast House of Industry adhered to the general mendicity society model by providing only day accommodation for the poor – namely, 'that class of poor who have no place of residence convenient for working in'.[74] The institution encouraged industrious individuals to engage in employment, mostly the spinning of flax or wool (either on-site or at the paupers' abode), knitting and picking oakum. One year after opening, 309 spinners of linen yarn were employed, as well as stocking knitters and oakum pickers.[75] The destitute

69 Ibid., p. 48.
70 *PI, Appendix C, Part II*, p. 35.
71 Dublin Mendicity Society minute book, 13 July 1830; McHugh, *Drogheda before the Famine*, p. 47; *Second report, state of the poor select committee, 1830*, p. 376; Report on the state of the poor in Waterford city, 1834, ff. 18ʳ–19ʳ; *Second report of the Mendicity Association, Londonderry*, p. 6; Frederick Page, *Observations on the state of the indigent poor in Ireland, and the existing institutions for their relief* (London, 1830), p. 25.
72 *Sligo Journal*, 13 May 1828; *PI, Appendix A*, p. 702.
73 *The fourth report of the general committee of the Mendicity Association, instituted in Londonderry, 13th May, 1825; with a statement of the accounts, and a list of the subscribers for the last year* (Derry, 1829), p. 10.
74 *BNL*, 14 July 1809; *PI, Appendix C, Part I*, p. 11; Jordan, *Who cared?*, pp. 20–1; *Martin's Belfast directory for 1841–42 ...* (1841; repr. Belfast, 1992), pp. 246–7.
75 *BNL*, 15 May 1810; 'Rules and regulations for the House of Industry, Belfast', p. 267.

poor were also incentivised away from mendicancy by the Belfast society's provision of food, fuel and straw to deserving cases approved by visitors.[76] Mendicity societies, particularly in large cities, were designed, in the words of the Dublin society's officials, to 'resemble as much as possible a factory' as opposed to a prison.[77]

The guiding principle of these institutions was similar to that used by the New Poor Law workhouses in England (and later in Ireland) from the 1830s – namely, 'that the condition of persons within charitable institutions should not be raised above the level of the lower class of the working orders out of doors'.[78] These charities did not wish to undermine the incentive and moral virtue of 'honest' and independent industry to the working classes. Those who entered these institutions were subject to strict discipline and order, and relief had to be earned, either through genuine distress or hard labour. Removing these individuals from the streets and from a state of idleness for a few hours each day decreased their chances of resorting to alms-seeking. However, mendicity societies did not – and could not – completely prevent this eventuality. It was noted that many relieved at the Limerick Mendicity Society during the day would 'take up the trade of begging on their return home each night, to the great annoyance of the shopkeepers'.[79] In Dublin, a number of women, 'notoriously prostitutes', were reported as attending the institution during the day and being 'on the streets at night', while a police magistrate in the city told the Poor Inquiry commissioners that 'Many of the beggars at night are persons who are in the Mendicity all day'.[80] To these individuals the mendicity societies were clearly yet another survival option to be utilised. They could enter the asylums voluntarily and receive shelter and food during the day before returning to their habitual practices in the evening. The poor exerted agency and made decisions for themselves, drawing on their knowledge of the various welfare options available to them in the 'economy of makeshifts'.

76 For the work of the Belfast asylum, see Cooke, *Sermon preached in aid of the Belfast House of Industry.*

77 *FJ*, 21 Feb. 1838.

78 *Second report, state of the poor select committee, 1830*, p. 342.

79 *Deane's Limerick almanack, directory and advertiser, 1838*, p. 37.

80 Dublin Mendicity Society minute book, 12 Oct. 1824; *PI, Appendix C, Part II, Report upon vagrancy and mendicity in the City of Dublin*, p. 40a*.

Lack of Legal Powers

The ability of mendicity societies to apprehend and confine street beggars varied from place to place, and in many cases the lack of powers physically to remove mendicants was the source of much debate and complaint by the managing committees and local householders, who were critical of this weakness. Some mendicity societies employed beadles to suppress mendicancy, but the exact nature of their work is difficult to ascertain. Did they physically man-handle beggars out of public streets or did they use persuasion, intimidation or threats to ward off mendicants? In 1831, the Coleraine Mendicity Society and poor house was paying its 'bang-beggar' an annual salary of £7 16s., while the following year, this figure increased substantially to £17 11s. 8d. for 'persons to prevent street begging'.[81] More definitive information on the powers exercised by such individuals is available for the Belfast House of Industry, whose two constables apprehended and confined street beggars under authority deputed from the town's Charitable Society, which had been granted such powers by a 1774 statute.[82] Beggars were confined in a 'miserable vault' in the House of Industry for up to 24 hours before being released, while the most 'incorrigible' inmates were taken before a magistrate.[83] The Londonderry Mendicity Society's constables also possessed powers of apprehension: two, or sometimes three, officers called 'bangbeggars' were employed 'to go round the City in every direction, and to apprehend any one they may find begging', who were then confined in the city bridewell.[84] After being sent away by the master 'over the bridge', the mendicants were allegedly discouraged from re-entering the town by the one penny toll on the bridge. If caught a second time, the beggars were confined in a bridewell attached to the mendicity asylum.[85]

81   *OSM*, xxxiii, p. 71; *Municipal corporations (Ireland). Appendix to the first report of the commissioners. Part III. – Conclusion of the north-west circuit*, pp. 1050–51, H.C. 1836 [C 26], xxiv, 50–1. It appears that this parliamentary report formed the basis of Maxwell Given's presentation of the mendicity society's accounts for the years 1831–2 in 'Historical notes compiled by Maxwell Given' 1906, pp. 1707–10.

82   13 & 14 Geo. III, c. 46 [Ire.] (2 June 1774).

83   *PI, Appendix C, Part I*, p. 12. In 1810 the House of Industry advertised for a 'stout active man, to take up all persons found begging in the Streets of Belfast, and to keep the Streets free from Mendicants': *BNL*, 28 Sept. 1810.

84   *The third report of the general committee of the Mendicity Association, instituted in Londonderry, 13th May, 1825; with a statement of the accounts, and a list of the subscribers for the last year* (Derry, 1828), p. 6.

85   *Second report of Geo. Nicholls, Poor Laws, Ireland*, p. 11; *Third report of the Mendicity Association, Londonderry*, p. 6; *Colby's Ordnance Survey memoir of Londonderry* (1837; 2nd edn, Limavady, 1990), p. 168.

Upon its foundation in 1818, the Dublin Mendicity Society employed inspectors to clear beggars from the city streets. The efficacy of this method was undermined, however, by the absence of legal powers for these inspectors to remove or detain mendicants. To overcome this problem the institution's officers accompanied members of the Dublin police 'on the beat' and the former's role was limited to 'pointing out persons in the act of begging to the police' who would subsequently arrest and detain the culprit.[86] According to the Poor Inquiry commissioners, these weaknesses were such that the system which prevailed in Dublin 'presents far less facilities for their [the beggars'] apprehension than that adopted in London'.[87] M.J.D. Roberts has argued that the employment by the London Mendicity Society of its own constables resulted from the belief 'that existing police agents in London were demonstrably uninterested in enforcing the begging provisions' of the English vagrancy legislation.[88] Just as the formation of the professional Metropolitan Police in 1829 led the London Mendicity Society to relinquish its policing duties regarding mendicants,[89] it appears that the Dublin society waned in its deployment of street inspectors in the mid-1830s, around the time of the establishment of the Dublin Metropolitan Police along the lines of Robert Peel's London force. Indeed, the 1830s witnessed the unusual phenomenon of private residents and businesses employing extra-legal street inspectors, who possessed no legal powers of any kind, for the sole purpose of removing beggars from outside their respective homes and places of business.

Inter-Denominational Appeal of Mendicity Societies

In a period marked by increasing sectarian tensions, and when public charity was closely linked to confessional identities, the establishment and management of mendicity societies provided opportunities for inter-denominational collaboration in the public sphere of philanthropy. Public figures who differed in their religious views co-operated through these charities, as the mendicity society model was agreeable to the doctrinal views of the different Irish churches and religious societies, as well as the social, economic and cultural outlook of the middle-class men who formed and ran the organisations. The 19-man committee of the Ballyshannon Mendicity Society, for example,

---

86 *PI, Appendix C, Part II, Report upon vagrancy and mendicity in the City of Dublin*, p. 33a*; Dublin Mendicity Society minute book, 17 May 1836.
87 *PI, Appendix C, Part II, Report upon vagrancy and mendicity in the City of Dublin*, p. 33a*.
88 Roberts, 'Reshaping the gift relationship', p. 217.
89 Ibid., p. 218.

comprised nine Catholics and ten Protestants.[90] The cross-denominational nature of the management of mendicity societies can also be seen in the raising of income from collections in different churches and meeting houses. The Carrickfergus Mendicity Society was supported through collections in the local Church of Ireland church and Presbyterian meeting house, as well as by voluntary subscriptions,[91] while the local Catholic priest in Ballymena collected subscriptions upon the establishment of the town's society.[92] The income for the Sligo society, the chairman of which was Presbyterian minister Rev. Heron,[93] included donations collected at sermons preached at the town's Anglican, Presbyterian and Independent places of worship.[94] In 1837, 'the few Jews residing in Dublin' contributed £7 14s. to the city's mendicity society.[95]

These charities were secular in nature and embraced all denominations, in terms both of their serving members and those paupers relieved. The fact that the Antrim Mendicity Society relieved Catholics, who comprised 'the least competent in means and numbers to contribute' to the charity's income, was hailed as a 'practical illustration of disinterested benevolence'.[96] As with most large secular charities in urban centres, Protestants formed a dispro- portionately large number of the members, reflecting the greater social and economic prominence of Protestants in nineteenth-century urban Ireland. But, the rising strength and confidence of the Catholic middle classes was also represented in the membership of the mendicity societies. Catholic priest, Poor Law advocate and member of the Dublin Mendicity Society managing committee, Rev. Thaddeus O'Malley pointed to the collaboration between clergy of all denominations in mendicity societies as evidence for the suitability of having priests and ministers serve on Poor Law boards of guardians.[97] (The subsequent stipulation[98] that clergymen could not serve as guardians was one of the features of the 1838 Irish Poor Law Act which distinguished it from the English act of four years previously.) Testifying to a parliamentary select committee, O'Malley asserted:

Now I have been acting for many Years on the Mendicity Committee in Dublin; we had Clergymen of the different Churches there; and

90 *PI, Appendix C, Part I*, p. 118.
91 *Third report, state of the poor select committee, 1830*, Appendix, p. 698.
92 *PI, Appendix A*, p. 718.
93 Fióna Gallagher, *The streets of Sligo: urban evolution over the course of seven centuries* (Sligo, 2008), p. 169.
94 *Sligo Journal*, 22 Apr., 13 May 1828.
95 *Twentieth annual report of the managing committee of the Association for the Suppression of Mendicity in Dublin. For the year 1837* (Dublin, 1838), p. 21.
96 *BNL*, 14 June 1831.
97 O'Malley, *Poor Laws – Ireland*, p. 67.
98 1 & 2 Vict., c. 56, s. 19 (31 July 1838).

I never knew any thing approaching to an Unpleasantness to occur between them. I think it most desirable to bring the Clergy of both Churches together, and I do not know any more fitting Occasion than the administering [of] Poor Relief.[99]

The evidence suggests that, notwithstanding a small number of instances where political and religious tensions found their way into the board rooms of managing committees,[100] mendicity societies were successful in serving as cross-denominational forums wherein Catholics and Protestants could co-operate in the relief of poverty and suppression of mendicancy.

Decline of the Mendicity Societies: The 1838 Poor Law and 'Double Taxation'

In most cases, the mendicity societies ceased to operate in the late 1830s and early 1840s and this decline was directly related to the introduction of the 1838 Poor Law. The main supporters of the mendicity societies were the middle classes and petty bourgeois (such as small shopkeepers), who were also liable for the new poor rate. With the introduction of the new compulsory assessment, these ratepayers were more reluctant to subscribe to the mendicity societies, which catered for the same class of destitute poor now eligible for admission to the workhouses. The problem of perceived 'double taxation' impacted on other charities' level of subscriptions and donations, as former supporters became more selective in how they distributed their disposable income in light of the new poor rate. Throughout the 1830s, while the Poor Law question was prominent in public discourse in Ireland and Britain, mendicity societies were conscious of the likely impact that the introduction of a poor rate would have on their voluntarily generated income. The threat of a compulsorily assessed Poor Law was regularly used with great effect by charitable societies to pressure the public into parting with some of their money. In the late 1820s, the Dublin Mendicity Society warned the city's inhabitants that in the event that insufficient income was raised from the usual voluntary sources, the organisation would petition parliament to legislate for a compulsory rate for the support of the society. 'That resolution', managing committee member Anthony Richard Blake informed a parliamentary inquiry, 'appeared to have a very beneficial effect;

---

99 *Report from the select committee of the House of Lords on the laws relating to the relief of the destitute poor, and into the operation of the medical charities in Ireland; together with the minutes of evidence taken before the said committee*, p. 836, H.C. 1846 (694), xi, 872.

100 Binns, *Miseries and beauties of Ireland*, ii, pp. 257–8; *Sligo Journal*, 13, 30 May 1828.

subscriptions came in almost immediately upon it'. When asked for his opinion as to what would have been the effect on voluntary contributions had a compulsory rate been introduced, Blake replied that such sources of income would have ceased. The committee was told by Blake that in towns and cities where institutions such as mendicity societies existed and operated, people refused to give alms to beggars in the streets. His explanation was: 'It results, I apprehend, from their feeling that they already contribute to the support of the poor, and partly from knowing that the distressed may be relieved through the mendicity establishment'.[101]

Blake's assertion here that the existence of mendicity societies ended public alms-giving does not ring true, though, as it was the near-universal experience of these charities to criticise the continued practice of alms-giving to street beggars even after the mendicity asylum had been established.[102] The period between the passing of the Poor Law in 1838 and the first admission of paupers into workhouses was an interval period marked by uncertainty, when the managers of charities urged the public to continue to contribute to their local mendicity society until such a time as the workhouse was open for the reception of paupers. In May 1840, in Downpatrick, the defunct mendicity society was revived 'to relieve the poor of this district in their present distressed state', by means of home-based assistance and badging.[103] At this juncture, the poor rate valuator had been appointed (March 1840), yet the contracts for the construction of the workhouse would not be signed for another four months (September 1840).[104] In spring 1842, the delay in opening the workhouse (the first paupers were not admitted until September 1842)[105] required a final burst of publicity to seek continued donations to the mendicity fund which 'ceases when the Workhouse opens'.[106] In its final report, for the year ending July 1838, the Londonderry Mendicity Society expressed its support for the recently enacted Poor Law under which, it hoped, 'apprehended abuses will

---

101 *Second report, state of the poor select committee, 1830*, pp. 341–2.
102 *Sixth report, Dublin Mendicity Society, 1823*, p. 28; *Galway Weekly Advertiser*, 1 Jan. 1825; *Third report, Londonderry Mendicity Association*, p. 6; *OSM*, iii, p. 101. The London society hit out at this continued practice, asserting that 'indiscriminate almsgiving is not charity. So long as this habit is indulged in, so long must all efforts to suppress Mendicity prove abortive': London Mendicity Society minute book, 24 Feb. 1819.
103 *Downpatrick Recorder*, 30 May 1840.
104 *Appendices B. to F. to the eighth annual report of the Poor Law Commissioners*, appendix E, no. 10, p. 385, H.C. 1842 [C 399], xix, 397; *Appendices A. to D. to the ninth annual report of the Poor Law Commissioners*, Appendix C, no. 9, p. 286, H.C. 1843 [491], xxi, 294.
105 *Appendices, ninth annual report, Poor Law Commissioners*, Appendix C, no. 9, p. 286.
106 *Downpatrick Recorder*, 30 Apr. 1842.

be checked, the evils will be corrected, and the measure be attended with advantage to all'. Yet, noting that the Poor Law had yet to be enforced in the city, the society, acknowledging its own imminent demise, beseeched the public to continue their subscriptions and donations, and urged that the poor 'must not be left to perish between the old and the new mode of relief'.[107] In February 1840, it was reported that the workhouse was 'considerably advanced and will, when completed, be a magnificent edifice. [T]he Mendicity establishment will be surrendered'.[108] When the Derry workhouse opened in November 1840, 'the inmates of the Mendicity and a few others' were admitted into the new institution.[109]

Most mendicity societies were dissolved around the time when people witnessed the most tangible evidence that the Poor Law was operating in their area – the collection of poor rates and the opening of the local workhouse.[110] The Waterford society appears to have declined around 1840–1. A newspaper notice published in February 1840 referred to the continued difficulties in keeping the institution open, and announced a special public meeting to consider the urgent problem.[111] When the Waterford city workhouse admitted its first 60 paupers in April 1841, 54 were inmates of the mendicity asylum.[112] The decision to close the Belfast House of Industry was taken at a meeting on 31 May 1841, less than three weeks after the first paupers were admitted into the town's workhouse, while in Limerick, city paupers from the Mendicity Society were among the first inmates of the workhouse in 1841.[113] Two exceptions to this trend were the mendicity societies in Dublin and Ballymoney, the latter of which remained in existence until 1902, surviving on the proceeds of the bequest of £1,000 by Presbyterian woollen draper, Neal Kennedy, who died circa 1821.[114]

The decline of the Irish mendicity societies manifested itself differently from that of the British anti-begging charities. From what little information that can be gathered on the fate of these latter institutions, there does not appear to have been much immediate impact from the introduction

107 *Thirteenth report, Londonderry Mendicity Association*, pp. 6–7. For similar sentiments in Newry, see *Belfast Commercial Chronicle*, 8 Oct. 1838.

108 *Clare Journal, and Ennis Advertiser*, 6 Feb. 1840.

109 *Londonderry Journal*, n.d., cited in *Clare Journal, and Ennis Advertiser*, 30 Nov. 1840.

110 The declarations of the first poor rate and the opening of the workhouses for the reception for paupers occurred almost invariably in the years 1841–2 in the country's 130 Poor Law Unions: *Appendices B. to F. to the eighth annual report of the Poor Law Commissioners*, appendix E, no. 10, pp. 384–6.

111 Ó Cearbhaill, 'A memory that lived and a charity that died', pp. 169–70.

112 *Clare Journal, and Ennis Advertiser*, 22 Apr. 1841.

113 Ibid., 31 May 1841.

114 Ballymoney Mendicity Committee minute book, 1846–1902 (PRONI, J.B. Hamilton papers, D1518/4/3/4. Location: TQ 1–075/A3 B37504).

of the 1834 New Poor Law in England and Wales. Given the existence of a rate-based Poor Law there for more than two centuries, the 1830s did not witness a sudden shift from the voluntary to compulsory mode of poor relief and the funding of this relief. The relatively rapid nationwide closure of charitable societies that was witnessed in Ireland following the introduction of the Poor Law was not replicated in the rest of Britain; on the contrary, in 1840, six years after the introduction of the New Poor Law, numerous new mendicity societies were established in English towns, most likely in response to the increased levels of poverty, destitution and beggary arising from the nationwide economic depression of 1839–42.[115] Lionel Rose suggests that many provincial societies ceased operating by the late 1840s owing to continued alms-giving by the benevolent and pleas from fraudulent applicants.[116] The formation of so-called mendicity societies experienced a revival in mid- to late Victorian Britain; however, these later charities ought to be regarded as part of the emerging Charitable Organisation Society movement, which pioneered the use of scientific methods of social casework to the investigation of poverty and charity, and in this regard differed from the rudimentary *modus operandi* of earlier mendicity societies.[117] In certain cases, the decline of British mendicity societies was due to localised circumstances. The Edinburgh Mendicity Society (also known as the Society for Suppressing Begging) was merged into the city's House of Refuge in 1836, owing to the mendicity society's diminishing finances and the latter institution's greater capacity to allocate resources towards the relief of destitution and suppression of street begging.[118] The London society continued to operate throughout the Victorian period but its purpose was largely superseded by the establishment of the Charity Organisation Society in 1869 and the charity declined in significance and prominence until its dissolution in 1959.[119]

Ireland's Houses of Industry also ceased to exist following the introduction of the Poor Law, under which Houses of Industry and all associated assets

---

115 *Coventry Herald*, 10 Jan. 1840; *Warwick and Warwickshire Advertiser*, 2 May 1840; *Bucks Herald*, 7 Mar. 1840.

116 Lionel Rose, *'Rogues and vagabonds': vagrant underworld in Britain, 1815–1985* (London and New York, 1988), p. 19.

117 R. Humphreys, *Sin, organized charity and the Poor Law in Victorian England* (Basingstoke, 1995), pp. 101–43, 204–5; Derek Fraser, *The evolution of the British welfare state: a history of social policy since the Industrial Revolution* (2nd edn, Basingstoke, 1984), pp. 130–2.

118 *Edinburgh Evening Courant*, 24 Mar. 1836. I am grateful to Joseph Curran for this reference.

119 Roberts, 'Reshaping the gift relationship', pp. 228–31; Rose, *'Rogues and vagabonds'*, p. 95.

were to be vested in the newly appointed Poor Law Commissioners.[120] In some instances, the new workhouses were established in the former Houses of Industry premises. Such measures made sense in locations where a large segregated institution designed for the poor already existed, thus avoiding the cost of acquiring a new site and building a workhouse. The North and South Dublin Union workhouses were established in the city's House of Industry and Foundling Hospital respectively, and in Cork the former House of Industry was used for meetings of the board of guardians between June 1839 and December 1841, when the new purpose-built workhouse was opened.[121] Upon the opening of the Limerick union workhouse in 1841, the 489 inmates of the city's House of Industry were transferred to the new institution.[122] Interestingly, among the first purchases of the Limerick Board of Guardians were 'tables and forms' from the city's Mendicity Society for £40.[123] What also made sense in many cases was the appointment of staff from the recently dissolved institutions to positions in the new workhouses; for example, a Mr Riordan, previously master in the Clonmel House of Industry, was appointed to the same position in the town's workhouse in late 1840.[124]

A Poor Law Survivor: The Dublin Mendicity Society

The case of Dublin makes for fascinating reading. The Dublin Mendicity Society was almost unique in remaining in existence after the introduction of the workhouses – and indeed in outliving the Poor Law system.[125] In seeking to explain this, one must consider the sheer size of the city and the number of destitute poor in this urban centre. In most other villages, towns and cities where mendicity societies were founded, these charities could not have been sustained alongside such a large institution as the local workhouse, in terms of both the ability of local ratepayers to support the two systems and the demand for the various institutions' welfare services. The sprawling metropolis of Dublin, on the other hand, possessed both a large enough pool of prospective supporters to continue subscribing to charitable causes concurrent to paying their Poor Law rates and the constant flow of local and non-native poor. The key to the Dublin Mendicity Society's

120 1 & 2 Vict., c. 56, s. 34.
121 Michelle O'Mahony, *Famine in Cork city: famine life at Cork union workhouse* (Cork, 2005), pp. 21–30.
122 Fleming and Logan, *Pauper Limerick*, p. xv.
123 *Clare Journal, and Ennis Advertiser*, 30 Nov., 7 Dec. 1840.
124 Ibid., 7 Dec. 1840.
125 The Dublin Mendicity Society (Institution) remains in existence at the time of writing, celebrating its bicentenary in 2018. See www.mendicity.org (accessed 5 Jan. 2017).

Table 5.2   Categories of inmates in the Dublin Mendicity Society on 25 April 1840

Males		Females		Totals
Able-bodied	102	Able-bodied	499	601
Infirm	204	Infirm	1,143	1,347
Extern sick	11	Extern sick	155	166
Children in upper schools	135	Children in upper schools	185	320
Children in infant schools	107	Children in infant schools	103	210
Young children	44	Young children	47	91
Totals	603		2,132	2,735

Source: *Twenty-second report, Dublin Mendicity Society, 1839*, p. 15.

Table 5.3   Categories of inmates in the Dublin Mendicity Society on an unspecified date in June 1840

Males		Females		Totals
Able-bodied	25	Able-bodied	225	250
Infirm	0	Infirm	0	0
Extern sick	0	Extern sick	0	0
Children in upper schools	35	Children in upper schools	42	77
Children in infant schools	31	Children in infant schools	45	76
Young children	0	Young children	0	0
Totals	91		312	403

Source: *Twenty-second report, Dublin Mendicity Society, 1839*, p. 15.

survival and longevity was its ability to adapt to new circumstances, tailoring its services to provide for newly defined and focused categories of the city's destitute poor.[126] Following the opening of the city's two workhouses, young children and infirm adults were no longer admitted into the mendicity institution, as these individuals were catered for in the Poor Law institutions. Tables 5.2 and 5.3 demonstrate the stark modification in the charity's inmate base arising from the introduction of the Poor Law

126   Cousins, 'Philanthropy and poor relief', p. 36.

system. On 25 April 1840, infirm females comprised almost 42 per cent of the mendicity society's 2,735 inmates, while just weeks later, following the opening of North and South Dublin Union workhouses, there were no infirm paupers (male or female) recorded in the institution. The able-bodied poor, while not gone completely, had diminished considerably in number, as had the child inmates; furthermore, there were no longer any 'young children' to be found on the charity's books.[127] Whereas the number of the mendicity society's inmates dropped by around 2,000, there were just more than 2,000 inmates in the newly opened workhouses, and most of these individuals had been previously catered for in the Mendicity Institution.[128] A clear connection can, thus, be established in the use of the city's poorer classes of these respective welfare institutions.

The Dublin Mendicity Society's long-held fears that a poor rate would impact detrimentally on its own income levels were borne out upon the introduction of the Poor Law system. Table 5.4 and Figure 5.2 (extrapolated from Table 5.4) demonstrate the rapid fall in income from both annual subscriptions and casual sources for the Society in these years. Subscriptions fell from £6,365 14s. 11d. in 1839 to £1,891 10s. 2d. just one year later, representing a drop of 70 per cent. In the following two years, the Society again witnessed a 70 per cent decrease in subscriptions, falling to £563 19s. 8d. in 1842. A brief surge in subscriptions was recorded during the early years of the Great Famine but by 1848 subscriptions had fallen to the relatively low amount of £708 4s. 8d. The drop in income around 1840 was caused by subscribers' knowledge that the Society was looking after a considerably smaller number of paupers, who were now catered for in the workhouses. Nonetheless, the 'double taxation' factor was undoubtedly the main reason behind this substantial decrease.

In considering the decline of the mendicity societies, whose duties were largely superseded by the Poor Law workhouse system, a number of issues may be analysed – one being whether the same men who served on the mendicity societies' managing committees became members of the workhouse boards of guardians upon the emergence of the new system. Clerics of all denominations, as noted above, frequently served as members of the managing committees of the mendicity charities: in its final year of operation, 12 of the Londonderry Mendicity Society's committee of 42 men (28.6 per cent) were clergymen, while the two secretaries were also clerics.[129] Under the 1838 Poor

127 *Twenty-second report, Dublin Mendicity Society, 1839*, p. 15. The total number of inmates is mistakenly given as 2,715 (ibid.).
128 Ibid.; *Seventh annual report of the Poor Law Commissioners, with appendices*, p. 44, H.C. 1841 Session I [C 327], xi, 342.
129 *Thirteenth report, Londonderry Mendicity Association, 1838*, p. 3.

Table 5.4   Subscriptions and other casual income received by the Dublin Mendicity Society, 1830–48

Year	Annual subscriptions	Casual income (fines, legacies, anonymous donations, etc.)	Total income
1830	£6,038	£4,609	£10,647
1831	£5,311	£4,236	£9,547
1832	£3,922	£2,908	£6,830
1833	£3,849	£2,848	£6,697
1834	£4,061	£2,951	£7,012
1835	£3,908	£2,611	£6,519
1836	£4,844	£3,399	£8,243
1837	£4,247	£5,177	£9,424
1838	£4,793	£3,877	£8,670
1839	£6,366	£4,815	£11,181
1840	£1,892	£2,915	£4,807
1841	£661	£1,330	£1,991
1842	£564	£1,336	£1,900
1843	£592	£974	£1,566
1844	£717	£1,209	£1,926
1845	£662	£1,321	£1,983
1846	£1,143	£1,165	£2,308
1847	£1,569	£2,015	£3,584
1848	£708	£977	£1,685

Source: *Thirty-first annual report of the managing committee of the Association for the Suppression of Mendicity in Dublin. For the year 1848* (Dublin, 1849), p. 21. Figures have been rounded to the nearest pound.

Law, clergymen were specifically prohibited from serving as Poor Law union guardians, thereby excluding from boards of guardians a large number of individuals who had considerable first-hand experience of relieving the poor as well as valuable administrative skills. Of the members of an eight-person sub-committee from among the Londonderry Poor Law Union board of guardians in 1842, one (Sir Robert A. Ferguson) can be definitively identified as having been a member of the city's mendicity society, while the names of two other Poor Law guardians (Messrs McClelland and Mehan) match those

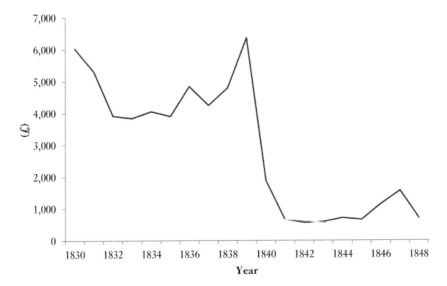

Figure 5.2   Subscriptions to the Dublin Mendicity Society, 1830–48

of two members of the earlier charity.[130] In Belfast, a John Cunningham and a Charles Thomson served as directors of the House of Industry (the former as treasurer) in 1810, and three decades later, individuals of the same names were among the guardians of the Poor Law union.[131] (A John Cunningham bequeathed £100 to the Belfast House of Industry but as it was dissolved by late 1842 this money was appropriated to the Surgical Hospital, with the sanction of the Commissioners for Charitable Bequests.)[132] James McTier and John Knox were also two officials of the Belfast House of Industry who served among the town's first Union guardians.[133] In Dublin, in 1841, Sir John Kingston James Bart and John Mackay were members of the mendicity society managing committee at the same time as they served as elected

130 Ibid.; *Londonderry Union. Return to an order of the honourable House of Commons, dated 11 March 1842; – for, copies of the contracts entered into for the building of the Londonderry Union poor-house* ... p. 35, H.C. 1842 (189), xxxvi, 231.

131 *BNL*, 4 May 1810; Belfast Board of Guardians minute book, 4 Jan. 1842 (PRONI, Belfast Board of Guardians papers, BG7/A/1); *Poor Law (Ireland). Copies of any communications, &c. by the Poor Law Commissioners to any boards of guardians in Ireland, in reference to 15th & 16th clauses of the amended Poor Law Act...*, p. 27, H.C. 1844 (346), xl, 659; Farrell, *The Poor Law and the workhouse in Belfast*, p. 28.

132 *BNL*, 23 Dec. 1842.

133 For their involvement with the House of Industry, see *BNL*, 25 Dec. 1840. Their service as Poor Law guardians is recorded at: Belfast Board of Guardians minute book, 4 Jan. 1842 for John Knox; Farrell, *The Poor Law and the workhouse in Belfast*, p. 28 for James McTier.

guardians in the North and South Dublin Unions respectively.[134] These cases appear, however, to have been merely a handful of instances where continuity in personnel can be identified and they must not necessarily be considered representative.

Perhaps most interesting of all is the case of the Dublin Mendicity Society's honorary secretary, Joseph Burke, who ended his involvement with the charity when he was appointed as an Assistant Poor Law Commissioner in April 1839.[135] Burke's appointment to a state position followed on the heels of years of correspondence with (or perhaps canvassing of) senior political figures, both Tory and Whig, as well as a direct request to Lord Morpeth for a Poor Law appointment.[136] To Burke, a member of the Irish Bar and clearly an ambitious man, a position with the new Poor Law administration was a natural progression from his employment with the Dublin Mendicity Society. Indeed, in his appeal to Morpeth, Burke specifically drew on his service to the mendicity society, 'which has given me an experience as to the state of the numerous poor of this city, that I submit might prove useful in the working or carrying into effect any legislative measure for the amelioration of their present & very deplorable state'.[137] These examples suggest that some level of continuity existed between the mendicity societies, and the new Poor Law workhouses and Poor Law system, in terms of the individuals who were responsible in overseeing the administration of the new system. Of course, a key difference was that while the administrators possessed great independence in the mendicity societies, which operated as private entities, the manner in which the workhouses were run, and relief provided therein, was governed by legislation and guardians were accountable to the centralised Poor Law Commissioners in Dublin.

134 *Twenty-fourth annual report of the managing committee of the Association for the Suppression of Mendicity in Dublin. For the year 1841* (Dublin, 1842), p. iii; *Dublin Almanac, and general register of Ireland, 1841*, pp. 815, 816.

135 *Twenty-second report, Dublin Mendicity Society, 1839*, p. 11; *Sixth annual report of the Poor Law Commissioners. With appendices*, p. 24, H.C. 1840 [C 245], xvii, 424; Letter of resignation of Joseph Burke as Honorary Secretary of Dublin Mendicity Society, 29 Apr. 1839, in Letter book of Joseph Burke (NAI, M 2591, f. 134ʳ). Joseph was the younger brother of genealogist John Burke, founder of *Burke's Peerage*: *FJ*, 4 May 1839; Letter book of Joseph Burke, f. 13ʳ⁻ᵛ; Helen Andrews, 'Burke, John' in *DIB*, ii, pp. 41–2.

136 Letter book of Joseph Burke, ff. 9ʳ–17ʳ. For the letter to Morpeth, dated 17 Jan. 1837, see ibid., ff. 17ʳ–18ᵛ. A similar petition was sent to Irish MP Richard Lalor Sheil and the English Poor Law Commissioner George Nicholls: Joseph Burke to Richard Lalor Sheil, 5 June 1837, ibid., ff. 86ᵛ–87ᵛ; Joseph Burke to George Nicholls, 22 Mar. 1838 ibid., f 114ʳ⁻ᵛ.

137 Letter book of Joseph Burke, f. 18ʳ (NAI, M 2591).

How Effective Were Mendicity Societies?

The crucial question remains: how effective were mendicity societies in supressing beggary and relieving destitution in Irish towns and cities? In considering this matter one may turn to the views of contemporaries, but caution must be exercised: in many cases where a judgement of the efficacy of a mendicity society is to be found, it was the opinion of an individual directly associated with the charity and with, therefore, an obvious interest in presenting a distorted picture. According to Thomas Brodigan, treasurer and secretary of the Drogheda Mendicity Society, the institution 'completely suppressed street begging, which was a great evil previous to the establishment of the asylum'.[138] Yet, the little information available on the Drogheda mendicity asylum depicts an under-resourced institution failing to meet its foundational aim of ridding the town's streets of beggars. The Poor Inquiry noted that while the society, founded in 1822, initially succeeded in mitigating the nuisance caused by mendicants, reduced subscriptions had limited the resources of the charity and limited its efficacy. The society was providing neither work for the able-bodied poor nor education for child inmates yet was still expending on average 1s. 9d. a week per pauper. 'We visited this institution and it appeared to us to be so conducted that little good could be expected to be derived from it', the report asserted, before opining that 'notwithstanding this asylum, the streets of Drogheda are much infested with beggars'.[139] This report presents a signifi-cantly different image of the Drogheda asylum from that provided just a few years earlier by Brodigan.

The society in Derry can be cited as a body which received praise beyond its own members. Londonderry MP George Hill claimed that 'there is no such thing as street begging in the city of Derry', attributing this to the work of the city's mendicity society.[140] Another observer identified noticeable decreases in street begging in a number of urban centres following the establishment of mendicity societies. 'I found no begging, certainly, in the streets, neither in Dublin or Limerick, very little in Cork, and very little at Waterford: I mean actual mendicants pestering you in the streets, I did not find that', the English magistrate, parochial overseer and Poor Law writer Frederick Page noted.[141] Page, who personally visited the mendicity asylums at Dublin, Cork, Waterford, Limerick and Belfast, was especially

---

138 *Second report, state of the poor select committee, 1830*, p. 376.
139 *PI, Appendix C, Part I*, pp. 54–5.
140 *First report, state of the poor select committee, 1830*, p. 172.
141 *Second report, state of the poor select committee, 1830*, p. 61.

complimentary towards these charities' ability to provide for their poor on such marginal budgets.[142]

The Dublin Mendicity Society was praised in the House of Commons by Henry Grattan (Junior) as alleviating the daily pressures and intimidation felt by shopkeepers by soliciting beggars:

> He knew that, but for the exertions of a Mendicity Society, supported by voluntary contribution, in the city of Dublin, it would be impossible, at that very moment, for any shop-keeper to keep his door open for the purpose of carrying on business. But for the exertions of that Society, the doors would be besieged with mendicants, that all passage must be impossible.[143]

The *Freeman's Journal* also extolled the benefits that accrued to the city traders from the mendicity society, 'which has so amply relieved their doors from a nuisance which, in no small degree, impeded their business, and injured their interests'.[144] In their survey of public institutions in late 1820s Ireland, the Quakers and social reformers, Elizabeth Fry and Joseph John Gurney, pointed to the mendicity asylums as appropriate models for the prevention of distress and starvation, and called on the government to facilitate some level of rated funding for these institutions through the grand juries. Mendicity societies were, they claimed, 'too important for the order and comfort of the whole community of Ireland ... to fall to the ground'.[145]

Just as praise for the mendicity societies transcended religious and social boundaries, so did criticism. Three members of the Whately Poor Inquiry – the Church of Ireland dean of the royal chapel at Dublin Castle, Rev. Charles Vignoles; the Catholic peer Lord Killeen; and a Protestant Tory landed gentleman from County Meath, J.W.L. Naper – dissented from the commission's recommendations for the direct provision of poor assistance through the encouragement of voluntary associations, and cited the insufficient financial support of mendicity societies across Ireland as among the reasons for their opposition.[146] In the main body of the commission's reports, the Clonmel Mendicity Society was described as having failed to suppress the increasing number of beggars in the town, estimated to total 150 in the mid-1830s.[147] Roman Catholic bishop James Doyle told the 1830

---

142 Page, *Observations on the state of the indigent poor in Ireland*, p. 25.
143 Hansard 2, xvi, 1090–1 (9 Mar. 1827).
144 *FJ*, 15 Sept. 1818.
145 Elizabeth Fry and John Joseph Gurney, *Report addressed to the Marquess Wellesley, Lord Lieutenant of Ireland* (2nd edn, Dublin, 1827), pp. 46, 93.
146 *PI, Appendix H*, pp. 8–9.
147 *PI, Appendix A*, p. 699.

select committee on the poor in Ireland that a short-lived mendicity asylum in Carlow town, with which he was involved, failed due to the organisation's lack of powers to apprehend and detain the mendicant poor. Doyle noted that contrary to the society's founding principles its activities actually contributed to an increase in street beggars in the provincial town.[148] The Quaker and Poor Law Assistant Commissioner Jonathan Binns painted a woeful picture of the Waterford Mendicity Society and its inmates, who were described as being sickly, wretched and largely idle.[149] Yet, Binns perceived the mendicity society movement as a worthwhile cause, as shown in his lamenting that in Tralee, where pauperism prevailed to a great extent, there was no mendicity asylum, 'that which almost every town in Ireland should possess, in the absence of some legislative provision for the poor'.[150] In his account of visiting Dublin in 1834, Henry Inglis contrasted his negative impression of the mendicity society's asylum with the House of Industry, the latter of which was 'as fine an institution of the kind as I have any where seen'. In the mendicity society's premises, on the other hand, a small number of paupers were at work while 'hundreds, for whom no employment could be found, [were] lying and sitting in the court, waiting for the mess which had tempted them from their hovels, and the incertitude of mendicancy'. He noted the rudimentary education facilities for children and seemed to criticise the practice of sending children home to their abodes at the end of the day, thus returning them 'to the hovels in which vice and misery are so often united'.[151] A few years later, the editor of the *Cambridge Independent Press* felt it necessary to record his own dismissal of the utility of the Cambridge Mendicity Society, inserting the following opinion beneath a standard report of the charity's 1852 annual meeting: 'We state this as requested, but for ourselves we consider the Society calculated to increase mendicancy, favour the improvident, and in all respects do more harm than good: although its promoters are, no doubt, actuated by good motives'.[152]

Conclusion

In his 1843 article, 'Mendicancy in Ireland', the influential English economist and Poor Law commentator Nassau Senior analysed in considerable detail the state of Irish mendicancy and whether its extent had fluctuated following

---

148   *Second report, state of the poor select committee, 1830*, p. 406.
149   Binns, *Miseries and beauties of Ireland*, ii, p. 257.
150   Ibid., ii, p. 370. See also Gray, *Making of the Irish Poor Law*, p. 15.
151   Inglis, *Ireland in 1834*, i, pp. 16–18.
152   *Cambridge Independent Press*, 23 Oct. 1852.

the introduction of the Poor Law. It is significant that in the 20-page article Senior did not once mention mendicity societies, reflecting their disappearance from Ireland's welfare landscape and the discourse of poor relief in the preceding five years.[153]

Mendicity societies were part of the middle classes' embracing of an associational culture in approaching social and moral problems of the early nineteenth century. These charities differed from the earlier Houses of Industry in being voluntary-funded charities, not founded on foot of legislation and (typically) providing only daytime accommodation to mendicant inmates. It has been argued that these societies constituted part of a mendicity society movement, which spread across Ireland, Britain and parts of western Europe in the first half of the nineteenth century. Supporting Robert Morris's argument that voluntary societies were stimulated by the example provided by earlier bodies, mendicity societies built upon the experience gained and precedents set by other societies, and all members of this movement shared mutual backgrounds, interests, objectives and methods of operation. Significantly, the members of these charities engaged in exchanges of information, reflecting the transnational discourse of social improvement in this period. Yet, while constituting a movement, mendicity societies did not answer to a central entity, and were established and supported through local initiatives.

The Irish entities within this movement shared many features with their international counterparts, yet, within Ireland, there were distinct regional features. Most notable was, first, the concentration of societies in Ulster and, secondly, the prevalence of mendicity charities in relatively small towns and villages in the northern province. It has been argued that a prime reason for this geographic concentration was the popularity of the Scotch model of poor assistance, wherein voluntarism and corporate minimalism were cherished. The distinctive Presbyterian feature of Ulster society, which shared many world views and ecclesiastical structures with the Calvinist Church of Scotland, is crucial to explaining this. Financial uncertainty marred the existence of all mendicity societies and their eventual decline, with the exceptions of the Dublin and Ballymoney societies, arose directly from the introduction of the Irish Poor Law and compulsory assessments for the support of the workhouse system, which catered for a similar class of the poor as the mendicity societies. Figures for Dublin reveal the direct transfer of inmates from the Mendicity Society to the city's newly opened workhouses in 1840. The ethos of mendicity societies conformed with the middle classes' desire for the promotion of industry and restraint among the poor, and their appeal transcended religious boundaries.

---

153 [Senior], 'Mendicancy in Ireland', pp. 391–411.

In assessing the efficacy of Irish mendicity societies, an important question relates to the resources – both material and legal – at these institutions' disposal. What was it possible for these charities to do in terms of suppressing street begging? Financial uncertainty plagued mendicity societies throughout their relatively short existence. Some fluctuated between dissolution and re-establishment, while others experienced a constant struggle to make ends meet. Funded through voluntary and casual sources, mendicity societies were subject to the whim and appetite of the public for anti-mendicancy measures, and this appetite was tempered by the number of beggars seen on local streets at any given time. In this light, mendicity societies' efforts were constantly guided by limited budgets.

These societies were innovative in catering specifically for that class of the poor who were prone or vulnerable to resorting to street begging for survival. The provision of relief, in the form of food, daytime shelter and occasional paid labour, resembled the widespread contemporary emphasis on the virtues of industry and the evils of unqualified assistance. Succour was to be earned, either through sweat or true suffering. This rudimentary system conformed to the distinction between the 'deserving' and 'undeserving' poor. Paupers had the opportunity of learning skills, such as spinning, by which they could gain economic self-dependency, yet their in-house labour was such that it did not undercut the independent labouring classes. Children received a basic education in many mendicity societies, while the Dublin society in particular published reports of former child inmates who had secured respectable positions: in 1820, the charity reported that 42 of its children had been employed by shopkeepers, while 24 had entered domestic service.[154] This is not to deny that conditions for paupers inside these institutions were difficult and strict. The able-bodied were put to 'hard labour' and inmates, at all times, were required to conform to moralising middle-class expectations; regrettably, as with most forms of charity and philanthropy, the perspectives of the recipients – that is, the beggars who sought relief from mendicity societies – are wholly absent from the available source material.[155] As well as the provision of material and moral succour, mendicity societies also endeavoured to remove refractory beggars from the streets. The ability of the societies, in this regards, varied from place to place. The Belfast and Derry societies, for instance, employed constables who exerted legal powers, and the apprehension and confinement of mendicants appears to have been regular undertakings by these paid

---

154 *Report, Dublin Mendicity Society, 1820*, p. 16.
155 Laurence M. Geary has noted this important point in another context: "'The best relief the poor can receive is from themselves'", p. 58.

officers. In Dublin, on the other hand, the lack of these powers prevented the mendicity society from enacting similar policies.

In assessing the efficacy of mendicity societies, it is here argued that this network of charities were innovative developments in a society devoid of a statutory provision for the poor. Limited by uncertain sources of income and the niggardliness of many potential subscribers, these charities succeeded in putting large numbers of individuals, otherwise likely to resort to mendicancy, to work and in education, however rudimentary. For the urban middling classes who founded, supported and ran these charities, street begging was not only a nuisance and a moral evil, but, as demonstrated in Chapter 3, constituted a very real threat to the economic survival of businesses, and was the means of disseminating contagious disease. Emerging from the aftermath of the Napoleonic Wars and declining with the introduction of the long-awaited Irish Poor Law, the mendicity society movement constituted an important, yet overlooked, element in the welfare landscape of pre-Famine Ireland.

III Responses II:
Denominational Approaches

6

Roman Catholic Approaches
to Begging and Alms-Giving

Introduction

Mary Aikenhead, foundress of the Irish Sisters of Charity (later Religious Sisters of Charity), attributed her conversion to Catholicism and her call to devote her life to the poor to the influence of hearing the parable of Lazarus the beggar (Luke 16:19–25) as a young girl. Around 1802, shortly after the deathbed conversion of her father from Anglicanism to Catholicism, Aikenhead heard a preacher recount the gospel parable, in which the starving mendicant Lazarus pleads for crumbs from the table of the rich man (Dives); Lazarus subsequently dies and is accepted into the bosom of Abraham, while Dives is banished to Hell. Aikenhead subsequently followed her late father in converting to the Roman church and in 1815, with the assistance of Fr (later Archbishop) Daniel Murray, she founded the Sisters of Charity, whose fourth vow of service of the poor distinguished this congregation of female religious as a significant presence within Irish Catholicism and Irish society.[1] Aikenhead serves as a useful entry-point into this discussion of Catholic perceptions of and responses to beggary in pre-Famine Ireland. Her congregation was founded for the express purpose of attending to the poor and their foundation in 1815 represented an important moment in the history of Catholicism and also philanthropy in Ireland. Through her private and public utterances, Aikenhead expressed views of poverty and charity that differed noticeably from those of many (male) clergy, yet the charity practised by Aikenhead and other female religious nonetheless framed the recipients of assistance

---

1 [Mary Padua O'Flanagan], *The life and work of Mary Aikenhead, foundress of the congregation of Irish Sisters of Charity 1787–1858* (London, 1924), pp. 8–9; S.A. [Sarah Atkinson], *Mary Aikenhead: her life, her work, and her friends, giving a history of the foundation of the congregation of the Irish Sisters of Charity* (3rd edn, Dublin, 1911).

in terms of the meritorious and the unworthy. Aikenhead's example not only allows for a consideration of women's perspectives on perceived social problems, but, crucially, highlights the difficulty in talking universally about the attitudes and responses of members of a particular confession. This discussion will analyse distinctions in how Catholic teachings on charity and good works were understood by Catholics and Protestants, with both sides perceiving disparate moral consequences for both giver and receiver in the alms-giving transaction. As Brian Pullan has urged,[2] consideration of distinctly Catholic approaches to poverty and begging ought not to be confined to the question of good works and alms-giving. Instead, the evolution of Catholic attitudes and responses to poverty and beggary in the pre-Famine period requires contextualisation with reference to the wider movement within European Catholicism for revival and reform, as reflected in the archbishopric of Daniel Murray. The exploration of Catholic approaches to poverty, mendicancy and alms-giving will be presented in two sections – the first analysing discourses, the second examining actions. Such an approach, to be mirrored in the succeeding chapter on Protestantism, facilitates a discussion of how Catholics perceived and responded to beggary and alms-giving. Owing to the predominant position of men in the public sphere, and particularly within the patriarchal Roman church, male clerics dominated the discourses discussed in the first section. The second section will centre attention on how Catholics responded to mendicancy, either on an individual or a corporate level.

Discourses

Roman Catholic Teaching on Alms-Giving
In considering Roman Catholic approaches to charity in this period, it is useful to start with a contemporary Catholic catechism which outlined the church's basic teaching on such matters. Bishop of Kildare and Leighlin, James Doyle published a revised catechism in 1828, based upon the earlier version of the Archbishop of Cashel, Dr James Butler.[3] The publication of a revised catechism was part of Doyle's wider programme of pastoral

---

2 Brian Pullan, 'Catholics and the poor in early modern Europe' in *Transactions of the Royal Historical Society*, 5th series, xxvi (1976), pp. 15–34; Brian Pullan, 'Catholics, Protestants and the poor in early-modern Europe' in *Journal of Interdisciplinary History*, xxxv, no. 3 (Winter 2005), pp. 441–56.

3 Butler's catechism proved extremely popular and the Catholic Book Society published a 26th edition in 1836: *The Most Rev. Dr James Butler's Catechism: revised, enlarged, approved and recommended by the four R.C. Archbishops of Ireland, as a general catechism for the kingdom* (26th edn, Dublin, 1836).

revival in his diocese, where he oversaw the development and expansion of Sunday school catechesis, confraternities and chapel libraries.[4] Unlike the Roman Catechism, which was disseminated among parish priests, Doyle's publication was designed to be accessible to Catholic children, who were urged to be diligent in studying the text at home and in school.[5] While alms-giving was not specifically addressed in the catechism, a section pertaining to good works is pertinent to the question:

Q. Will strict honesty to every one, and moral good works, insure salvation, whatever church or religion one professes?

A. No; unless such good works be enlivened *by faith that worketh by charity*. Galatians 5:6.

Q. Why must our good works be enlivened by faith?

A. Because the scriptures say, without faith is it impossible to please God – and he that believeth not shall be condemned. Hebrews 11:6. Mark 16:16.

Q. Are we justified by faith alone, without good works?

A. No; *as the body without the spirit is dead, so also faith without works is dead*. James 2:26.[6]

Here, the Catholic emphasis on good works is clear, but good works must complement faith in God. Through good works, an active and living faith is fostered. The Presentation Sisters, for instance, were beseeched in the mid-nineteenth century to 'lay up treasures of virtue and good works which shall follow us beyond the tomb'.[7] According to the Catholic archdeacon of Limerick, Michael Fitzgerald: 'Faith is a vital and active principle. Faith, working in charity, is a fire that consumes the dross of selfishness, lights up generous emotions, and warms the heart with the glow of high and holy purposes'.[8] *The poor man's catechism*, a tenth edition of which was published

---

4 Thomas McGrath, 'Doyle, James ('J.K.L.')' in *DIB*, iii, pp. 444–6.
5 James Doyle, *The general catechism, revised, corrected, and enlarged, by the Right Reverend James Doyle, D.D., Bishop of Kildare and Leighlin, and prescribed by him to be taught throughout the dioceses of Kildare and Leighlin* (Dublin, 1843), p. 2.
6 Ibid., p. 21.
7 'Short sketches of the lives of some of the nuns who entered the community from 1790 to 1870', [c.early twentieth century], p. 38 (Presentation Convent, George's Hill Archive, Dublin, GHAD/P/16). The language here was inspired by Matt. 6:20–21: 'Lay not your treasure on earth, where moth and rust doth corrupt, but lay up for yourself treasures in Heaven'.
8 Fitzgerald, *Wickedness and nullity of human laws against mendicancy*, p. 50.

by the Catholic Book Society in Dublin in 1832, outlined that a perfect faith was one which was firm, entire and active:

> As you believe, so you must practice; you must join good works with faith. A faith without good works, is a dead faith, and will turn to your confusion at the last day. God will then examine not only how you believed, but also how you lived. As the body is but a dead carcase without the soul, so faith also is dead without charity and good works. *Though your faith be strong enough to move mountains, without charity it availeth nothing.* – I Corinthians 13:2.[9]

Such views contrast with Protestant teachings, which since the sixteenth century stressed salvation by faith alone (*sola fide*).[10] Indeed, the twelfth of the Thirty-Nine Articles of the Anglican Communion asserts that good works 'cannot put away our sins'.[11] As will be seen, for some Protestant commentators in this period it was to these fundamental tenets of Roman Catholicism that Ireland's endemic poverty and beggary was to be attributed.

Roman Catholics and Indiscriminate Alms-Giving
Throughout Europe since the Reformation, among the most common perceptions of Roman Catholics long held by Protestants was that the Catholic emphasis on good works encouraged indiscriminate alms-giving to the poor, which in turn supported pauperism and beggary among the lower orders.[12] This argument centred on the perception that Catholics believed they could atone for sin by engaging in good works. It followed that it was in an individual's interest not to distinguish between the 'deserving' and

---

9 [John Mannock], *The poor man's catechism; or, the Christian doctrine explained; with suitable admonitions* (10th edn, Dublin, 1832), p. 9. This work was first published by Mannock (1681–1764), an English Benedictine monk, in 1752: see Philip Jebb, 'Mannock, John' in *ODNB*, xxxvi, pp. 520–1.

10 Another Catholic catechism from this period explicitly contrasts the Roman church's doctrine of good works with the teachings of 'Luther, and other heretics': [John Joseph] Hornihold, *The real principles of Catholics; or, a catechism by way of general instruction, explaining the principal points of the doctrine & ceremonies of the Catholic Church* (4th edn, Dublin, 1821), p. 314.

11 'Thirty-Nine Articles of Religion', from the Church of Ireland website (https://www.ireland.anglican.org/our-faith/39-articles-of-religion) (accessed 5 Jan. 2017). A useful discussion of Protestant theological views of good works, rewards and merit is contained in Emma Disley, 'Degrees of glory: Protestant doctrine and the concept of rewards hereafter' in *Journal of Theological Studies*, new series, xliv, pt. 1 (Apr. 1991), pp. 77–105. See also Carter Lindberg, '"There should be no beggars among Christians": Karlstadt, Luther, and the origins of Protestant poor relief' in *Church History*, xlvi, no. 3 (Sept. 1977), pp. 313–34.

12 Pullan, 'Catholics, Protestants and the poor', pp. 441–56.

'undeserving'; the more alms one gave, the more likely it was for their sins to be forgiven. The indiscriminate furnishing of alms was incentivised for the giver, as well as encouraging dependency in the receiver. Self-sanctification bred beggary. Alleged Catholic recklessness in alms-giving undermined the traditional distinction between the 'deserving' and 'undeserving' poor. Beggary was, thus, not merely enabled, but encouraged. The natural conclusion which Protestants drew from this line of reasoning was that Roman Catholic views and practices regarding poverty and charity led to moral and temporal impoverishment. Among the proponents of this argument was the Church of Ireland minister Rev. John Graham (1766–1844), an evangelical controversialist and author at the height of the 'Second Reformation' of the 1820s and 1830s who was 'a zealous and even fanatical participant in Protestant commemorations of the Williamite period'.[13] For Graham, who identified 'a very perceptible connection between Popery and idleness, mendicity and disease', 'the Papist' was habituated into idleness and vice. 'He is taught that poverty confers a degree of merit, both upon him who suffers under it, and the person who relieves him'.[14] The reverence for mendicant clergymen – 'the bare-footed Friar' – diminished the 'horror of beggary': 'he is led insensibly to admire not only the costume of mendicity, but the address and the artifice of the mendicant; he smiles at the assumed crutches of the light-footed cripple, or the pretended blindness of the clamorous impostor on the bridge'.[15] Turning his attention to the question of the distinctive Catholic emphasis on good works, Graham held forth on the inherent relationship between this distinctly Catholic belief and the country's endemic beggary:

The doctrine of works atoning for sin, is the sheet-anchor of mendicity in Ireland: and it would require an East Indian Treasury to remedy this progressive evil – if no other remedy exists but almsgiving. The most selfish and uncharitable contribute to perpetuate this nuisance, by giving alms to all who solicit it with sufficient importunity, merely because they trust it will purchase to themselves a licence to commit sin with impunity, or prove the means of liberating their departed relatives from purgatory.[16]

Graham's views must be seen in their particular historical context. During the 1810s, a small group of ultra-Protestants were exhibiting a disproportionate

13 Norman Moore (rev. Colm Lennon), 'Graham, John' in *ODNB*, xxiii, pp. 222–3.
14 John Graham, *God's revenge against rebellion: an historical poem on the state of Ireland, with notes and an appendix, consisting of a pastoral epistle from Rome, and two letters to the editor of the* Dublin Evening Post (Dublin, 1820), p. 48.
15 Ibid.
16 Ibid., p. 50.

level of influence in Dublin city in their campaign of opposition to Catholic Emancipation, while a growing evangelical sentiment would become emboldened two years after the publication of Graham's work, with the launching of the 'Second Reformation'.[17] Graham's work was but one of many in which polemicists sought to convince their Protestant audiences of the moral impoverishment of a rapidly advancing Irish Catholicism. To these commentators, the trope of the beggar was a useful rhetorical device which personified the nefarious impact of indiscriminate alms-giving.

The Presbyterian minister Rev. James Carlile, based at the Abbey Street congregation in Dublin, wrote to the evangelical Church of Scotland preacher and Poor Law reformer Rev. Thomas Chalmers on the misguided Catholic practice of indiscriminate alms-giving, noting that this was carried out largely through a belief that such works atoned for sin. In his letter, dated April 1830, Carlile wrote of Irish Catholics: 'They regard giving to the poor as one of the first if not the very first duty of Christianity', adding that there was 'much error & superstition' associated 'with their means of charity. The idea of its being highly meritorious in the will of God is almost universal and accompanied I fear not infrequently with the notion that it makes atonement for sin'.[18] This last point is crucial to understanding how non-Catholics, such as Carlile, viewed Catholics' seeming overindulgence when it came to relieving beggars. The cause of the mendicant's penury did not matter and was not to be considered. What counted was that charity was being sought and the prospective giver was presented with an opportunity to atone for sin. According to Carlile, 'much of the alms giving however that is provided on this principle is given to beggars indiscriminately, crowds of whom are usually to be found at the doors of certain places of worship on occasions of peculiar solemnity'.[19]

The novelist William Carleton, who converted from Catholicism to the Church of Ireland in the early 1820s, also drew his readers' attention to what he alleged was the distinctly Roman Catholic practice of indiscriminate alms-giving to beggars. 'They act under the impression that eleemosynary good works possess the power of cancelling sin to an extent almost incredible'.

---

17 Jacqueline Hill, 'Dublin after the Union: the age of the ultra-Protestants, 1801–1822' in Michael Brown, Patrick M. Geoghegan and James Kelly (eds), *The Irish Act of Union, 1800: bicentennial essays* (Dublin, 2003), pp. 144–56; Irene Whelan, *The Bible war in Ireland: the 'Second Reformation' and the polarization of Protestant–Catholic relations, 1800–1840* (Dublin, 2005).

18 James Carlile to Thomas Chalmers, 26 Apr. 1830 (PRONI, Cooke and Chalmers papers, T3307/12B).

19 Carlile to Chalmers, 26 Apr. 1830. For his thoughts on the nature of repentance, see James Carlile, *A series of sermons, on the nature and effects of repentance and faith* (London, 1821), pp. 22–42.

Such a belief led directly, Carleton argued, to the conclusion that any sin, no matter how gross, can be atoned for through alms-giving. 'The principle of assisting our distressed fellow-creatures, when rationally exercised, is one of the best in society; but here it becomes entangled with error, superstition, and even with crime – acts as a bounty upon imposture, and in some degree predisposes to guilt, from an erroneous belief that sin may be cancelled by alms and the prayers of mendicant impostors'.[20] These words were first published in 1833, a crucial point in Carleton's literary career, when he was moving in evangelical Church of Ireland circles in Dublin and had formed an important friendship with the polemicist and publisher Rev. Caesar Otway, who published Carleton's first writings in his *Christian Examiner.*[21]

Outside of Ireland, the association between Catholic teaching and indiscriminate alms-giving was stressed by Protestant commentators. According to one contributor to the *Westminster Review* in 1844:

> The duty of public and most indiscriminate almsgiving is one of the most fatal errors of the Roman Catholic church. When proclaimed from the pulpit, as it often is, a country is inevitably demoralized. Protestantism was favourable to industry, for it led men to reflect that heaven could not be purchased. Catholics do not say that it can, but they dwell more upon what are called good works. Beggars therefore swarm, and swarm most in Roman Catholic states; witness Ireland, Italy, Spain.[22]

The Church of England minister and Poor Law commentator Joseph Townsend (1739–1816) attributed the abundant number of beggars in the Spanish city of León to the alms received (in the form of food) at convents and the bishop's palace: 'On this provision they live, they marry, and they perpetuate a miserable race'.[23] Negative views of Catholic charity were

---

20 Carleton, 'Tubber derg', p. 386. In an infamously anti-Catholic passage in his first published short story, but omitted from later reprints, Carleton expounded on this simplified thesis that a life-long sinner can effectively wipe his slate clean through the Catholic sacrament of penance: [Carleton], 'A pilgrimage to Patrick's Purgatory', pp. 268–71.

21 James H. Murphy, *Irish novelists and the Victorian age* (Oxford, 2011), pp. 45–69; Owen Dudley Edwards, 'William Carleton and Caesar Otway: a problem in Irish identity' in John Cunningham and Niall Ó Ciosáin (eds), *Culture and society in Ireland since 1750: essays in honour of Gearóid Ó Tuathaigh* (Dublin, 2015), pp. 64–85.

22 Anon., 'Coningsby' in *Westminster Review*, xlii (1844), p. 54, quoted in Ó Ciosáin, *Ireland in official print culture*, p. 121.

23 Joseph Townsend, *A journey through Spain in the years 1786 and 1787; with particular attention to the agriculture, manufactures, commerce, population, taxes and revenue of that country; and remarks in passing through a part of France* (3 vols, London, 1791), i, p. 379.

not unique to Ireland and Britain and, as demonstrated by Alan Forrest and Olwen Hufton, the second half of the eighteenth century in France saw Enlightenment thinkers question the indiscriminate nature of Catholic charity, with abbeys and monasteries receiving the butt of criticism for allegedly attracting and encouraging groups of vagrant beggars. This manner of charity, it was argued, benefited not the poor but the givers of alms. Furthermore, Catholic practice was actually failing the poor, by increasing their numbers and providing no incentive to industry and self-dependence.[24]

Implicit in these criticisms was that Catholic poor relief was confined to casual, private exchanges and did not benefit from organisation, inspection, and oversight, reflecting the general backwardness and irresponsibility of 'Popery'. The reality, however, was more complex. The multiplication of charitable societies throughout Ireland from the middle of the eighteenth century included many Catholic-ethos organisations, mirroring their Protestant counterparts in having a formal structure of patrons and personnel, a system for the investigation and relief of distress, and published annual reports including accounts. The *Catholic Directory* for 1821 lists numerous Roman Catholic orphan schools, free schools, Magdalene asylums and widows' homes in Dublin city,[25] while the emphasis on inspection and discrimination is evident in the *First report [of the Society of St. Vincent de Paul in Limerick]*, which assured its supporters that the charity carried out 'the strictest enquiry into the circumstances and merits of each case' and 'has never encouraged the practice of casual and indiscriminate relief to the poor'.[26] The success of the Society of St Vincent de Paul movement within global Catholicism in the mid-1800s – in the two decades following the founding of the first society in Paris in 1833, 500 conferences were established throughout the United Kingdom, Europe and North America – further attests to the importance of organised, corporate poor relief initiatives within nineteenth-century Catholicism.[27]

24　Alan Forrest, *The French Revolution and the poor* (Oxford, 1981), p. 18; Hufton, *The poor of eighteenth-century France*, p. 194.

25　Patrick Cunningham, 'The *Catholic Directory* for 1821' in *Reportorium Novum*, ii, no. 2 (1960), pp. 324–63.

26　*First report [of the Society of St. Vincent de Paul in Limerick, 1849]*, reprinted in Bob Ryan, *An open door: the history of the Society of St. Vincent de Paul in Limerick 1846–1996* (Limerick, 1996), pp. 40, 45.

27　Bernard Aspinwall, 'The welfare state within the state: the Saint Vincent de Paul Society in Glasgow, 1848–1920' in W.J. Sheils and Diana Wood (eds), *Voluntary religion. Papers read at the 1985 summer meeting and the 1986 winter meeting of the Ecclesiastical History Society*, Studies in Church History, xxiii (Oxford, 1986), pp. 445–59; Mary Lassance Parthun, 'Protestant and Catholic attitudes towards poverty: the Irish community and the development of the Saint Vincent de Paul Society in nineteenth-century Toronto' in Robert O'Driscoll and Lorna Reynolds (eds), *The untold story: the Irish in Canada* (2 vols, Toronto, 1988), ii, pp. 853–69.

The matter of Catholic teaching surrounding sin and atonement was one of the questions asked of a number of senior Catholic clergymen by an 1825 parliamentary select committee.[28] The committee's predominant objective was to investigate the state of Ireland, with particular regard to the agrarian disturbances and outrages of the early 1820s. Throughout the extensive reports and witness testimonies, however, it is clear that the state of Irish Catholics and their religion 'formed, as might have been expected, the leading topic of Examination'.[29] In his testimony, Archbishop of Dublin Daniel Murray gave a comprehensive and convincing denunciation of the suggestion that Catholics operated under the principle that a certain amount of good works would cancel out an equal number of sins; by this argument, Catholic doctrine thus facilitated the committing of bad works in the expectation that a subsequent good work would negate the sin. 'I cannot find any language sufficiently strong to mark my abhorrence of that demoralizing doctrine', said Murray, adding that he felt 'wounded' and 'grieved' at the suggestion being made.[30] Murray explained that good and bad works were not credits which could be accumulated, with the goal of merely collecting more of the former than the latter. Rather, the only means by which sin could be annulled was through true repentance:

How then, according to our doctrine, is this sin, once committed, to be blotted out? Upon no other condition, than that of sincere and deepfelt repentance. No other good works that we can perform, will ever remove the stain that has been fixed upon the soul. We may fast, we may pray, we may give alms, we may go to confession and receive absolution; all is nothing towards the effacing of that sin, until the heart is changed by contrition and repentance, and that repentance must be so intense, and our hatred to that sin must be so sincere; that rather than commit the same or another grievous sin in future, our resolution should be to incur in preference a thousand deaths.

Having expressed genuine contrition, the sinner ought to seek an amendment of the wrong and also seek absolution through the sacrament of penance, administered by the appropriate authority – that is, an ordained priest.[31]

---

28 These clerics were Bishop of Kildare and Leighlin James Doyle, Archbishop of Armagh Patrick Curtis, Archbishop of Dublin Daniel Murray, Archbishop of Tuam Oliver Kelly, and Bishop of Ardagh James Magaurin.

29 *Report from the select committee on the state of Ireland: 1825*, p. 3, H.C. 1825 (129), viii, 3.

30 *Second report from the select committee on the state of Ireland*, pp. 225–26, H.C. 1825 (129), viii, 235–6.

31 Ibid., p. 226. This was also asserted by Archbishop Kelly (ibid., p. 251). For Archbishop Doyle, see ibid., pp. 193–5.

Leaving aside the rights or wrongs of the aforementioned Protestant writers' conclusions (a matter, surely, for theologians), one can at least appreciate how their views may have been formed. John Mannock's Catholic-ethos *Poor man's catechism*, for instance, appears to advocate for indiscriminate poor relief in line with scripture: 'let your *beneficence extend itself to all* (Galatians 6:10), both good and bad, thankful and ungrateful, deserving and worthless; for it is in this manner that God does good to us'.[32] Similarly, the widely read Augustinian friar William Gahan spoke of the spiritual rewards of alms-giving: 'Water does not so easily wash away the spots off our clothes, says St. John Chrysostom, as alms wash off the spots of our souls, and blot out the stains of our sins ... In fine, alms deeds are more beneficial to the charitable giver than to the distressed receiver'.[33] As Catholic theology asserted that Christ manifested himself in the poor, to relieve the beggar was to relieve Christ; on the other hand, to turn away from the soliciting mendicant was to refuse assistance to Christ. The poor possessed a spiritual significance, given that they presented the prospective giver with the opportunity to provide alms and to sanctify oneself. Their distress served as a reminder of Christ's suffering on the cross and to many Catholic charity workers and commentators, the poor constituted 'the elect of God'.[34]

In the view of Rev. Michael Fitzgerald, the Catholic archdeacon of Limerick, alms-giving was a sacred duty for better-off Christians as much as alms were an imperishable right for the poor. Fitzgerald shaped his views around what he considered to be the benevolent mode of poor assistance in Catholic countries, contrasting this with the follies and cruelties of Protestantism, the English workhouse system and the science of political economy. For Fitzgerald, the Calvinist portrayal of good works as being non-essential for salvation was contrary to fundamental Christian principles and served to 'cut up the roots of good works and seal up the fountains

---

32 [Mannock], *Poor man's catechism*, p. 241. A later example of such sentiment is the use by Archbishop of Dublin, Paul Cullen of a passage from the Book of Tobit (4:11): 'Alms deliver all from sin', *Weekly Telegraph*, 21 Feb. 1852. Interestingly, while being included among the books of the Bible in Roman Catholicism, Tobit is not considered a canonical text in Protestantism and appears in the Apocrypha in the Authorised (King James) Version.

33 William Gahan, 'On the necessity and signal advantages of alms and works of mercy' in William Gahan, *Sermons and moral discourses, for all the Sundays and principal festivals of the year, on the most important truths and maxims of the gospels* (3rd edn, 2 vols, Dublin, 1825), ii, p. 25.

34 William J. Callahan, 'The problem of confinement: an aspect of poor relief in eighteenth-century Spain' in *Hispanic American Historical Review*, li, no. 1 (Feb. 1971), pp. 2–3; *Ladies' Association of Charity, of St. Vincent de Paul. Under the patronage of His Grace the Lord Archbishop. The first annual report* (Dublin, 1852), p. 5.

of Christian benevolence'.[35] The Irish Poor Law system post-1838, which centred on indoor relief limited to the workhouse, represented the ultimate degradation of the poor exemplified in the dehumanising label of 'pauper' being applied to inmates. He asserted:

> The word pauper – that horrible word which Christian lips should never apply to a fellow-being – is of pure English coinage. To English ears it sounds as something worse than felon; and it was evidently devised for the purpose of conveying as much of hatred, contempt, and abhorrence for the poor, as two small syllables could be made to contain.[36]

Furthermore, the increasingly popular science of political economy, charac-terised by its 'iron-hearted calculations as to the treatment of the poor', served to criminalise and vilify alms-giving.[37]

Fitzgerald argued not only that alms-giving was 'a sacred duty – a part of the sacrificial duty of Christianity' but also that the poor enjoyed a moral entitlement to assistance from their fellow men. 'If your brother be poor, he has a right to your alms by the *magna charta* [*sic*] of the everlasting empire of Christ'.[38] Obligation and right were correlative concepts which shaped how Fitzgerald viewed this relationship between giver and receiver. To refuse alms to a beggar was to refuse assistance to Christ, who preached, 'Verily, I say unto you, in as much as ye did it not to one of the least of these, ye did it not to me' [Matt. 25:45].[39] Fitzgerald's views were part of a wider discourse in which medieval monastic systems of charity were contrasted with modern Poor Law initiatives, which were associated with Catholicism and Protestantism respectively. The *First report of the Society of St. Vincent de Paul* (1846), founded in 1844, bemoaned the Elizabethan Poor Law in England 'which was passed as a substitute for the relief formerly given freely and received gratefully at the doors of monasteries, in the name of God and the saints; and which turned out to be one of the most devouring plagues of England'.[40] An early nineteenth-century English pamphlet which sought 'to vindicate the Catholic Clergy and People' from the frequent accusations of superstition, ignorance and error defended in a fascinating manner the medieval monastic approach to assisting the poor. The anonymous author sarcastically contrasted, through text and imagery, 'The Dark Ages of

---

35 Fitzgerald, *Wickedness and nullity of human laws against mendicancy*, p. 6.
36 Ibid., p. 19.
37 Ibid., p. 5.
38 Ibid., p. 27.
39 For the use of this scriptural passage, see ibid., p. 3.
40 *First report of the Society of St. Vincent de Paul* (Dublin, 1846), p. 20.

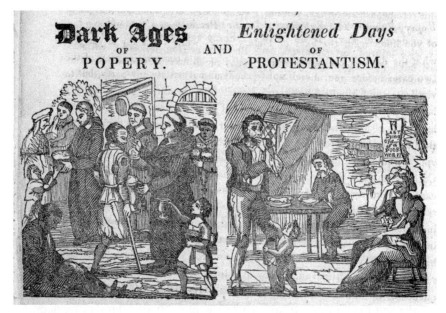

Figure 6.1   Contrasting Catholic and Protestant approaches to poverty, as
portrayed in a Catholic-ethos publication; from Anon., *People of England!*
([London? early 19th cent.]) (reproduced courtesy of National Library of Ireland)

Popery' and the 'Enlightened Days of Protestantism'.[41] As seen in Figure 6.1,
the former were represented by a group of regular clergy bestowing generous
portions of food upon a group of paupers. The countenances on the faces
of both givers and receivers are ones of contentment and affability. 'The
Enlightened Days of Protestantism', on the other hand, were represented
by a labouring family in their wretched abode, with ragged clothes and no
food. Each member of the family is idle, while a famished infant cries at its
mother's breast. The contrast between the two images – Christian endeavour
versus idleness, abundance of food versus penury and malnourishment,
sociability versus loneliness, contentment versus despondency – is stark.

Catholics and a Statutory Provision for the Poor
Part of the challenge in discussing attitudes and responses within Catholicism
towards poverty and beggary is that 'Catholics did not always think or act
in the same way, that there was a spectrum of opinion in the Church
rather than a core of agreed and accepted precept'.[42] On what was arguably

41 Anon., *People of England!* (n.p. [London?]), [early nineteenth century]), pp. 1–2,
     consulted at NLI (P 1211(3)).
42 Pullan, 'Catholics and the poor in early modern Europe', p. 26.

the central social question of the first half of the nineteenth century in Ireland – whether a Poor Law should be introduced – Irish Catholics were by no means united. Archbishop Murray and Anthony Richard Blake were among the Poor Inquiry commissioners whose final report in 1836 rejected the suitability of the English workhouse system for Ireland and instead proposed a system based on the voluntary model of relief,[43] while Lord Killeen was one of three commissioners who dissented from the inquiry's conclusions regarding the suitability of voluntary relief.[44] Since the 1820s, Daniel O'Connell had been making ambivalent statements about an Irish Poor Law, before finally committing himself to opposing what became the Irish Poor Relief Act of 1838.[45] On the other hand, many priests and senior clerics, such as the archbishop of Armagh, Dr William Crolly, and most notably the bishop of Kildare and Leighlin, James Doyle, supported a legal provision for the poor.[46] Doyle's arguments for a state provision for the poor arose from his perception of a moral and economic crisis in the mid-1820s and he believed that the state was the only possible agent capable of effecting the long-term alleviation of Ireland's endemic distress.[47]

Among the most prominent Roman Catholic clergymen who promoted a statutory provision was Rev. Thaddeus Joseph O'Malley, a curate at the Marlborough Street chapel in Dublin city. O'Malley was a well-known social radical who engaged with various political theories and among whose most controversial proposals was for a commune-style system of residence and employment for the urban working classes.[48] O'Malley followed in the tradition of Bishop Doyle in espousing a liberal Catholic viewpoint that has been identified by Peter Gray as exerting a significant influence on

43 *PI, third report.* In his testimony to the 1830 parliamentary committee on the state of the poor in Ireland, Blake asserted that 'a compulsory provision for the poor would tend to prevent the growth of those independent feelings and industrious habits, through which alone I look for the regeneration of Ireland': *Second report, state of the poor select committee, 1830*, p. 343.
44 *PI, Appendix H*, pp. 8–9.
45 Gray, *Making of the Irish Poor Law*, pp. 87–91, 178–218.
46 *PI, Appendix C, Part I*, p. 14; Gray, *Making of the Irish Poor Law*, pp. 27–33.
47 Gray, *Making of the Irish poor law*, pp. 27–33. For Doyle's writings, see Thomas McGrath (ed.), *The pastoral and education letters of Bishop James Doyle of Kildare and Leighlin, 1786–1834* (Dublin, 2004).
48 Thaddeus O'Malley, *An address to mechanics, small farmers, and the working classes generally, upon a feasible means of greatly improving their condition; with a word in their behalf to employers and landlords* (Dublin, 1845). O'Malley's proposals were dismissed in a review published in the politically nationalist *The Nation* as Benthamism bordering on socialism, with the reviewer writing that 'we would rather see the family of a tradesman inhabiting the poorest room in the Liberty, with his wife and children, than crowded in Mr. O'Malley's household, if they were to gain by it the diet and lodging of Prince Albert': *The Nation*, 4 Oct. 1845.

government policy in the 1830s. 'The Irish Catholic case, paralleling that of French liberal Catholicism, was principally for public welfare relief as a social entitlement, a moral bonding agent which would create equitable relationships in a fractured society by imposing fiscal responsibilities on the propertied, while offering the destitute poor an alternative to self-defeating agrarian or trade-unionist violence'.[49] O'Malley mirrored the views of fellow social commentators of this period in espousing a paternalistic concept of society, according to which the profligate lower orders were in need of moral guidance from the wealthier classes. To O'Malley, 'the best if not the only chance of giving them a right direction is, to subject them like children to the guiding control of a parental authority'.[50]

As well as in his published works,[51] O'Malley's views can be gleaned from contributions he made to public meetings and which were subsequently published in the press. At the 1838 annual meeting of the Dublin Mendicity Society, the Church of Ireland Archbishop of Dublin, Richard Whately, a well-known critic of an entitlement to relief for the able-bodied poor, claimed that the experience of England demonstrated that a legal provision aggravated, rather than mitigated, the levels of misery and pauperism. For Whately, the only effective way to suppress street begging was for inhabitants to support the mendicity society financially. O'Malley responded by claiming that, on the contrary, the case of England pointed to the virtues of a legal entitlement to relief, and beseeched Whately to name a country in which there were fewer mendicants than in England, adding 'and to what other cause can we attribute that most striking result than to its assured legal provision for the poor? ... And how could we compulsorily put down the trade of mendicancy without a compulsory provision for the really destitute?' Taking up O'Malley's challenge, Whately asserted that there was less pauperism in Scotland than in England – implicitly championing the traditional Scottish system of voluntarism and minimalism in poor relief – to which O'Malley replied: 'There is a legal provision for the poor there also'.[52] Some degree of tension can be identified in this exchange between Whately and O'Malley,

---

49 Peter Gray, 'The Irish Poor Law and the Great Famine', p. 7, paper presented to the International Economic History Congress conference, Helsinki, 2006 www.helsinki.fi/iehc2006/papers3/Gray.pdf (accessed 25 Feb. 2014).

50 O'Malley, *Poor Laws – Ireland*, pp. 59–60.

51 Ibid.; Thaddeus O'Malley, *A sketch of the state of popular education in Holland, Prussia, Belgium, and France* (2nd edn, London and Dublin, 1840); Thaddeus O'Malley, *An address to mechanics, small farmers, and the working classes.*

52 *FJ*, 17 Jan. 1838. Just weeks later at another public meeting called by the Mendicity Society, Whately's contribution was directly followed by a sharp rebuttal by O'Malley: *FJ*, 21 Feb. 1838. Whately's admiration for the Scottish system can be identified in the reports of the Poor Inquiry, which he chaired, wherein the voluntarist model was credited with keeping Scotland free from the 'extensive, exhausting, demoralizing

which is compounded by the newspaper report's recording of cries of 'Hear, hear' to some of O'Malley's – and only O'Malley's – assertions. While it is tempting to attribute this friction to interdenominational tensions seeping into the meetings of the non-denominational Mendicity Society, it is also possible that Whately was merely the latest target of O'Malley's notoriously disputatious temperament.[53] The tension of the exchange was certainly compounded by the fact that the question of poor relief was one about which both these men thought deeply and felt strongly. Interestingly, just a few months earlier, O'Malley had expressed his support for Whately's thoughts on the need for encouraging civilising influences among the lower orders.[54]

In setting out a vision for a national provision for the poor, O'Malley addressed general Catholic, as well as his own, attitudes to mendicancy and alms-giving. He presented beggary as an evil practice which the vast majority of Irish Catholics, both lay and clergy, would gladly see suppressed. When asked by a parliamentary inquiry whether alms-giving to beggars at the door was a duty for Catholics, he replied: 'But I would not have the Beggar come to their Door. The Trade of Mendicancy I look upon as almost necessarily immoral. The impudent Hypocrite fares best by it. For the really deserving and silently suffering Poor it is a cruel Resource, to which it is a Disgrace to the Legislature to condemn them'. He added that only beggars themselves would complain of the prohibition of mendicancy and a vagrancy act which criminalised this practice would, therefore, serve as a measure for the relief of the industrious poor.[55]

Roman Catholics and the 'Deserving'/'Undeserving' Distinction
The distinction between the 'deserving' and 'undeserving' poor prevailed in Catholic thought, as promulgated by the clergy. Archbishop Daniel Murray shared the views of most senior clerics (including his successor in the see, Paul Cullen)[56] in singling out the 'virtuous poor' for charity, exhorting his flock, in a pastoral letter in favour of the Dublin Mendicity Society, 'that

mendicancy' as seen in Ireland or the 'still more extensive and ruinous public pauperism' created by the English Old Poor Law: *PI, Appendix H*, p. 464.

53 During his life, O'Malley fell out with a priest and bishop in Philadelphia, for which he was briefly excommunicated; clashed with Archbishop John McHale, for which he was suspended in 1840; was dismissed two years later by the government from his position as rector of the University of Malta; was dismissed in 1862 from the chaplaincy of the Westmoreland Lock Hospital; and on foot of writing a controversial pamphlet in 1870, which proposed changes to ecclesiastical discipline, O'Malley was dismissed as chaplain to the Presentation Sisters and forbidden to perform sacramental functions: David Murphy and Sinéad Sturgeon, 'O'Malley, Thaddeus Joseph' in *DIB*, vii, pp. 681–2.

54 O'Malley, *Poor Laws – Ireland*, p. 59.

55 *Report, select committee, relief of the destitute poor, and medical charities, Ireland*, p. 837.

56 Virginia Crossman, '"Attending to the wants of poverty": Paul Cullen, the relief of

in the distribution of your Charities, you will have that excellent Institution in view, as it is certain that your Alms would be much more profitably employed, for the relief of the real Poor, if given thro' it, than when bestowed indiscriminately on the Mendicants, who solicit your aid thro' the Streets'.[57] Among lower clergy, such views were also to be found. Rev. Patrick Coleman, Parish Priest of St Michan's parish in Dublin, told the Poor Inquiry in the mid-1830s that 'By far the greater number [of the parochial poor] are deserving of Charity',[58] while other priests in Dublin city parishes marked out their local poor as being genuine by way of their being 'disposed to work'.[59] To the Augustinian friar and renowned preacher William Gahan, whose works were widely published and disseminated among the populace, alms-giving was an 'indispensable duty' for good Christians, yet he refrained from recommending indiscriminate charity:

> Prudence and discretion are indeed to be used in the choice of proper objects; but as St. John Chrysostom observes too anxious an inquiry and an over-great suspicion of imposture are to be avoided, as being contrary to Christian simplicity and fraternal charity.[60]

Kilkee parish priest Rev. Michael Comyn described a class of beggars known to be impostors and the local habit of not entertaining such individuals' pleas: 'Strollers often bring recommendations with them, but we pay little attention to them ... because we know them to be forged. There is a set of people going about the country, called wandering sailors, who are in general impostors, and these carry about plenty of letters and documents'.[61] The existence of a category of 'undeserving' poor was also alleged by the Franciscan Christopher Fleming, labelling some mendicants as 'half-naked assemblies of vagrants,

poverty and the development of social welfare in Ireland' in Dáire Keogh and Albert McDonnell (eds), *Cardinal Paul Cullen and his world* (Dublin, 2011), pp. 146–65.

57 Daniel Murray, *A sermon, preached on the nativity of our Blessed Saviour, in the Church of the Conception, Marlborough-Street, on the 25th December, 1837, by the most Rev. Doctor Murray, and published for the benefit of St. Vincent's Hospital, Stephen's Green, at the desire of some friends of that charitable institution* (Dublin, 1838), p. 16; Draft of pastoral by Archbishop Daniel Murray regarding the Dublin Mendicity Society, 12 Nov. 1836 (DDA, DMP, 31/5/27).

58 Return of answers to queries from the Poor Inquiry, by Rev. P. Coleman, P.P. St Michan's parish, Dublin, [*c*.1833–4] (DDA, DMP, 31/4/34).

59 Return of answers to queries from the Poor Inquiry, by Rev. Paul Long, P.P. Barony of Thomas Court and Donore, Dublin, [*c*.1833–4] (DDA, DMP, 31/4/88); Return of answers to queries from the Poor Inquiry, by Rev. A. O'Connell, P.P. St Michael and St John's parish, Dublin, [*c*.1833–4] (DDA, DMP, 31/4/90).

60 Gahan, 'On the necessity and signal advantages of alms and works of mercy', pp. 21, 26.

61 *PI, Appendix A*, p. 625.

[with] their oaths, their blasphemies, their riots, their ignorance, [and] their total neglect of religion'.[62] These instances, however, are not necessarily representative, as they only reveal the views of (male) clergy. They exclude the perspectives of Catholic women (both lay and religious) and lay men, and they do not illuminate how Catholics of both sexes and all social classes *actually responded* to beggary on a practical level. In dealing with a soliciting mendicant, did the actions of the Catholic laity conform to the moralising urgings of their clergymen? The evidence makes clear that indiscriminate alms-giving was widespread among the largely Catholic lower classes, suggesting the limitations of priests' influence over the private lives of their flock. Yet, the poor were known to employ models of discernment.[63] According to a priest in County Galway, those living in his locality drew a line between the public solicitation of alms and private requests for charity, supporting the thesis that the lower classes exhibited some level of discrimination in how they negotiated mendicants' solicitations: 'There is a feeling against street or public beggary peculiar to the inhabitants of this country. Alms are given privately in provisions, and to some in money'.[64] The suggestion here is that the line of demarcation centred on the visibility of beggary and alms-giving, practices which ought to be kept out of public sight.

Female Religious and Alms-Giving: The Case of the Religious Sisters of Charity

Donal Kerr identified Daniel Murray's role in the establishment of the Sisters of Charity, of Mercy, and of Loreto as his greatest achievement,[65] and the particular instance of Mary Aikenhead and the Irish Sisters of Charity serves as an interesting case study for examining how female religious approached poverty and alms-giving. A number of female religious orders and congregations targeted the poverty and ignorance of the lower classes and driven by a zeal characteristic of philanthropists of all denominations in this period they undertook moralising missions among the poor of towns and cities. While these female religious sought to improve the temporal conditions of the impoverished, the main thrust of their work was to introduce the poor to religious instruction through catechesis.[66] Outlining

---

62 Christopher Fleming, *Sermons on different subjects* (2 vols, Dublin, 1822–3), i, p. 127, quoted in Ó Ciosáin, *Ireland in official print culture*, p. 119.

63 Ó Ciosáin, 'Boccoughs and God's poor', pp. 93–9.

64 *PI, Supplement to Appendix A*, p. 4.

65 Donal Kerr, 'Dublin's forgotten archbishop: Daniel Murray, 1768–1852' in James Kelly and Dáire Keogh (eds), *History of the Catholic diocese of Dublin* (Dublin, 2000), p. 248.

66 Rosemary Raughter, 'Pious occupations: female activism and the Catholic revival in eighteenth-century Ireland' in Rosemary Raughter (ed.), *Religious women and their history: breaking the silence* (Dublin, 2005), pp. 25–49.

the system of instruction for poor girls in her institution in George's Hill in Dublin city, founded in 1766, Teresa Mullally stated that 'besides the spiritual instructions I hope they will be trained to morality, decency & industry which is so much wanting among our poor'.[67] The founding documents of the Presentation Sisters' convent in Cork stated explicitly: 'The Principal End of This Religious Institute is the Instruction of Poor Girls in the Principles of Religion and Christian Piety'.[68]

While numerous female congregations and orders were founded in Ireland between the late eighteenth and the late nineteenth centuries,[69] the establishment of the Religious Sisters of Charity in Dublin in 1815 marked a new departure in Irish social and religious history, as this nascent congregation pioneered social work by female religious in the wider community. Aikenhead's congregation adopted the model of non-enclosure pioneered by the Daughters of Charity in seventeenth-century France, who, in not being restricted within the convent walls, were unique in publicly working among the sick and poor of their locality.[70] The observation of the French community's co-founder, St Vincent de Paul, that 'their monastery being generally no other than the abode of the sick; their cell, a hired room; their chapel, the parish church; their cloister, the streets or wards of hospitals; their enclosure, obedience'[71] may be applied to the nineteenth-century Irish Sisters of Charity. Aikenhead's entry into religious life was encouraged by Daniel Murray, who arranged for Aikenhead to serve her noviceship in the Institute of the Blessed Virgin Mary at York, escorting her and an associate there in 1812 and making the same journey three years later to accompany them back to Dublin. During Aikenhead's time in the northern English convent, Murray was a regular correspondent, outlining his plans for a new congregation and the rules upon which the new body would be based. In one letter Murray wrote to Aikenhead: 'you will not

---

67 Teresa Mullaly to Archbishop John Thomas Troy, [c.1802] (Presentation Sisters, George's Hill Archive, GHAD/FD/146).

68 'Rules and constitutions of the Religious Congregation of the Charitable Instruction established in the Convent of the Presentation of our Blessed Lady in Cork agreeable to the bull of His Present Holiness Pope Pius VI', [c.1809] (Presentation Sisters, George's Hill Archive, GHAD/C/5). See also *Rules and constitutions of the Institute of the Religious Sisterhood of the Presentation of the Ever Blessed Virgin Mary, established in the City of Cork, for the charitable instruction of poor girls conformably to the rules of the late Pope, Pius VI* ... (Cork, 1809), pp. 11–15, held at GHAD/C/7(1).

69 In 1800, there were 120 nuns living in 18 houses across Ireland; by 1851, the number had increased to 1,500 nuns in 95 convents: Luddy, 'Religion, philanthropy and the state', p. 160.

70 Susan E. Dinan, *Women and poor relief in seventeenth-century France: the early history of the Daughters of Charity* (Aldershot, 2006), pp. 45–6.

71 Cited ibid., p. 46.

be surprised at my reminding you that your family in future are to be the poor of Jesus Christ'.[72] Until his death, Murray retained a close association with Aikenhead and the Sisters of Charity, preaching sermons on behalf of the community's poor schools and orphan houses[73] and bequeathing money to the congregation 'for the purpose of being distributed amongst the Sick Poor whom they shall visit'.[74] Concern for the poor was central to Murray and Aikenhead's world view and this was reflected in the distinctive stipulation that the Sisters take a fourth vow of 'perpetual service of the poor' in addition to the three vows of poverty, chastity and obedience commonly taken by female religious congregations and orders.[75]

The emergence of lay and religious female activists at this time was influenced by a number of factors: the growth of a Catholic middle class from the mid-eighteenth century, confident in its strengthening social and economic influence; the Catholic revival in the early years of the new century; and the broader appeal of philanthropy to women of the wealthier classes. Female philanthropy flourished across all denominations, as well-off women brought to their work with the poor a middle-class sense of morality which was 'suffused with religious rhetoric and imagery'.[76] The work of female religious, however, was influenced by a distinctly Catholic framework, wherein charity benefited both the giver and the receiver, as the bestowing of relief served to bring about the spiritual redemption of both parties. The constitution of the Sisters of Charity asserts this sentiment: 'The end of this Congregation is, not only that its members, aided by Divine Grace, attend to the salvation and perfection of their own souls, but also that, assisted by the same, they labour seriously in works of spiritual and corporal mercy, for the salvation and consolation of their neighbour'.[77] To Mary Aikenhead, providing assistance to the poor contributed towards 'our own perfection and the salvation of our neighbour'.[78]

72 Daniel Murray to Mary Aikenhead, 26 Jan. 1813 (Religious Sisters of Charity Archives, Caritas, Sandymount (RSCA), 1/B/4) cited in 'Dublin cause for the beatification and canonization of the servant of God Mary Aikenhead foundress of the Sisters of Charity (1787–1858). Positio on the life, the witness and the fame of sanctity of the servant of God (2 vols, 1994), volume I', held at RSCA. For Murray's involvement in Aikenhead's novitiate in York, see [O'Flanagan], *Life and work of Mary Aikenhead*, pp. 20–36.

73 *FJ*, 14 Mar. 1817, 10 Feb. 1821, 11 Dec. 1830.

74 Evelyn Bolster, 'The last will and testament of Archbishop Daniel Murray of Dublin (d. 1852)' in *Collectanea Hibernica*, nos. 21–2 (1979–80), p. 158.

75 [O'Flanagan], *Life and work of Mary Aikenhead*, pp. 39–42.

76 Luddy, *Women and philanthropy*, p. 2.

77 Cited in Mary Aikenhead to unidentified priest, 13 June 1840, in *Letters of Mary Aikenhead* (Dublin, 1914), p. 519.

78 Mary Aikenhead to Mother Francis Magdalen, 5 Sept. 1840, ibid., p. 327.

A letter (dated December 1833) from Mary Aikenhead to the Whately Poor Inquiry, outlining the work of the Sisters of Charity, constitutes a rare public statement by a Catholic woman, and illuminates Aikenhead's views on the causes and nature of poverty:

> The object of our institution is to attend to the comforts of the poor, both spiritual and temporal, to visit them at their dwellings and in hospitals, to attend them in sickness, to administer consolation in their afflictions, and to reconcile them to the dispensations of an all-wise Providence in the many trials to which they are subject. The education and relief of orphans, and religious instruction of the lower orders, is part of our duty.

The prevalence of destitution in the suburbs and villages to the south-east of the city (Irishtown, Ringsend, Beggar's Bush and Ballsbridge) was attributed to a want of employment, the unavailability of satisfactory medical treatment and the consumption of unwholesome food. Poverty was caused by external factors, not by the poor themselves. While the taking of spirituous liquors by the poor was acknowledged by Aikenhead, this practice was explained away with the qualifying statement: 'they often resort to it in despair, to drown the recollection of their sufferings'. Aikenhead asserted: 'The poor are, generally speaking, very docile and remarkably patient under their sufferings and privations; they are grateful beyond measure for the least kindness shown to them, and are most anxious to procure employment even at the lowest wages'.[79] Her fellow Sister of Charity, Mother Catherine (née Alicia Walshe) identified the suffering of the poor as being caused by their sheer poverty and not by any moral flaw on their part: 'poverty seems for the most part the causes of most of their sufferings. That is the general cause of their sickness'.[80] To these female religious, the poor of Dublin suffered temporal poverty with admirable fortitude and were presented as possessing the traits of appreciation and industriousness. The language used by the female religious speaks of the sanctifying impact on the poor of their suffering the trials of poverty and want. They were not the idle, imprudent and wicked poor so often criticised in public discourse. Yet, while there is an absence of explicit moral judgement of the poorer classes in Aikenhead's letter, and indeed an absence of direct references to mendicancy and the giving of alms to beggars, this does not allow one to conclude that the Sisters did not distinguish between the 'deserving' and 'undeserving' poor. Women-run philanthropic initiatives – those run

79 *PI, Appendix C, Addenda to Appendix A*, p. 25e.
80 Diary of Mother Catherine, 12 Mar. 1818, p. 12 (RSCA, MS RSCG/1/C/15).

by either lay or religious, Catholic or Protestant women – focused their resources on women and children, the archetypal virtuous poor, while the category of 'fallen women' were admitted into Magdalen asylums so as to be, in the views of the institutions' managers, reconstructed as 'members of the 'deserving' poor, entitled to the support of the public'.[81]

In assessing the views of male and female religious towards alms-giving and begging, the fact that these individuals were themselves engaged in alms-seeking is of interest. Priests sought alms 'when at mass and at other times they solicited contributions to fund church expenditure of various kinds, including the parish's own informal poor relief structures, such as they were'.[82] Ó Ciosáin suggests that priests, therefore, looked on beggars with suspicion, as potential rivals to the alms of their congregations. This sentiment was expressed by Michael Comyn, parish priest of Kilkee, County Clare to the Poor Inquiry:

> Notwithstanding the influx of beggars to this place in summer, I never saw more than two of them begging at the chapel; this is because I beg myself for the chapel to pay for its building, and the people give to me in preference to them. If I were to stop there would be plenty of them.[83]

Meanwhile, female religious communities also largely survived on voluntary donations, in addition to the dowries brought by its members. Colin Jones notes that the seventeenth-century French Daughters of Charity were both charitable donors and recipients, receiving and providing 'spiritual as well as material benefits'.[84] The same can be said of the main female communities in pre-Famine Ireland, who both collected and dispensed charity. When the Sisters of Mercy arrived in Charleville in 1836 to establish a new convent, the apparent absence of a local middle class caused dismay, as it threw into doubt the prospect of support 'for the sisters or for the poor'.[85] The financial uncertainty that characterised such sources of income for religious communities was appreciated by Catherine McAuley, foundress of the Sisters of Mercy, who in 1839–40 blamed the newly introduced Poor Law rate for 'breaking up all contributions' and for having 'deprived us

81 Maria Luddy, *Prostitution and Irish society, 1800–1940* (Cambridge, 2007), p. 87; Jacinta Prunty, *The monasteries, Magdalen asylums and reformatory schools of Our Lady of Charity in Ireland 1853–1973* (Dublin, 2017), pp. 93–108.

82 Ó Ciosáin, *Ireland in official print culture*, p. 119.

83 *PI, Appendix A*, p. 625.

84 Jones, 'Some recent trends in the history of charity', pp. 58–9.

85 Quoted in Caitriona Clear, 'The limits of female autonomy: nuns in nineteenth-century Ireland' in Luddy and Murphy, *Women surviving*, p. 253.

of much help. We find it very difficult to keep up the poor Institution'.[86] Aikenhead and her colleagues in the Sisters of Charity oftentimes took to soliciting donations directly from the public, either through door-to-door canvassing or, in one instance, sending out 3,000 'begging notes' to Dublin's citizens.[87] The language of mendicancy was common in the parlance of female religious communities, especially regarding their own endeavours in collecting donations and subscriptions; for example, members of the Sisters of Nazareth in England went on 'begging tours' in the second half of the nineteenth century to raise income for their community.[88] However, this is not to suggest that female religious saw themselves as beggars on the same level as the mendicant poor. Many of the members of religious congregations in the nineteenth century came from middle-class Catholic families, and life within these communities mirrored wider social divisions, most notoriously in the division between lay and choir nuns;[89] as such, it is not surprising that female religious adhered to the conventional moral framework of distinguishing between the 'deserving' and 'undeserving' poor.

Shifting the focus from male and female religious towards the Catholic laity, we see that another viewpoint can be gleaned from Irish-language sources. The lower classes appear regularly in the diary of the Callan schoolteacher and draper Amhlaoibh Ó Súilleabháin (1783–1838), whose Irish-language journal, although clearly written for a public readership, contains copious observations on the weather, nature and social conditions, and is a rare example of this genre of writing. Ó Súilleabháin was a prominent member of his local community, being actively involved in the local branch of the Catholic Association (Daniel O'Connell's mass political movement that campaigned for Catholic Emancipation), serving on a number of coroners' juries and socialising with shopkeepers, clergy and the local doctor. As such, his attitudes towards poverty and other social matters reflected the perspectives of his social position and peers.[90] Ó Súilleabháin

---

86 Mary C. Sullivan (ed.), *The correspondence of Catherine McAuley, 1818–1841* (Dublin and Baltimore, MD, 2004), pp. 199, 322.

87 Mary Aikenhead to Mary de Chantal, 3 Jan. 1837 in *Letters of Mary Aikenhead*, p. 71. See also Mary Aikenhead to Mary de Chantal, Feast of the Epiphany 1842, ibid., p. 126; Mary Aikenhead to Mary de Chantal, 16 Dec. 1843, ibid., p. 158; [O'Flanagan], *Life and work of Mary Aikenhead*, p. 301; Diary of Mother Catherine, 29 Aug. 1819, p. 26.

88 Carmen Mangion, 'Faith, philanthropy and the aged poor in nineteenth-century England and Wales' in *European Review of History – Revue européenne d'histoire*, xix, no. 4 (Aug. 2012), pp. 518, 521.

89 Caitriona Clear, 'Walls within walls: nuns in nineteenth-century Ireland' in Chris Curtin, Pauline Jackson and Barbara O'Connor (eds), *Gender in Irish society* (Galway, 1987), pp. 134–51.

90 Desmond McCabe, 'Ó Súilleabháin, Amhlaoibh (O'Sullivan, Humphrey)' in *DIB*, vii, pp. 953–5.

wrote sympathetically of the poor, noting the high price of potatoes at a
times of crisis; his observation in April 1827 that 'There are not even alms
for the paupers'[91] points to mendicants' dependency on the poor (that is,
those only slightly removed from destitution) for assistance. Later, the diarist
recorded that 'The small farmers are very good people. It is they who, almost
on their own, feed the poor people of Ireland … Tradesmen and shopkeepers
are also generous in giving alms to God's poor'.[92] The reference to beggars
as 'God's poor' displays an inherently Catholic perspective and the giving
of alms is portrayed in a positive light. Despite this sympathy for what we
may term the 'deserving' poor, Ó Súilleabháin identified an immoral element
among the local lower classes, perhaps revealing an urban prejudice against
the rural poor: 'The street mob were very noisy at three in the morning.
Some of them are still very drunk. It's not harm to call them 'mob' (*coip*)
for they are the froth (*coipeadh*) of the lake-dwellers, bog-dwellers, and dirty
mountain-dwellers with no respect of manners'.[93] He later refused to support
'the town rabble going from door to door with a wren in a holly brush' (a
reference to the St Stephen's Day Wren's Boys tradition in Ireland); when
recording the 1832 phenomenon of crowds of people running through the
countryside with lumps of burning turf, in the belief that dividing the turf
would stave off the rapidly advancing cholera epidemic, the diarist's tone
displays his condescension towards the 'credulous' and 'foolish' 'poor people
of Ireland', but also his embarrassment at the conduct of his co-religionists,
who made themselves 'a laughing-stock for the Protestants'.[94]

In his poem '*Ceol na mBacach*' ('The song of the beggars') the Ulster
poet Aodh Mac Domhnaill (1802–67) lashed out at the Roman Catholic
authorities in Famine-era Belfast for what he considered their collusion with
the Presbyterian and Anglican authorities in suppressing beggary with an
unduly heavy hand and, according to one recent commentator, 'trying to
ingratiate themselves with Belfast's ruling classes at the expense of their
own flock'.[95] The target of the poem was the Bishop of Down and Connor,
Cornelius Denvir, who in July 1847 was among a number of the town's
clergymen and gentlemen of different denominations who agreed at a public
meeting to impose a strict regime of clearing the streets of beggars and

---

91 Tomás de Bhaldraithe (ed.), *The diary of an Irish countryman 1827–1835: a translation
   of Cín Lae Amhlaoibh* (Cork, 1979), p. 16. See also ibid., p. 84.
92 Ibid., p. 84.
93 Ibid., p. 20.
94 Ibid., pp. 68, 119–20. This incident is best described by S.J. Connolly, 'The "blessed
   turf": cholera and popular panic in Ireland, June 1832' in *IHS*, xxiii, no. 91 (May 1983),
   pp. 214–32.
95 Antain Mac Lochlainn, 'The Famine in Gaelic tradition' in *Irish Review*, no. 17/18
   (Winter 1995), p. 102.

quarantining the sick poor in an effort to prevent the spread of contagion.[96]
Mac Dhomhnaill wrote:

> There sat a Bishop from the Church of the Pope
> And a hundred parsons of the English kind
> To issue decrees and warrants of arrest
> Against those who supported them all of their lives ...
> But I'll never believe, from priest or from brother
> That it's wicked to be destitute, abandoned or poor
> For I've heard it said, by poets and authors
> That Jesus was born among those who were poor.
> Colm Cille preached to men and to women
> From the time of the prophets it's always been taught
> That every proud man who places his trust in riches
> Will never gain entry to the kingdom of God.[97]

To Mac Dhomhnaill, Denvir's co-operation with the mostly Protestant
authorities constituted a traitorous abandonment of his own flock. Yet, other
themes emerge from this piece, namely the corruption of Denvir's (Catholic)
benevolence through his association with Protestants, but, more significantly, the undermining of the bishop's humane empathy, and subsequently
his pastoral efficiency, through his fraternising with the moral trappings
of wealth. To the poet, the poor were not to be dismissed as a category of
people that can be coldly pigeonholed and vilified as being deviant but were
in fact those who demonstrated the true virtue of Christian suffering.

Actions

The approaches of the Catholic middle-class laity differed significantly
from their poorer co-religionists: the former partook in organised corporate
relief initiatives, reflecting the associational culture popular in 'respectable'
society in the Atlantic world, while the latter's responses were largely
limited to individual and casual exchanges with mendicants. The survival
of source material relating to these varied approaches is weighted heavily in
favour of the middle-classes' charity work and, as such, the historian must
be careful not to ignore the extent and significance of private, unrecorded
charity. In urban centres men from the rising Catholic mercantile middle

---

96 For this municipal crack-down on beggars, see *BNL*, 30 July 1847.
97 'Song of the Beggars' in Colm Beckett, *Aodh Mac Domhnaill, Dánta* (Dublin, 1987),
    pp. 63–4, cited in Mac Lochlainn, 'The Famine in Gaelic tradition', pp. 102–3.

classes engaged in religious and philanthropic initiatives, influenced by a combination of economic self-interest and a genuine feeling of religious benevolence.[98] These men joined members of the Protestant middle classes in establishing and running mendicity societies. An 1832 return from the Dublin Mendicity Society, sent to the Commissioners of National Education regarding the charity's poor schools, identified 12 Roman Catholics among its managing committee of 58 men. Of these 12 (comprising just more than one-fifth of the membership of the committee), four were clergymen, while the remaining eight were laymen.[99] These Catholic laymen included barrister and MP Daniel O'Connell (1775–1847), lawyer and government adviser Anthony Richard Blake (1786–1849) and Queen's Counsel and Commissioner of the National System of Education John Richard Corballis (c.1797–1879).[100] Within Irish Catholicism at this time, a wave of philanthropic endeavour reflected a spirit of revival and reform, drawing inspiration from precedents within European Catholicism. The numerous confraternities that emerged since the mid-to-late eighteenth century were part of the Church's infrastructure to reform the spiritual guidance of Catholics. While most confraternities concerned themselves with the encouragement of devotional practices among members, some bodies carried out poor relief work, most notably the Society of St Vincent de Paul, a lay Catholic charity. The Society was founded in Paris by Frederic Ozanam in 1833 and by the time the first Irish conference was established in Dublin 11 years later, there were 130 societies across Europe.[101] The emergence and rapid nationwide growth of the Society of St Vincent de Paul local conferences occurred during the Famine and post-Famine period, and within six years of the founding of the inaugural Dublin society, 50 conferences were established throughout Ireland. While the early development of this movement regrettably falls outside the scope of this study, a few brief remarks, drawing on sources from the late 1840s, will add to our understanding of contemporary Catholic thinking on social problems, such as poverty and mendicancy. The Society advanced Vincentian traditions of poor assistance, seeing the presence of

---

98 Patrick J. Corish, *The Irish Catholic experience: a historical survey* (Dublin, 1986), p. 153.

99 Dublin Mendicity Society application to National Commissioners for Education, 19 Jan. 1832 (NAI, Commissioners of National Education papers, ED/1/28/1).

100 O'Connell and Corballis were also among the general members of the Dublin Chamber of Commerce in 1836, although the officers appear to have all been Protestants, mainly Anglicans and Quakers: *Report of the council of the Chamber of Commerce of Dublin, to the annual assembly of the members of the association, held on the 1st of March 1836* (Dublin, 1836), pp. 34, 38.

101 Máire Brighid Ní Chearbhaill, 'The Society of St. Vincent de Paul in Dublin, 1926–1975' (PhD thesis, Maynooth University, 2008), p. 5. For an outline of the Dublin society's early history, see ibid., pp. 1–19.

Christ in the poor person, whose suffering was sanctified by that very presence. Charity sanctified the givers of alms, who were beseeched to conduct themselves with humility in their charity work, which centred on visiting the sick and poor in their own homes. Local conferences of the Society employed moralising and gospel-driven language similar to that used by Protestant charities, seeing the relief of temporal poverty as of equal importance as attending to the spiritual privation of the poor. Reports spoke of their objectives as being 'to stimulate and encourage industry and habits of religion among the poor'. The societies wished to encourage independence in the poor and during the Famine years particular emphasis was placed on removing children from the streets and exposing them to the fruitful rewards of education and religious instruction. The St Mary's conference in Clonmel paid particular attention in 1848 to those children who 'spent the day in the street exposed to the worst examples of vice and immorality, mendicancy, and idleness'.[102]

Wealthy Catholics also carried out their philanthropic duties through their wills and charitable bequests, and charities aimed at suppressing beggary regularly benefited. Among the 12 charities and causes which each received £50 through the bequest of the Catholic gentleman John Moore of Portland Street, Dublin were the Mendicity Society and the Sick and Indigent Roomkeepers' Society, both flag-bearers for the urban middle classes' drive to suppress street begging and distribute alms according to strict criteria of eligibility.[103] The Dublin Mendicity Society, as well as poor relief schemes in Galway, was included in the will of a Thomas Bennet, who bequeathed more than £2,000 to relatives, friends and charitable causes.[104] As well as their lay co-religionists, Catholic clergymen responded to beggary through corporate means, most notably through their support for and involvement in running charitable societies. Daniel Murray's archbishopric of Dublin (1823–52) witnessed an upsurge in corporate philanthropic endeavour and the multiplication of bodies with a duty of service to the poor, particularly through his encouragement of male and female religious communities that focused on educating the poor.[105] It was during Murray's

---

102 *Report of the proceedings of the Society of St. Vincent de Paul, in Ireland, during the year 1848* (Dublin, [c.1848]), pp. 14, 16.
103 Extract from the will of John Moore (d. 7 June 1828), Portland Street, Dublin, [c.1833] (DDA, JHP, 35/2/77).
104 Last will and testament of Thomas Bennett, 9 May 1828 (DDA, DMP, 33/9/14/1).
105 To focus here on charity work during Murray's episcopacy is not to ignore the fact that his predecessor, Archbishop Troy, was also engaged on such social questions and his reign also witnessed an upsurge in the number of religious communities in Dublin relieving the poor: Cormac Begadon, 'Laity and clergy in the Catholic renewal of Dublin, c.1750–1830' (PhD thesis, Maynooth University, 2009), pp. 71–2.

episcopate that the Sisters of Mercy, the Sisters of Charity, the Ladies' Association of Charity of St Vincent de Paul and the Society of St Vincent de Paul, all of whom worked among the poorest classes, were established in Dublin city and it was upon Murray's suggestion that Edmund Rice deputed two of his Christian Brothers to establish the congregation in Dublin, with the aim of catering for poor boys in St Andrew's parish.[106] That Archbishop Murray and his predecessor, Dr John Troy, were prepared to co-operate with other denominations in tackling the city's social problems, and most relevantly to this study, in suppressing street begging, is seen in their service as Vice-Presidents of the Mendicity Society.[107] They were not the only Catholic clerics to serve cross-denominational corporate initiatives suppressing mendicancy, with clergymen in Galway, Sligo, Ballymena and Drogheda active in the work of their local society as well as in encouraging their flock to contribute to the charities.[108] The members of the Dublin society's managing committee included Fr Thaddeus O'Malley, Fr James Monks (who had previously served as the Catholic chaplain to the House of Industry) and Fr Matthew Flanagan.[109] The Bishop of Down and Connor William Crolly subscribed to and chaired meetings of the Belfast House of Industry (mendicity society),[110] while his successor in the see, Cornelius Denvir, served as a collector of donations for the same institution alongside a number of Protestant ministers and laymen.[111] Denvir also served as governor of the town's Charitable Society[112] while the temperance campaigner Fr Theobald Mathew served as a governor of the House of Industry in Cork city.[113] In April 1840, the proceeds of one of Fr Mathew's public speaking engagements in the Royal Exchange in Dublin city, attended

106 William Meagher, *Notices of the life and character of His Grace Most Rev. Daniel Murray, late Archbishop of Dublin, as contained in the commemorative oration pronounced in the Church of the Conception, Dublin, on occasion of His Grace's months' mind. With historical and biographical notes* (Dublin, 1853), p. 93; Kerr, 'Dublin's forgotten archbishop', p. 248.

107 *Report, Dublin Mendicity Society, 1818*, [unpaginated], f. 2ʳ. Troy and Murray also chaired meetings of the society at times: *FJ*, 15 Feb. 1820, 1 Feb., 27 Apr., 3 May 1830; Dublin Mendicity Society minute book, 5 June 1821.

108 *Galway Weekly Advertiser*, 17 July, 21 Aug. 1824, 21 May 1825; *Sligo Journal*, 13 May 1828; *PI, Appendix A*, p. 718; McHugh, *Drogheda before the Famine*, pp. 48–9.

109 *Twenty-second report, Dublin Mendicity Society, 1839*, p. 5. For Monks, see John Thomas Troy to Charles Grant, 30 Nov. 1820 (NAI, CSORP, CSO/RP/1820/1300).

110 *BNL*, 4 Apr. 1834, 5 Mar. 1830. On at least one occasion Crolly also preached a charity sermon in aid of the House of Industry: *BNL*, 17 June 1817.

111 *BNL*, 24 Nov. 1837. In 1817 a charity sermon was held in the Catholic chapel in Belfast in aid of the town's House of Industry: *BNL*, 13 June 1817.

112 *BNL*, 16 July 1847.

113 O'Neill, 'The Catholic Church and relief of the poor', p. 140.

by an estimated 2,000 persons paying 6*d*. per head, were allocated to the city's Mendicity Society.[114]

Edmund Rice, founder of the Christian Brothers in Waterford at the turn of the nineteenth century, was also active in corporate efforts to suppress beggary, through his involvement in the southern city's mendicity society. Rice served as chairman of this charity, which, like other mendicity associations, attracted the financial support and goodwill of both Catholic and Protestant middle-class supporters, and drawing on his substantial wealth from his mercantile career was a relatively generous contributor to the charity's coffers.[115] Rice, whose piety was influenced by European Catholic spirituality, especially the lives and teachings of Ignatius of Loyola and St Teresa, founded schools for poor boys in Waterford, which sought to effect a moral reformation in these children by introducing them to Catholic instruction, through catechesis, and by encouraging discipline, industry and sobriety.[116] The Catholic middle classes (both lay and clerical) were as likely as their Protestant counterparts to champion poor relief initiatives that sought to instil 'habits of industry' among the lower orders without undermining the independent, industrious working poor. Bishop of Dromore, Michael Blake, promoted the work of the Newry Mendicity Society, which relieved 'poor strolling mendicants in the manner best adapted to reconcile them to a life of labour and to virtuous habits'.[117]

Daniel Murray's interest in poverty and charity extended beyond his involvement with the Dublin Mendicity Society. The archbishop was one of three Catholic prelates appointed to serve on the newly established Board of Charitable Bequests in 1844,[118] and was also an active member of the Commissioners of National Education (who oversaw the establishment of the national school system from 1831) and the Poor Inquiry of 1833–6. Murray also chaired meetings of the civic and cross-denominational Mansion House Relief Committee, and served on the managing committee of the Charitable Infirmary.[119] The fact that these positions were open to Catholic clergymen

---

114 *Nenagh Guardian*, 11 Apr. 1840.

115 Ó Cearbhaill, 'A memory that lived', pp. 159–71.

116 Dáire Keogh, 'Evangelising the faithful: Edmund Rice and the reformation of nineteenth-century Irish Catholicism' in Lennon, *Confraternities and sodalities*, pp. 57–75.

117 Draft of letter from Michael Blake to editor of *Newry Commercial Telegraph*, *c*.1833 (PRONI, Dromore Diocesan papers, DIORC/3/1, ff. 30–31).

118 The others were Archbishop William Crolly of Armagh and Cornelius Denvir of Down and Connor. The three prelates' involvement with the Board attracted criticism from some quarters, as the recommendations of the Board were seen as being anti-Catholic and infringing on episcopal independence: see *FJ*, 20 Jan. 1845.

119 *FJ*, 12 Feb. 1831; 'List of the governors of the Charitable Infirmary, in Jervis-street, for 1830', [*c*.Jan. 1830] (DDA, DMP, 31/2/134).

reflected, as Seán Connolly has illustrated, 'the new respectability of the Irish Catholic hierarchy', as 'the first half of the nineteenth century saw a steady growth in the degree of recognition offered to Catholic churchmen by the Irish establishment'.[120] This growing recognition of the Catholic Church's role in the public sphere was reflected in the decision to postpone the 1838 annual meeting of the largely Protestant-run Dublin Mendicity Society owing to the absence, due to illness, of Archbishop Murray; the meeting was adjourned to a future date 'so as that it should be honoured by his grace's presence'.[121] In February 1831, at the annual general meeting of the Sick and Indigent Roomkeepers' Society, the chairman, Lord Mayor Sir Robert Harty, was accompanied on the speakers' platform by two represent-atives of the city's Roman Catholic and Anglican communities – Archbishop Murray and Rev. Franc Sadleir of Trinity College respectively.[122] The Sick and Indigent Roomkeepers' Society and the Mendicity Society were both cross-denominational bodies, as seen by the various shades of Christianity represented among its officers and membership, and the fact that these two charities were listed alongside Catholic-ethos societies in the *Catholic directory* further affirms that they were viewed by church authorities as acceptable organisations which Catholics could support.[123]

Conclusion

Can we speak of a Catholic attitude to poverty, beggary and alms-giving in pre-Famine Ireland, as being distinct from a Protestant approach? In the above discussion, some nuance has been brought to our understanding of the most frequently arising tropes pertaining to Catholic charity prevalent in the discourse of poverty and poor relief. The accusation of indiscriminate alms-giving arising from an emphasis on good works was common, yet when levelled at the Roman faith was usually couched in sectarian vituperation. Alms were commonly doled out without discrimination by Catholics to mendicants but, as will be seen in the next chapter, Protestants were also known to engage in this practice. Furthermore, the poorer classes, along with their wealthier co-religionists, were known to draw upon concepts of deservedness when dealing with mendicants. Catholic charitable works, and Catholics' dealings with beggars, were not confined to casual, unorganised

120 Connolly, *Priests and people*, p. 10.
121 *FJ*, 11 Jan. 1838.
122 *FJ*, 5 Feb. 1831.
123 *Complete Catholic registry, 1836*, pp. 108–9; *Complete Catholic directory, almanac, and registry for the year of our Lord, 1838*, pp. 337–9.

exchanges. Rather, the pre-Famine period witnessed the introduction of a level of sophistication in Catholics' work with the poor, whether through denominationally based initiatives or in cross-denomination entities. Middle-class Catholic men co-operated with their Protestant social peers in mendicity institutions and other charitable societies, while the majority of Catholic clergymen who contributed to the discourse on poverty stressed the virtues of honesty, industry and self-dependence among the poor, and the evils of reckless alms-giving. In all of these examples, the similarities between Catholic and Protestant approaches are greater than the differences.

Catholic commentators on social questions regularly turned their attention to the questions of begging and alms-giving. A concern with the ubiquity of beggary was not limited to Protestants, as Catholics were also prominent in the public discourses on poverty, Poor Laws and mendicancy. Contributions by Catholics to these debates were not, however, marked by consensus. Archbishop Daniel Murray and Thaddeus O'Malley echoed wider middle-class concerns over indiscriminate alms-giving, seeing this practice as encouraging pauperism rather than industry and self-dependence. Other figures, such as Michael Fitzgerald, appealed to the monastic tradition of indiscriminate assistance to the sick and poor, associating this tradition with Catholicism and contrasting it with the perceived harshness of Protestant approaches to poverty. While Fitzgerald did not appear to frame his world view in terms of the 'deserving'/'undeserving' poor distinction, many of his co-religionists, both clerical and lay, did embrace such concepts, either explicitly, such as Murray or O'Malley, or implicitly, such as Aikenhead. What is clear is that Murray and O'Malley's views were more in line with those of their fellow Catholic clergymen than Fitzgerald's, as Catholic clergy in the pre-Famine period 'appear to have fully absorbed the conventional economic and social doctrines of their day, and there is little to indicate that their outlook on most issues would have been significantly different to that of their Protestant counterparts'.[124]

One field in which a distinctive Catholic 'flavour' to charity work was evident was in the work of Irish convents.[125] Convents became the most important providers of charity in nineteenth-century Ireland and were influential in cementing the power of the Church in Irish society, largely through their running of schools. Despite the prominence of poverty and charity within the public and private writings of these communities and the women therein, we do not know how they dealt with beggars on a

---

124 Connolly, 'Religion, work-discipline and economic attitudes', pp. 237–8.
125 A study of the post-Famine period could also draw upon the proliferation of conferences of the Society of St Vincent de Paul as evidence of a distinctly Catholic approach to poor relief.

practical level. It is noteworthy that while Aikenhead and her fellow Sister of Charity, Mother Catherine, did not appear to blame the poor for their indigence – perhaps owing to the Sisters' regular visiting with the sick and poor, circumstances which could enliven sympathy and empathy with the poor, and humility among the nuns – there was no attempt in their writings to grapple with the underlying structural causes of poverty in Irish society. Contributing to the public discourse pertaining to such matters fell outside the remit, and the gendered roles shaped by social expectations, of nineteenth-century philanthropic women, whose work was focused on the provision of spiritual and temporal assistance to the most 'deserving' – namely, women and children. There were no equivalent communities within Irish Protestantism, which will be examined in the next chapter.

7

Protestant Approaches
to Begging and Alms-Giving

Introduction

Addressing the annual general meeting of the Dublin Mendicity Society in January 1838, the city's Church of Ireland archbishop, Richard Whately, boasted of having never given money to a beggar. Whately rejected the notion that one should give alms out of sympathy: instead, Christian feelings ought to prevent one from indiscriminately doling out alms to paupers 'who most practised deception on the public, and to give them money was but to pay them for the purpose of keeping up the system of public misery and street begging'.[1] This refusal to give alms seems to have been a well-known trait of Whately's. W.R. Le Fanu, whose father was one of the prelate's acquaintances, relates Whately's recollection of one particular mendicant who solicited alms from him: '[Whately] used to tell of a beggar who followed him asking alms, to whom he said, "Go away; I never give anything to a beggar in the streets." The beggar replied, "And where would your reverence wish me to wait on you?"'[2]

The case of Whately provides a useful entry-point into considering how Protestants perceived and responded to street begging in the subject period, as it brings to light the complexities in negotiating how different people negotiated begging and alms-giving. Whately was a Church of Ireland archbishop and theologian but not an evangelical; his views on begging and alms-giving were grounded in scripture but also in political economy; he never gave alms to a beggar but was a regular and relatively generous contributor to charitable causes. Yet, Whately was a senior cleric and the

---

1 *FJ*, 17 Jan. 1838.
2 W.R. Le Fanu, *Seventy years of Irish life being anecdotes and reminiscences* (2nd edn, London, 1893), p. 78. See also E. Jane Whately, *Life and correspondence of Richard Whately, D.D. late Archbishop of Dublin* (2 vols, London, 1866), i, p. 150.

question must be asked as to how representative were his views, either of his fellow Episcopalians or of the clergy (regardless of denomination) in general. How did his views tally with those of Protestant women? Mirroring the approach taken in the preceding chapter, this discussion will pivot on the questions of what Protestants said and did about begging and alms-giving in pre-Famine Ireland. The influence of evangelicalism on concepts of poverty and charity will be considered, before analysing how Protestant commentators contributed to the prolonged and fraught Poor Law debates of this period. Public discussion on matters of social concern did not escape the sectarian nature of contemporary political and religious discourses, and the questions of Ireland's endemic poverty and prevalent mendicancy were no different. In this light, beggary became associated with the Roman Catholicism of a majority of Ireland's poorer classes and this chapter will examine how the tropes of beggary and Catholicism became fused together in Protestant social discourse. Attention will then shift to the actions taken by Protestants within their own congregations, wherein internal mechanisms unique to each church or religious society were adopted in corporate responses to destitution and mendicancy, and the role of Protestant women in such initiatives.

Discourses

Evangelicalism, Begging and Alms-Giving

The role of Protestant evangelicalism in shaping how contemporaries approached poverty and begging in this period is indispensable to any study of how the main Protestant churches negotiated these social questions. Arising from British Protestantism in the eighteenth century, evangelicalism was a movement of reform and revival which is difficult, if not impossible, strictly to define, for, in Boyd Hilton's words, 'it was not a precise phenomenon';[3] Jonathan Wright has described evangelicalism as 'a complex and varied phenomenon, which cut across both denominational and theological lines'.[4] What can be identified are doctrinal traits largely shared by evangelicals of all denominations. Evangelicals stressed four central doctrines: Christ's atoning death on the Cross for the sins of mankind; the Bible as the chief source of religious authority; conversion to a new life of faith in Christ and assurance of one's personal salvation; and an activism in spreading the gospel.[5] Evangelicals' beliefs were not new, being grounded

3 Hilton, *Age of atonement*, p. 7.
4 Wright, *'Natural leaders'*, p. 204.
5 D.W. Bebbington, *Evangelicalism in modern Britain: a history from the 1730s to the 1980s* (London, 1989), pp. 2–17. For a critical discussion on the viability of this

in Judeo-Christian theology, but 'what distinguished evangelicals was the emphasis they gave to particular doctrines, and the fervour with which they practised "vital religion"'.[6]

Evangelicalism, as understood by historians of the nineteenth century, was a movement which transcended national boundaries. Its roots can be traced to the missionary zeal of John Wesley (1703–91) and the early Methodists from the 1730s onwards, and successfully developed in north America by George Whitefield (1714–70). A later manifestation of this movement's evolution emerged from within the Church of England in the 1790s and was associated with the Clapham Sect group of merchants, barristers and politicians in London, of whom William Wilberforce (1759–1833), the author of *Practical view of the prevailing religious system* (which reached its 14th edition in Britain in 1820), was the most influential.[7] Evangelicalism built upon the movement for the reformation of manners and morals that emerged in the 1780s and the impetus provided by millennial expectation, which, in itself, had been created by the momentous political crises in France, Britain and Ireland. Furthermore, evangelicals' zeal for conversion and activism was complemented by the emerging associational culture of middle-class life and spurred the formation of numerous voluntary societies. As Irene Whelan has observed, 'the evangelical movement throughout the British Isles entered the new century on a wave of enthusiasm expressed through the phenomenal spread of voluntary organisations devoted to everything from Bible and tract distribution to Sunday Schools, home and overseas missions, and countless other charitable and philanthropic concerns'.[8] The various denominations' own manifestations of evangelicalism are not to be treated as identical entities, yet, differences aside, Irish evangelicals – Church of Ireland, Presbyterian and Methodist – shared many interests.[9] Irish evangelicalism

four-pronged model of evangelicalism, see J.N. Ian Dickson, *Beyond religious discourse: sermons, preaching and evangelical Protestants in nineteenth-century Irish society* (Milton Keynes, 2007), pp. 5–8.

6 Hilton, *Age of atonement*, p. 8.

7 Stewart J. Brown, *The national churches of England, Ireland, and Scotland 1801–1846* (Oxford, 2001), pp. 55–6; William Wilberforce, *A practical view of the prevailing religious system of professed Christians, in the higher and middle classes in this country, contrasted with real Christianity* (London, 1797). A Dublin edition of *Practical view* was published in the same year.

8 Irene Whelan, 'The Bible gentry: evangelical religion, aristocracy, and the new moral order in the early nineteenth century' in Gribben and Holmes, *Protestant millennialism, evangelicalism and Irish society*, p. 55. Also David Hempton, 'Evangelicalism in English and Irish society, 1780–1840' in Mark A. Noll, David W. Bebbington and George A. Rawlyk (eds), *Evangelicalism: comparative studies of popular Protestantism in North America, the British Isles, and beyond, 1700–1900* (New York and Oxford, 1994), p. 156.

9 Andrew Holmes, *The shaping of Ulster Presbyterian belief and practice, 1770–1840* (Oxford, 2006), p. 306; Andrew Holmes, 'The experience and understanding of

also evolved differently from its British counterpart, owing to political developments particular to Ireland. The growing assertiveness and success of Catholic reform movements under the leadership of Daniel O'Connell, most notably the campaigns for Catholic Emancipation and repeal of the Act of Union, which saw the mobilisation of priests as political activists, drove evangelicals to advocate the protection of the rights and privileges of an embattled Protestant minority, the various branches of which co-operated in the Bible society and Sunday School movements in pursuit of common interests.[10]

Turning to the questions of poverty, begging and alms-giving, it can be seen that evangelicalism greatly influenced how the evolving discourses were shaped. Evangelicals placed greater emphasis on the sufferer's spiritual impoverishment than on his/her bodily wants, as it was salvation through personal conversion that was ultimately sought, and which was the focus of evangelicals' associational and voluntary work. The emphasis on spiritual salvation reflected a shift in the language of philanthropy when compared with the middle of the previous century; then, the provision of temporal relief guided how charity was framed and bestowed. An English evangelical controversialist at the turn of the century captured the shift in emphasis: 'How preferable is that bread which endureth to everlasting life, to that which perisheth; and how much more to be dreaded is a famine of the word of truth, than a dearth of earthly food'.[11] John Bird Sumner, the evangelical bishop of Chester (later archbishop of Canterbury) who also served on the English Poor Inquiry Commission in the early 1830s, saw alms-giving as duly relieving immediate temporal poverty – 'this it may and ought to do' – but failing to strike at the root of the pauper's destitution, namely his soul weighed down by original sin: 'No effort of man can take away the consequences of the first sin'.[12] Sumner drew on the biblical story of the crippled beggar who asked alms of John and Peter as they entered the temple, to whom Peter replied: 'Silver and gold have I none; but such as I have give

religious revival in Ulster Presbyterianism, c.1800–1930' in *IHS*, xxxiv, no. 136 (Nov. 2002), p. 362.

10 Miriam Moffitt, *The Society for Irish Church Missions to the Roman Catholics, 1849–1950* (Manchester, 2010), pp. 12–13; R.F.G. Holmes, *Our Irish Presbyterian heritage* (n.p. [Belfast], 1985), p. 110.

11 Richard Hill to a clergyman, 10 Nov. 1800, Edwin Sidney, *The life of Sir Richard Hill, Bart.* (London, 1839), p. 472, quoted in Boyd Hilton, 'The role of Providence in evangelical social thought' in Derek Beales and Geoffrey Best (eds), *History, society and the churches: essays in honour of Owen Chadwick* (Cambridge, 1985), p. 220. See also Hilton, *Age of atonement*, pp. 88, 98.

12 John Bird Sumner, 'Sermon VII. The surest mode of benefitting the poor' in John Bird Sumner, *Christian charity; its obligations and objects, with reference to the present state of society. In a series of sermons* (2nd edn, London, 1841), p. 109.

I thee: In the name of Jesus Christ of Nazareth rise up and walk'. Instead of bestowing alms, the apostle assisted the indigent to his feet, 'and he leaping up stood, and walked, and entered with them into the temple, walking, and leaping, and praising God' (Acts 3: 1–8). According to Sumner, alms would have provided mere temporary sustenance and the beggar's wants would have remained. 'But by what he [Peter] did, when he bid him to *rise up and walk*, he removed his wants, instead of relieving them; he lifted him up to a state which before he could not have reached; the man became a new creature'.[13] Just as Christians of all denominations grounded their charity in scripture, Sumner here presented a biblical precedent underpinning the evangelical zeal for personal conversion and rebirth in Christ. While salvation trumped bodily relief, the former was inextricably linked to the improvement of the social conditions of the poor.[14] How could the slum dweller or the rural peasant be convinced to turn to Christ and be assured of salvation when living in the morally polluting environments of filth, idleness, intemperance, illiteracy and nakedness among other vices, not to mention irreligion? In disseminating the gospel to the irreligious poor, the personal, face-to-face encounter was the preferred means. This method drew inspiration from the pastoral work of Christ and facilitated the personal evangelisation of the poor by missionaries; the focus of evangelical charity was on the individual and his/her salvation.

Yet, despite these shared approaches, evangelicals could hold contrasting opinions on poverty and charity. These differences were caused by a disparity in views among evangelicals as to the working of divine providence in the world, with a distinction being drawn between 'moderates' and 'extremists' who perceived worldly happenings as being mostly consequences of man-made actions or divine interferences respectively.[15] Church of Scotland minister and social reformer Thomas Chalmers railed against a state provision for the poor, championing private charity by individuals and, at most, minimal interventions by corporate bodies. In terms of temporal wants, Chalmers's target was not poverty but pauperism, and he saw the evangelising work of Christian missionaries, visiting the homes of the poor and detecting genuine cases and imposture through their moralising inspections, as, in Hilton's words, 'the only sure way to effect a moral regeneration of society'.[16] Chalmers's opposition to a compulsory poor scheme stood in stark contrast to, for instance, the views of the evangelical Church of Ireland rector of Powerscourt,

---

13 Sumner, 'Sermon VII. The surest mode of benefitting the poor', p. 111.
14 Brian Dickey, '"Going about doing good": evangelicals and poverty *c*.1815–1870' in John Wolffe (ed.), *Evangelical faith and public zeal: evangelicals and society in Britain 1780–1980* (London, 1995), p. 44.
15 Hilton, *Age of atonement*, pp. 15–17.
16 Ibid., p. 81.

Rev. Robert Daly, who shifted from a position of outright hostility to a Poor Law to one whereby he believed that a statutory provision was necessary for the temporal and moral alleviation of the poorer classes.[17] Daly's interesting argument was that a statutory provision would alleviate the pastoral pressures on clergymen, whose duties were overly concerned with relieving the worldly poverty of their flock. Under the proposed Poor Law these clerics would have greater liberty to attend to the spiritual wants of the poor. These instances demonstrate that while common traits can be identified among nineteenth-century evangelicals, their approaches to social questions could vary greatly. Yet, evangelicals considered these questions with an eye to a common ultimate objective – the salvation of the souls of sinners through personal conversion. In a charity sermon in aid of the Belfast House of Industry the evangelical Presbyterian minister Rev. Henry Cooke drew on a passage from Proverbs 3:27 ('Withhold not good from them to whom it is due, when it is in the power of thine hand to do it') to make a distinction between relieving true, genuine distress and 'undeserving' imposture. Beggary was presented by Cooke as an immoral practice, which exposed the poor to 'continual temptations ... [and] to the contagion of bad example', as well as leaving many 'almost totally devoid of the means of education, or religious instruction'; furthermore, mendicancy also had wider societal consequences – for example, in the economic value of the individual's lost labour. Cooke evoked images of ill-health to suggest that beggary exerted a cancerous influence on the social body: the Belfast House of Industry, established to suppress mendicancy and its causes, sought 'not a temporary palliative, but a radical cure' to this 'disease' through the use of 'proper remedies' – namely, a system of home visitations and inspections that constituted 'a kind of domestic police, which preserves order, so essential to industry; promotes cleanliness, so essential to health; and stimulates to diligence, by the dread of censure, and the hope of reward'.[18]

Protestants, Irish Mendicancy and the Poor Law Question
Anglican clergy were the leading contributors to public debate on poor relief in eighteenth-century Ireland.[19] The condition of the poor did not escape the attention of the Archbishop of Dublin, William King, who established alms houses, granted begging badges to the poor and forbade the destitute to beg outside their own parish.[20] Dean of St Patrick's, Jonathan Swift, was widely known for his philanthropic endeavours, and his published work includes

17 [Robert Daly], 'Improvement of Ireland – Poor Laws' in *Christian Examiner and Church of Ireland magazine*, x, no. 55 (Jan. 1830), pp. 1–8.
18 Cooke, *Sermon preached in aid of the Belfast House of Industry*, pp. 3–22.
19 Gray, *Making of the Irish Poor Law*, pp. 19–27.
20 William Edward Hartpole Lecky, *A history of Ireland in the eighteenth century* (5 vols, London, 1913–19), i, p. 230.

tracts on the state of indigence and beggary in Dublin city. Swift drew a firm line between the local Dublin beggars, who were to be badged and relieved by their own parish, and 'the Evil of Foreign Beggars', whom he wished to see whipped and driven out of the city, 'and let the next country Parish do as they please'.[21] Swift viewed the vast majority of the city's mendicants as 'undeserving Wretches', too lazy to work and whose destitution was owed to 'their own Idleness, attended with all Manner of Vices, particularly Drunkenness, Thievery, and Cheating'.[22]

The most significant eighteenth-century contribution to the debate on provision for the poor were two pamphlets by Dean of Clogher, Richard Woodward, proposing the erection of multi-faceted poor houses for various categories of the poor, to be established in every county in Ireland. Woodward was critical of the prevailing manner of relief which was devoid of any statutory provision for the poor and railed against the iniquity of the system based on voluntary and unsystematic relief, whereby almsgiving frequently arose 'from the Sympathy of Wretches almost as poor as those whom they relieve', while 'the Thoughtless, the Unfeeling, and the Absentee contribute nothing'.[23] The clergyman's scheme did not propose an unqualified right to relief for all in distress but echoed the widespread disdain for the 'undeserving' idle poor, suggesting that habitual beggars and vagrants be branded, imprisoned, whipped and, as a last resort for recidivists, transported.[24] In a more detailed pamphlet, published two years later, a 1 per cent tax on agricultural and commercial output to fund a national system of poor assistance was suggested.[25] Woodward's proposals constituted the most coherent reflection, until that point, of the question of Ireland's poverty and influenced the Houses of Industry legislation of the early 1770s.[26] Woodward's pamphlets provide an insight into the evolving philosophical treatment of poverty and begging by contemporary clerics. The language used by Woodward focused on relieving the temporal plight of the destitute, while punishing the bodily frailties of 'undeserving' mendicants. His concern was with the provision of suitable lodgings, food and clothing to the poor, as well as increasing 'the Aggregate of National Industry, and the Security of Property'.[27] There was none of the evangelical emphasis on securing the soul of the sinner which

---

21 [Swift], *Proposal for giving badges to the beggars*, p. 6.
22 Ibid., pp. 8–9.
23 [Richard Woodward], *A scheme for establishing county poor-houses, in the kingdom of Ireland* (Dublin, 1766), p. 5.
24 Ibid., p. 10.
25 Woodward, *Argument in support of the poor*.
26 Cousins, 'The Irish parliament and relief of the poor', pp. 95–115; Gray, *Making of the Irish Poor Law*, pp. 21–5.
27 [Woodward], *A scheme for establishing county poor-houses*, p. 6.

shaped the language of charity in the following decades. While Woodward spoke about 'humanity', 'compassion' and 'justice', nowhere did he suggest the importance of personal salvation or spiritual regeneration.

Woodward's somewhat utilitarian model contrasted sharply with the sentiments echoed three decades later by Rev. Robert Daly of Powerscourt in his outline of a proposal for inducing the Irish poor to lift themselves out of poverty. A 'renowned preacher and militant evangelical', Daly was a leading figure in the 'Second Reformation' of the 1820s, and from 1843 until his death three decades later served as bishop of the united dioceses of Cashel, Emly, Waterford and Lismore.[28] His activism included running local schools and supporting various evangelical missionary societies, leading to accusations of proselytism. He was well placed to drive, together with the evangelical members of the landed Wingfield family, a religious revival on the Powerscourt estate throughout the 1820s and 1830s.[29] In evidence to the Poor Inquiry, Daly extolled the virtues of a charitable scheme he had witnessed first-hand in Brighton which promoted a savings scheme among the poor and was supplemented by a cash sum doled out by the charity in question. The scheme was based on the principle that, where possible, gratuitous relief should not be provided, and it taught the poor 'the importance of very small, if habitual, savings'. The encouragement of prudence and self-sufficiency benefited both the giver and the receiver. Noting that the Brighton scheme led to 'the suppression of mendicancy and imposture', Daly contrasted the previous system of poor relief in his County Wicklow parish with the system prevailing in the 1830s (and which was based on the Brighton initiative): 'Under our former system of almsgiving, it seems to be the object of the poor to be as miserable and squalid as possible, in order to extort alms; under this it is the object of the poor to vie one with the other in comfort and decency of appearance'.[30]

Elsewhere, Daly outlined the development of his views on a statutory poor provision, evolving from a standpoint of outright opposition to his later belief that 'a national legal provision for the poor is a national duty'.[31] Writing in 1830, in Caesar Otway's *Christian Examiner*, an evangelical Church of Ireland magazine, Daly argued that a disproportionate amount of the clergy's time was exerted on handling requests for poor relief. As such, they could not devote sufficient time to the spiritual well-being of their congregation.

28 Eoghan Ó Raghallaigh, 'Daly, Robert' in McGuire and Quinn (eds), *DIB*, iii, pp. 32–3; Desmond Bowen, *Souperism: myth or reality? A study in souperism* (Cork, 1970), pp. 90, 119–20.

29 Gray, *Making of the Irish Poor Law*, p. 26; Whelan, 'The Bible gentry', pp. 62, 66–7.

30 *PI, Appendix C, Part II, Addenda to Appendix A*, p. 40e.

31 [Daly], 'Improvement of Ireland', p. 2.

A statutory relief scheme, which would remove the burden from the parish, would benefit both clergymen and their parishioners, Daly argued:

> I conceive, that among other blessings to be derived from a national provision for the poor, one, and not the least, will be the improvement it will introduce in the intercourse between the minister and the poor of his flock; *temporal wants will not form the main subject of every conversation, and his visits will not be sought with the hope of extracting some pecuniary assistance, but with the view of receiving that instruction which can make wise unto salvation.* I am, moreover, induced to give my opinion on this subject, because I know that no one has more opportunity of learning by experience, the real state of the poor under the present system, than the clergyman of a parish.[32]

Not surprisingly, the author had much to say on the topic of mendicancy and saw the practice of indiscriminate alms-giving to beggars as a greater evil than any faults in the English Speenhamland Poor Law system, which was becoming the subject of increasing public controversy.[33] While acknowledging the merits of the argument that a compulsory poor rate would diminish much of the charitable spirit in the alms-giver and the gratitude of the recipient, Daly asserted:

> but I have long and attentively watched the spirit in which alms are given and received, under the system of sturdy mendicancy which exists in our country, and I do unhesitatingly say, that nothing was ever levied more in the shape of a tax, than the contributions extracted in this country by the noise and importunate clamour of beggars.

For the clergyman, the prevailing Irish system only encouraged unqualified relief, thus fostering idleness and dependency. In his analysis of Irish poverty, the author adhered to the traditional model of the 'deserving' and 'undeserving' poor, and identified the archetypal threats long associated with the mendicant poor – crime, vice, sedition and disease:

> [T]he strolling mendicant utters his imprecations against those who do not contribute according to the scale which he has laid down,

---

32 Ibid., p. 7 (emphasis added).
33 Under the Speenhamland system, which was first introduced in 1795, the English parish supplemented labourers' wages and indexed this provision to the fluctuating price of bread. Opponents of the system perceived it as an encouragement to idleness, dependency and pauperism.

and spends the produce of his day's collection in drunkenness and profligacy; passing through the country he sows the seeds of dishonesty, immorality, and vice, increases sedition, and discontent, and in times of the prevalence of fever, carries its infection throughout the land.[34]

Daly's views provide a useful comparison with those of Woodward decades earlier and reflect the shift in the lexicon of the Poor Law debate. The influence of evangelicalism and moralism ensured that for some influential reformers spiritual salvation trumped temporal assistance, yet the latter remained a matter of utmost urgency and importance.

This view of the mendicant poor posing a threat to civil order is reflected in another contribution to *Christian Examiner* a year later. The author, who signed off as 'Hibernicus', adopted a different tone from the earlier contribution, and alleged that Roman Catholicism, in particular its mass of priests, was the fundamental source of all that was evil in Ireland. In presenting his argument, the author drew on the popular motif of the beggar as a personification of Popish error and deceit. 'Hibernicus' stated that Popery was 'adverse to all improvement, either of body or mind', before continuing:

It is unquestioned, that wandering beggars are the chief agents of the priests, in mock miracles and prophecies, deceptions, and impostures of every kind; they are still more useful in the frightful system of *espionage*, which forms, perhaps, a more powerful source of dominion, than even the confessional itself. They form also a fluctuating medium for the conveyance of sedition and agitation from one district to another.[35]

For the author, whose views reflected the evangelical obsession with Popish 'error' and 'priestcraft', wandering mendicants constituted not only a threat to the state but a cancerous influence on the spiritual and moral well-being of the impressionable poor. The beggar's deviance transcended the temporal and spiritual spheres of human existence. Applying these beliefs to his argument in favour of a Poor Law, 'Hibernicus' stated that one advantage of a statutory poor provision would be to remove responsibility for such paupers – almost invariably Catholics – from the priests to appointed officers, who would presumably be Protestants. The intensity of this piece, with its unbridled focus on the perceived moral wickedness of Catholicism, must be seen in the context of increasing sectarian tensions in public discourse in Ireland throughout the 1820s and into the 1830s.

34 [Daly], 'Improvement of Ireland', p. 5.
35 'Hibernicus', 'On the Poor Laws' in *Christian Examiner*, xi, no. 73 (July 1831), p. 508.

This period witnessed the continued refinement of distinct identities and cultures among the Catholics and Protestants of Ireland, as political issues, most notably Catholic Emancipation, tithes and the proposed repeal of the Act of Union, came to the fore of widely mobilised mass movements. Other factors, such as an increasingly confident and assertive Catholic middle class demanding to be placed on an equal footing as their Established Church counterparts, the emergence of evangelical movements in each of the main Protestant denominations and the radicalisation of the Orange movement, fanned the flames of sectarian hatred and suspicion, and moulded the language employed by commentators and polemicists in discourse on poverty, education and other contentious matters.[36]

Among the clerics who publicly and regularly addressed the questions of poverty, beggary and the suitability (or otherwise) of a statutory Poor Law for Ireland was Richard Whately, the Church of Ireland archbishop of Dublin from 1831 to 1863. Whately was among a number of leading Christian political economists in Ireland and Britain in the first half of the nineteenth century who were, in Peter Gray's words, 'concerned with reconciling universal truths of classical political economics with the moral teaching of Christianity, arguing that the two were complementary and must be united in the service of good governance'.[37] While not an evangelical, Whately shared the moralising conceptions of poverty with the revivalist wings of the Established Church and flavoured them with political economy, drawing particular influence from the theories of demographic (un)sustainability put forward by the evangelical political economist, Rev. Thomas Malthus.

The archbishop's notorious eccentricities were evident in the manner in which he dealt with street beggars. During his time in Oxford, where he served as a member of the town's mendicity society, Whately personally inspected beggars' pockets to ensure that they were not hiding money.[38] Whately's views on begging and alms-giving, outlined in considerable detail in a sermon preached in aid of Dr Steevens' Hospital in the mid-1830s, drew on 'Christ's example' in drawing distinctions between the sick poor, who were almost invariably deserving of assistance, and able-bodied beggars, from whom indiscriminate charity must be withheld. The numerous instances in the gospels wherein Christ aided the sick and cured illnesses contrasted sharply, Whately argued, with the two instances of him providing alms – in the form of food – to the hungry, as told in the parable of the Loaves

---

36 Whelan, *Bible war in Ireland*.
37 Gray, *Making of the Irish Poor Law*, p. 123. See also Hilton, *Age of atonement*, pp. 36–70.
38 Whately, *Life and correspondence of Richard Whately*, i, p. 149.

and the Fishes.[39] After feeding the multitudes, Christ sent them away, 'not allowing them to remain in expectation of a daily renewal of the like miracle', Whately observed.[40] Thomas Chalmers, in evidence to the 1830 Irish poor committee, also drew upon the parable of the Loaves and the Fishes to argue that Christ's teachings supported voluntarist models of poor assistance: Christ identified the 'sordid principle upon which [the multitudes] ran after Him' and accordingly exerted discretion in his charity, as the indiscriminate manner of doling out assistance 'would have disorganized and put into disorder the whole population'.[41]

Whately's concept of charity was based on personal activism, stressing the need for the better-off to go out and work among the distressed. Underpinning this work was the moral requirement for '*discrimination* in charity'.[42] Relieving the poor was a Christian duty, but assistance must be bestowed warily so as not to foster mendicancy: 'if no one gave alms, there would be no beggars'.[43] Indiscriminate alms-giving exerted a corruptive influence on both parties within a charitable transaction – the benefactor and the recipient. The former negated his duty to ascertain the credentials of the soliciting poor person and determine 'whether they are doing good or mischief', while the mendicant was being induced to continue 'the wretched and demoralizing trade of begging'.[44] Indiscriminate alms-giving actually constituted a 'sin' on the part of the giver, Whately believed, as this misspent charity maintained the beggar in his life of idleness and vice.[45] Furthermore, the morally debilitating effect of this transaction extended beyond the two immediate parties to 'real objects of compassion', whose 'modest and simple' pleas for assistance were dwarfed by the extravagant fabrications or the grotesque bodily exposures of the fraudulent and professional mendicant. Indiscriminate alms-giving only served to facilitate and encourage 'this wretched kind of lottery', in which style won out over substance.[46] Whately's emphasis on the economic and moral evils which arise from feckless alms-giving – hence his urging for 'discrimination in charity' – reflects the influence of Malthus, who asserted that 'experience has proved, I believe without a single exception, that poverty and misery have always increased in proportion to the quantity of indiscriminate

---

39 The first instance is told in Matt. 14:13–21, Mark 6:31–44, Luke 9:10–17 and John 6:5–15, and the second in Matt. 15:32–39 and Mark 8:1–9.

40 Whately, *Christ's example*, p. 10.

41 *Second report, state of the poor select committee, 1830*, p. 320.

42 Whately, *Christ's example*, p. 25.

43 Ibid., p. 21.

44 Ibid., pp. 23, 21.

45 Ibid., p. 22. See also *FJ*, 17 Jan. 1838.

46 Whately, *Christ's example*, p. 20.

charity'.[47] Whately's use of the lottery metaphor further displays the intellectual reach of Malthus, who regularly deployed this rhetorical device – for example, in asserting the unavoidable extent of suffering and poverty in the human condition, he referred to 'the unhappy persons who in the great lottery of life have drawn a blank'.[48]

In late 1833, Whately was appointed to chair the Royal Commission of Inquiry into the Condition of the Poorer Classes in Ireland.[49] The inquiry's third and final report forwarded Whately's views, previously articulated in public and in private, which were shared by most of the commissioners and other influential commentators such as Nassau Senior, a lifelong friend and former pupil of the archbishop's. The inquiry rejected the workhouse-based New Poor Law in England, instead championing the 'Scottish system' of minimalist state action, wherein assistance would be provided with discretion largely through voluntary agencies and without a compulsory poor rate, thus preventing a right to relief for the poor and the burden of an additional tax for ratepayers. (A limited state provision was to be made for certain categories of the poor, such as the impotent and sick poor.)[50] On the question of mendicancy, the inquiry echoed Whately's disdain for indiscriminate alms-giving, stating that 'the abundant alms which are bestowed, in particular by the poorer classes, unfortunately tend … to encourage mendicancy with its attendant evils'.[51] Voluntary charities, such as mendicity societies, were to fall under the regulation of a Poor Law Commission, yet the direct provision of relief was to remain in the hands of the voluntary organisations. The report also advocated for revised vagrancy laws, empowering magistrates either to transport convicted vagrants to the colonies as labourers (this was aimed at the mendicant poor who were willing to work) or confine them in Irish penitentiaries for an indefinite period of time, a measure targeting the refractory, able-bodied and idle beggar.[52] In the end, the commission's

47 T.R. Malthus, *An essay on the principle of population; or, a view of its past and present effects on human happiness; with an inquiry into our prospects respecting the future removal or mitigation of the evils which it occasions* (new edn, London, 1803), book iv, chapter ix, p. 564.

48 Ibid., book iii, chapter ii, p. 378. For Malthus's influence on the debate on Irish poverty, see Gray, *Making of the Irish Poor Law*, pp. 47–50, 123–9.

49 Gray, *Making of the Irish Poor Law*, pp. 92–129; Ó Ciosáin, *Ireland in official print culture*, pp. 26–69.

50 Among the measures proposed by the Poor Inquiry were: a state-assisted emigration scheme; a system of agricultural education and improvement, including land drainage and reclamation, to be overseen by a Board of Improvement; and improved housing for the rural poor, the expense of which to be met partly by the landlord and partly through local rates.

51 *PI, third report*, p. 25.

52 Ibid., p. 27.

proposed system was rejected by the government, which subsequently adopted George Nicholls's workhouse- and poor rate-based relief system, modelled on the New English Poor Law.

Whately's criticism of a rate-based relief provision bestowed upon the able-bodied poor as an entitlement, as per the Speenhamland system in England from 1795, countenanced both 'the moral and economic hazards involved'.[53] This system tempted the diligent labourer away from industry and independence, and served as a 'bounty on idleness ... a bounty upon lying ... a bounty on theft'.[54] In his evidence to an 1832 parliamentary inquiry on the tithes system, Whately expressed his unyielding opposition to the introduction of a compulsory Poor Law for the able-bodied in Ireland, asserting that the provision in Ireland of a legal right to relief would encourage dependency and idleness among the lower orders, thereby encumbering any attempt to foster industry:

> It would tend to make them leave their parents and their children to parish support, instead of attending to them as they do now, and to prevent them from laying by any thing for a time of distress. They would work as little as possible, and get all they could from the parish. I have seen that operate a great deal in England, and I think it would operate with much more rapid and destructive effect in Ireland.[55]

Whately's unrelenting criticism of Poor Law provision was shared by perhaps the leading intellectual and social commentator in the first half of the nineteenth century, Rev. Thomas Chalmers. An evangelical Church of Scotland minister, political economist and prolific writer, Chalmers's championing of voluntary private charity was influenced by his Calvinist theology, evangelical disposition, an adherence to Christian political economy and his own practical experience of overseeing an urban experiment of voluntary poor relief and moral inspection in his Glasgow parish of St John's (1819–23). Chalmers's scheme was based on romantic impressions of a rural, familial and communal basis for alleviating distress, and the inherently Christian practice of visitation to the sick and poor was central to this idealistic model of benevolence. Chalmers's influence extended to

---

53 Gray, *Making of the Irish Poor Law*, p. 125.
54 Letter from Richard Whately to directors of Bulcamp House of Industry, 2 June 1823, reprinted in *Report from His Majesty's commissioners for inquiring into the administration and practical operation of the Poor Laws*, Appendix C, pp. 260c–261c, H.C. 1834 (44), xxxvii, 264–5.
55 *The evidence of His Grace the Archbishop of Dublin, as taken before the select committee of the House of Lords, appointed to inquire into the collection and payment of tithes in Ireland, and the state of the laws relating thereto* (London, 1832), p. 97.

Ireland and the Irish Poor Law debate: he appeared as a 'star witness' to the 1830 Irish poor committee's inquiry;[56] he was in frequent correspondence with Irish Presbyterian ministers, who regularly invited him to preach charity sermons;[57] his writings were sold and republished in Belfast and Dublin;[58] and he took an active interest in Irish social conditions – for instance, inquiring into the management of the poor in Dublin city and the Presbyterian Church's relief efforts in Connaught during the Great Famine.[59] As Jonathan Wright has convincingly argued, Chalmers's views on poverty and charity echoed those of Irish Presbyterians (particularly among the middle classes of Belfast), as opposed to shaping them.[60] These views were shared by other Presbyterian ministers in Ireland, most prominently by Rev. James Carlile of Mary's Abbey congregation in Dublin. In his letter to Chalmers in 1830, Carlile suggested that 'the poor would eagerly grasp at a compulsory provision and readily give out all their habits of helping one another', thus mirroring Chalmers's own views based on his experiment in St John's. A compulsory provision, in encouraging dependency and discouraging 'spontaneous charity', would only serve as 'a premium on pauperism'.[61] Almost a decade later, Carlile publicly expounded these views while addressing a meeting of representatives of Dublin's charitable societies on the topic of the forthcoming rates-funded Poor Law system. He pointed to the English Poor Law system, which conferred a right to relief upon the poor, the effects of which were, he claimed, 'enormous vagrancy ... [and] public pauperism'. This stood in stark contrast to the Scottish system, which excluded the able-bodied, except in cases of emergency wherein assistance was funded through the voluntary raising of subscriptions, thus preventing 'public pauperism'.[62]

Quakers were also active contributors to the Poor Law debate, which encompassed the related topics of mendicancy and charity. This question was one which demonstrated how the independence of spirit, thought and action that characterised Quakerism filtered through to Irish Friends' approaches to social issues. Quakers did not adhere, en masse, to particular social and economic theories, and, thus, approached social questions 'unencumbered

56 Peter Gray, 'Thomas Chalmers and Irish poverty' in Frank Ferguson and James McConnel (eds), *Ireland and Scotland in the nineteenth century* (Dublin, 2009), p. 96.
57 Cooke and Chalmers papers (PRONI, T3307).
58 *BNL*, 1 Dec. 1820; *FJ*, 17 Jan. 1822, 15 Feb. 1827.
59 James Carlile to Thomas Chalmers, 28 Jan. 1829 (PRONI, Cooke and Chalmers papers, T3307/15); Hamilton Magee, *Fifty years in the Irish mission* (Belfast and Edinburgh, [*c*.1905]), p. 55.
60 Wright, '*Natural leaders*', pp. 221–6.
61 James Carlile to Thomas Chalmers, 26 Apr. 1830.
62 *FJ*, 21 Feb. 1838.

by theory ... [and] unfettered by untested preconceptions'.[63] For instance, Ebenezer Shackleton's 1832 pamphlet in favour of a statutory Poor Law in Ireland did not concern itself with attributing blame for Ireland's structural poverty to any party but, rather, with finding a satisfactory solution; for Shackleton, a statutory Poor Law, based on the English precedent of 'a right to a sufficiency of wholesome food', constituted the best means not only of relieving the poor but also of curtailing agrarian unrest.[64] A proposed plan, framed and published by 13 Quaker men in 1825, attributed Ireland's social, economic and political misery to landlord absenteeism and high rents. Proposing to encourage resident proprietary of land and capital investment, the plan aimed to create an expanding class of small farmers: 'instead of an oppressed, defrauded, turbulent, lawless, uninformed, idle, poor, miserable peasantry; would spring up an industrious, independent, well-instructed, affluent and contented yeomanry'.[65]

The travel account of the English Quaker Jonathan Binns contains an array of colourful mendicant characters whom the author encountered throughout Ireland. Binns served as an agricultural assistant commissioner on the Whately Poor Inquiry in the mid-1830s and travelled across Ireland in this capacity, carrying out investigations into the social conditions of the poor. In various locations (predominantly in large provincial towns), Binns distinguished between the 'deserving' and 'undeserving' poor yet nuanced these concepts through a consideration of the reality of existence for large numbers of the Irish poor. In Philipstown (Daingean), in King's County, Binns's emphasis was on the practical complexities inherent in doling out alms to beggars: 'the windows were frequently crowded with miserable women, carrying children upon their backs, and soliciting charity with pitiful lamentations. To relieve all was impossible – and to relieve only a few increased the number of those who begged'. Nonetheless, Binns drew comfort from the significance of the work in which he was engaged and the long-term consequences of the Poor Inquiry's investigations: 'Under such distressing circumstances, my consolation was, that I was engaged in preparing a full and honest statement of their wretched condition, with a view to the introduction of legislative measures of relief'.[66] His comments

63 Helen E. Hatton, *The largest amount of good: Quaker relief in Ireland, 1654–1921* (Kingston, Ontario and London, 1993), p. 27.

64 Ebenezer Shackleton, *Poor Laws: the safest, cheapest and surest cure for boyism of every kind in Ireland* (Dublin, 1832), p. 7.

65 *Statement of some of the causes of the disturbances in Ireland, and of the miserable state of the peasantry; with a plan for commencing on sound principles, an amelioration of their condition, thereby removing the causes of the disturbances, and bringing the country into a state of peace and quietness* (Dublin, 1825), pp. 8–11.

66 Binns, *Miseries and beauties*, ii, p. 40. See also ibid., ii, p. 23.

regarding mendicancy in Cork city reveal that while he drew the common distinction between the 'deserving' and 'undeserving' poor he perceived beggary to be a legitimate resort in lieu of a statutory provision, as per the status quo in Ireland: 'But what can be said in denunciation of a custom which seems to be *obliged* by the absence of an legal provision for the aged, the infirm, and the deserving needy?'[67]

Protestants and the Trope of the (Catholic) Beggar

Political and social discourse in nineteenth-century Ireland was regularly coloured by confessional allegiances and sectarian mistrust, and this regularly carried over into debates on poverty and charity. For Protestant commentators, the undeniable economic success of the largely Protestant, industrialising north-east of the island contrasted sharply with the rest of the country, whose economic backwardness was attributed to the prevalence of 'Popery' and 'priestcraft'. The north-east was commonly presented as a prosperous and morally upright region while economic and moral impoverishment characterised those parts outside of Ulster. A significant feature of such rhetoric was the deployment of the trope of the beggar to personify the dissoluteness of non-Ulster regions: the perceived ubiquity of mendicancy outside the north-east reflected the idleness, improvidence and misplaced benevolence among the largely Catholic poorer classes, while the supposed absence of beggary in the north-east pointed to a spirit of industry, 'true religion', thrift and relief mechanisms that did not encourage pauperism. In an influential address to an anti-Repeal crowd in Belfast, in 1841, Rev. Henry Cooke attributed the prosperity of Ulster under the Union to the 'genius of industry' combined with the 'genius of Protestantism'.[68] Niall Ó Ciosáin has written of how begging distinguished Ireland from Britain in the nineteenth century, and, in some contemporary discourse, came to represent Ireland. 'This was so not just because the beggars themselves demonstrated the poverty and character flaws of the Irish, but also because, to Protestant observers, their existence represented the Catholicism of those who gave to them'.[69] By the 1830s, the motif of the beggar was applied to the Irish Catholic MP Daniel O'Connell, who became, in conservative Protestant discourse, 'the big beggarman' or 'the king of the beggars'. The association with mendicancy arose from O'Connell's innovative fundraising campaign, through which even the poor could contribute small amounts to the annual 'Catholic Rent' or the 'O'Connell tribute', the Catholic Association's funding system for remunerating O'Connell during his

67　Ibid., ii, p. 147.
68　*BNL*, 26 Jan. 1841.
69　Ó Ciosáin, *Ireland in official print culture*, p. 122.

parliamentary career.[70] His enemies dismissed the 'O'Connell tribute' as 'collecting the annual alms for the Mendicant-General of Ireland', through the means of the 'beggarly Repeal Society' and the 'Repeal begging box';[71] in Ó Ciosáin's succinct judgement, 'this was a big beggar begging from many smaller ones'.[72]

In 1830, two clergymen attached to the London-based Irish Evangelical Society recorded their impressions of their recent visit to Ireland, noting that:

> The moment we put our feet on the shore of poor Ireland we were met by the most disgusting evidence of the pauperism and the superstition of its population, as our alms were solicited with those obtestations which at once betrayed the baneful tenets of the religion its inhabitants profess. This characterised every stage of our journey in the southern and central parts of the kingdom.[73]

Without asserting the explicit comparison, the authors made clear that mendicancy was endemic in those parts of Ireland where Catholicism predominated among the population and the Protestant north was excluded from this sweeping statement. The point, however, was made more explicitly ten years later in a newspaper article entitled 'The Irish Presbyterians: effects of Presbyterianism in Ireland', published in the Edinburgh-based *The Witness*, an evangelical Church of Scotland title, and reprinted in the *Belfast News-Letter*. The anonymous author, recounting a recent trip to Ireland and writing for a Scottish Presbyterian audience, contrasted 'the smiling comfort, prosperous agriculture, busy enterprise, and quiet security of the Presbyterian North' with the rest of the country, where 'crowds of beggars … swarm in those districts where Popery sits like a night-mare on the energies of the population'. The recurring image of ubiquitous beggary prevailing in the largely Catholic south and west was deployed effectively by the author, and the reader could not be unaware of the associations made between 'Popery', idleness and mendicancy:

> Let any man pass from Drogheda, where this pestilence of beggary and moral degradation first meets the stranger as he goes south, to Dublin, where may be seen, not only in the streets, but at the

---

70 Ibid., pp. 121–4.
71 *Downpatrick Recorder*, 20 Nov. 1841, 24 Apr. 1841.
72 Ó Ciosáin, *Ireland in official print culture*, p. 123.
73 Irish Evangelical Society minute book, 14 Sept. 1830 (PRONI, Irish Evangelical Society papers, CR7/2/A/1/5).

Mendicity House, appalling exhibitions of teeming wretchedness. Let him pass on to Limerick, marking, as he journeys, the striking contrast between the richness of the soil, the greenness of the natural verdure, and the starved and ragged-looking population, who besiege the coach with their importunities, and pour out their fluent blessings or ready imprecation at every halting place, according to their success or failure in extorting money.

In Galway, the writer observed 'crowds of beggars on every side' and implicitly linked this mendicancy to the fact that there was 'no trade flourishing but priestcraft – none well-fed but Priests'. To demonstrate the stark contrast between the extent of Irish beggary outside of Ulster and the alleged absence of this practice in the north-east, the author concluded by figuratively conveying his readers to Belfast, 'the capital of Presbyterianism'. He wrote: 'Arrived at Belfast, let him observe the stir and enterprise, the wide streets, the handsome buildings, the well-dressed people, the nearly total absence of importunate beggars, the harbour filled with vessels which trade with all the world, and the signs of comfort and industry which everywhere prevail'.[74]

These comments, made by and for Presbyterians, reflected wider Protestant fears and suspicions towards Roman Catholic priests, who were seen as the disseminators of superstitious error and political radicalism, and who consciously ensnared their impoverished flock in conditions of poverty and, worse still, pauperism. To Protestants fired up with the zeal of evangelicalism and the 'Second Reformation', eager to disseminate the Bible and to fortify their missionary work through conversions to 'true religion', priests were accused of actively thwarting scripture reading among their parishioners, indicating the contrasting emphasis placed by Protestants and Catholics on the significance of the Bible in their religious practice.[75] Many of the social, economic and political ills of Ireland were attributed to the dominance of 'Popery' and 'priestcraft' throughout the country, a centuries-old association in the Protestant mind between Roman Catholicism and

---

74 *BNL*, 8 Sept. 1840. A post-Famine instance of northern prosperity being contrasted with southern mendicancy is to be found in James Macauly, *Ireland in 1872: a tour of observations. With remarks on Irish public questions* (London, 1873), p. 157.

75 *State of Ireland select committee, fourth report, 1825*, pp. 494–501; *A review of the existing causes which at present disturb the tranquillity of Ireland, recommended to the serious attention of landholders, the established clergy, and the Hibernian Sunday School Society: also, an exposure of the system adopted by the Roman Catholic clergy to deter their flocks from reading the sacred scriptures* (Dublin, 1822), pp. 14–15; [James Carlile], *Memorial recommending the establishment of a mission to the Roman Catholics of Ireland* (Dublin, 1825), p. 7.

superstition which resurfaced during the sectarian tensions of the 1820s and 1830s.[76]

Ironically, as S.J. Connolly has shown, this period saw in the Irish Catholic prelates and clergy a determination to rein in folkloric, non-orthodox practices. This suppression of 'all incantations, charms and spells; all superstitious observations of omens and accidents; and such nonsensical remarks'[77] was undertaken with such zeal that some commentators remarked of Catholic priests becoming more Protestant in their manners and customs.[78] Crucially, this period also witnessed the growing confidence of Irish Catholicism, mobilised into a significant political force by Daniel O'Connell with the support of Irish priests.[79] In a Famine-era tract, Rev. John Edgar conveyed to 'Presbyterian Ulster [and] Presbyterian Scotland' the need to bring enlightenment, regeneration and spiritual freedom to the poor of Ireland, thus negating the effects of what he termed 'The Priest's Curse'.[80] In a later publication on the Presbyterian missions in Connaught, Edgar lamented: 'Whatever other ills have been driven from Connaught, Popery is there still, with all its priests, palsying human energy, darkening human intellect, crushing human liberty, besotting human mind'.[81] Whereas the missionaries toiled daily in teaching poor girls skills so as to encourage them to become self-reliant and economically independent, the local priest was accused of subjecting these families to 'persecution' in keeping them 'ignorant, and idle, and ragged, penniless, and hopelessly poor'.[82]

Turning to Belfast, it will be seen that these Presbyterian fears and suspicions of Catholics must be placed in the context of demographic changes in the northern town. Eighteenth-century Belfast had been, in Gillespie and Royle's words, 'an overwhelmingly Presbyterian town', with an estimated two-thirds of its population being Presbyterian in 1792. Furthermore, wealth in the region was firmly in Protestant hands: an 1818 estimate of the capital employed by Belfast's merchants listed just seven Catholics whose capital totalled between £49,500 and £70,000, while 134 Protestant merchants were calculated as cumulatively possessing between

76 Moffit, *Society for Irish Church Missions*, pp. 1–45. For the perception of priests as instigators of sectarian violence and murder in the 1798 Rebellion, see James Kelly, *Sir Richard Musgrave, 1746–1818: Ultra-Protestant ideologue* (Dublin, 2009), pp. 71–83; Holmes, *The shaping of Ulster Presbyterian belief and practice*, pp. 101–2.

77 *Butler's Catechism*, p. 41.

78 Connolly, *Priests and people*, pp. 110–15.

79 Patrick M. Geoghegan, *King Dan: the rise of Daniel O'Connell, 1775–1829* (Dublin, 2008), pp. 231–2, 258.

80 John Edgar, *The General Assembly's Irish schools. The priest's curse* (n.p. [Belfast?], [c.1847]), p. 16.

81 John Edgar, *Connaught harvest* (Belfast, 1853), p. 5.

82 Ibid., p. 6.

£1.7 million and nearly £2.2 million.[83] However, the position of Catholics quickly transformed from being a miniscule proportion of the town's population (1,000 in 1784, or less than 7 per cent) to a sizeable minority (19,712 in 1834, or around one-third of the population). The immense growth in the town's Catholic population was reflected in the fact that three of the four Roman Catholic churches in Belfast in 1837 had been erected in the previous 22 years.[84] Migrating Catholics came into Belfast from the surrounding countryside and mainly comprised the impoverished, poorly educated and unskilled. In 1802, Martha McTier, from a well-known radical Presbyterian family, bemoaned the fact that the 'R Catholics here [are] now a large though poor and unknown body'.[85] That the town's first sectarian riots occurred in this period is not insignificant and was emblematic of the simmering community tensions.[86] Catholics constituted a disproportionately large element of Belfast's destitute classes, thus ensuring that the respectable Presbyterian middle classes' fears of the lower orders were somewhat coloured by confessional mistrust and animosity.

Actions

Irish Protestants were active in cross-denominational efforts to curtail mendicancy, through parish vestries and voluntary charitable societies, such as mendicity societies. In an attempt to gauge whether any unique characteristics of denominational charity can be ascribed to the main Protestant churches and religious societies, attention now turns to how Protestants responded within their own denominations to social problems. In considering the responses of Protestants, in individual and corporate capacities, to mendicancy, it is helpful to start by tackling a fundamental question: did Protestants give alms to beggars? The evidence shows that the answer is yes, many Protestants of all denominations distributed alms to the mendicant poor; furthermore, alms-giving was oftentimes undertaken without discrimination. This is borne out by the evidence

---

83 Listing of Catholic and Protestant merchants in Belfast, 1818 (BL, Liverpool papers, Add MS 38368, ff. 159–197).

84 Raymond Gillespie and Stephen A. Royle, *Belfast, Part I, to 1840*, Irish Historic Towns Atlas, no. 12 (Dublin, 2003), pp. 8, 21. This increase in church-building was not unique to northern Catholicism and of the 31 places of worship across all denominations in Belfast in 1840, 22 (71 per cent) had been built since 1801: ibid., figure 4 (p. 7).

85 Martha McTier to William Drennan, [1802] in Jean Agnew (ed.), *The Drennan-McTier letters, 1802–19* (3 vols, Dublin, 1999), iii, p. 92. McTier added in the same letter: 'I begin to fear these people, and think like the Jews they will regain their native land'.

86 Marianne Elliott, *The Catholics of Ulster* (London, 2000), p. 321; Wright, *'Natural leaders'*, pp. 80–3.

presented to the Poor Inquiry in the mid-1830s, taking County Antrim, the heartland of Irish Presbyterianism, as a case study. In Ahoghill parish, where Protestants comprised 79 per cent of the population according to the 1834 revised census,[87] 'the character of the beggar is seldom considered ... Alms would be given even when the character of the applicant is unknown'.[88] In Antrim parish, 'Those who give relief to strangers have no knowledge of their character, no criterion whereby to judge of their destitution, except their appearance'.[89] In a series of questionnaires which were sent out by the Poor Inquiry to local elites throughout the country, respondents in County Antrim (among whom Protestant clergymen and public figures predominated) acknowledged the practice of alms-giving in their localities.[90] In the above examples it was predominantly the lower and lower-middle classes who provided this assistance through indiscriminate alms-giving – cottiers, small farmers and small shopkeepers – and this raises the important question of the extent to which the laity followed the urgings of their preachers. Despite the public utterances of Protestant ministers and commentators, many of their flock continued to dole out alms to beggars without regard to their supposed deservedness, suggesting a discord between the attitudes of the clergy and the lower classes among the laity. As such, the extent to which social class was a factor in guiding how beggars and begging were perceived is essential. In addition to these non-specific comments about Protestant alms-giving, a small number of individual instances can be identified. For instance, the Presbyterian army surgeon John Gamble was won over by the solicitations of beggars in County Monaghan.[91] In November 1820, a Dublin mendicant named Anne Marie Byrne, who subsisted 'by writing begging petitions', appealed to the British authorities in Dublin Castle for assistance. In her petition, Byrne praised a Quaker grocer, Stephen Dalton of the Coombe, for previously assisting her:

Only for M Daltons family I should be starved to Death with cold and hunger – my shoes was wore out going to the Park. Mr Dalton gave me money to get shoes. Quakers is good to every one. The[y] never ask the person where the[y] go to worship, the[y] show charity to every perswasion, [sic] according as the[y] know the want.[92]

---

87 OSM, xxiii, p. 16.
88 PI, Appendix A, p. 703.
89 PI, Appendix A, p. 704.
90 PI, Supplement to Appendix A, pp. 270–93. The existence of indiscriminate alms-giving in this region was also recorded in the Ordnance Survey memoirs: OSM, xxvi, p. 22.
91 Gamble, Sketches of history, politics, and manners, pp. 165, 184–5.
92 Papers relating to Anne Marie Byrne, Nov. 1820 (NAI, CSORP, CSO/RP/1821/909).

Elsewhere in the British Isles, Protestants proved the fallacy in the belief that alms-giving was mostly confined to Catholics: Methodist founder John Wesley was a lifelong distributor of alms to the mendicant poor, while the Scottish Poor Inquiry commissioners in the 1840s recorded the prevalence of Church of Scotland parishes licensing local, known beggars, adding that 'begging is in many places a recognised means of subsistence for paupers'.[93]

Each of the main Protestant and Dissenting denominations oversaw internal relief measures for impoverished and distressed members of their ecclesiastical community; in some instances, however, it is not clear whether the organised relief extended to non-congregants. These initiatives fulfilled the Christian imperative to relieve one's neighbours, while also concentrating limited resources to known, 'deserving' individuals and families. Anglican canon law set down how members of the Church of Ireland were to contribute on a communal level towards the relief of the poor. The 96th canon required churchwardens to provide a 'strong chest, with a hole in the upper part thereof' for use as a collection box for the poor, 'knowing that to relieve the poor, is a sacrifice which pleaseth God'. The collected alms, 'to be truly and faithfully delivered to their most poor and needy neighbours', were to be distributed 'in the presence of most of the parish', underlining the public nature of parochial alms-giving within the Anglican communion.[94] This was the context for the requirement that parishes maintain a poor box. In Bumlin parish, County Roscommon (incorporating the town of Strokestown), among the initiatives in the early nineteenth century of the new curate, seemingly eager to introduce order into the administration of parochial affairs, was the purchase of 'Vestry & Registry Books, & book of common prayer, & two copper boxes for collecting the poor money'.[95] This sense of communal responsibility for the local poor is reflected in the memorials of the dead in Enniskillen parish church, which record two bequests of 'copper poor-boxes' from parishioners, dating from 1753

For the identification of Dalton as a grocer, see *Wilson's Dublin directory for the year 1822 ...* p. 60.

93   John Walsh, 'John Wesley and the urban poor' in *Revue française de civilisation britannique*, vi, no. 3 (1991), p. 26; George Nicholls, *A history of the Scotch Poor Law* (London, 1856), p. 142. See also Sarah Lloyd, '"Agents in their own concerns?" Charity and the economy of makeshifts in eighteenth-century Britain' in King and Tomkins, *The poor in England 1700–1850*, p. 124.

94   E.D. Bullingbrooke, *Ecclesiastical law; or, the statutes, constitutions, canons, rubricks, and articles, of the Church of Ireland. Methodically digested under proper heads, with a commentary, historical and juridical* (2 vols, Dublin, 1770), i, pp. 275–6. Preachers' books also reveal the regular distribution of alms from weekly collections: Preachers' book, St Jude's parish, Muckamore, County Antrim, 1842–56 (PRONI, St Jude's parish records, CR/1/75/E/1).

95   Bumlin parish vestry minute book, n.d. (RCBL, Bumlin parish records, P 737.5.1, f. 1ʳ).

and 1842.[96] The order for the administration of the Holy Communion, as
outlined in the Book of Common Prayer, stipulated a point in the service for
the collection of 'Alms for the Poor … in a decent Bason to be provided by
the Parish for that purpose',[97] while the minister could substitute his sermon
for one of 21 homilies on prescribed topics, including 'Of alms-doing'.[98]

Just as in Britain,[99] Irish dissenting communities maintained their
own poor and occasionally operated systems for regulating beggary. In
Presbyterian congregations, this operated through the kirk session, a meeting
of the minister and elected lay elders of each congregation and represented
the base of Presbyterianism's hierarchical series of church courts. The
session largely operated as a disciplinary body, 'trying' congregants for
moral misdemeanours, such as fornication, Sabbath-breaking and habitual
drunkenness; these bodies also oversaw the congregation's distribution of
alms to the poor.[100] The Irish kirk session differed from its Scottish
counterpart in that it was not the instrument of the state church, a contrast
that filtered down to how congregations managed poverty and mendicancy:
Irish kirks had no legal powers to curtail mendicancy, whereas in Scotland,
since 1592, legislation recognised the session as the appropriate instrument
'for punishment of masterful beggaris and relief of the puir'.[101] Among the
assistance given by Irish kirk sessions to impoverished congregants was the
payment of pew rents (negating a regular cause of non-attendance at service)[102]
and funeral expenses,[103] the maintenance of 'deserving' congregants (such
as widows and the blind)[104] and the operation of alms houses and charity

---

96 *Association for the Preservation of the Memorials of the Dead, Ireland. Journal for the
     year 1892*, ii, no. 1 ([1892]), p. 113.
97 *The Book of Common Prayer* (Edinburgh, 1818), p. 194. See also Bullingbroke,
     Ecclesiastical law, i, p. 479.
98 Bullingbroke, *Ecclesiastical law*, i, pp. 390–1.
99 Joanna Innes, 'The "mixed economy of welfare" in early modern England: assessments
     of the options from Hale to Malthus (*c*.1683–1803)' in Daunton, *Charity, self-interest
     and welfare*, p. 145.
100 Holmes, *The shaping of Ulster Presbyterian belief and practice*, pp. 35, 166–75.
101 '[An act] for punishment of masterful beggars and relief of the poor', James VI, c. 149,
     no. 69 (5 June 1592), cited in Rosalind Mitchison, 'The making of the old Scottish Poor
     Law' in *Past & Present*, no. 63 (May 1974), p. 63. See also Nicholls, *History of the Scotch
     Poor Law*, pp. 27–9.
102 Holmes, *The shaping of Ulster Presbyterian belief and practice*, pp. 63, 69; Memorial of
     the Presbyterian congregation of May Street, Belfast to the Lord Lieutenant, 4 Apr.
     1832 (NAI, CSOOP, CSO/OP1832/404/16).
103 'Funeral account book, Rosemary St. Presbyterian Church (3rd), Belfast, 1752–70'
     (PRONI, Presbyterian Church records, MIC1P/7/2, microfilm).
104 'Report of the session of the Scots Church [Dublin] to the congregation', 23 May 1831,
     p. 1 (Abbey Presbyterian Church, Dublin archives, Mary's Abbey congregation records,
     book no. 18); Mary's Abbey poor list account book, 1814–31 (Abbey Presbyterian
     Church, Dublin archives, Mary's Abbey congregation records, book no. 13).

schools.[105] Poor assistance was provided to certain of the 'deserving' poor
from monies received at weekly voluntary church collections and distributed
by the kirk sessions. The collection and distribution of this money was carried
out on a voluntary basis by ministers and lay elders, and was not conferred
on the needy as a matter of right.[106] Surviving Irish kirk sessions books reveal
that in the seventeenth and eighteenth centuries financial assistance was
provided to certain of the deserving poor, such as the sick, widows, victims
of crime and those who suffered for the sake of their religious beliefs.[107]

Whereas Scottish kirks oversaw into the early nineteenth century a
system of parochial badging of local mendicants, known as 'Kingsmen' or
'Bluegownsmen', owing to the blue coat granted annually by the parish, no
such system appears to have been practised by their Irish counterparts.[108] A
rare recorded case of an Irish Presbyterian congregation providing begging
licences to its local poor arose in 1774 in Ballycarry, County Antrim. Located
8 kilometres north of Carrickfergus and 23 kilometres north of Belfast,
Ballycarry (or Broadisland) is the oldest Presbyterian congregation in Ireland;
it was here that Rev. Edward Brice established a presbytery in 1613. In
February 1774, the congregation's kirk session adopted a detailed resolution
which ordered its members not to give alms to 'foreign Vagrants' and divided
the local poor into three categories.[109] The division, and the prescribed
manner of dealing with such individuals, adhered to Calvinist views of the
virtue of private, voluntary charity: John Calvin pointed to St Paul's writings
in his championing of the virtue of 'the rich spontaneously and liberally
relieving the wants of their brethren, and not grudgingly or of necessity',[110]
while the Scottish Reformation leader John Knox distinguished between
'stubborne and idill beggaris, quho … mak a craft of their beggyng' and

105 Wright, *Historical guide to Dublin*, pp. 97–100.
106 W.T. Latimer, 'The old session book of the Presbyterian congregation at Dundonald,
     Co. Down' in *Ulster Journal of Archaeology*, 2nd series, iii, no. 4 (July 1897), pp. 227–32;
     William Fee McKinney, 'Old session books of Carnmoney, Co. Antrim' in *Ulster
     Journal of Archaeology*, 2nd series, vi, no. 1 (Jan. 1900), pp. 9–10.
107 For instance, see Aghadowey Presbyterian Church kirk session minute book, printed
     note inside front cover (Presbyterian Historical Society of Ireland Archive, Aghadowey
     Presbyterian Church records, no reference number); ibid., 7 Aug. 1704, f. 16ʳ; Carnmoney
     Presbyterian Church kirk session poor list, 18 Mar. 1782 (Presbyterian Historical
     Society of Ireland Archive, Carnmoney Presbyterian Church records, MIC/1P/37/6,
     microfilm).
108 Anon., 'The Scottish system of Poor Laws' in *Dublin University Magazine*, iii, no. 17
     (May 1834), p. 510.
109 Typed copy of the Ballycarry (Broadisland) Presbyterian Congregation kirk session
     minute book, 20 Feb. 1774 (PRONI, Calwell papers, D3784/4/11). I am grateful to
     Dr Andrew Holmes for pointing me in the direction of this source.
110 John Calvin, *Commentaries on the four last books of Moses arranged in the form of a
     harmony*, trans. Charles William Bingham (4 vols, Grand Rapids, MI, 1950), i, p. 279.

'personis of honestie' whose indigence ought to be relieved.[111] According to the 1774 Ballycarry kirk session resolution, those poor 'who are incapable of using any Industry; but capable of moving from House to House' were to be provided with begging badges and were to receive no alms from the public collections. Those 'who are capable of using some Industry; but not sufficient for their support' were to be afforded assistance from local inhabitants 'in a private Way according to their several abilities'. They were also entitled to receive no more than 6½d. per month from the public collections. The third class, 'who are neither capable of any Industry, nor yet able to crawl from House to House for support', were to receive alms from the Sabbath collections.[112]

A number of points merit discussion. Persons in the first category of paupers were to be provided with the means to support themselves, through licensed begging. Any alms proffered to them were at the discretion of local inhabitants, thus avoiding the burden of a compulsory rate and any entitlement to relief for the destitute. Similarly, regarding the second category, it was merely *recommended* to locals that such persons be assisted – there was to be no compulsion – and the amount allowed to the poor from the collections was, by public consensus, subject to a maximum figure. Those of the third category were to be assisted through the public collections, but in the event that such funds were found to be insufficient, it was ordered that 'the Minister Do make Representations of such Insufficiency to the Congregation'. Again, the importance of avoiding compulsion was underlined. Local inhabitants were, moreover, subject to expected behavioural norms and duties. As these measures were internal communal agreements, and had no grounding in civil law, the penalty for failing to meet the expected standards was congregational disapproval and possible expulsion. The resolution continued:

Resolved that any Inhabitant within the Bounds of this congregation, who gives alms of Lodging to a Vagrant Beggar (unless in a case of Starving) is and will be deemed an Enemy to industry and the real Poor, as well as to the good order of this Cong[regatio]n. – and that any of our own Poor, who shall hereafter lodge or harbour a foreign Beggar shall be deemed to have thereby forfeited the Protection and Support of this Cong[regatio]n.

For local named persons to be approved for a begging badge, their nomination had to be sanctioned at a 'publick Meeting'.[113] The relief of poverty and

111 David Laing (ed.), *The works of John Knox* (6 vols, Edinburgh, 1895), ii, pp. 200–1.
112 Typed copy of the Ballycarry kirk session minute book, 20 Feb. 1774.
113 Ibid.

handling of beggars within the Presbyterian congregation was subject to the public approval of the community, wherein operated an independent system of social welfare and moral regulation.

The detailed outline here of the agreed manner for negotiating mendicancy is fascinating. Yet, it raises the question of just how representative this instance was within Irish Presbyterian congregations. Consultation of kirk session books for congregations throughout Ireland reveals examples of assistance being provided to the distressed, but no other instance of such a detailed process for dealing with beggars has yet come to light. The evidence for Scotland suggests that the rarity of beggars' appearance in kirk session books does not mean that alms-giving was not carried out; rather, that it was conducted by individuals acting in a private capacity, usually at communions and other public occasions.[114] Such poor relief 'was part of the general social obligation of a Christian community, an obligation so central that it was very rarely explicitly laid down ... Silence on the subject ... comes from the assumptions of basic morality, not from indifference'.[115]

Within Irish and British Methodism, beggary and destitution were managed through a network of charities called Strangers' Friend Societies (SFSs). This movement emerged in the late eighteenth century and societies were specifically designed to cater for the non-local, non-Methodist poor in large urban centres. Methodists also organised relief funds for impoverished members of their own congregation.[116] As with most charities founded in this period, the SFSs allocated their resources to the assistance of the 'respectable', typically industrious poor, who were too ashamed to resort to public begging; such individuals were assisted with money, food and clothes. The establishment of these charities was in response to the social problems associated with a rapidly growing population, the surge of industrialisation and the influx of non-local rural dwellers into towns and cities in search of work or relief, who were in want of a support network on which to fall back in times of distress. These charities drew explicitly upon the example of Christ in developing their *modus operandi*, which centred on home visitations. Their name was inspired by a passage from the gospel of Matthew (25:35–36): 'For I was an hungred, and ye gave me meat: I was thirsty, and ye gave me drink: I was a stranger, and ye took me in: Naked, and ye clothed me: I was sick, and ye visited me: I was in prison, and ye came unto me', and this extract was usually included on the title page of

---

114 Mitchison and Leneman, *Sexuality and social control*, pp. 36–7.
115 Mitchison, 'Making of the old Scottish Poor Law', pp. 62–3.
116 William Smith, *A consecutive history of the rise, progress, and present state of Wesleyan Methodism in Ireland* (Dublin, 1830), p. 204.

annual reports. By the early nineteenth century, approximately twenty SFSs had been founded by Methodists throughout Ireland and Britain, invariably in large urban centres where there were significant and active Methodist communities. In Ireland, they were to be found in Dublin, Belfast, Cork, Waterford and Armagh.[117]

Strict rules specifically omitted habitual mendicants from the remit of the SFSs. Such an exclusionary policy was enforced by the Dublin SFS, founded by Methodist preacher Dr Adam Clarke in 1790. In a 1799 pamphlet, Clarke, also influential in the foundation of SFSs in Bristol (1786), Liverpool (1789) and Manchester (1791), informed his readers that 'however deplorable the state of street Beggars may appear, they are not in general the most necessitous', while advising subscribers that mendicants 'are not proper objects of your Charity'.[118] Instead, the Dublin organisation focused its resources on the poor who inhabited wretched cellars and garrets throughout the city's slums, who did not resort to public begging and, in many instances, had no network of relatives or friends on which to fall back; the redeeming of artisans' pawned tools and the payment of prisoners' debts, allowing them to return of 'habits of industry', was typical of the form of assistance provided.[119] The suffering of these 'deserving' individuals could only be truly relieved through home-visiting, an innovation of Methodist charity volunteers, who built upon the precedent of Methodism's founder John Wesley.[120] Drawing inspiration from the example of Christ in working among the sick and distressed, Wesley demanded that he and other Methodists had personal contact with the people they were relieving:

How better is it, when it can be done, to carry relief to the poor than send it! And that both for our own sakes and theirs. For theirs, as it is so much more comfortable to them, and as we may then assist them in spirituals as well as temporals; and for our own, as it is far more apt to soften our hearts and makes us naturally care for each other.[121]

117 Ciarán McCabe, 'The early years of the Strangers' Friend Society, Dublin: 1790–1845' in *Bulletin of the Methodist Historical Society*, xix (2014), pp. 65–93.

118 [Adam Clarke], *The nature, design, and general rules of the Strangers' Friend Society, as established in Dublin, 1790* (Dublin, 1799), pp. 3, 6.

119 *Annual report of the Strangers' Friend Society (founded in 1790) for visiting and relieving distressed strangers and the resident sick poor, in Dublin and its vicinity; with an account of some of the cases relieved, and list of subscribers for 1840* (Dublin, 1841), p. 18; *For the year 1806. The annual report of the Strangers' Friend Society, as established in Dublin, in 1790* (Dublin, 1807), pp. 11–12.

120 Frank Prochaska, *The voluntary impulse: philanthropy in modern Britain* (London, 1988), p. 44.

121 Quoted in Henry D. Rack, *Reasonable enthusiast: John Wesley and the rise of Methodism* (London, 1989), p. 363.

Subscribers to SFSs were assured that those relieved formed 'a most deserving class of the community. It will at once be seen that they are not the noisy importunate beggars, who impede our progress in the streets, hang about our doors, taking every opportunity to exhibit their misery'.[122] The testimonies of several officers of the Dublin society to the Poor Inquiry reveal that the merits of helping the 'deserving' poor, while excluding those whose destitution was self-inflicted, prevailed throughout the institution. Such sentiments were not merely for the purposes of public pronouncements but were deeply held by the Methodist members of the charity. Treasurer Francis White spoke of the fundamental importance of the visitors investigating each case so as to determine the moral disposition of the applicants. 'The grounds of refusal of relief are want of good character, or the same person attempting to obtain relief from more than one visitor, or having been recently relieved; by want of character I mean where distress has been brought on by drunkenness, extravagance, or indolence, or breach of moral duties'. White added that, 'there is nothing exclusive in the institution; all persons in distress and of good character are eligible for relief, except common beggars'.[123] Secretary John Ouseley Bonsall, a bookseller by occupation, explained that those whose descent into destitution arose 'from their own faults' were excluded from the charity's remit.[124] The Belfast SFS insisted in its public pronouncements that its beneficiaries were visited by volunteers before being relieved, 'to prevent imposition' and ensure that 'real distress' was being targeted.[125]

British members of the SFS movement framed their charitable works according to the same model of deservedness. Just as the Manchester Strangers' Friend Society insisted that it only relieved 'proper objects', thus excluding 'all kinds of Street Beggars [and] Vagrants',[126] the Bristol society promoted the idea that 'giving alms to mendicants, without any inquiry as to their necessities, appears to be an encouragement to an idle *profession*; and as a system of *intimidation* is now adopted by these vagrants, it is a duty incumbent to resist their demands'.[127] An interesting question is whether these charities, in drawing strict distinctions between who was and was not eligible to receive assistance, had veered significantly from the world view

---

122 *Annual report of the Strangers' Friend Society (founded in 1790) for visiting and relieving distressed strangers, and the resident sick poor, in Dublin and its vicinity; with an account of some of the cases relieved, and the list of subscribers for 1831* (Dublin, 1832), p. 4.
123 *PI, Appendix C, Part II*, p. 17.
124 Ibid., p. 18.
125 *BNL*, 30 Dec. 1808.
126 Quoted in G.B. Hindle, *Provision for the relief of the poor in Manchester, 1754–1826* (Manchester, 1975), p. 85.
127 *Bristol Mercury*, 21 Dec. 1830.

espoused by Methodism's founder, John Wesley, whose lifelong mission of extending a charitable hand to all persons in need included doling out alms to beggars with, according to one historian, 'almost Franciscan abandon'.[128]

Quakers' monthly meetings, the lowest rung on the denomination's organisational ladder, operated a poor committee to cater for local distressed Friends. The corporate responses of Quakers to poverty were, therefore, limited to their own community. It was left to individual Quakers' own initiative to engage in charity aimed at other denominations.[129] One explanation of this may be that the profoundly individualistic nature of Quaker life and the structure of Quaker meetings encouraged greater personal responsibility than in other denominations. On a more practical level, the limited nature of Quaker corporate relief may be attributed to the small size of the Irish Quaker community, which paled in comparison to Catholics, Anglicans and Presbyterians. The assistance which could be generated from within the community was limited and most effective when focused at the distressed within the same community.

The utility of assisting distressed Friends, so as to keep them from penury and pauperism, was also stressed in Quaker meetings, which promoted industrious habits and the education of children. In the mid-seventeenth century, a meeting in north Yorkshire was advised that 'each particular Meeting should be expected to care for its own poor; to find employment for such as want work or cannot follow their former callings for reason of the evil therein ... and to help parents in the education of their children, that there may not be a beggar amongst us'.[130] A mid-eighteenth-century query form distributed to meetings throughout Ireland enquired into the moral condition of the community, asking: 'Are the Poor taken due care of, and do their Children partake of necessary learning to fit them for Trades?'[131] Monthly meetings relieved the temporal suffering of Friends in a variety of ways: in Waterford the provision of cash sums 'for the use of a friend in straitened circumstances' was a regular item of expenditure at the turn of the century;[132] the Lisburn meeting's poor committee outlined its object as providing 'for the care of poor friends in the Bounds of the Mo[nthly]

128 Walsh, 'John Wesley and the urban poor', p. 17; Rack, *Reasonable enthusiast*, p. 361.

129 Richard S. Harrison, 'Dublin Quakers in business 1800–1850' (MLitt thesis, 2 vols, University of Dublin, 1987), ii, p. 454.

130 Olive C. Goodbody, *Guide to Irish Quaker Records, 1654–1860* (IMC, Dublin, 1967), p. 11.

131 Thomas Wight (rev. John Rutty), *A history of the rise and progress of the people called Quakers in Ireland ...* (Dublin, 1751), pp. 323–4.

132 Waterford Friends monthly meeting poor house accounts, 13 July 1799 (FHLD, Waterford monthly meeting records, MM XI P2); ibid., 9 Nov. 1799, 28 June 1800, 14 Feb. 1801.

Meeting of Lisburn';[133] the Cork city meeting maintained pensioners on its poor list, purchased medicines for poor Friends and even paid for mentally ill members to be treated at the York Retreat, an English asylum which catered solely for insane Quakers.[134] The importance of self-reliance and independence is evident in the Cork monthly meeting's decision in September 1844 to discontinue Mary Corlett's weekly allowance 'as her son in law disapproves of her being dependent on the Society for support and is desirous of making adequate provision for her himself'. The same meeting discontinued Thomas Sinton's weekly allowance:

> as it appears not only that he is of ability to earn a livelihood, suited to his present condition but also that he has sufficient open and opportunity so to do, and it is the judgement of this committee that a man so circumstanced, and in the prime of life and health, is not of the class for whom the Society's provision was ever designed or with whose maintenance it ought to be burdened.[135]

The decision by Martha Robinson to refuse the offer of 'suitable apartments both to reside, and to work in' was not met with approval and it was resolved 'it is not reasonable that our Monthly meeting should any longer contribute to her rent'.[136] These instances, all taken from the minutes of the same meeting, demonstrate communal approval for personal responsibility and taking care of one's own relatives, as well as disapproval for unwarranted idleness and aversion to industry.

Protestant Women, Poverty and Mendicancy

Women are noticeably absent from the above discussion on Protestant approaches to poverty, charity and beggary, reflecting the relatively limited role for women in the realm of public philanthropy in this period. Women were not members of mendicity societies or Strangers' Friend Societies, and they did not generally serve on parish vestries or kirk sessions. Where Protestant women were active within the philanthropic sphere was, first, in

---

133 Lisburn Friends monthly meeting poor committee minutes, n.d. (PRONI, Records of the Religious Society of Friends in Ulster, MIC16/21, f. 1, microfilm).
134 Cork Friends Poor Committee minutes, 5 Mar. 1826 (FHLD, Cork monthly meeting records, MM VIII P1, first book, f. 18ʳ); Cork Friends Poor Committee minutes, 3 Nov. 1810 (FHLD, Cork monthly meeting records, MM VIII P4); Cork Friends Poor Committee minutes, 3 Aug. 1848 (FHLD, Cork monthly meeting records, MM VIII P5); ibid., 26 July 1849, 25 Feb. 1863. See also Richard S. Harrison, *Merchants, mystics and philanthropists: 350 years of Cork Quakers* (Cork, 2006), pp. 56–7.
135 Cork Friends Poor Committee minutes, 9 Sept. 1844 (FHLD, Cork Monthly Meeting records, MM VIII P1, third book, f 8ᵛ); ibid., ff. 8ᵛ–9ʳ.
136 Cork Friends Poor Committee minutes, 9 Sept. 1844.

auxiliaries to male-run Bible societies, involved directly in the distribution of Bibles to the poor, and, secondly, in charities that focused on sick and poor women and children, such as lying-in charities, orphan houses and educational establishments. The two types of charitable initiatives complemented each other, as an ignorance of the teachings of Christ and 'true religion' was held to cause poverty. As with their Catholic counterparts, Protestant women's role in charity was focused on providing temporal and spiritual succour to poor women and children while attempting to instil 'habits of industry', independence and self-restraint. 'The foundation of charity for these women was the example of Christ and its purpose was to provide the poor with the means of taking responsibility for their own lives. They did not provide alms indiscriminately but attempted to teach the poor thrift and religion'.[137]

Instances of Protestant women's involvement in the direct provision of relief include (to select just a small sample) the ladies' poor committees within Quaker meetings,[138] the Ladies' Association 'for attending to the poor of the [Presbyterian] Scots Church' at Mary's Abbey, Dublin[139] and, in a later period, Ellen Smyly's Anglican-ethos ragged schools in the Dublin slums.[140] However, the most relevant example to this study of approaches to mendicancy is the work of Mary Ann McCracken and the Ladies' Committee of the Belfast Charitable Society in the town's poorhouse, which opened in 1774 for the suppression of street begging through institutional-based relief initiatives and a system of badging. The Charitable Society was founded and run by members of Belfast's largely Presbyterian, liberal middle classes.[141] McCracken, whose own family was steeped in the political, intellectual, cultural, social and economic life of the growing town, was the main driver of the Ladies' Committee, being a joint-founder in 1824 and regularly the only attendee at meetings; the committee's eventual decline in 1851 came about through McCracken's advanced years and the lack of enthusiasm for a successor. The committee served as a subsidiary to the

---

137 Luddy, *Women and philanthropy*, pp. 58–9.
138 Dublin Friends women's monthly meeting poor committee minutes, 1791–1855 (FHLD, women's monthly meeting, Dublin papers, MM II B3, MM II B4, MM II B5); Cork Friends women's monthly meeting poor committee minutes, 1786–1883 (FHLD, women's monthly meeting, Cork papers, MM VIII P2).
139 Scotch Church, Mary's Abbey annual reports, 1830–62 (Abbey Presbyterian Church, Dublin, Mary's Abbey congregation records, book no. 18).
140 Preston, *Charitable words*, pp. 74–82.
141 The most comprehensive account of this institution remains Strain, *Belfast and its Charitable Society*. For the town's Presbyterian middle classes at this period, see Wright, *'Natural leaders'*, *passim*; W.H. Crawford, 'The Belfast middle-classes in the late eighteenth century' in David Dickson, Dáire Keogh and Kevin Whelan (eds), *The United Irishmen: republicanism, radicalism and rebellion* (Dublin, 1993), pp. 62–73.

Charitable Society's all-male management committee and oversaw gendered work among the female paupers, such as laundry work, needlework and straw-plaiting. However, McCracken devoted particular attention to the fate of pauper children apprenticed to tradespeople in the town, reflecting the wider gendered pattern within Irish and British philanthropy for poor children to be dealt with by women, owing to the 'maternal role attributed to women'.[142] In proposing a system of regular visitation on the apprentices, as well as inviting them back to the poorhouse for an annual dinner, McCracken sought 'to inspire self-respect and raise them from their present degraded state of neglected outcasts'. The moral condition of the children also concerned her and the encouragement of attendance at Sunday school and public worship would, she suggested, contribute to their overall moral improvement.[143] For philanthropic women such as McCracken, keeping poor children out of the public streets and training them to 'habits of industry' was the most effective means of mitigating the moral and social 'evil' of unrestrained beggary.

Conclusion

Protestant discourses and actions on the questions of poverty, the Poor Law and beggary in pre-Famine Ireland were shaped by different theological and political influences from Roman Catholic approaches. In considering poverty and the place of the poor in society, Protestant evangelicals laid more emphasis on the spiritual state of the distressed than on their temporal wants, as seen in the contrasting views put forward by Richard Woodward in the third quarter of the eighteenth century and contributors to the *Christian Examiner*, such as Robert Daly, decades later. The bestowing of any amount of alms to the poor would not mitigate the fact that they remained weighed down by original sin until such a time as they were reborn in Christ. Evangelicalism also manifested itself in the proliferation of religious and philanthropic societies, many of which concentrated their efforts on the threat and impact of mendicancy. Yet, this examination of Protestant views on beggary is not limited to a consideration of evangelicalism. The case of Richard Whately reflects the significance of thinkers such as Malthus on a generation of Protestant social reformers, who perceived a natural relationship between the moral teachings of Christianity and the benefits accruing from theoretical and statistical studies in political economy. Each

---

142 Luddy, *Women and philanthropy*, p. 69.
143 Strain, *Belfast and its Charitable Society*, pp. 116–22; Mary McNeill, *The life and times of Mary Ann McCracken, 1770–1866: a Belfast panorama* (Belfast, 1988), pp. 257–87.

of the main Protestant churches and religious societies operated their own system of managing poverty and the poor, and in regulating mendicancy, either directly or indirectly. The Irish kirk sessions mirrored their Church of Scotland counterparts in adhering to a traditional Calvinist model of collecting and distributing alms on a voluntary basis, it being held that such an approach protected, first, the recipient from the corruptive power of dependency and, secondly, the giver from the burden of compulsory assessment. Alms were not distributed without qualification to beggars but were doled out to 'deserving' paupers who were subject to communal regulation and moral judgement; similar practices were in place in Irish Quakerism and Methodism. The Church of Ireland's congregationally based responses are strikingly different, with more stringent guidelines, as set out in ecclesiastical law, on the operation of a poor box and the place of charity within the liturgy. Yet, despite these nuances, many of the attitudes and responses of Protestants to beggary mirrored those of Catholics: distinctions were commonly drawn between 'deserving' and 'undeserving' supplicants; alms-giving was, nonetheless, widely carried out and done so largely by members of the lower classes; clergy and middle-class commentators and reformers were most likely to decry the indiscriminate alms-giving and extol the virtues of 'discrimination in charity'; and women's performance of public charity was limited and determined by gendered expectations on the propriety of such works, with ladies' charitable initiatives focused on poor women and children.

Conclusion

It was stated at the start of this book that begging was a ubiquitous feature of pre-Famine Irish society. Many beggars begged out of necessity and the practice was not just ingrained in the culture of the poor – what Fuchs has termed 'the cultures of expediency'[1] – but was a necessary source of income for many in distress. Poor families could descend rapidly into destitution through the illness of a family member, particularly a breadwinner, and for persons who found themselves in these situations beggary was a survival strategy always open to them, yet one which carried social stigma and required skill in the practice of exciting compassion in others. In a period before any legal entitlement to assistance, the need to subsist by begging was incontrovertibly real for many. Just as Timothy P. O'Neill described pre-Famine Ireland as a 'fever-ridden country',[2] it could also be described as a beggar-ridden country. What requires assertion, however, is that alms-giving to beggars was also prevalent in this period. People who begged subsisted, either completely or in part, upon the alms provided to them. In this light, not only beggars but alms-givers were ubiquitous in pre-Famine Ireland. The solicitation and provision of alms was an exchange requiring two parties, driven by different motivations. The reasons why people gave assistance to mendicants included a sense of Christian duty to the poor, a desire to be rid of an inconvenience, or a superstitious fear of the repercussions of refusal. Individuals resorted to mendicancy only if they possessed a reasonable expectation of receiving some assistance. Even in cases of desperation, it was assumed that among the many passers-by the beggar accosted and the many doors on which he or she knocked, a certain proportion of individuals would bestow alms. This understanding of the nature of charity – 'the knack of presenting a cogent case and the places and

---

1 Fuchs, *Gender and poverty*, pp. 14–17.
2 O'Neill, 'Fever and public health', p. 1.

situations under which they would receive the most sympathy[3] – informed
how beggars, either casual or professional, plied their trade.

The present book highlights and explores the many complexities
inherent in the practices of begging and alms-giving in pre-Famine Ireland.
Contemporary discourse on the poor and on beggary was beset with the
difficulties of defining just who and what was being discussed. Definitions of
begging and vagrancy were imprecise, shifting and problematic. The socio-
economic categories of individuals who begged were fluid and ever-evolving.
Was there ever a 'typical' beggar? The mid-1820s economic downturn, which
impacted severely on urban textile workers, led to an increased proportion
of artisans among the mendicant classes of Irish cities, while the case of
charwomen raises the question of where casual employment ended and
begging commenced. The wording and enforcement of legislation is another
way in which society framed definitions of beggar and vagrants, yet, the law
can be problematically wide-ranging, ambiguous and antiquated, and this
was the case with vagrancy laws in Ireland. Begging is, by definition, the
solicitation of alms, yet it regularly encompassed the sale of trivial items or
the offering of a service. Begging was part of the 'economy of makeshifts'
which the poor negotiated on a daily basis. Mendicancy in nineteenth-
century Ireland was also a practice which involved and enforced gendered
attitudes and roles. Poor women were acutely vulnerable to destitution
and pauperism, a fact reflected by their predominance among Ireland's
mendicants, mirroring trends in other countries. While many sources speak
of a singularly male sense of shame towards begging, one must countenance
Laurence Geary's assertion that women ultimately carried the responsibility
for ensuring that their children were fed, and this urgency superseded all
possible notions of shame. Children were prominent among the mendicant
classes and various contributors to public discourse portrayed these child
beggars as victims of the moral pollution of city slums. Beggary was part of
the decline into more serious grades of degradation, typically thievery for
boys and prostitution for girls.

Measuring mendicancy was also plagued with difficulties. How does one
satisfactorily estimate the numbers of an imprecisely defined category of
inherently marginalised individuals, to many of whom seasonal migration,
vagrancy and rootlessness were a way of life? It is argued in this book that
contemporaries' concern with the extent of mendicancy is to be seen in the
context of the wider societal debate on a proposed statutory Poor Law. In
the 1830s, the cost of the prospective rates-funded system of relief needed
to be set against the prevailing casual and voluntary system of alms-giving.
Through the calculation of average estimates as to the level of alms-giving

3 Hufton, *The poor of eighteenth-century France*, pp. 109–10.

(largely by shopkeepers in provincial towns), subscriptions to mendicity societies and poor rates, it has been demonstrated that the amount paid out in casual, private alms to beggars far outweighed subscriptions and rates. Mendicancy was one of the most prominent matters of social and moral concern that exercised the membership of statistical societies across Ireland and the transatlantic world from the 1830s onwards. Statistics, infused with possibility and excitement, heralded, its new disciples believed, an opportunity to arrive at fully informed conclusions through the negotiation of objective facts.

Perceptions of beggars in pre-Famine Ireland were varied. These included fears that mendicants spread disease and impeded the successful running of businesses. Beggary was associated, by some, with the supernatural, and the extent to which beggars' prayers and curses were heeded varied from person to person. The ubiquity and visibility of mendicants offended the sensibilities of the wealthier classes but could be creatively utilised by those same 'respectable' classes, as represented by the members of mendicity societies in striking fear into inhabitants who failed to subscribe to their charity. Mendicity societies constituted a movement wherein charities not only shared mutual motivations and objectives but exchanged information amongst each other. The transmission of information (and sometimes personnel), as well as the offering of assistance between societies, marked them out as more than merely a mass of unconnected bodies. They constituted a movement, not rule-bound or pivoting around a central entity but linked by an exchange of ideas and common interests. The decline of these societies can be directly linked to the introduction of the 1838 Irish Poor Law Act; ratepayers feared the prospect of 'double taxation', by way of poor rates in addition to subscriptions to their local mendicity society, for the support of the same category of paupers. These fears led directly to the dissolution of most Irish mendicity societies in the same period as the introduction of the poor-rate assessment and the establishment of the workhouse system.

The research on which this book is based supports the conclusions of historians of welfare regimes throughout Europe in playing down the traditional and crude pigeon-holing of Catholic charity as characteristically indiscriminate and personable, and Protestant approaches as cold, harsh and administrative.[4] Colin Jones stresses that the Catholic–Protestant distinction is not as significant as the rural–urban model,[5] and, just as Seán Connolly concluded that the 'idea of a simple causal link between religion and the presence or absence of habits of industry ... does not stand up to

4 Pullan, 'Charity and poor relief in early modern Italy', p. 84.
5 Jones, 'Some recent trends in the history of charity', p. 53.

examination',[6] this book's findings support the work of recent historians of European welfare regimes in asserting that confessional affiliation did not account for differences in approaches to mendicancy and alms-giving.[7] Each denomination's negotiation of mendicancy certainly incorporated a 'flavour' distinct to that denomination – most notably seen in the corporate initiatives from within the community – but of greater significance were the overlaps in how individuals with opposing theological doctrines negotiated beggary and charity.

The rise of evangelicalism in transatlantic Protestantism in the mid- to late eighteenth century influenced the manner in which many Protestants viewed issues surrounding poverty. In seeking a remedy for the condition of the country's paupers and beggars, emphasis shifted from concern for the mendicant's temporal wants, as emphasised by Bishop Richard Woodward in his 1760s scheme for a national provision for the poor, to his spiritual poverty, as argued by the evangelical rector of Powerscourt, Rev. Robert Daly in 1830. The Church of Scotland minister Thomas Chalmers emerged as an influential commentator on the question of Irish poverty, championing a voluntary approach to poverty and mendicancy and drawing on the example of Christ to defend his opposition to indiscriminate alms-giving. A disdain for undiscerning charity was not limited to evangelicals, and the theologically liberal Richard Whately was perhaps the most prominent advocate of voluntarism and discrimination in the distribution of alms, drawing influence from Malthusian theory and expounding his beliefs in, among other places, the reports of the mid-1830s Poor Inquiry. The trope of beggary was used by Protestant (especially Presbyterian) commentators to present the north-east of the island as being fundamentally different from the 'priest-ridden' rest of the country. The perceived beggary and economic backwardness of the largely Catholic south and west was contrasted with the industriousness and economic vibrancy of 'Protestant Ulster', and this association between mendicancy and Catholicism coloured political discourse, wherein Daniel O'Connell was regularly portrayed as a deviant mendicant, fattening himself on the alms procured from impoverished Irish Catholics.

The internal social measures that were deployed within Protestant congregations to alleviate distress focused on the local 'deserving' poor, who

---

6 Connolly, 'Religion, work-discipline and economic attitudes', p. 241.
7 Pullan, 'Catholics, Protestants and the poor', pp. 441–56; Steven King, 'Welfare regimes and welfare regions in Britain and Europe, c.1750s to 1860s' in *Journal of Modern European History*, ix, no. 1 (2011), pp. 48–51; Steven King and John Stewart, 'Welfare peripheries in modern Europe' in Steven King and John Stewart (eds), *Welfare peripheries: the development of welfare states in nineteenth- and twentieth-century Europe* (Berne, 2007), pp. 9–38.

were to be restored to honest poverty, while the 'undeserving' idle poor were to be scorned. Internal structures within the different communities, such as Anglican service, Presbyterian kirk sessions, Quaker meetings and Methodist Strangers' Friend Societies, were the means through which Irish Protestants responded within their confessional communities to the problem of beggary. Individuals could also involve themselves in other corporate initiatives, such as non-denominational mendicity societies and civil parish vestries. The instance of Mary Ann McCracken, and her work with the Ladies' Committee of the Belfast Charitable Society, suggests that middle-class Protestant women shared their male counterparts' concern with instilling 'habits of industry' into the 'respectable poor'.

Middle-class philanthropists and social commentators, regardless of their confessional allegiance, largely held shared beliefs on the merits of discrimination in charity and the evils of unqualified alms-giving to street beggars: an aversion to indiscriminate charity was held as strongly by members of the Catholic hierarchy as by an Ulster Presbyterian minister. In considering these matters, emphasis must be given to the influence of middle-class interests and expectations from the early decades of the century onwards, and how these shaped the language of philanthropy. In an era of moral and material 'improvement', the poor were to be assisted in removing themselves from idleness, misery and pauperism, yet were not to be lifted beyond their natural rank in society. Limited social mobility was the experience of the poor in this period. Every man, woman and child was born into a particular station in life, and that rank carried with it expectations of one's behaviour and responsibilities. While the language of charity deployed in the public sphere was invariably condescending towards the poorer classes, wealthier members of society understood that their material comfort depended on the labour of the poor. Thus, by his neglect of his duties to be industrious, the idle labourer or artisan not only sinned against God but failed to uphold his responsibility towards his fellow man. Religious reform, the rise of evangelicalism, the strengthening conservative impulse in reaction to the horrors of the French Revolution, the impact of industrialisation and urbanisation of the impact of these societal changes contributed in part to the creation of middle-class identity in Ireland and Britain, adherents of which championed the virtues of industry, sobriety, religious devotion and piety, self-help, personal cleanliness, political obedience, and 'moral restraint'. While not forgetting the example of Christ in working among the poor, middle-class philanthropists and commentators believed that, to borrow from Lord Acton, absolute charity tended to corrupt absolutely.

Moving down the social ladder, the matter becomes more complex. It is clear that most of the alms-giving to beggars was undertaken by members of the labouring and poorer classes. For example, the middle-class members of mendicity societies regularly implored domestic servants to desist in giving alms, in the form of food, to beggars calling at the doors of the wealthy. In both rural and urban Ireland, most of these poor alms-givers were Catholics. Yet, some evidence, such as the Poor Inquiry testimony from north-east Ulster, reveals that indiscriminate alms-giving was practised there too by labouring Protestants. Sources agree that most of the country's beggars were supported largely by those only slightly better-off than themselves: in urban locations, these were usually labourers, artisans and shopkeepers; in rural areas, agricultural labourers, cottiers and small farmers. In this light, Timothy P. O'Neill's focus on denominational differences, which was outlined in the introduction to this book, is open to question, and Seán Connolly's claim that social class was the true line of demarcation in how individuals negotiated mendicancy is closer to the truth. The poor were the main supporters of beggars, but the drawing of distinctions between various categories of mendicants was not unknown among the lower orders. Members of all classes distinguished between the 'deserving' and 'undeserving' poor. This terminology is found in abundance in the contemporary language of charity, as reflected in pamphlets, charity sermons, addresses to public meetings and private correspondence – all reflecting the views of the wealthier classes – yet these moralising categorisations are also to be found, for instance, in the extensive Poor Inquiry testimony from materially humble members of society.

Cultures of welfare specific to certain regions of Ireland can also be identified. Mendicity societies were established in abundance in the north-east, owing to the prominence of Irish Presbyterianism in that corner of the island, as well as the localised experience of industriali-sation and urbanisation, which fostered an urban middle class that was sufficiently concerned to initiate associational means to combat the scourge of mendicancy. Furthermore, the near-complete absence of these charities along the western seaboard reflects the poverty, as well as the relative absence of industry, urbanisation and middle-class associational life, in this region. Certain practices were also carried out along regional trends: for instance, the doling out of alms at church doors appears not to have been practised in Ulster. Perceptions of begging and alms-giving in pre-Famine Ireland also forwarded regional differences: in a time of heightened sectarian tensions, many Protestant writers pointed to the alleged absence of beggars and beggary in 'Protestant Ulster' to prove the economic and moral strength of the northern province, thereby asserting the moral impoverishment of Catholicism and its adherents.

As well as analysing beggary and alms-giving, this study has raised questions and pointed to themes that require further research by historians of nineteenth-century Ireland. As the focus of Section II has been on the viewpoints and actions of the churches and charities in responding to beggary, the role of the state did not receive the same level of attention, and this is a matter which warrants further attention – for instance, in regard to the powers of the police to apprehend and detain street beggars and the study of vagrancy as a crime. While there have been histories of the many associations that managed the various categories of poor in eighteenth- and nineteenth-century Ireland, the Dublin House of Industry is an institution long in need of extensive analysis. The provision of informal private support within a kinship network remains largely unexamined in an Irish context, and a study of this subject would deepen our understanding of how the poor viewed their distress and the relief options available to them, as well as exploring the extent to which friends, families and neighbours were important features in the lives of the poor. It is clear, however, that such a study would be difficult given the paucity of sources. The prevalence of children in begging, particular in urban areas, was remarked upon by countless commentators, but this phenomenon has not been subjected to detailed analysis by Irish historians. Perceptions of the corruptive nature of the urban environment, particularly the morally corrosive effect these 'debilitating environments'[8] had on vulnerable and impressionable children, would be sure to reward the researcher and such a study would complement the work of Felix Driver and Tristram Hunt on nineteenth-century British cities.[9]

While focused on the questions of begging and alms-giving, this study has probed numerous aspects of nineteenth-century Irish society. It is here suggested that mendicancy can be deployed as a vehicle with which to drive a wide-ranging analysis of Irish society in the first half of the nineteenth century. While the present work has been concerned with perceptions of and responses to begging and alms-giving in the period 1815–45, this topic has provided insights into wider social and cultural developments: the growing confidence and assertiveness of the Catholic middling classes; the rise of Protestant evangelicalism and its influence in shaping social thought; the evolving role of the parish vestries in the civil life of local communities; and the importance of the culture of association in spurring the formation of hundreds of charitable societies across Ireland and Britain. A persistent theme has been the transnational exchange of social thought on questions such as poverty and begging, and this is proven by the proliferation of the various social, philanthropic and intellectual movements identified and analysed above. These include the statistical societies, Strangers' Friend Societies and, most pertinently to this study, the mendicity societies. The

8 Shore, *Artful dodgers*, p. 2.

9 Felix Driver, 'Moral geographies: social science and the urban environment in mid-nineteenth-century England' in *Transactions of the Institute of British Geographers*, new series, xiii, no. 3 (1988), pp. 275–87; Hunt, *Building Jerusalem*, pp. 13–185.

debates on begging and alms-giving need to be viewed in a transnational context; Irish mendicity societies, while arising from local initiative, were part of a transnational movement, drawing inspiration from the pioneering Hamburg institution and, in some cases, exchanging information directly with similar institutions in Britain. The Irish Poor Law debate was heavily influenced by parallel discourses in Britain. The aforementioned movements of social improvement transcended national boundaries and were international phenomena. The impact of religious revivals also introduced an international element into the Irish context. Evangelical Protestantism flourished in North America, as well as in Ireland and Britain, while the Catholic revival in Ireland mirrored the growing assertiveness of the Catholic Church in Europe. To study begging and alms-giving in pre-Famine Ireland is to study a variety of social, cultural, economic, political and religious factors, both internal and external to Ireland, which shaped how all classes of society, from British parliamentarians to Dublin artisans, and from Belfast clergymen to Connaught labourers, perceived and responded to the intractable question of the mendicant poor and their relief.

Bibliography

Primary Sources

Manuscript Material

Republic of Ireland

Abbey Presbyterian Church, Dublin
Mary's Abbey congregation records, books no. 9, 13, 14 and 18

Dublin Diocesan Archives
Daniel Murray papers (30/7–34/6)
John Hamilton papers (35/1–37/4)

Friends Historical Library, Dublin
Cork monthly meeting records (MM VIII)
Dublin monthly meeting records (MM II)
Waterford monthly meeting records (MM XI)

National Archives of Ireland, Dublin
Australian Transportation Database
Chief Secretary's Office Official Papers
Chief Secretary's Office Registered Papers
Commissioners of National Education papers
Criminal Index Files
Irish Prison Records (accessed through www.findmypast.ie)
Miscellaneous (Letter book of Joseph Burke (M 2591))
State of the Country papers

National Library of Ireland, Dublin
Association for the Suppression of Mendicity in Dublin papers (MSS 32,599/1–32,616)
Report on the state of the poor in Waterford city and on the charitable institutions of
    that city, 5 Apr. 1834 (MS 3,288)

Presentation Convent, George's Hill Archive, Dublin
'Rules and constitutions of the Religious Congregation of the Charitable Instruction
established in the Convent of the Presentation of our Blessed Lady in Cork
agreeable to the bull of His Present Holiness Pope Pius VI', [c.1809] (GHAD/C/5)
'Short sketches of the lives of some of the nuns who entered the community from 1790
to 1870', [c.early twentieth century] (GHAD/P/16)
Teresa Mulally to Archbishop John Thomas Troy, [c.1802] (GHAD/FD/146)

Religious Sisters of Charity Archive, Caritas, Sandymount, Dublin
Diary of Mother Catherine, 2 June 1812–29 Aug. 1825 (RSCG/1/C/15)
'Dublin cause for the beatification and canonization of the servant of God Mary
Aikenhead foundress of the Sisters of Charity (1787–1858). Positio on the life, the
witness and the fame of sanctity of the servant of God' (2 vols, 1994)

Representative Church Body Library, Dublin
Vestry Minute Books (arranged by County)

Cork
St Finbar's parish, vestry minute book, 1764–1837 (P 497.5.1)
St Paul's parish, vestry minute book, 1796–1926 (P 349.5.1)
St Peter's parish, vestry minute book, 1752–1846 (P 342.5.1)

Dublin
St Andrew's parish, vestry minute book, 1757–1817 (P 59.5.1)
St Andrew's parish, vestry minute book, 1819–47 (P 59.5.2)
St Bride's parish vestry minute book, 1826–85 (P 327.3.3)
St Catherine's parish, vestry minute book, 1785–1815 (P 117.5.5)
St Catherine's parish, vestry minute book, 1816–35 (P 117.5.7)
St Mary's parish, vestry minute book, 1788–1819 (P 277.7.4)
St Michan's parish, vestry minute book, 1800–28 (P 276.5.4)
St Michan's parish, vestry minute book, 1828–1922 (P 276.5.5)
St Thomas's parish, vestry minute book, 1823–41 (P 80.5.2)
St Werburgh's parish, vestry minute book, 1780–1859 (P 326.5.2)

Galway
St Nicholas's parish, vestry minute book, 1805–1909 (P 519.5.1)

Kildare
Naas parish, vestry minute book, 1805–85 (P 487.5.1)

Kilkenny
St Canice's parish, vestry minute book, 1775–1824 (P 622.5.1)
St Mary's parish, vestry minute book, 1792–1872 (P 792.5.2)

Louth
St Peter's parish, vestry minute book, 1748–1803 (P 854.5.1)

Roscommon
Bumlin parish vestry minute book, 1811–70 (P 737.5.1)

Westmeath
Mullingar parish, vestry minute book, 1806–1983 (P 336.5.1)

Thurles Library
Thurles Poor Law Union records (BG151)

Northern Ireland

Methodist Historical Society of Ireland Archives, Belfast
Strangers' Friend Society register of relief recipients, 1794–9 (IrBe.MS.OS42.02)

Public Record Office of Northern Ireland (arranged by archival reference number)
Belfast Poor Law Union Board of Guardians papers (BG/7)
Church of Ireland records (CR1)
Presbyterian Church records (CR3)
Irish Evangelical Society papers (CR7/2)
Records of the Religious Society of Friends in Ulster (CR8)
Abercorn papers (D623)
Caledon papers (D847/5)
Fintona papers (D1048)
Cunningham and Clarke papers (D1108)
J.B. Hamilton papers (D1518)
Calwell papers (D3784)
Maxwell Given papers (D4164)
Dromore Diocesan papers (DIORC/3)
Lisburn (Blaris) parish records (MIC1/4)
Ardtrea parish records (MIC1/319/1)
Rosemary Street, Belfast, Presbyterian Church papers (MIC1P/7)
Ordnance Survey memoirs (MIC6C)
Census return and testamentary documents (T715)
Groves manuscripts (T808)
Cooke and Chalmers papers (copies) (T3307)

Presbyterian Historical Society of Ireland Archive, Belfast

Presbyterian Church Records
Aghadowey Presbyterian Church kirk session minute book, 1702–65 (no reference number)
Carnmoney Presbyterian Church kirk session poor list, 1718–1878 (MIC/1P/37/6; microfilm)

Great Britain

British Library, London
Liverpool papers (Add. MS 38368)
London Mendicity Society minute book, 1818–24 (Add. MS 50136)
Place papers (Add. MS 35145)

Linnean Society Archives, London
James Edward Smith papers (GB-110/JES), accessed online at http://linnean-online.
    org/62487/

National Records of Scotland, Edinburgh
Dundas family (Viscounts Melville) papers (GD51)
Dukes of Buccleuch papers (GD224)

The National Archives, Kew
Home Office Correspondence, HO 44

Printed Material

Modern Editions of Manuscript Material
Agnew, Jean (ed.), *The Drennan-McTier letters, 1776–1819* (IMC, 3 vols, Dublin, 1999).
Brown, William (ed.), *Yorkshire Deeds*, Yorkshire Archaeological Society Record Series
    (10 vols, n.p., 1922).
Crawford, W.H. and B. Trainor (eds), *Aspects of Irish social history, 1750–1800* (Belfast,
    1969).
Day, Angélique and Patrick McWilliams (eds), *Ordnance Survey memoirs of Ireland* (40
    vols, Belfast, 1990–8).
Ellis, Eilish and P. Beryl Eustace (eds), *Registry of deeds, Dublin: abstracts of wills, vol. 3,
    1785–1832* (IMC, Dublin, 1984).
Fleming, David and John Logan (eds), *Pauper Limerick: the register of the Limerick
    House of Industry 1774–1793* (IMC, Dublin, 2011).
Gillespie, Raymond (ed.), *The vestry records of the parish of St John the Evangelist,
    Dublin, 1595–1658* (Dublin, 2002).
—— *The vestry records of the parishes of St Catherine and St James, Dublin, 1657–1692*
    (Dublin, 2004).
Gillespie, Raymond and Alison O'Keeffe (eds), *Register of the parish of Shankill, Belfast,
    1745–1761* (Dublin, 2006).
Letters of Mary Aikenhead (Dublin, 1914).
McGrath, Thomas (ed.), *The pastoral and education letters of Bishop James Doyle of
    Kildare and Leighlin, 1786–1834* (Dublin, 2004).
Ní Mhurchadha, Maighréad (ed.), *The vestry records of the united parishes of Finglas, St
    Margaret's, Artane and the Ward, 1657–1758* (Dublin, 2007).
Sokoll, Thomas (ed.), *Essex pauper letters, 1731–1837* (Oxford, 2001).
Sullivan, Mary C. (ed.), *The correspondence of Catherine McAuley, 1818–1841* (Dublin
    and Baltimore, MD, 2004).
Wallace, W.J.R. (ed.), *The vestry records of the parishes of St Bride, St Michael le Pole and
    St Stephen, Dublin, 1662–1742* (Dublin, 2011).

Legislation
10 & 11 Chas. I, c. 4 [Ire.], 'An act for the erecting of houses of correction, and for the
    punishment of rogues, vagabonds, sturdy beggars and other lewd and idle persons'
    (1635).

17 & 18 Chas. II, c. 7 [Ire.], 'An act for provision for ministers in cities and corporate towns, and making the church of St. Andrew's, in the city of Dublin, presentative for ever' (1665).

2 Ann., c. 12 [Ire.], 'An act for the reviving an act for taking away the benefit of clergy in some cases and for transporting of felons' (4 Mar. 1704).

12 Geo. I, c. 9 [Ire.], 'An act for the more effectual erecting and the better regulating free schools, and for rebuilding and repairing churches' (8 Mar. 1726).

11 & 12 Geo. III, c. 11 [Ire.], 'An act for better regulating the foundling hospital and workhouse in the city of Dublin, and increasing the fund for the support thereof, also for making a provision for appointing a locum tenens in case of the death or absence of the lord mayor or the president of the court of conscience' (2 June 1772).

11 & 12 Geo. III, c. 30 [Ire.], 'An act for badging such poor as shall be found unable to support themselves by labour, and otherwise providing for them, and for restraining such as shall be found able to support themselves by labour or industry from begging' (2 June 1772).

13 & 14 Geo. III, c. 10 [Ire.] (session 1773–74), 'An act to explain and amend an act made in the 3rd year of the reign of his late majesty King George II entitled an act for better keeping churches in repair' (4 May 1774).

13 & 14 Geo. III, c. 46 [Ire.], 'An act for amending an act made the last session of parliament entitled an act for badging such poor as shall be found unable to support themselves by labour, and otherwise providing for them, and for restraining such as shall be found able to support themselves by labour or industry from begging' (2 June 1774).

15 & 16 Geo. III, c. 14 [Ire.], 'An act for repealing an act made in the 13th and 14th years of the reign of his present majesty entitled an act to explain and amend an act made in the 3rd year of the reign of his late majesty King George II entitled an act for better keeping churches in repair, and for other purposes' (7 Mar. 1776).

15 & 16 Geo. III, c. 35 [Ire.] 'An act for amending an act made in the 11 and 12th years of his present majesty's reign entitled an act for badging such poor as shall be found unable to support themselves by labour industry from begging, so far as the said act relates to the county of Limerick, and to the county of the city of Limerick, and for extending the provisions of the said law to the town of Coleraine in the county of Londonderry' (4 Apr. 1776).

35 Geo III, c. 36 [Ire.], 'An act for more effectually preserving the peace within the city of Dublin, and the district of the metropolis, and establishing a parochial watch in the said city' (5 June 1795).

36 Geo. III, c. 20 [Ire.], 'An act more effectually to suppress insurrections, and prevent the disturbance of the public peace' (24 Mar. 1796).

59 Geo. III, c. 41, 'An act to establish regulations for preventing contagious diseases in Ireland' (14 June 1819).

7 Geo. IV, c. 72, 'An act to consolidate and amend the Laws which regulate the levy and application of church rates and parish cesses, and the election of churchwardens, and the maintenance of parish clerks, in Ireland' (31 May 1826).

3 & 4 Will. IV, c. 37, 'An act to alter and amend the laws relating to the temporalities of the Church in Ireland' (14 Aug. 1833).

1 & 2 Vict., c. 56, 'An act for the more effectual relief of the destitute poor in Ireland' (31 July 1838).

10 & 11 Vict., c. 84, 'An act to make provision for the punishment of vagrants and persons offending against the laws in force for the relief of the destitute poor in Ireland' (22 July 1847).

27 Vict., c. 17, 'An act for the abolition of vestry cess in Ireland, and for other purposes relating thereto' (13 May 1864).

29 & 30 Vict., c. 90, 'An act to amend the law relating to the public health' (7 Aug. 1866).

Parliamentary Debates and Parliamentary Papers (Returns, Reports, Minutes and Appendices, Arranged in Chronological Order)

The journals of the House of Commons of the Kingdom of Ireland (19 vols, Dublin, 1796–1800).

Hansard's parliamentary debates, second series 1820–9.

Hansard's parliamentary debates, third series, 1830–91.

A statement of the number of offenders committed to the several goals in Ireland, for trial at the different assizes, commission, and quarter sessions, in the years 1805, 1806, 1807, 1808, 1809 & 1810 ... H.C. 1812 (246), v, 1005.

Report from committee on the state of mendicity in the metropolis, H.C. 1814–15 (473), iii, 231.

First report from the select committee on the state of disease and condition of the labouring poor, in Ireland, H.C. 1819 (314), viii, 365.

(Ireland). Report of the commissioners appointed by the Lord Lieutenant of Ireland to inspect the House of Industry, and to report upon the management thereof, with a view to the introduction of such reforms and improvements, as would render it, not only less expensive, but more efficient for the purposes for which it was originally designed, H.C. 1820 (84), viii, 227.

Report from the select committee on the state of Ireland: 1825, H.C. 1825 (129), viii, 1.

First report from the select committee on the state of Ireland: 1825, H.C. 1825 (129), viii, 7.

Second report from the select committee on the state of Ireland: 1825, H.C. 1825 (129), viii, 179.

Third report from the select committee on the state of Ireland: 1825, H.C. 1825 (129), viii, 303.

On the state of Ireland. Fourth report: viz. minutes of evidence, 26 April – 21 June, 1825, H.C. 1825 (129), viii, 471.

First report of the commissioners on education in Ireland, H.C. 1825 (400), xii, 1.

Minutes of evidence taken before the select committee of the House of Lords, appointed to inquire into the state of Ireland, more particularly with reference to the circumstances which may have led to the disturbances in that part of the United Kingdom. 24 March–22 June, 1825, H.C. 1825 (521), ix, 249.

Dublin vestries. Returns of the several sums of money assessed in the several parishes in the city of Dublin, by vestries holden during Easter week, in the year 1830 ... H.C. 1830 (523), xxxi, 299.

First report of evidence from the select committee on the state of the poor in Ireland. Minutes of evidence: 24 March–14 May, H.C. 1830 (589), vii, 218.

Second report of evidence from the select committee on the state of the poor in Ireland. Minutes of evidence: 18 May–5 June, H.C. 1830 (654), vii, 451.

Third report of evidence from the select committee on the state of the poor in Ireland. Minutes of evidence: 8 June–7 July. With an appendix of documents and papers, and likewise a general index, H.C. 1830 (665), vii, 649.

Report of the select committee on the state of the poor in Ireland; being a summary of the first, second and third reports of evidence taken before that committee: together with an appendix of accounts and papers, H.C. 1830 (667), vii, 1.

Population, Ireland. Census of the population, 1831. Comparative abstract of the population in Ireland, as taken in 1821 and 1831, H.C. 1833 (23), xxxix, 3.

Report from His Majesty's commissioners for inquiring into the administration and practical operation of the Poor Laws, Appendix (C). Communications, H.C. 1834 (44), xxxvii, 264.

Prisons of Ireland. Thirteenth report of Inspectors General of Prisons, Ireland: 1835, H.C. 1835 (114), xxxvi, 381.

First report from His Majesty's commissioners for inquiring into the condition of the poorer classes in Ireland, with appendix (A) and supplement, H.C. 1835 (369), xxxii, 1.

Poor Inquiry (Ireland), Appendix (C) – Parts I and II. Part I. Reports on the state of the poor, and on the charitable institutions in some of the principal towns; with supplement containing answers to queries. Part II. Report on the city of Dublin, and supplement containing answers to queries; with addenda to appendix (A)., and communications, H.C. 1836 [C 35], xxx, 35.

Third report of the commissioners for inquiring into the condition of the poorer classes in Ireland, H.C. 1836 [C 43], xxx, 1.

Poor Inquiry (Ireland), Appendix (H) – Part I. containing reasons for recommending voluntary associations for the relief of the poor; and reasons for dissenting from the principle of raising funds for the relief of the poor by the voluntary system, as recommended in the report. Also, Tables No I, II, II, referred to in third report, H.C. 1836 [C 41], xxxiv, 643.

Municipal corporations (Ireland). Appendix to the first report of the commissioners. Part III. – Conclusion of the north-west circuit, H.C. 1836 [C 26], xxiv, 1.

Second annual report of the Poor Law Commissioners for England and Wales; together with appendices A. B. C. D., H.C. 1836 (595), xxix, 1.

Report of Geo. Nicholls, Esq., to His Majesty's Principal Secretary of State for the Home Department, on Poor Laws, Ireland, H.C. 1837 [C 69], li, 201.

Second report of Geo. Nicholls, Esq., to Her Majesty's Principal Secretary of State for the Home Department, on Poor Laws, Ireland, H.C. 1837–8 [C 104], xxxviii, 657.

Sixth annual report of the Poor Law Commissioners. With appendices, H.C. 1840 [C 245], xvii, 397.

Seventh annual report of the Poor Law Commissioners, with appendices, H.C. 1841 Session I [C 327], xi, 291.

Londonderry Union. Return to an order of the honourable House of Commons, dated 11 March 1842; for, copies of the contracts entered into for the building of the Londonderry Union poor-house … H.C. 1842 (189), xxxvi, 197.

Appendices B. to F. to the eighth annual report of the Poor Law Commissioners, H.C. 1842 [C 399], xix, 119.

Appendices A to D. to the ninth annual report of the Poor Law Commissioners, H.C. 1843 [C 491], xxi, 53.

Poor Law (Ireland). Copies of any communications, &c. by the Poor Law Commissioners to any boards of guardians in Ireland, in reference to 15th & 16th clauses of the amended Poor Law Act … H.C. 1844 (346), xl, 633.

Report from Her Majesty's commissioners for inquiring into the administration and practical operation of the Poor Laws in Scotland, H.C. 1844 [C 557], xx, 1.

Report from the select committee of the House of Lords on the laws relating to the relief of the destitute poor, and into the operation of the medical charities in Ireland; together with the minutes of evidence taken before the said committee, H.C. 1846 (694), xi, 1.

Reports and communications on vagrancy, H.C. 1847–8 [C 987], liii, 240.

Prisons of Ireland. Twenty-eighth report of the Inspectors-General on the general state of the prisons of Ireland, 1849; with appendices, H.C. 1850 [C 1229], xxix, 305.

The census of Ireland for the year 1851. Part III. Report on the status of disease, H.C. 1854 [C 1765], lviii, 1.

The census of Ireland for the year 1851. Part v. Table of deaths. vol. 1, H.C. 1856 [C 2087-I], xxix, 263.

Ninth annual report of the Commissioners for Administering the Laws for Relief of the Poor in Ireland, with appendices, H.C. 1856 [C 2105], xxviii, 415.

Contemporary Newspapers and Periodicals

The Advocate; or Irish Journal
Belfast Commercial Chronicle
Belfast Monthly Magazine
Belfast News-Letter
Bristol Mercury
Bucks Herald
Cambridge Independent Press
Christian Examiner and Church of Ireland Magazine
Clare Journal, and Ennis Advertiser
Constitution; or Cork Advertiser
Cork Constitution
Cork Mercantile Chronicle
The Correspondent (Dublin)
Coventry Herald
Downpatrick Recorder
Dublin Evening Mail
Dublin Evening Packet and Correspondent
Dublin Morning Register
Dublin Penny Journal
Dublin University Magazine
Edinburgh Evening Courant
Edinburgh Review
Enniskillen Chronicle and Erne Packet
Freeman's Journal
Galway Weekly Advertiser
Journal of the Statistical Society of London
Leinster Journal (Kilkenny) (known as *Finn's Leinster Journal* between 1766 and 1802)
Londonderry Sentinel
The Moderator (Kilkenny)
Morning Chronicle
The Nation
Nenagh Guardian
Saunder's News-Letter

Sligo Journal
Southern Reporter and Cork Commercial Courier
Transactions of the Dublin Statistical Society
Tuam Herald
Ulster Journal of Archaeology
Warwick and Warwickshire Advertiser
Waterford Chronicle
Weekly Telegraph
Wexford Independent

Contemporary Reports of Charitable and other Welfare Organisations (Arranged in Chronological Order, by Organisation)

Dublin House of Industry

An account of the proceedings and state of the fund of the Corporation instituted for the Relief of the Poor, and for Punishing Vagabonds and Sturdy Beggars in the County of the City of Dublin, published by order of the corporation, March 22d, 1774 (Dublin, 1774).

Observations on the state and condition of the poor, under the institution, for their relief, in the city of Dublin; together with the state of the fund, &c. published by order of the Corporation instituted for the Relief of the Poor and for punishing Vagabonds and Sturdy Beggars, in the County of the City of Dublin, March 25th, 1775 (Dublin, 1775).

Observations on the House of Industry, Dublin; and on the plans of the association for suppressing mendicity in that city (Dublin, 1818).

Dublin Mendicity Society

Report of the Association for the Suppression of Mendicity in Dublin. For the year 1818 (Dublin, 1819).

Second report of the Association for the Suppression of Mendicity in Dublin, 1819 (Dublin, 1820).

Report of the general committee of the Association for the Suppression of Mendicity in Dublin. For the year 1820 (Dublin, 1821).

Sixth report of the general committee of the Association of Mendicity in Dublin. For the year 1823 (Dublin, 1824).

Tenth report of the general committee of the Association for the Suppression of Mendicity in Dublin. For the year 1827 (Dublin, 1828).

Nineteenth annual report of the managing committee of the Association for the Suppression of Mendicity in Dublin. For the year 1836: with resolutions upon the subject of the Poor Laws (Dublin, 1837).

Twentieth annual report of the managing committee of the Association for the Suppression of Mendicity in Dublin. For the year 1837 (Dublin, 1838).

Twenty-second annual report of the managing committee of the Association for the Suppression of Mendicity in Dublin. For the year 1839 (Dublin, 1840).

Twenty-third annual report of the managing committee of the Association for the Suppression of Mendicity in Dublin. For the year 1840 (Dublin, 1841).

Twenty-fourth annual report of the managing committee of the Association for the Suppression of Mendicity in Dublin. For the year 1841 (Dublin, 1842).

Thirty-first annual report of the managing committee of the Association for the Suppression of Mendicity in Dublin. For the year 1848 (Dublin, 1849).

London Mendicity Society

The first report of the society established in London for the suppression of mendicity (London, 1819).

The third report of the society for the suppression of mendicity, established in London, 1818 (London, 1821).

The thirty-second report of the society for the suppression of mendicity, established in London, 1818 (London, 1850).

Londonderry Mendicity Society

The first report of the general committee of the Mendicity Association, instituted in Londonderry, 13th May, 1825; with a statement of the accounts, and a list of the subscribers for the last year (Derry, 1826).

The second report of the general committee of the Mendicity Association, instituted in Londonderry, 13th May, 1825; with a statement of the accounts, and a list of the subscribers for the last year (Derry, 1827).

The third report of the general committee of the Mendicity Association, instituted in Londonderry, 13th May, 1825; with a statement of the accounts, and a list of the subscribers for the last year (Derry, 1828).

The fourth report of the general committee of the Mendicity Association, instituted in Londonderry, 13th May, 1825; with a statement of the accounts, and a list of the subscribers for the last year (Derry, 1829).

The fifth report of the general committee of the Mendicity Association, instituted in Londonderry, 13th May, 1825; with a statement of the accounts, and a list of the subscribers for the last year (Derry, 1830).

The thirteenth report of the general committee of the Mendicity Association, instituted in Londonderry, May 13, 1825; with a statement of the accounts, and a list of the subscribers for the year ending July 31, 1838 (Derry, 1838).

Strangers' Friend Society, Dublin

[Clarke, Adam], *The nature, design and general rules of the Strangers' Friend Society, as established in Dublin, 1790* (Dublin, 1799).

For the year 1806. The annual report of the Strangers' Friend Society, as established in Dublin, in 1790 (Dublin, 1807).

Annual report for the year 1818, of the Benevolent or Strangers' Friend Society (originated in the year 1790) (Dublin, 1819).

Annual report of the Strangers' Friend Society; (founded in 1790) for visiting and relieving distressed strangers, and the resident sick poor, at their habitations, in Dublin and its vicinity: with an account of some of the cases relieved, and a list of subscribers, for 1823 (Dublin, 1824).

Annual report of the Strangers' Friend Society (founded in 1790) for visiting and relieving distressed strangers, and the resident sick poor, in Dublin and its vicinity; with an account of some of the cases relieved, and a list of subscribers for 1831 (Dublin, 1832).

Annual report of the Strangers' Friend Society (founded in 1790) for visiting and relieving distressed strangers and the resident sick poor, in Dublin and its vicinity; with an account of some of the cases relieved, and [a] *list of subscribers for 1840* (Dublin, 1841).

Other Organisations (Arranged in Chronological Order)

The first report of the society, instituted in Edinburgh on 25th January 1813, for the suppression of beggars, for the relief of occasional distress, and for the encouragement of industry among the poor. With an account of receipts and disbursements from 27th February to 1st November 1813 (Edinburgh, 1814).

Barker, F., *Medical report of the house of recovery and fever-hospital, in Cork-street, Dublin* (Dublin, 1818).

First annual report, of the Association for the Suppression of Mendicity in the City of Waterford (Waterford, 1822).

Report of the council of the Chamber of Commerce of Dublin, to the annual assembly of the members of the association, held on the 1st of March 1836 (Dublin, 1836).

First report of the Society of St. Vincent de Paul (Dublin, 1846).

Report of the proceedings of the Society of St. Vincent de Paul, in Ireland, during the year 1848 (Dublin, [*c*.1848]).

First report [*of the Society of St. Vincent de Paul in Limerick, 1849*], reprinted in Bob Ryan, *An open door: the history of the Society of St. Vincent de Paul in Limerick 1846–1996* (Limerick, 1996), pp. 39–50.

Ladies' Association of Charity, of St. Vincent de Paul. Under the patronage of His Grace the Lord Archbishop. The first annual report (Dublin, 1852).

Other Books, Pamphlets, Reports, Directories and Journal Articles

'A barrister', *The Vagrant Act, in relation to the liberty of the subject* (London, 1824).

An address to the mechanics, workmen, and servants, in the city of Dublin (Dublin, 1828).

Anon., 'Abolition of Mendicity' in *Belfast Monthly Magazine*, ii, no. 11 (30 June 1809), pp. 435–8.

Anon., *Arguments in proof of the necessity and practicality of suppressing street begging in the city of Dublin* ... (Dublin, 1817).

Anon., *The constable's assistant: being a compendium of the duties and powers of constables, and other peace officers; chiefly as they relate to the apprehending of offenders, and the laying of information before magistrates* (3rd edn, London, 1818).

Anon., 'Introduction' in *Journal of the Statistical Society of London*, i, no. 1 (May 1838), pp. 1–5.

Anon., *A letter to the Right Hon. Lord Goderich, on the deplorable condition of the helpless poor in Ireland, with a plan of relief, as at present partly in operation in several districts of the province of Ulster. By a member of a parochial poor relief committee* (Dublin, 1827).

Anon., 'Management of the poor in Hamburg' in *Belfast Monthly Magazine*, iii, no. 13 (31 Aug. 1809), pp. 94–9.

Anon., *People of England!* (n.p. [London?], [*c*.early nineteenth century]).

Anon., *The real grievance of the Irish peasantry, as immediately felt and complained of among themselves, a fruitful source of beggary and idleness, and the main support of the Rock system* ... (London, 1825).

Anon., 'The Scottish system of Poor Laws' in *Dublin University Magazine*, iii, no. 17 (May 1834), pp. 508–22.

Anon., 'Tenant right, repeal and Poor Laws: dangers and duties of the Conservative Party and landed interest in Ireland' in *Dublin University Magazine*, xxxi, no. 181 (Jan. 1848), pp. 134–58.

Association for the Preservation of the Memorials of the Dead, Ireland. Journal for the year 1892, ii, no. 1 ([1892]).

Atthill, Lombe, *Recollections of an Irish doctor* (1911; repr. Whitegate, 2007).

Barker, F. and J. Cheyne, *An account of the rise, progress, and decline of the fever lately epidemic in Ireland, together with communications from physicians in the provinces, and various official documents* (2 vols, Dublin, 1821).

Barrow, John, *A tour round Ireland through the sea-coast counties in the autumn of 1835* (London, 1836).

Bicheno, J.E., *Ireland, and its economy; being the result of observations made in a tour through the country in the autumn of 1829* (London, 1830).

Binns, Jonathan, *The miseries and beauties of Ireland* (2 vols, London, 1837).

Boileau, John P., 'Statistics of mendicancy' in *Journal of the Statistical Society of London*, xii, no. 1 (Feb. 1849), pp. 43–8.

The Book of Common Prayer, and administration of the sacraments and other rites and ceremonies of the Church, according to the use of the United Church of England and Ireland; together with the psalter, or psalms of David, pointed as they are to be sung or said in churches (Edinburgh, 1818).

Breakey, William Alex, *Handbook for magistrates, clerks of petty sessions, solicitors, coroners, &c., being a comprehensive index and synopsis of the common and statute law in Ireland* (Dublin, 1895).

Bullingbrooke, E.D., *Ecclesiastical law; or, the statutes, constitutions, canons, rubricks, and articles, of the Church of Ireland. Methodically digested under proper heads, with a commentary, historical and juridical* (2 vols, Dublin, 1770).

Calvin, John, *Commentaries on the four last books of Moses arranged in the form of a harmony*, trans. Charles William Bingham (4 vols, Grand Rapids, MI, 1950).

Carberry, Mary, *The farm by Lough Gur: the story of Mary Fogarty (Sissy O'Brien)* (London, 1937).

[Carleton, William], 'A pilgrimage to Patrick's Purgatory' in *Christian Examiner*, vi, no. 34 (Apr. 1828), pp. 268–86.

—— *Traits and stories of the Irish peasantry* (1844; 2 vols, repr. Gerrards Cross and Savage, MD, 1990).

—— *Traits and stories of the Irish peasantry* (new edn, 2 vols, London, 1852).

—— *The autobiography of William Carleton* (1896; repr. London, 1968).

Carlile, James, *A series of sermons, on the nature and effects of repentance and faith* (London, 1821).

[Carlile, James], *Memorial recommending the establishment of a mission to the Roman Catholics of Ireland* (Dublin, 1825).

Carlyle, Thomas, *Chartism* (London, 1840).

Colby's Ordnance Survey memoir of Londonderry (1837; 2nd edn, Limavady, 1990).

Colquhoun, Patrick, *A treatise on indigence; exhibiting a general view of the natural resources for productive labour; with propositions for ameliorating the condition of the poor …* (London, 1806).

A complete Catholic registry, directory, and almanac ... 1836, 1838, 1845.

Cooke, Henry, *A sermon, preached in the meeting-house of the Third Presbyterian Congregation, Belfast, on Sunday, the 18th December, 1814, in aid of the funds of the House of Industry* (3rd edn, Belfast, 1815).

Cunningham, Patrick, 'The *Catholic directory* for 1821' in *Reportorium Novum*, ii, no. 2 (1960), pp. 324–63.

[Daly, Robert], 'Improvement of Ireland – Poor Laws' in *Christian Examiner*, x, no. 55 (Jan. 1830), pp. 1–8.

de Bhaldraithe, Tomás (ed.), *The diary of an Irish countryman 1827–1835: a translation of Cín Lae Amhlaoibh* (Cork, 1979).

Deane's Limerick almanack, directory and advertiser, 1838.

Dickens, Charles, *The adventures of Oliver Twist* (1839; Oxford, 1987).

Dobbs, Arthur, *An essay on the trade and improvement of Ireland* (2 parts, Dublin, 1729–31).

Dorian, Hugh, *The outer edge of Ulster: a memoir of social life in nineteenth-century Donegal*, ed. Breandán Mac Suibhne and David Dickson (Dublin, 2001).

Douglas, John, *Observations on the necessity of a legal provision for the Irish poor, as the means of improving the condition of the Irish people, and protecting the British landlord, farmer and labourer* (London, 1828).

Doyle, James, *The general catechism, revised, corrected, and enlarged, by the Right Reverend James Doyle, D.D., Bishop of Kildare and Leighlin, and prescribed by him to be taught throughout the dioceses of Kildare and Leighlin* (Dublin, 1843).

Dublin almanac, and general register of Ireland, 1841.

Dubourdieu, John, *Statistical survey of the county of Antrim, with observations on the means of improvement; drawn up for the consideration, and by direction of the Dublin Society* (Dublin, 1812).

Eden, Frederic Morton, *The state of the poor: a history of the labouring classes in England, with parochial reports*, ed. A.G.L. Rogers (1797; repr. London, 1928).

Edgar, John, *The General Assembly's Irish schools. The priest's curse* (n.p. [Belfast?], [c.1847]).

—— *Connaught harvest* (Belfast, 1853).

The evidence of His Grace the Archbishop of Dublin, as taken before the select committee of the House of Lords, appointed to inquire into the collection and payment of tithes in Ireland, and the state of the laws relating thereto (London, 1832).

'E.W.', 'The beggarman's tale' in *Dublin Penny Journal*, i, no. 51 (15 June 1833), pp. 406–7.

'Extract from the report of the establishments at Hamburg, in 1799' in *Belfast Monthly Magazine*, iii, no. 13 (31 Aug. 1809), pp. 99–101.

Finlay, John, *The office and duty of church-warden and parish officer* (Dublin, 1824).

Fitzgerald, Michael, *Wickedness and nullity of human laws against mendicancy, and the anti Christian character of the Irish Poor-law, proved from the consideration of alms-giving, mendicancy, and Poor Laws, on Christian and Catholic principles, in a sermon, preached in St. Michael's, Limerick (on Whitsunday, the 4th of June, 1843,) on behalf of the Thomond-gate male and female schools* (Dublin, 1843).

Flood, Henry, *Poor Laws: arguments against a provision for paupers, if it be parochial or perpetual* (Dublin, 1830).

Fry, Elizabeth and Joseph John Gurney, *Report addressed to the Marquess Wellesley, Lord Lieutenant of Ireland, respecting their late visit to that country* (London, 1827).

Full and true account of the trial of two most barbarous and cruel beggar-women, Sarah Mullholland & Maria Burke, who were found guilty of strangling a child, for the purpose of extorting charity!!! Together with various particulars concerning the impostures of other street beggars ([Dublin?], [*c*.1830]).

Gahan, William, 'On the necessity and signal advantages of alms and works of mercy' in William Gahan, *Sermons and moral discourses, for all the Sundays and principal festivals of the year, on the most important truths and maxims of the gospels* (3rd edn, 2 vols, Dublin, 1825).

Gamble, John, *Views of society and manners in the north of Ireland, in a series of letters written in the year 1818* (London, 1819).

—— *Sketches of history, politics, and manners in Dublin, and the north of Ireland, in 1810* (new edn, London, 1826).

The gentleman's and citizen's almanac (Watson's) for 1820.

Graham, John, *God's revenge against rebellion: an historical poem on the state of Ireland, with notes and an appendix, consisting of a pastoral epistle from Rome, and two letters to the editor of the* Dublin Evening Post (Dublin, 1820).

Griscom, John, *A year in Europe, comprising a journal of observations in England, Scotland, Ireland, France, Switzerland, the north of Italy, and Holland, in 1818 and 1819* (2 vols, New York, 1823).

Hackett, William, 'The Irish bacach, or professional beggar, viewed archaeologically' in *Ulster Journal of Archaeology*, 1st series, ix (1861–2), pp. 256–71.

Hall, [Mrs] S.C., *Tales of Irish life and character* (Edinburgh and London, 1910).

Harty, William, *Historic sketch of the causes, extent, and mortality of contagious fever, epidemic in Ireland in 1741, and during 1817, 1818, and 1819: together with a review of the causes, medical and statistical productive of epidemic fever in Ireland* (Dublin, [1820]).

Haughton, James, 'What is doing for the people in Dublin?' in *People's Journal* (London), ii (1846), pp. 232–6.

Haughton, Samuel, *Memoir of James Haughton, with extracts from his private and published letters* (Dublin, 1877).

[Haywood, Eliza], *A present for a servant-maid. Or, the sure means of gaining love and esteem* (Dublin, 1744).

'Hibernicus', 'On the Poor Laws' in *Christian Examiner*, xi, no. 73 (July 1831), pp. 506–12.

—— 'On the Poor Laws' in *Christian Examiner*, xi, no. 74 (Aug. 1831), pp. 590–7.

Hincks, Thomas Dix, *A short account of the different charitable institutions of the city of Cork, with remarks* (Cork, 1802).

Hornihold, [John Joseph], *The real principles of Catholics; or, a catechism by way of general instruction, explaining the principal points of the doctrine & ceremonies of the Catholic Church* (4th edn, Dublin, 1821).

Inglis, Henry D., *Ireland in 1834. A journey through Ireland, during the spring, summer, and autumn of 1834* (2nd edn, 2 vols, London, 1835).

Ireland. An account of all sums of money levied in the several parishes of Ireland, by authority of vestry, for building and repairing of churches, salaries of parish clerks and other officers, and other incidents; particularly distinguishing any sums which may have been raised for purchase of organs or stoves, or salaries of organists or choristers. Part I (n.p., [1824]).

Laing, David (ed.), *The works of John Knox* (6 vols, Edinburgh, 1895).

Lawson, James A., 'On the connexion between statistics and political economy' in *Transactions of the Dublin Statistical Society*, i, session 1 (1847–8), pp. 3–9.

Le Fanu, W.R., *Seventy years of Irish life being anecdotes and reminiscences* (2nd edn, London, 1893).

Lewis, Samuel, *A topographical dictionary of Ireland, comprising the several counties, cities, boroughs, corporate, market and post towns, parishes and villages, with historical and statistical descriptions ...* (2 vols, London, 1837).

Logan, William, *An exposure, from personal observation, of female prostitution in London, Leeds and Rochdale, and especially in the city of Glasgow, with remarks on the cause, extent, results and remedy of the evil* (2nd edn, Glasgow, 1843).

Longfield, Mountiford, *Four lectures on Poor Laws, delivered in Trinity term, 1834* (Dublin, 1834).

Macauly, James, *Ireland in 1872: a tour of observations. With remarks on Irish public questions* (London, 1873).

McCrea, J.B., *Protestant poor a conservative element of society; being a sermon preached in Ebenezer Church, Dublin, for the Protestant Colonisation Society of Ireland* (Dublin, [*c.*1840]).

Mac Doinnléibhe, P., 'Castleblaney Poor Law rate book (1847)' in *Clogher Record*, v, no. 1 (1963), pp. 131–48.

MacNally, Leonard, *The justice of the peace for Ireland: containing the authorities and duties of that officer ...* (2 vols, Dublin, 1808).

Magee, Hamilton, *Fifty years in the Irish Mission* (Belfast and Edinburgh, [*c.*1905]).

Malthus, T.R., *An essay on the principle of population; or, a view of its past and present effects on human happiness; with an inquiry into our prospects respecting the future removal or mitigation of the evils which it occasions* (new edn, London, 1803).

[Mannock, John], *The poor man's catechism; or, the Christian doctrine explained; with suitable admonitions* (10th edn, Dublin, 1832).

Martin, Matthew, *Letter to the Right Hon. Lord Pelham, on the state of mendicity in the Metropolis* (London, 1803).

—— *Substance of a letter, dated Poet's Corner, Westminster, 3d March, 1803, to the Right Hon. Lord Pelham, on the state of mendicity in the Metropolis* (London, 1811).

Martin's Belfast directory for 1841–42 ... (1841; repr. Belfast, 1992).

Mason, William Shaw, *A statistical account, or parochial survey of Ireland, drawn up from the communications of the clergy* (3 vols, Dublin, 1814).

M[athison]., G.F.G., *Journal of a tour in Ireland during the months of October and November 1835* (London, 1836).

Meagher William, *Notices of the life and character of His Grace Most Rev. Daniel Murray, late Archbishop of Dublin, as contained in the commemorative oration pronounced in the Church of the Conception, Dublin, on occasion of His Grace's months' mind. With historical and biographical notes* (Dublin, 1853).

Moncrieff Wilson, James, *Statistics of crime in Ireland, 1842 to 1856. A paper read before the section of Economic Science and Statistics of the British Association. At Dublin, on Saturday, 29th of August, 1857* (Dublin, 1857).

The Most Rev. Dr James Butler's Catechism: revised, enlarged, approved, and recommended by the four R.C. archbishops of Ireland, as a general catechism for the kingdom (26th edn, Dublin, 1836).

Murray, Daniel, *A sermon, preached on the nativity of our Blessed Saviour, in the Church of the Conception, Marlborough-Street, on the 25th December, 1837, by the most Rev. Doctor Murray, and published for the benefit of St. Vincent's Hospital, Stephen's Green, at the desire of some friends of that charitable institution* (Dublin, 1838).

[Newport, John], *A slight peep into the Church vestry system in Ireland* (London, [c.1825]).

Nicholls, George, *A history of the Irish Poor Law, in connexion with the condition of the people* (London, 1856).

—— *A history of the Scotch Poor Law, in connexion with the condition of the people* (London, 1856).

Nicholson, Asenath, *Annals of the Famine in Ireland*, ed. Maureen Murphy (1851; Dublin, 1998).

O'Connor, Denis Charles, *Seventeen years' experience of workhouse life: with suggestions for reforming the Poor Law and its administration* (Dublin, 1861).

[O'Flanagan, Mary Padua], *The life and work of Mary Aikenhead, foundress of the Congregation of Irish Sisters of Charity 1787–1858* (London, 1924).

O'Hanlon, W.M., *Walks among the poor of Belfast, and suggestions for their improvement* (Belfast, 1853).

O'Hara Family [John and Michael Banim], *Father Connell* (3 vols, London, 1842).

O'Malley, Thaddeus, *Poor Laws – Ireland. An idea of a Poor Law for Ireland* (2nd edn, London, 1837).

—— *A sketch of the state of popular education in Holland, Prussia, Belgium, and France* (2nd edn, London and Dublin, 1840).

—— *An address to mechanics, small farmers, and the working classes generally, upon a feasible means of greatly improving their condition; with a word in their behalf to employers and landlords* (Dublin, 1845).

[Otway, Caesar], *Sketches in Ireland: descriptive of interesting, and hitherto unnoticed districts, in the north and south* (Dublin, 1827).

—— *Sketches in Erris and Tyrawly* (Dublin, 1841).

Page, Frederick, *Observations on the state of the indigent poor in Ireland, and the existing institutions for the relief* (London, 1830).

Pichot, Amédee, *L'Irlande et Le Pays de Galles, esquisses de voyages, d'économie politique, d'histoire, de biographie, de littérature, etc., etc., etc.* (2 vols, Paris, 1850).

'Proceedings of statistical societies' in *Journal of the Statistical Society of London*, i, no. 1 (May 1838).

[Pückler-Muskau, Hermann von], *Tour in England, Ireland, and France, in the years 1826, 1827, 1828, and 1829, with remarks on the manners and customs of the inhabitants, and anecdotes of distinguished public characters. In a series of letters* (Philadelphia, 1833).

Quennell, Peter (ed.), *Mayhew's London underworld* (London, 1987).

Report of the committee for investigating the causes of the alarming increase of juvenile delinquency in the metropolis (London, 1816).

A report upon certain charitable establishments in the city of Dublin, which receive aid from parliament (Dublin, 1809).

Revans, John, *Evils of the state of Ireland; their causes and their remedy – a Poor Law* (London, [c.1836]).

A review of the existing causes which at present disturb the tranquillity of Ireland, recommended to the serious attention of landholders, the established clergy, and the

Hibernian Sunday School Society: also, an exposure of the system adopted by the Roman Catholic clergy to deter their flocks from reading the sacred scriptures (Dublin, 1822).

Rules and constitutions of the Institute of the Religious Sisterhood of the Presentation of the Ever Blessed Virgin Mary, established in the City of Cork, for the charitable instruction of poor girls conformably to the rules of the late Pope, Pius VI ... (Cork, 1809).

'Rules and regulations for the House of Industry, in Belfast ... ' in *Belfast Monthly Magazine*, iv, no. 21 (30 Apr. 1810), pp. 261–9.

[Senior, Nassau William], 'Mendicancy in Ireland' in *Edinburgh Review*, lxxvii, no. 156 (Apr. 1843), pp. 391–411.

Shackleton, Ebenezer, *Poor Laws: the safest, cheapest and surest cure for boyism of every kind in Ireland* (Dublin, 1832).

Skelton, Philip, *The necessity of tillage and granaries. In a letter to a member of parliament living in the county of ___* (Dublin, 1741).

Slater's national commercial directory for Ireland ... 1846.

Smith, William, *A consecutive history of the rise, progress, and present state of Wesleyan Methodism in Ireland* (Dublin, 1830).

Statement of some of the causes of the disturbances in Ireland, and of the miserable state of the peasantry; with a plan for commencing on sound principles, an amelioration of their condition, thereby removing the causes of the disturbances, and bringing the country into a state of peace and quietness (Dublin, 1825).

'Statistical Society of Ulster' in *Journal of the Statistical Society of London*, i, no. 1 (May 1838), p. 52.

Stokes, Whitley, *Observations on contagion* (2nd edn, Dublin, 1818).

Sumner, John Bird, 'Sermon VII. The surest mode of benefitting the poor' in John Bird Sumner, *Christian charity; its obligations and objects, with reference to the present state of society. In a series of sermons* (2nd edn, London, 1841), pp. 104–20.

[Swift, Jonathan], *A proposal for giving badges to the beggars in all the parishes of Dublin* (London, 1737).

Thackeray, William Makepeace, *The Irish sketchbook of 1842* (1843; repr. Dublin, 2005).

'Thirty-Nine Articles of Religion', accessed from Church of Ireland website https://www.ireland.anglican.org/our-faith/39-articles-of-religion (5 Jan. 2017).

Toone, William, *The magistrate's manual; or, a summary of the duties and powers of a justice of the peace, carefully compiled from the best authorities; with extracts from adjudged cases and the statutes to the 56th George III. 1816 ...* (2nd edn, London, 1817).

Townsend, Joseph, *A journey through Spain in the years 1786 and 1787; with particular attention to the agriculture, manufactures, commerce, population, taxes and revenue of that country; and remarks in passing through a part of France* (3 vols, London, 1791).

[Voght, Caspar von], *Account of the management of the poor in Hamburgh, since the year 1788: in a letter to some friends of the poor in Great Britain* (Dublin, 1796).

Warburton, J., J. Whitelaw and Robert Walsh, *History of the city of Dublin, from the earliest accounts to the present time ...* (2 vols, London, 1818).

Weld, Isaac, *Statistical survey of the county of Roscommon, drawn up under the direction of the Royal Dublin Society* (Dublin, 1832).

Whately, E. Jane, *Life and correspondence of Richard Whately, D.D. late Archbishop of Dublin* (2 vols, London, 1866).

Whately, Richard, *Christ's example, an instruction as to the best modes of dispensing charity. A sermon delivered for the benefit of the Relief and Clothing Fund, in Doctor Steevens' Hospital* (Dublin, 1835).

White, Francis, *Report and observations on the state of the poor of Dublin* (Dublin, 1833).

Whitelaw, James, *An essay on the population of Dublin. Being the result of an actual survey taken in 1798, with great care and precision, and arranged in a manner entirely new* (Dublin, 1805).

Wight, Thomas (rev. John Rutty), *A history of the rise and progress of the people called Quakers in Ireland* … (Dublin, 1751).

Wilberforce, William, *A practical view of the prevailing religious system of professed Christians, in the higher and middle classes in this country, contrasted with real Christianity* (London, 1797).

Wilde, W[illiam] R., *Irish popular superstitions* (Dublin, [1852]).

[Wilde, William R.], 'The food of the Irish' in *Dublin University Magazine*, xliii, no. 154 (Feb. 1854), pp. 127–46.

Wilson's Dublin directory for the year 1822.

[Woodward, Richard], *A scheme for establishing county poor-houses, in the kingdom of Ireland* (Dublin, 1766).

Woodward, Richard, *An argument in support of the right of the poor in the kingdom of Ireland to a national provision; in the appendix to which, an attempt is made to settle a measure of the contribution due from each man to the poor, on the footing of justice* (Dublin, 1768).

—— *An address to the public, on the expediency of a regular plan for the maintenance and government of the poor…* (Dublin, 1775).

Wright, G.N., *An historical guide to the city of Dublin, illustrated by engravings, and a plan of the city* (2nd edn, London, 1825).

Young, Arthur, *A tour in Ireland: with general observations on the present state of the kingdom. Made in the years 1776, 1777, and 1778, and brought down to the end of 1779* (2 vols, Dublin, 1780).

Secondary Sources

Reference Material

McGuire, James and James Quinn (eds), *Dictionary of Irish biography: from the earliest times to the year 2002* (9 vols, Cambridge, 2009).

Matthew, H.C.G. and Brian Harrison (eds), *Oxford dictionary of national biography: from the earliest times to the year 2000* (60 vols, Oxford, 2004).

Vaughan, W.E. and A.J. Fitzpatrick (eds), *Irish historical statistics: population, 1821–1971* (Dublin, 1978).

Books and Articles

Akenson, Donald Harman, *The Church of Ireland: ecclesiastical reform and revolution, 1800–1885* (New Haven, CT and London, 1971).

Ashton, T.S., *Economic and social investigations in Manchester, 1833–1933: a centenary history of the Manchester Statistical Society* (1934; repr. Brighton, 1977).

Aspinwall, Bernard, 'The welfare state within the state: the Saint Vincent de Paul Society in Glasgow, 1848–1920' in W.J. Sheils and Diana Wood (eds), *Voluntary religion. Papers read at the 1985 summer meeting and the 1986 winter meeting of the Ecclesiastical History Society*, Studies in Church History, xxiii (Oxford, 1986), pp. 445–59.

[Atkinson, Sarah], *Mary Aikenhead: her life, her work, and her friends, giving a history of the foundation of the congregation of the Irish Sisters of Charity* (3rd edn, Dublin, 1911).

Bardon, Jonathan, *A history of Ulster* (Belfast, 1992).

Barnard, Toby, *A new anatomy of Ireland: the Irish Protestants, 1649–1770* (New Haven, CT and London, 2003).

—— 'Hamilton's "Cries of Dublin": the society and economy of mid-eighteenth-century Dublin' in William Laffan (ed.), *The cries of Dublin &c: drawn from the life by Hugh Douglas Hamilton, 1760* (Dublin, 2003), pp. 26–37.

—— *The kingdom of Ireland, 1641–1760* (Basingstoke, 2004).

Barrett, Sam, 'Kinship, poor relief and the welfare process in early modern England' in Steven King and Alannah Tomkins (eds), *The poor in England 1700–1850: an economy of makeshifts* (Manchester, 2003), pp. 199–227.

Bebbington, D.W., *Evangelicalism in modern Britain: a history from the 1730s to the 1980s* (London, 1989).

Beier, A.L., 'Vagrants and the social order in Elizabethan England' in *Past & Present*, lxiv (Aug. 1974), pp. 3–29.

—— *Masterless men: the vagrancy problem in England 1560–1640* (London and New York, 1985).

Bolster, Evelyn, 'The last will and testament of Archbishop Daniel Murray of Dublin (d.1852)' in *Collectanea Hibernica*, nos. 21–2 (1979–80), pp. 149–59.

Bowen, Desmond, *Souperism: myth or reality? A study in souperism* (Cork, 1970).

Brown, Michael, Patrick M. Geoghegan and James Kelly (eds), *The Irish Act of Union, 1800: bicentennial essays* (Dublin, 2003).

Brown, Stewart J., *The national churches of England, Ireland, and Scotland, 1801–1846* (Oxford, 2001).

Bulmer, Martin, Kevin Bales and Kathryn Kish Sklar (eds), *The social survey in historical perspective, 1880–1940* (Cambridge, 1991).

—— 'The social survey in historical perspective' in Martin Bulmer, Kevin Bales and Kathryn Kish Sklar (eds), *The social survey in historical perspective, 1880–1940* (Cambridge, 1991), pp. 1–48.

Burke, Helen, *The people and the Poor Law in 19th-century Ireland* (Littlehampton, 1987).

Burns, Arthur and Joanna Innes (eds), *Rethinking the age of reform: Britain 1780–1850* (Cambridge, 2003).

Callahan, William J., 'The problem of confinement: an aspect of poor relief in eighteenth-century Spain' in *Hispanic American Historical Review*, li, no. 1 (Feb. 1971), pp. 1–24.

Clear, Caitriona, 'Walls within walls: nuns in nineteenth-century Ireland' in Chris Curtin, Pauline Jackson and Barbara O'Connor (eds), *Gender in Irish society* (Galway, 1987), pp. 134–51.

—— 'The limits of female autonomy: nuns in nineteenth-century Ireland' in Maria Luddy and Cliona Murphy (eds), *Women surviving* (Dublin, 1990), pp. 15–50.

——— 'Homelessness, crime, punishment and poor relief in Galway, 1850–1914: an introduction' in *Journal of the Galway Archaeological and Historical Society*, 1 (1998), pp. 118–34.

Coll, Blanche D., 'The Baltimore Society for the Prevention of Pauperism, 1820–1822' in *American Historical Review*, lxi, no. 1 (Oct. 1955), pp. 77–87.

Comerford, R.V. and Jennifer Kelly (eds), *Associational culture in Ireland and abroad* (Dublin, 2010).

Comerford, W.J.V., 'Some notes on the borough of Tuam and its records, 1817–1822' in *Journal of the Galway Archaeological and Historical Society*, xv, no. iii (1931), pp. 97–120.

Connolly, S.J., 'The "blessed turf": cholera and popular panic in Ireland, June 1832' in *Irish Historical Studies*, xxiii, no. 91 (May 1983), pp. 214–32.

——— 'Religion, work-discipline and economic attitudes: the case of Ireland' in T.M. Devine and David Dickson (eds), *Ireland and Scotland 1600–1850: parallels and contrasts in economic and social development* (Edinburgh, 1983), pp. 235–45.

——— *Priests and people in pre-Famine Ireland, 1780–1845* (Dublin, 1985).

——— *Religion and society in nineteenth-century Ireland* (Dundalk, 1994).

——— (ed.), *Belfast 400: people, place and history* (Liverpool, 2012).

——— 'Improving town, 1750–1820' in S.J. Connolly (ed.), *Belfast 400: people, place and history* (Liverpool, 2012), pp. 161–97.

Connolly, S.J. and Gillian McIntosh, 'Whose city? Belonging and exclusion in the nineteenth-century urban world' in S.J. Connolly (ed.), *Belfast 400: people, place and history* (Liverpool, 2012), pp. 237–69.

Corish, Patrick J., *The Irish Catholic experience: a historical survey* (Dublin, 1986).

Cousins, Mel, 'The Irish parliament and relief of the poor: the 1772 legislation establishing houses of industry' in *Eighteenth-Century Ireland*, xxviii (2013), pp. 95–115.

——— 'Philanthropy and poor relief before the Poor Law, 1801–30' in Laurence M. Geary and Oonagh Walsh (eds), *Philanthropy in nineteenth-century Ireland* (Dublin, 2015), pp. 23–37.

Crawford, John, *The Church of Ireland in Victorian Dublin* (Dublin, 2005).

Crawford, W.H., 'The Belfast middle-classes in the late eighteenth century' in David Dickson, Dáire Keogh and Kevin Whelan (eds), *The United Irishmen: republicanism, radicalism and rebellion* (Dublin, 1993), pp. 62–73.

Cronin (née Murphy), Maura, 'The economic and social structure of nineteenth-century Cork' in David Harkness and Mary O'Dowd (eds), *The town in Ireland*, Historical Studies XIII (Belfast, 1981), pp. 125–54.

Crossick, Geoffrey, 'From gentlemen to the residuum: languages of social description in Victorian Britain' in Penelope J. Corfield (ed.), *Language, history and class* (Oxford and Cambridge, MA, 1991), pp. 150–78.

Crossman, Virginia, *The Poor Law in Ireland, 1838–1948* (Dundalk, 2006).

——— 'Middle-class attitudes to poverty and welfare in post-Famine Ireland' in Fintan Lane (ed.) *Politics, society and the middle class in modern Ireland* (Basingstoke, 2010), pp. 130–47.

——— '"Attending to the wants of poverty": Paul Cullen, the relief of poverty and the development of social welfare in Ireland' in Dáire Keogh and Albert McDonnell (eds), *Cardinal Paul Cullen and his world* (Dublin, 2011), pp. 146–65.

——— *Poverty and the Poor Law in Ireland 1850–1914* (Liverpool, 2013).

Crossman, Virginia and Peter Gray (eds), *Poverty and welfare in Ireland, 1838–1948* (Dublin, 2011).

——— 'Introduction: poverty and welfare in Ireland, 1838–1948' in Virginia Crossman and Peter Gray (eds), *Poverty and welfare in Ireland, 1838–1948* (Dublin, 2011), pp. 1–20.

Cullen, Bob, *Thomas L. Synnott: the career of a Dublin Catholic 1830–1870* (Dublin, 1997).

Cullen, Mary, 'Breadwinners and providers: women in the household economy of labouring families, 1835–6' in Maria Luddy and Cliona Murphy (eds), *Women surviving* (Dublin, 1990), pp. 85–116.

Cullen, Michael J., *The statistical movement in early Victorian Britain: the foundations of empirical social research* (Hassocks and New York, 1975).

Cunningham, Hugh and Joanna Innes (eds), *Charity, philanthropy and reform from the 1690s to 1850* (Basingstoke, 1998).

Cunningham, John, *'A town tormented by the sea': Galway, 1790–1914* (Dublin, 2004).

D'Arcy Wood, Gillen, *Tambora: the eruption that changed the world* (Princeton, NJ, 2015).

Daunton, Martin (ed.), *Charity, self-interest and welfare in the English past* (London, 1996).

Dickey, Brian, '"Going about doing good": evangelicals and poverty *c.*1815–1870' in John Wolffe (ed.), *Evangelical faith and public zeal: evangelicals and society in Britain 1780–1980* (London, 1995), pp. 38–58.

Dickson, David (ed.), *The gorgeous mask: Dublin, 1700–1850* (Dublin, 1987).

——— 'In search of the old Irish Poor Law' in Rosalind Mitchison and Peter Roebuck (eds), *Economy and society in Scotland and Ireland, 1500–1939* (Edinburgh, 1988), pp. 149–59.

——— *Arctic Ireland: the extraordinary story of the great frost and forgotten famine of 1740–41* (Belfast, 1998).

Dickson, David, Dáire Keogh and Kevin Whelan (eds), *The United Irishmen: republicanism, radicalism and rebellion* (Dublin, 1993).

Dickson, J.N. Ian, *Beyond religious discourse: sermons, preaching and evangelical Protestants in nineteenth-century Irish society* (Milton Keynes, 2007).

Digby, Anne, *British welfare policy: workhouse to workforce* (London, 1989).

Dillon, Charles and Henry A. Jeffries (eds), *Tyrone: history and society* (Dublin, 2000).

Dinan, Susan E., *Women and poor relief in seventeenth-century France: the early history of the Daughters of Charity* (Aldershot, 2006).

Disley, Emma, 'Degrees of glory: Protestant doctrine and the concept of rewards hereafter' in *Journal of Theological Studies*, new series, xliv, pt. 1 (Apr. 1991), pp. 77–105.

Dudley, Rowena, 'The Dublin parish, 1660–1730' in Elizabeth FitzPatrick and Raymond Gillespie (eds), *The parish in medieval and early modern Ireland: community, territory and building* (Dublin, 2006), pp. 277–96.

Dudley Edwards, Owen, 'William Carleton and Caesar Otway: a problem in Irish identity' in John Cunningham and Niall Ó Ciosáin (eds), *Culture and society in Ireland since 1750: essays in honour of Gearóid Ó Tuathaigh* (Dublin, 2015), pp. 64–85.

Dupré Atkinson, Edward, *An Ulster parish: being a history of Donaghcloney (Waringstown)* (Dublin, 1898).

Dyson, Richard, 'Welfare provision in Oxford during the latter stages of the Old Poor Law, 1800–1834' in *Historical Journal*, lii, no. 4 (2009), pp. 943–62.

Dyson, Richard and Steven King, '"The streets are paved with beggars": experiences and perceptions of beggars in nineteenth-century Oxford' in Beate Althammer (ed.), *Bettler der europäischen Stadt der Moderne: Zwischen Barmherzigkeit, Repression und Sozialreform* (Frankfurt am Main, 2007), pp. 59–89.

Eccles, Audrey, *Vagrancy in law and practice under the Old Poor Law* (Farnham, 2012).

Elliott, Marianne, *The Catholics of Ulster* (London, 2000).

Evans, Eric J. (ed.), *Social policy, 1830–1914: individualism, collectivism and the origins of the Welfare State* (London and Boston, 1978).

Farrell, Michael, *The Poor Law and the workhouse in Belfast, 1838–1948* (Belfast, 1978).

Fitzgerald, Patrick, 'A sentence to sail: the transportation of Irish convicts and vagrants to colonial America in the eighteenth century' in Patrick Fitzgerald and Steve Ickringill (eds), *Atlantic crossroads: historical connections between Scotland, Ulster and North America* (Newtownards, 2001), pp. 114–32.

Fitzpatrick, David, '"A peculiar tramping people": the Irish in Britain, 1801–70' in W.E. Vaughan (ed.), *A new history of Ireland, vol. 5, Ireland under the Union, I, 1801–70* (Oxford, 1989), pp. 623–60.

Foley, Tadhg and Seán Ryder (eds), *Ideology and Ireland in the nineteenth century* (Dublin, 1998).

Fontaine, Laurence and Jürgen Schlumbohm, 'Household strategies for survival: an introduction' in *International Review of Social History*, xlv (2000), pp. 1–17.

Forrest, Alan, *The French Revolution and the poor* (Oxford, 1981).

Fraser, Derek, *The evolution of the British welfare state: a history of social policy since the Industrial Revolution* (2nd edn, Basingstoke, 1984).

Fuchs, Rachel, *Gender and poverty in nineteenth-century Europe* (Cambridge, 2005).

Gallagher, Fióna, *The streets of Sligo: urban evolution over the course of seven centuries* (Sligo, 2008).

Garnham, Neal, 'The criminal law, 1692–1760: England and Ireland compared' in S.J. Connolly (ed.), *Kingdoms united? Great Britain and Ireland since 1500: integration and diversity* (Dublin, 1999), pp. 215–24.

Geary, Laurence M., '"The whole country was in motion": mendicancy and vagrancy in pre-Famine Ireland' in Jacqueline Hill and Colm Lennon (eds), *Luxury and austerity*, Historical Studies XXI (Dublin, 1999), pp. 121–36.

—— *Medicine and charity in Ireland, 1718–1851* (Dublin, 2004).

—— '"The best relief the poor can receive is from themselves": the Society for Promoting the Comforts of the Poor' in Laurence M. Geary and Oonagh Walsh (eds), *Philanthropy in nineteenth-century Ireland* (Dublin, 2015), pp. 38–58.

Geary, Laurence M. and Oonagh Walsh (eds), *Philanthropy in nineteenth-century Ireland* (Dublin, 2015).

Geoghegan, Patrick M., *King Dan: the rise of Daniel O'Connell, 1775–1829* (Dublin, 2008).

Gillespie, Raymond, 'Rev. Dr John Yarner's notebook: religion in Restoration Dublin' in *Archivium Hibernicum*, lii (1998), pp. 30–41.

—— 'The coming of reform, 1500–58' in Kenneth Milne (ed.), *Christ Church Cathedral, Dublin: a history* (Dublin, 2000), pp. 151–73.

—— 'Making Belfast, 1600–1750' in S.J. Connolly (ed.), *Belfast 400: people, place and history* (Liverpool, 2012), pp. 123–59.

Gillespie, Raymond and Stephen A. Royle, *Belfast. Part I, to 1840*, Irish Historic Towns Atlas, no. 12 (Dublin, 2003).

Goodbody, Olive C., *Guide to Irish Quaker records, 1654–1860* (IMC, Dublin, 1967).

Gray, Peter, 'The Irish Poor Law and the Great Famine', paper presented to the International Economic History Congress conference, Helsinki, 2006, accessed at University of Helsinki website www.helsinki.fi/iehc2006/papers3/Gray.pdf (accessed 25 Feb. 2014).

—— *The making of the Irish Poor Law, 1815–43* (Manchester, 2009).

—— 'Thomas Chalmers and Irish poverty' in Frank Ferguson and James McConnel (eds), *Ireland and Scotland in the nineteenth century* (Dublin, 2009), pp. 93–107.

—— 'Irish social thought and the relief of poverty, 1847–1880' in *Transactions of the Royal Historical Society*, xx (2010), pp. 141–56.

Griffin, Brian, *The Bulkies: police and crime in Belfast, 1800–1865* (Dublin, 1997).

Harrison, Richard S., *Merchants, mystics and philanthropists: 350 years of Cork Quakers* (Cork, 2006).

Hatton, Helen E., *The largest amount of good: Quaker relief in Ireland, 1654–1921* (Kingston, Ontario and London, 1993).

Hempton, David, 'Evangelicalism in English and Irish society, 1780–1840' in Mark A. Noll, David W. Bebbington and George A. Rawlyk (eds), *Evangelicalism: comparative studies of popular Protestantism in North America, the British Isles, and beyond, 1700–1900* (New York and Oxford, 1994), pp. 156–76.

Hill, Jacqueline, 'The Protestant response to repeal: the case of the Dublin working-class' in F.S.L. Lyons and R.A.J. Hawkins (eds), *Ireland under the Union: varieties of tension. Essays in honour of T.W. Moody* (Oxford, 1980), pp. 35–68.

—— 'Artisans, sectarianism and politics in Dublin, 1829–48' in *Saothar*, vii (1981), pp. 12–27.

—— 'Dublin after the Union: the age of the ultra-Protestants, 1801–1822' in Michael Brown, Patrick M. Geoghegan and James Kelly (eds), *The Irish Act of Union, 1800: bicentennial essays* (Dublin, 2003), pp. 144–56.

Hill, Jacqueline and Colm Lennon (eds), *Luxury and austerity*, Historical Studies XXI (Dublin, 1999).

Hill, Myrtle, 'Expressions of faith: Protestantism in nineteenth-century Tyrone' in Charles Dillon and Henry A. Jeffries (eds), *Tyrone: history and society* (Dublin, 2000), pp. 637–63.

Hilton, Boyd, 'The role of Providence in evangelical social thought' in Derek Beales and Geoffrey Best (eds), *History, society and the churches: essays in honour of Owen Chadwick* (Cambridge, 1985), pp. 215–33.

—— *The age of atonement: the influence of evangelicalism on social and economic thought, 1795–1865* (Oxford, 1988).

Himmelfarb, Gertrude, 'Mayhew's poor: a problem of identity' in *Victorian Studies*, xiv, no. 3 (Mar. 1971), pp. 307–20.

Hindle, G.B., *Provision for the relief of the poor in Manchester, 1754–1826* (Manchester, 1975).

Hindle, Steve, 'Dependency, shame and belonging: badging the deserving poor, c.1550–1750' in *Cultural and Social History*, i, no. 1 (2004), pp. 6–35.

—— *On the parish? The micro-politics of poor relief in rural England* c.*1550–1750* (Oxford, 2004).

Hitchcock, David, *Vagrancy in English culture and society, 1650–1750* (London, 2016).

Hitchcock, Tim, 'Begging on the streets of eighteenth-century London' in *Journal of British Studies*, xliv, no. 3 (July 2005), pp. 478–98.

—— *Down and out in eighteenth-century London* (London, 2007).

Hitchcock, Tim and Robert Shoemaker, *London lives: poverty, crime and the making of the modern city, 1690–1800* (Cambridge, 2015).

Holmes, Andrew R., 'The experience and understanding of religious revival in Ulster Presbyterianism, c.1800–1930' in *IHS*, xxxiv, no. 136 (Nov. 2002), pp. 361–85.

—— *The shaping of Ulster Presbyterian belief and practice, 1770–1840* (Oxford, 2006).

Holmes, R.F.G., *Our Irish Presbyterian heritage* (n.p. [Belfast], 1985).

Hufton, Olwen H., *The poor of eighteenth-century France, 1750–1789* (Oxford, 1974).

Hughes, S.C., *The church of S. Werburgh, Dublin* (Dublin, 1889).

Humphreys, R., *Sin, organized charity and the Poor Law in Victorian England* (Basingstoke, 1995).

Hunt, Tristram, *Building Jerusalem: the rise and fall of the Victorian city* (London, 2005).

Innes, Joanna, 'The "mixed economy of welfare" in early modern England: assessments of the options from Hale to Malthus (c.1683–1803)' in Martin Daunton (ed.), *Charity, self-interest and welfare in the English past* (London, 1996), pp. 139–80.

Innes, Joanna and Arthur Burns, 'Introduction' in Arthur Burns and Joanna Innes (eds), *Rethinking the age of reform: Britain 1780–1850* (Cambridge, 2003), pp. 1–70.

Irwin, Clarke H., *A history of Presbyterianism in Dublin and the south and west of Ireland* (London, 1890).

Jones, Colin, 'Some recent trends in the history of charity' in Martin Daunton (ed.), *Charity, self-interest and welfare in the English past* (London, 1996), pp. 51–63.

Jones, D.J.V., '"A dead loss to the community": the criminal vagrant in mid-nineteenth-century Wales' in *Welsh History Review*, viii (1976–7), pp. 312–44.

Jones, E.L., 'The agricultural labour market in England, 1793–1872' in *Economic History Review*, new series, xvii, no. 2 (1964), pp. 322–38.

Jordan, Alison, *Who cared? Charity in Victorian and Edwardian Belfast* (Belfast, [1992]).

Jütte, Robert, *Poverty and deviance in early modern Europe* (Cambridge, 1994).

Kelly, James, 'Transportation from Ireland to North America, 1703–1789' in David Dickson and Cormac Ó Gráda (eds), *Refiguring Ireland: essays in honour of L.M. Cullen* (Dublin, 2003), pp. 112–35.

—— *Sir Richard Musgrave, 1746–1818: Ultra-Protestant ideologue* (Dublin, 2009).

—— 'Charitable societies: their genesis and development, 1720–1800' in James Kelly and Martyn J. Powell (eds), *Clubs and societies in eighteenth-century Ireland* (Dublin, 2010), pp. 89–108.

Keogh, Dáire, 'Evangelising the faithful: Edmund Rice and the reformation of nineteenth-century Irish Catholicism' in Colm Lennon (ed.), *Confraternities and sodalities in Ireland: charity, devotion and sociability* (Dublin, 2012), pp. 57–75.

Kerr, Donal [A.], 'Dublin's forgotten archbishop: Daniel Murray, 1768–1852' in James Kelly and Dáire Keogh (eds), *History of the Catholic diocese of Dublin* (Dublin, 2000), pp. 247–67.

King, Steven, *Poverty and welfare in England, 1700–1850: a regional perspective* (Manchester, 2000).

—— 'Welfare regimes and welfare regions in Britain and Europe, *c.*1750s to 1860s' in *Journal of Modern European History*, ix, no. 1 (2011), pp. 42–64.

King, Steven and Alannah Tomkins (eds), *The poor in England 1700–1850: an economy of makeshifts* (Manchester, 2003).

—— 'Introduction' in Steven King and Alannah Tomkins (eds), *The poor in England 1700–1850: an economy of makeshifts* (Manchester, 2003), pp. 1–38.

King, Steven and John Stewart (eds), *Welfare peripheries: the development of welfare states in nineteenth- and twentieth-century Europe* (Berne, 2007).

—— 'Welfare peripheries in modern Europe' in Steven King and John Stewart (eds), *Welfare peripheries: the development of welfare states in nineteenth- and twentieth-century Europe* (Berne, 2007), pp. 9–38.

Laffan, William (ed.), *The cries of Dublin &c: drawn from the life by Hugh Douglas Hamilton, 1760* (Dublin, 2003).

Laragy, Georgina, 'Poor relief in the south of Ireland, 1850–1921' in Virginia Crossman and Peter Gray (eds), *Poverty and welfare in Ireland, 1838–1948* (Dublin, 2011), pp. 53–66.

Latimer, W.T., 'The old session book of the Presbyterian congregation at Dundonald, Co. Down' in *Ulster Journal of Archaeology*, second series, iii, no. 4 (July 1897), pp. 227–32.

Lavelle, Ruth and Paul Huggard, 'The parish poor of St. Mark's' in David Dickson (ed.), *The gorgeous mask: Dublin, 1700–1850* (Dublin, 1987), pp. 86–97.

Law Reform Commission, *Report on vagrancy and related matters* (Dublin, 1985).

Lawrence, Paul, 'The Vagrancy Act (1824) and the persistence of pre-emptive policing in England since 1750' in *British Journal of Criminology*, lvii, no. 3 (2017), pp. 513–31.

Lecky, William Edward Hartpole, *A history of Ireland in the eighteenth century* (5 vols, London, 1913–19).

Lennon, Colm, '*Dives* and Lazarus in sixteenth-century Ireland' in Jacqueline Hill and Colm Lennon (eds), *Luxury and austerity*, Historical Studies XXI (Dublin, 1999), pp. 46–65.

—— (ed.), *Confraternities and sodalities in Ireland: charity, devotion and sociability* (Dublin, 2012).

Lindberg, Carter, '"There should be no beggars among Christians": Karlstadt, Luther, and the origins of Protestant poor relief' in *Church History*, xlvi, no. 3 (Sept. 1977), pp. 313–34.

Lucey, Donnacha Seán, 'Poor relief in the west of Ireland, 1861–1911' in Virginia Crossman and Peter Gray (eds), *Poverty and welfare in Ireland, 1838–1948* (Dublin, 2011), pp. 37–51.

Luddy, Maria, *Women and philanthropy in nineteenth-century Ireland* (Cambridge, 1995).

—— '"Abandoned women and bad characters": prostitution in nineteenth-century Ireland' in *Women's History Review*, vi, no. 4 (1997), pp. 485–504.

—— 'Religion, philanthropy and the state in late-eighteenth- and early-nineteenth-century Ireland' in Hugh Cunningham and Joanna Innes (eds), *Charity, philanthropy and reform from the 1690s to 1850* (Basingstoke, 1998), pp. 148–67.

—— *Prostitution and Irish society, 1800–1940* (Cambridge, 2007).

Luddy, Maria and Cliona Murphy (eds), *Women surviving* (Dublin, 1990).

McCabe, Ciarán, 'The early years of the Strangers' Friend Society, Dublin: 1790–1845' in *Bulletin of the Methodist Historical Society of Ireland*, xix (2014), pp. 65–93.

McCartney, Donal, *The dawning of democracy: Ireland 1800–1870* (Dublin, 1987).

Mac Donagh, Oliver, *Ireland: the Union and its aftermath* (rev. edn, London, 1977).

McDowell, R.B., 'Ireland on the eve of the Famine' in R. Dudley Edwards and Desmond Williams (eds), *The Great Famine: studies in Irish history, 1845–52* (1956; Dublin, 1994), pp. 3–86.

McHugh, Ned, *Drogheda before the Famine: urban poverty in the shadow of privilege, 1826–45* (Dublin, 1998).

McKinney, William Fee, 'Old session books of Carnmoney, Co. Antrim' in *Ulster Journal of Archaeology*, second series, vi, no. 1 (Jan. 1900), pp. 6–11.

McLellan, David, *The thought of Karl Marx: an introduction* (3rd edn, London, 1995).

Mac Lochlainn, Antain, 'The Famine in Gaelic tradition' in *Irish Review*, no. 17/18 (Winter 1995), pp. 90–108.

McLoughlin, Dympna, 'Workhouses and Irish female paupers, 1840–70' in Maria Luddy and Cliona Murphy (eds), *Women surviving* (Dublin, 1990), pp. 117–47.

McNeill, Mary, *The life and times of Mary Ann McCracken, 1770–1866: a Belfast panorama* (Belfast, 1988).

Malcolm, Elizabeth, *The Irish policeman, 1822–1922: a life* (Dublin, 2006).

Mangion, Carmen, 'Faith, philanthropy and the aged poor in nineteenth-century England and Wales' in *European Review of History – Revue européenne d'histoire*, xix, no. 4 (Aug. 2012), pp. 515–30.

Maxwell, Constantia, *The stranger in Ireland from the reign of Elizabeth to the Great Famine* (London, 1954).

Mitchison, Rosalind, 'The making of the old Scottish Poor Law' in *Past & Present*, no. 63 (May 1974), pp. 58–93.

—— 'Who were the poor in Scotland, 1690–1830?' in Rosalind Mitchison and Peter Roebuck (eds), *Economy and society in Scotland and Ireland 1500–1939* (Edinburgh, 1988), pp. 140–8.

—— *The Old Poor Law in Scotland: the experience of poverty, 1574–1845* (Edinburgh, 2000).

Mitchison, Rosalind and Leah Leneman, *Sexuality and social control: Scotland 1660–1760* (Oxford, 1989).

Moffitt, Miriam, *The Society for Irish Church Missions to the Roman Catholics, 1849–1950* (Manchester, 2010).

Morris, R.J., 'Voluntary societies and British urban elites, 1780–1850: an analysis' in *Historical Journal*, xxvi, no. 1 (Mar. 1983), pp. 95–118.

Moylan, Thomas King, 'Vagabonds and sturdy beggars, I: poverty, pigs and pestilence in medieval Dublin' in *Dublin Historical Record*, i, no. 1 (Mar. 1938), pp. 11–18.

Munck, Ronnie, 'The formation of the working class in Belfast, 1788–1881' in *Saothar*, xi (1986), pp. 75–89.

Murphy, James H., *Irish novelists and the Victorian age* (Oxford, 2011).

Murray, J.P., *Galway: a medico-social history* (Galway, [*c*.1993]).

Neal, Frank, 'The English Poor Law, the Irish migrant and the laws of settlement and removal, 1819–1879' in D. George Boyce and Roger Swift (eds), *Problems and perspectives in Irish history since 1800: essays in honour of Patrick Buckland* (Dublin, 2004), pp. 95–116.

Noll, Mark A., David W. Bebbington and George A. Rawlyk (eds), *Evangelicalism: comparative studies of popular Protestantism in North America, the British Isles, and beyond, 1700–1900* (New York and Oxford, 1994).

O'Brien, Gerard, 'The new Poor Law in pre-Famine Ireland: a case history' in *Irish Economic and Social History*, xii (1985), pp. 33–49.

Ó Cearbhaill, Seán E., 'A memory that lived and a charity that died: Edmund Rice and the Mendicity Institute' in Peter S. Carroll (ed.), *A man raised up: recollections and reflections on Venerable Edmund Rice presented in 1994 on the occasion of the 150th anniversary of his death* (Dublin, 1994), pp. 159–71.

Ó Ciosáin, Niall, 'Introduction' in Maureen Comber (ed.), *Poverty before the Famine, County Clare, 1835* (Ennis, 1996), pp. iii–vii.

—— 'Boccoughs and God's poor: deserving and undeserving poor in Irish popular culture' in Tadhg Foley and Seán Ryder (eds), *Ideology and Ireland in the nineteenth century* (Dublin, 1998), pp. 93–9.

—— *Print and popular culture in Ireland 1750–1850* (new edn, Dublin, 2010).

—— *Ireland in official print culture, 1800–1850: a new reading of the Poor Inquiry* (Oxford, 2014).

O'Connor, John, *The workhouses of Ireland: the fate of Ireland's poor* (Dublin, 1995).

Ó Gráda, Cormac, 'Malthus and the pre-Famine economy' in *Hermathena*, no. 135 (Winter 1983), pp. 75–95.

—— *The Great Irish Famine* (Basingstoke and London, 1989).

—— *Ireland before and after the Famine: explorations in economic history, 1800–1925* (2nd edn, Manchester, 1993).

—— *Ireland: a new economic history 1780–1939* (Oxford, 1994).

Ollerenshaw, Philip, 'Industry, 1820–1914' in Liam Kennedy and Philip Ollerenshaw (eds), *An economic history of Ulster, 1820–1940* (Manchester, 1985), pp. 62–108.

O'Mahony, Michelle, *Famine in Cork city: famine life at Cork union workhouse* (Cork, 2005).

O'Neill, Timothy P., 'The Catholic Church and relief of the poor 1815–45' in *Archivium Hibernicum*, xxxi (1973), pp. 132–45.

—— 'Fever and public health in pre-Famine Ireland', in *Journal of the Royal Society of Antiquaries of Ireland*, ciii (1973), pp. 1–34.

—— 'Poverty in Ireland 1815–45' in *Folk-Life*, xi (1973), pp. 22–33.

—— 'A bad year in the Liberties' in Elgy Gillespie (ed.), *The Liberties of Dublin* (2nd edn, Dublin, 1974), pp. 76–83.

O'Toole, David, 'The employment crisis of 1826' in David Dickson (ed.), *The gorgeous mask: Dublin, 1700–1850* (Dublin, 1987), pp. 157–71.

Palmer, Stanley H., *Police and protest in England and Ireland 1780–1850* (Cambridge, 1988).

Parthun, Mary Lassance, 'Protestant and Catholic attitudes towards poverty: the Irish community and the development of the Saint Vincent de Paul Society in nineteenth-century Toronto' in Robert O'Driscoll and Lorna Reynolds (eds), *The untold story: the Irish in Canada* (2 vols, Toronto, 1988), ii, pp. 853–69.

Pickstone, John V., 'Dearth, dirt and fever epidemics: rewriting the history of British "public health", 1780–1850' in Terence Ranger and Paul Slack (eds), *Epidemics and ideas: essays on the historical perception of pestilence* (Cambridge, 1999), pp. 125–48.

Post, John D., *The last great subsistence crisis in the western world* (Baltimore, MD and London, 1977).

Pounds, N.J.G., *A history of the English parish: the culture of religion from Augustine to Victoria* (Cambridge, 2000).

Prochaska, Frank, *The voluntary impulse: philanthropy in modern Britain* (London, 1988).

Preston, Margaret H., *Charitable words: women, philanthropy and the language of charity in nineteenth-century Dublin* (Westport, CT and London, 2004).

Prunty, Jacinta, *Dublin slums, 1800–1925: a study in urban geography* (Dublin, 1998).

—— 'Mobility among women in nineteenth-century Dublin' in David J. Siddle (ed.), *Migration, mobility and modernization* (Liverpool, 2000), pp. 131–63.

—— 'Battle plans and battlegrounds: Protestant mission activity in the Dublin slums, 1840s–1880s' in Crawford Gribben and Andrew R. Holmes (eds), *Protestant millennialism, evangelicalism and Irish society, 1790–2005* (Basingstoke, 2006), pp. 119–43.

—— *The monasteries, Magdalen asylums and reformatory schools of Our Lady of Charity in Ireland 1853–1973* (Dublin, 2017).

Pullan, Brian, 'Catholics and the poor in early modern Europe' in *Transactions of the Royal Historical Society*, 5th series, xxvi (1976), pp. 15–34.

—— 'Charity and poor relief in early modern Italy' in Martin Daunton (ed.), *Charity, self-interest and welfare in the English past* (London, 1996), pp. 65–89.

—— 'Catholics, Protestants and the poor in early-modern Europe' in *Journal of Interdisciplinary History*, xxxv, no. 3 (Winter 2005), pp. 441–56.

Rack, Henry D., *Reasonable enthusiast: John Wesley and the rise of Methodism* (London, 1989).

Raughter, Rosemary, 'Pious occupations: female activism and the Catholic revival in eighteenth-century Ireland' in Rosemary Raughter (ed.), *Religious women and their history: breaking the silence* (Dublin, 2005), pp. 25–49.

Roberts, M.J.D., 'Reshaping the gift relationship: the London Mendicity Society and the suppression of begging in England, 1818–1869' in *International Review of Social History*, xxxvi (1991), pp. 201–31.

—— *Making English morals: voluntary association and moral reform in England, 1787–1886* (Cambridge, 2004).

Robins, Joseph, *The lost children: a study of charity children in Ireland, 1700–1900* (Dublin, 1980).

—— *The miasma: epidemic and panic in nineteenth-century Ireland* (Dublin, 1995).

Rose, Lionel, *'Rogues and vagabonds': vagrant underworld in Britain, 1815–1985* (London and New York, 1988).

Samuel, Raphael, 'Comers and goers' in H.J. Dyos and Michael Wolff (eds), *The Victorian city: images and realities*, vol. 1, *Past and present, and numbers of people* (London, 1976), pp. 123–60.

Seaby, W.A. and T.G.F. Paterson, 'Ulster beggars' badges' in *Ulster Archaeological Journal*, third series, xxxiii (1970), pp. 95–106.

Sharpe, J.A., *Crime in early modern England, 1550–1750* (London and New York, 1984).

Shore, Heather, *Artful dodgers: youth crime in early-nineteenth-century London* (Woodbridge, 2002).

—— 'Crime, criminal networks and the survival strategies of the poor in early eighteenth-century London' in Steven King and Alannah Tomkins (eds), *The poor in England 1700–1850: an economy of makeshifts* (Manchester, 2003), pp. 137–65.

Slack, Paul, 'Vagrants and vagrancy in England, 1598–1664' in *Economic History Review*, xxvii, no. 3 (Aug. 1974), pp. 360–79.

Strain, R.W.M., *Belfast and its Charitable Society: a story of urban social development* (London, 1961).

Tobias, J.J., *Crime and industrial society in the nineteenth century* (Harmondsworth, 1972).

Thompson, F.M.L., 'Social control in Victorian Britain' in *Economic History Review*, 2nd series, xxxiv, no. 2 (May 1981), pp. 189–208.

Vaughan, W.E. (ed.), *A new history of Ireland*, vol. 5, *Ireland under the Union, I, 1801–70* (Oxford, 1989).

Wallach Scott, Joan, 'A statistical representation of work: *La statistique de l'industrie à Paris, 1847–1848*' in Joan Wallach Scott, *Gender and the politics of history* (New York, 1988), pp. 113–38.

Walsh, John, 'John Wesley and the urban poor' in *Revue française de civilisation britannique*, vi, no. 3 (1991), pp. 17–30.

Whelan, Irene, *The Bible war in Ireland: the 'Second Reformation' and the polarization of Protestant–Catholic relations, 1800–1840* (Dublin, 2005).

—— 'The Bible gentry: evangelical religion, aristocracy, and the new moral order in the early nineteenth century' in Crawford Gribben and Andrew R. Holmes (eds), *Protestant millennialism, evangelicalism and Irish society, 1790–2005* (Basingstoke, 2006), pp. 52–82.

Woods, Audrey, *Dublin outsiders: a history of the Mendicity Institution, 1818–1998* (Dublin, 1998).

Woolf, Stuart, *The poor in western Europe in the eighteenth and nineteenth centuries* (London and New York, 1986).

Wright, Jonathan Jeffrey, *The 'natural leaders' and their world: politics, culture and society in Belfast, c.1801–1832* (Liverpool, 2012).

Young, G.M., *Portrait of an age: Victorian England* (annotated edn, London, 1977).

Unpublished Theses

Begadon, Cormac, 'Laity and clergy in the Catholic renewal of Dublin, c.1750–1830' (PhD thesis, Maynooth University, 2009).

Dalgleish, Andrew J., 'Voluntary associations and the middle class in Edinburgh, 1780–1820' (PhD thesis, University of Edinburgh, 1991).

Dudley, Rowena, 'Dublin parishes 1660–1729: the Church of Ireland parishes and their role in the civic administration of the city' (PhD thesis, 2 vols, University of Dublin, 1995).

Harrison, Richard S., 'Dublin Quakers in business 1800–1850' (MLitt thesis, 2 vols, University of Dublin, 1987).

McCabe, Ciarán, 'Begging and alms-giving in urban Ireland, 1815–1850' (PhD thesis, Maynooth University, 2015).

Ní Chearbhaill, Máire Brighid, 'The Society of St. Vincent de Paul in Dublin, 1926–1975' (PhD thesis, Maynooth University, 2008).

Tumilty, Kathryn, 'The Church of Ireland and the Famine in Ulster, 1845–52' (PhD thesis, Queen's University Belfast, 2009).

Index

References to images printed in the book are presented in bold.